Organizational
LISTENING

This book is part of the Peter Lang Media and Communication list.
Every volume is peer reviewed and meets
the highest quality standards for content and production.

PETER LANG
New York • Bern • Frankfurt • Berlin
Brussels • Vienna • Oxford • Warsaw

Jim Macnamara

Organizational
LISTENING

The Missing Essential
in Public Communication

PETER LANG
New York • Bern • Frankfurt • Berlin
Brussels • Vienna • Oxford • Warsaw

Library of Congress Cataloging-in-Publication Data
Macnamara, Jim, author.
Organizational listening: the missing essential
in public communication / Jim Macnamara.
Pages cm
Includes bibliographical references and index.
1. Communication in public administration.
2. Communication in organizations. 3. Listening. I. Title.
JF1525.C59M33   658.4'5—dc23   2015033940
ISBN 978-1-4331-3053-3 (hardcover)
ISBN 978-1-4331-3052-6 (paperback)
ISBN 978-1-4539-1739-8 (e-book)

Bibliographic information published by **Die Deutsche Nationalbibliothek**.
Die Deutsche Nationalbibliothek lists this publication in the "Deutsche
Nationalbibliografie"; detailed bibliographic data are available
on the Internet at http://dnb.d-nb.de/.

The paper in this book meets the guidelines for permanence and durability
of the Committee on Production Guidelines for Book Longevity
of the Council of Library Resources.

Printed in the United States of America

CONTENTS

ACKNOWLEDGEMENTS

Research and publication of new insights cannot happen without considerable time and effort of many people, not only the researcher. I gratefully thank all the organizations that agreed to participate in the research that informed this book, despite knowing that it would include critical analysis. Their openness and concern for their stakeholders, publics, and society are to be commended.

In particular, I must acknowledge and thank Alex Aiken, the head of government communication in the UK, who granted me largely unfettered access to senior communication staff in the UK Cabinet Office, Whitehall, and a range of UK government departments and agencies, and Paul Njoku who facilitated these interactions.

I also thank Mark Weiner, CEO of Prime Research (North America), Richard Bagnall, CEO of Prime Research (UK), and Frank Ovaitt, president and CEO of the Institute for Public Relations in the US 2011–2015, who assisted me in gaining access to communication heads in some of the world's largest corporations.

I am indebted also to a number of academic colleagues who provided valuable advice, encouragement, and reviews of drafts of this book, particularly Nick Couldry, professor of media, communication and social theory at the London School of Economics and Political Science; Stephen Coleman, professor of political communication at the University of Leeds; and Anne Gregory, professor of corporate communications at the University of Huddersfield and chair of the Global Alliance for Public Relations and Communication Management. As well, I thank colleagues and collaborators at the University of Technology Sydney including Roger Dunston, associate professor in public communication, and research associate, Dr Gail Kenning; along with organizational systems consultant Paul Long.

For the production and publication of this book, I thank Peter Lang, New York, and particularly senior acquisitions editor Mary Savigar who supported publication in hardcover and paperback editions as a key research output from the Organizational Listening Project.

Jim Macnamara PhD, FAMEC, FAMI, CPM, FPRIA

INTRODUCTION

While the following are anecdotal, three incidents prompted and inspired the research and analysis reported in this book. Unfortunately for organizations and citizens, such incidents are all too often typical of organization-public communication today.

In 2010 I wrote to my local council about what a number of residents in the street where I live considered to be mismanagement of an environmental reserve adjacent to our houses. There had been a long history of politics between the local government body and the federal government over the land and who was responsible for the cost of maintenance of the reserve as well as the verge.[1] Noxious weeds were growing in the reserve, undergrowth was creating a fire hazard, and plants and grass on the verge were dying. The local council's Web site stated that the contact point for residents' inquiries was the general manager and gave an e-mail address. So I wrote to the council as advised. But no response was received in the following three weeks. So I wrote again. Still no acknowledgement or action followed. Exasperated after writing two letters and leaving a phone message to no avail, I contacted the local newspaper and also wrote a story for an online community news site, with photos of the overgrown reserve and verge. Suddenly, within a day of media reports appearing, the council sprang into action. Council members and officials contacted me and maintenance workers were on the case within a few days. But until bad publicity appeared resulting in public embarrassment, the council was not listening to its ratepayers.

In 2012 I was looking around to buy a new four-wheel-drive, as my wife and I enjoy trips to the Australian Outback (yes, unlike many 4WD owners, we do go beyond the city limits). A new model from a leading global brand was due for release and I was keen to find out details including its off-road features and its environmental impact such as fuel consumption, carbon emissions, and so on. Because local dealers could not answer my questions, I logged on to the manufacturer's Web site and, under the 'contact us' section, submitted an inquiry. I made it clear that I was a seriously interested potential buyer and waited for a response. None came. Intrigued, I phoned the national sales manager and told him of my interest and the lack of response to my Web inquiry. He was apologetic and explained (made the excuse) that the company's Web site was outsourced and that there had "been some problems with the supplier" and that the company was "in the process of changing contractors". In the meantime, it seemed that public inquiries and comments to this multi-billion dollar corporation disappeared into the ether of cyberspace.

In 2014, after flying from Sydney to the UK for the first stage of interviews with government organizations and companies in this research project, I submitted an online complaint about an aspect of the international airline's service. On the return leg, the seat that I was allocated was faulty, with part of the metal frame able to be felt through the seat cushion. Being a 24-hour journey, this was not a minor matter, so I reported the problem to the crew before take-off. A cabin attendant explained that there were no other seats as the flight was full, but promised to bring me an extra pillow. She never returned with the extra pillow. A further discussion with the purser of the flight after take-off evoked sympathy and a promise to report the matter, but no resolution of my problem. I ended up sitting on my blanket and suffered an unpleasant flight. The Web site of the airline—a major international carrier—states explicitly that "we welcome your feedback and comments", so after returning home I entered a short report of my experience along with my contact details and waited. And waited. No response was ever received.

Chances are that you and most people you know have experienced an organization not listening on at least one occasion, if not many times. And it is almost certain that this caused you and them frustration and even anger because of the inconvenience, wasted time, disadvantage, or worse that was caused. In some cases, a failure of organizations to listen can cause serious jeopardy to people including financial losses, injury, and even death, as will be shown in this study.

In many cases, the 'unlistened to' have little choice but to tolerate the indignity and marginalization that are caused by their voice not being given attention and response. On other occasions, the 'unlistened to' and the 'insufficiently listened to' exercise agency and silently censure the offending organization by resigning, withdrawing their support, or taking their business elsewhere. In a few instances, but increasingly in the age of social media, long-suffering citizens, irate customers, frustrated members, and consumer activists retaliate by publicly criticizing the organization concerned. In such cases, an organization can be significantly damaged through loss of reputation, support, and sales.

Some of the incidents reported above are relatively minor matters. But at a more serious level, a lack of listening can cause voter frustration that can ultimately topple governments; poor employee morale leading to reduced loyalty and rising staff turnover; a loss of customers; and even life-threatening crises such as misdiagnoses in hospitals and accidents caused by failure to address complaints and reported faults.

But how extensive is this non-listening? Are these anecdotal examples isolated cases, or are they typical and symptomatic of a malaise in contemporary society? This is what research reported in this book set out to examine and, having found such instances alarmingly widespread, explore the reasons and identify ways in which organizational listening can be improved for the benefit of civil society as well as governments, businesses, and other types of organizations.

Research reported in this book shows that, while some social scientists and humanities researchers see a 'crisis of voice' in contemporary societies (e.g., Couldry, 2010), the real problem is a crisis of listening—something that Nick Couldry implicitly supports in pointing out that voice needs to have value and more explicitly contends in identifying the denial of what he calls "voice that matters" to many in neoliberal societies.

This particularly occurs at organizational level—the focus of this book. Governments including their myriad departments and agencies; corporations; institutions ranging from hospitals and the police to museums, libraries, and schools; non-government organizations (NGOs); non-profit organizations such as associations, institutes, and clubs; and countless other public and private sector organizations are expected and often required to engage with citizens, customers, members, employees, and other 'publics',[2] 'stakeholders',[3] and 'stakeseekers'.[4] But, in many cases, they don't—not in any open, meaningful, and mutually satisfactory way.

This conclusion is based on a two-year research project examining 36 case studies involving 104 interviews, analysis of more than 400 documents such as communication plans, reports of public consultations, and evaluations of communication, and 25 experimental tests of the listening capabilities of organizations. The extant literature informing this topic, the methodology of this study, its findings and conclusions, and recommendations for improving public communication and engagement are reported in detail in the following chapters.

Communication and dialogue are conceptualized as *two-way*, *interactive*, and *transactional* (Craig & Muller, 2007; Griffin, 2009; Littlejohn & Foss, 2008). But these concepts remain normative ideals in many cases, or are operationalized as turn-taking in speaking, with little if any focus on listening. Sometimes, these 'speech acts' do not even involve turn-taking, with research showing that so-called communication by organizations mainly involves speaking to represent the voice and transmit the messages of the organization. Citizens are conceptualized as *consumers* by corporations and even by governments in many neoliberal capitalist societies, perceived primarily in the context of *consuming* products, services, and messages.

While the rhetoric of democratic politics, contemporary business, and professional practices such as public relations (PR), customer relations, and community relations professes *dialogue, engagement, participation, consultation, collaboration*, and even *co-production*—sometimes with good intent—listening receives little focus in scholarly or professional literature in these fields, as is shown in Chapter 1.

Furthermore, there is little recognition and examination of the particular challenges faced by organizations, many of which have thousands, hundreds of thousands, or even millions of people with an interest in their affairs—what will be referred to as stakeholders and publics in this analysis for brevity. The term 'stakeholders' is used to denote those with a direct physical or emotional stake in an organization or its activities (e.g., shareholders, employees, and local communities), while 'publics' refers to others with a broad interest or entitlement to information, including stakeseekers. Engagement with such large and diverse groups requires large-scale listening. The well-documented practices of interpersonal communication and interpersonal listening cannot be simply transplanted into an organizational context.

In addition to identifying a crisis of listening permeating politics, government, business, and civil society, and the destructive effects that this is having, this book goes further to propose an *architecture of listening* as a necessary element in all public and private sector organizations, as well as the *work of listening*. Based on empirical research conducted inside a substantial sample of organizations internationally, it identifies that large-scale listening requires a number of features and elements to be designed into organizations. Organizational listening cannot be effectively achieved simply by adding a 'listening post' or installing a software application. The key features and elements of an architecture of listening are identified based on the case studies examined and examples drawn from reports of various initiatives around the world.

Finally, this analysis explores the benefits for organizations as well as citizens, voters, members, employees, and 'consumers' in neoliberal capitalist terms of undertaking the work of listening facilitated by an architecture of listening. This analysis shows that there are substantial, tangible benefits for government, business, institutions, and NGOs arising from effective ethical listening ranging from increased organizational legitimacy, public support, and reputation to increased employee satisfaction, retention, and productivity; increased brand and customer loyalty; improved policy making and decision making; and even reduced costs through participatory, collaborative, and co-production approaches, as well as reduced disruptions caused by complaints, regulatory interventions, and legal actions. Conversely, it shows that not listening creates serious threats to the stability and continuity of governments, businesses, and other types of organizations.

It is recognized that some forms of organizational listening are problematic—particularly some instances of 'listening in', in contrast to 'listening to' and 'listening out for'. For instance, while national security is an important issue, there is considerable concern that the listening activities of intelligence and security agencies can infringe privacy and civil rights and amount to spying on citizens. However, such abuses of listening are not the focus of this book, which examines the broad range of legitimate interactions between organizations and citizens.

Ultimately, given the central role of organizations in industrialized and post-industrial societies, effective ethical organizational listening will benefit all members of society and can contribute to social equity and help address the concerning "democratic deficit" (Couldry, 2010, p. 49; Curran, 2011, p. 86; Norris, 2011) to produce an enriched democracy and civil society.

Notes

1. The strip of land between houses and a road, sidewalk, or other public areas is called a verge in the UK, a tree lawn and other terms in the US, and a nature strip in Australia.
2. Public relations scholars Jim Grunig and Todd Hunt (1984) advocate the term 'publics' (plural) to refer to groups of people with whom interaction is desirable or necessary. The concept also is advocated by sociologists and political scientists such as Nina Eliasoph (2004), who has called for broad-based replacement of the singular term 'public' with the plural 'publics' to recognize social plurality and diversity. Kate Lacey says "the idea of a singular, overarching public is a rhetorical fiction" (2013, p. 15).

3. 'Stakeholders' is a term proposed by R. Edward Freeman (1984) in his book *Strategic Management: A Stakeholder Approach* to draw attention to those affected by or affecting organizations beyond stockholders. Stakeholders can include employees, suppliers, distributors, retailers, and local communities.
4. 'Stakeseekers' is a term that broadens the concept of stakeholders to include individuals and groups without a direct relationship with an organization but who seek to have a say or influence (Heath, 2002; Spicer, 2007).

· 1 ·

THE FUNDAMENTAL ROLE OF COMMUNICATION AND VOICE

To be means to communicate dialogically. When dialogue ends, everything ends.
—(Mikhail Bakhtin, 1963/1984, p. 252, writing about human society)

Communication theorists and sociologists identify communication as "the organizing element of human life" (Littlejohn & Foss, 2008, p. 4) and the basis of human society (Carey, 1989/2009; Dewey, 1916). John Dewey said "society exists ... in communication" (1916, p. 5) and famously added that "of all things, communication is the most wonderful" (1939, p. 385)—albeit Dewey's statements are often misinterpreted, as noted by James Carey (1989/2009). Dewey was not suggesting that communication is easy or that it is always a satisfying experience. Raymond Williams also wrote effusively about the importance of communication in creating and sustaining communities and societies, echoing Dewey in saying "society is a form of communication" (1976, p. 10). Other scholars note that humans "cannot not communicate" (Watzlawick, Beavin, & Jackson, 1967, p. 48). Even silence communicates— an important principle informing this analysis.

Public Communication in Society

Communication between two individuals (dyads) and within small groups, referred to as *interpersonal* communication, is a long-standing field of study in which there is a substantial body of literature. Some interpersonal communication is private, while in other cases it deals with matters of public concern. Communication is also essential inside organizations such as government departments, corporations, and institutions such as schools, universities, and hospitals. This is commonly referred to as *organizational communication*, although it would be more accurately called intra-organizational communication. This sphere of communication involves interpersonal communication between managers and individual employees as well as *mediated* communication through a range of channels such as newsletters and intranets.

Within societies communication also needs to occur on a larger scale between governments and citizens; between corporations and their customers and potential customers; between associations, clubs, libraries, institutes, and community groups and their members; between schools and universities and their students; between hospitals, clinics, doctors, nurses, and their patients; and so on. This broader sphere of communication, as well as organizational communication, is collectively referred to in this analysis as *public communication*. It is sometimes conducted interpersonally (i.e., face-to-face) such as in meetings, but it is public in the sense that it is commonly mediated to substantial numbers of people through advertising and publicity; publications such as brochures, pamphlets, and newsletters; public events; and increasingly Web sites and social media. Such communication is also public in the sense that it relates to matters in the public sphere (Habermas, 1962/1989, 2006) rather than the private sphere (Chartier, 1989; Hansson, 2007)—albeit the separation of private and the public is seen by some to denote a "false opposition" (D. Goodman, 1992, p. 2) and to be a blurred boundary in contemporary societies (Baxter, 2011). The Web site of the School of Communication at American University in Washington, DC, says of public communication:

> It's at the heart of our economy, society, and politics. Studios use it to promote their films. Politicians use it to get elected. Businesses use it to burnish their image. Advocates use it to promote social causes. (American University, 2015)

By way of clarification, the singular term *communication* is used in this analysis to refer to the processes of exchanging messages and meaning making between people, rather than communications (plural), except when directly quoting sources that use the latter term. While the words are used interchangeably in many cases, *communications* is widely used in the engineering and information technology fields to refer to systems and technologies for transmission and reception of signals and data (e.g., as in telecommunications). Telephones, computers, fibre optics, and satellites are used for communications. People do communication (Mazur, 2013)—including people acting on behalf of organizations. Hence, as a further clarification about this text, the terms 'organizational communication' and 'organizational listening' are not used anthropomorphically; rather they refer to people in organizations engaging with other people on behalf of organizations.

Throughout the twentieth century it was common to refer to *mass communication* in discussing public communication with large groups of people. However, this understanding of communication is mostly associated with *mass media* such as newspapers, radio, and television that dominated the mediascape during the twentieth century, the now questionable concept of *mass society* (Hoggart, 2004; Williams, 1962/1976), and related transmissional notions of communication that will be examined and challenged in Chapter 2. Public communication is a more inclusive term than mass communication as it incorporates a range of channels and methods such as meetings, events, the Internet, and social media as well as mass media, and it recognizes a range of groups with differing interests and views rather than one imagined static mass audience.

Communication between individuals and organizations may not always be public in the sense of being open for all to hear or see, but it is public in the sense of organization-public relationships, referred to in public relations practice as OPR (Heath, 2013). Organizations including governments, corporations, non-government organizations (NGOs), and various types of institutions routinely refer to 'the public' as well as publics (plural), along with a number of other terms such as 'stakeholders'[1] for those with whom they need to interact, such as voters, customers, members, students, patients, or citizens. It is appropriate therefore to include this interaction within the rubric of public communication and, indeed, this particular sphere of communication is the focus of this book. Public communication is used in this analysis to include government communication, organizational communication, political communication, corporate communication, marketing communication, and their constituent practices such as advertising, public relations, customer relations, and public consultation.

Near the end of the twentieth century, eminent media researchers Jay Blumler and Michael Gurevitch identified a "crisis in public communication" and, in particular, what they called a "crisis of civic communication" (1995, p. 1). Erik Bucy and Paul D'Angelo similarly have warned of "the crisis of communication for citizenship" (1999, p. 329). These researchers were referring to a decline of interest in news and information other than entertainment and a decline in civic and political participation—what a number of scholars term the "democratic deficit" (Couldry, 2010, p. 49; Curran, 2011, p. 86; Norris, 2011). However, this analysis shows that the crisis in public communication extends much further into contemporary civic life.

The Public Sphere

Much public communication takes place within what is widely referred to as the *public sphere*, the concept brought to prominence by Jürgen Habermas (1962/1989, 2006) to denote the domain in which public communication and debate related to democratic politics and civic life occurs. In particular, Habermas advocated a deliberative public sphere in which citizens and 'political actors' engage in rational-critical deliberation and debate to reach decisions. Such a concept of democracy frames how communication is conducted. Furthermore, whereas the public sphere was once a physical place, such as the famed but much-overstated *agora* of ancient Greece,[2] today the public sphere is largely mediated (Corner, 2007; Dahlgren, 2009; Keane, 2009a, 2009b). During the twentieth century, mass media—press, radio, and television— provided a primary site of the public sphere in developed societies, along with 'town hall' meetings and other forums for public communication. Today, the public sphere has expanded to include the Internet, particularly the Web and social media.

The Habermasian concept of the public sphere has been criticized on at least four grounds. First, critics see the deliberative public sphere as normative and unachievable because of its "idealization of public reason" (Curran, 2002, p. 45). Second, deliberative democracy is seen as an unrealistic and normative model because, as Peter Dahlgren says, "there is not much chance that a vast majority of people of a Western liberal democracy will become 'active citizens' or even well-informed citizens" (2009, p. 13). Lincoln Dahlberg (2014) identifies two other substantial critiques as the public sphere's propensity for *exclusion* of some groups and its focus on *consensus*.

Exclusion can occur at two levels, according to critics. At one level, whole groups of people who are marginalized in society can be excluded, such as the poor, those who are mentally ill, and Indigenous people. In particular,

Stephen Elstub notes that the widely applied democratic approach of "focus-sing on 'common' interests can exclude the more specific but still relevant interests of excluded and marginalized groups" (2010, p. 296). Also, exclu-sion can occur because some citizens do not have the sociopolitical resources and social capital to participate in deliberation and rational-critical debate (e.g., lack of education). Or they may choose to engage in different ways, such as agonistically through protests and other forms of activism. Dahlberg says that "in order to be considered legitimate deliberators, subjects must come to internalize the rules of the particular form of communication deemed to be the universally valid form of democratic engagement or be excluded from the public sphere" (2014, p. 27).

While consensus is often viewed as a positive characteristic within groups and society, the deliberative public sphere as described by Habermas (1962/1989, 2006) and others such as David Held (2006) is also criticized for imposing "homogeneity" on diverse groups of citizens through focus on consensus-seeking (Bickford, 1996) and recognition of singular 'public opin-ion' (Fraser, 1990). Chantal Mouffe (1999, 2005) and other poststructuralist critics who advocate agonistic modes of political discussion and participation call for greater recognition of plurality, diversity, and struggle in the public sphere and public communication. Roger Silverstone (2007) took up Edward Said's notion of *contrapuntal* (from the Italian *contra* meaning against and *punto* meaning point) to emphasize the different viewpoints and interests and dialectic tension between voices in the public sphere.

However, as Dahlberg (2014) and other Habermasian supporters argue, Habermas recognized problems of exclusion and also limitations of deliber-ation and rationality. Habermas acknowledged that "unequal distribution of attention, competencies, and knowledge", strategic manipulation of various kinds, and systemic coercion by state or corporate interests occur and cause exclusions from the public sphere (1996, pp. 307–308, 325). In his more recent writings he also recognized and expressed concern that public spheres are "dominated by the kind of mediated communication that lacks the defin-ing features of deliberation" (2006, p. 414), referring to mass media focus on entertainment and celebrity rather than substantial public information and education. Significantly for this analysis, Habermas identified advertising and public relations as part of the apparatus of media and potentially corrupting influences in the public sphere (1989, pp. 189–193). Noting these limita-tions, he stated that the deliberative public sphere should not be viewed as an "end state" and explicitly acknowledged that "the public sphere ideal is not perfectly reachable" (1992, p. 477). For Habermas, the public sphere is not a set of strict procedures for deliberation, as is often claimed, but an intentionally normative model to identify what he called the "functionally necessary" sociopolitical resources and conditions needed to enhance rational-critical deliberation qualitatively as well as quantitatively (Habermas, 1996, p. 325).

Many commentators on the public sphere also overlook or ignore that Habermas (1981/1984, 1981/1987) developed his *theory of communicative action* in the 1970s and incorporated this into his evolving concept of the public sphere to address some of the causes of exclusion and the limitations of consensus. Habermas's theory of communicative action calls for genuine *communicative* action designed to achieve understanding (and potentially consensus) in contrast with *strategic* action that, either openly or in a concealed way, uses communication for persuasion and even manipulation to serve individual or organizational self-interests. While noting Bickford's concern that Habermas's theory of communicative action narrows debate and represented interests by requiring participants to be focussed on "achieving, sustaining and renewing consensus" (1996, p. 17), this theory usefully draws attention to the importance of authentic communicative action rather than lobbying, persuasion, and propaganda (political or corporate), which utilize top-down, one-way approaches to communication.

The term 'strategic' arises many times in this analysis as an adjective used to describe actions and communication, both in the literature reviewed and in reporting research into public communication by organizations. It is important to understand the way that this term frames communication before proceeding too far. While strategic actions and *strategic communication* are often assumed to be positive concepts denoting purposefulness, prioritization, and effectiveness, a seminal paper on the topic by Hallahan, Holtzhausen, van Ruler, Verčič, and Sriramesh (2007) points out that strategic communication by an organization is widely understood as "purposeful use of communication to fulfil *its* mission" (p. 3) [emphasis added]. Kirk Hallahan and his co-researchers acknowledge that the traditional and widely applied approach to strategy "privileges a management discourse and emphasizes upper management's goals for the organization as given and legitimate" (2007, p. 11). As well as being widely used in business, Michael Schneider identifies "the rise of strategic communication" in government and public diplomacy (2015, p. 18). In a 2015 discussion of "the dark side of strategic communication", Ronald Dulek and Kim Campbell note that the term "shifts the focus from context and the recipient to purpose and the sender" (2015, p. 122).

Drawing on leading management texts in the field (e.g., Thompson, Peteraf, Gamble, & Strickland, 2013), they point out that strategy in communication "focuses on achieving the sender's predetermined aim" (2015, p. 123). This organization-centricity and sender-receiver hierarchy need to be borne in mind in considering claims and discussions of strategic communication.

Habermas's concept of the public sphere based on deliberation and rational debate grounded in communicative action rather than manipulative strategic action remains an enduring feature of contemporary democracies. In recent writing, Habermas has argued that the public sphere is "part of the bedrock of liberal democracies" (2006, p. 412). However, challenges to Habermas's demanding notion of deliberative democracy, coupled with elitist tendencies and citizen apathy, have led to some 'watered down' models of democracy in which there are low levels of participation by citizens and in which governments become remote from the people. On the other hand, concern about negative effects of declining citizen interest and participation in politics in many countries (Dahlgren, 2009) and declining citizens' trust in politicians and representative institutions (Coleman, 2013a; Gibson, Lusoli, & Ward, 2008, pp. 111–113; Lacey, 2013, p. 187; Tilley, 2005) has led some political and social scientists to seek more open participatory models to redress the 'democratic deficit'—what Carl Boggs (2000) calls "the great retreat" from civic and political engagement. Increasing disengagement from traditional politics and civic life by young people is of particular concern (Bennett, 2008; Bennett, Wells, & Freelon, 2011; Coleman, 2008, 2013a; Couldry, Livingstone, & Markham, 2007; Curran, 2011; Loader, Vromen, & Xenos, 2014).[3]

A number of types of democracy and public spheres exist around the world, and a number of others are proposed to increase social equity and the legitimacy of governments. The type of democracy that is practiced, or the one we want, sets the parameters for who speaks and who listens, and the types and levels of listening that should occur. Types of democracy in existence or envisaged include the following:

1. *Elite* democracy in which, as the name suggests, elites govern and there are limited opportunities for others to participate. Proponents argue that elites are the most equipped to provide leadership (e.g., in terms of education) and that most people do not wish to be actively involved in politics;

2. *Liberal* democracy, which privileges individual freedom, often adopting voluntary voting, and operates by leaders and power centres

informally identifying and representing the views of citizens aggregated into what is referred to as 'public opinion' (Fishkin, 1995; Lippmann, 1922);

3. *Plebiscitary* democracy, which emanates from the liberal theories of Max Weber on plebiscitary leadership (see Mommsen, 1959/1984), is a form of liberal democracy in which leaders allegedly reflect the will of the people and rule authoritatively, with checks and balances applied only occasionally through elections or referenda;

4. *Representative* democracy, which is closely aligned with what Habermas and some others refer to as *republican* democracy, involves political engagement through elected representatives who allegedly speak on behalf of and are accountable to citizens. Despite calls for deliberative and other more participatory forms of democracy, this model is the most widely adopted in contemporary Western societies;

5. *Deliberative* democracy as proposed by Habermas as a normative model in which substantial numbers if not all citizens deliberate (think deeply about) and rationally debate issues of public concern;

6. *Monitory* democracy as described by John Keane (2009b) in which Michael Schudson's (2003) notion of the "monitorial citizen" uses various forms of media to monitor social and political developments and becomes active only when he or she decides to intervene, supported by thousands of NGOs that engage in a watchdog role as well as advocacy and activist groups acting on behalf of citizens;

7. *Direct* democracy, or what some call *participatory* democracy (e.g., Carpentier, 2011), which seeks the involvement of citizens in a range of political activities beyond electing representatives and expressing opinion. These can include various citizen councils, juries, and committees, as well as national forums and other opportunities for political participation;

8. *Radical* (or *agonistic*) democracy, which has similarities to direct democracy in that it seeks high levels of engagement by citizens (Carpentier, 2011; Curran, 2011), but has other fundamental differences. Drawing on neomarxism and New Left thinking, radical democratic theory challenges liberal pluralist models for "ignoring the enormously unequal resources available to different groups in society" (Curran, 2011, p. 81) and the focus on consensus and unilateral public opinion, advocating instead an agonistic approach. Hence this model could also be called agonistic democracy;

9. *Dialogic* democracy proposed by Anthony Giddens (1994), who argues that Habermas's deliberative democracy is unrealistic because of its reliance on the 'ideal speech situation' and its overemphasis on *consensus*. Instead, dialogic democracy accepts "the essential contestability of the issues with which we are dealing" (Dobson, 2014, p. 120). Giddens says "dialogic democracy presumes only that dialogue in a public space provides a means of living along with the other in a relation of mutual *tolerance*" (1994, p. 115) [emphasis added];

10. *Communicative* democracy proposed by Iris Marion Young (2000), which claims that deliberative democracy is not sufficiently inclusive because its focus on rational forms of communication privileges dominant social groups and excludes others. Young proposes additional modes of political communication, which she refers to as greeting, rhetoric, and narrative to expand the range of voices and include alternative ways of speaking. However, as Andrew Dobson notes, Young's communicative democracy "has only told half of the story" as, despite its emphasis on communication, it does not address listening" (2014, p. 135).

Many argue that there is no single public sphere today, but rather a number of *public sphericles*—also called *sphericules* (Carpentier, 2011; Gitlin, 1998). Despite being seen negatively as social fragmentation by some, this concept recognizes the rise of activism and single issue politics that characterize contemporary democratic societies and is arguably more reflective of democratic practices in the twenty-first century than the notion of a homogeneous public sphere. Alternatively, like the term 'publics', the term 'public spheres' (plural) can serve to identify the range of forums and sites of democratic participation today.

Irrespective of whether democratic societies express their voice and engage in debate in a public sphere, public spheres, or public sphericles, elected governments and various institutions and organizations that make up the state—such as the White House, Number 10 Downing Street, cabinets, ministries, senates, congresses, councils, and civil service departments and agencies—need to listen to the voice of the people, as well as speak to and for citizens, to maintain a mandate and have legitimacy. Robert Dahl said that a key characteristic of democracy is "the continuing responsiveness of the government to the preferences of its citizens, considered as political equals" (1971, p. 1). How, and how well, these organizations communicate with citizens is therefore of particular interest.

Nancy Fraser (1992) makes a distinction between strong and weak publics and Bernard Miège (2010) discusses a three-tiered public sphere made up of an *elite sphere* of political actors from the organs of the state and the upper echelons of the corporate sector; a middle tier, which is the mainstream public sphere mostly mediated through mass media; and the *societal sphere* in which private unorganized citizens can participate in opinion-formation but are largely remote from the major centres or decision making and thus constitute a weak public or public sphere in Fraser's terms. The relative resources and circumstances of the weak societal sphere as well as the mainstream public sphere and elite sphere need to be considered in examining organizational listening, influence, and response.

The Market

For as long as people have engaged in politics and organized systems of government—or even longer—they also have created markets for trade and commerce that form the basis of business and economies. Along with the state (politics and government), the market makes up a key sector of contemporary societies, particularly capitalist societies. While early markets were mostly localized in villages and towns and involved barter and simple bilateral trade conducted largely through interpersonal communication, the market economies of industrialized countries are composed of large corporations operating nationally and increasingly as part of globalized markets, as well as small businesses and individual workers.

The market is an important and essential site for investigation, particularly in neoliberal capitalist economies, as scholars note that market values and logic have permeated almost all areas of society in such systems. In addition to political economy critiques, Nick Couldry is critical of neoliberalism from a sociological perspective, saying that a neoliberal discourse provides the organizing metaphors for contemporary life in capitalist societies. We hear this daily in references to people as 'consumers', rather than citizens, and descriptions of the development and success of societies in terms of gross domestic product (GDP), export earnings, retail sales, and overall economic growth—which Nobel Prize–winning economics writer Paul Krugman calls the "spectator sport" of our age (as cited in Greenhouse, 2009, p. 7). This trend is referred to as *marketization* by some (e.g., Couldry, 2010, p. 53). Neoliberalism has seen market values and logic such as efficiency and competition infiltrate and shape government, resulting in privatization, deregulation, free trade and open markets, reductions in government spending, and the handing over of many social services and public utilities such as railways and power supplies to private enterprise.

Colin Leys says that in neoliberal capitalist societies "politics are no longer about managing the economy to satisfy the demands of voters, they are increasingly about getting voters to endorse policies that meet the demands of capital" (2001, p. 68). In such societies, Evgeny Morozov says "it's the ratings agencies and bond markets—not the voters—who are in charge today" (2014, p. 29). Given these shifts, Couldry argues that "neoliberalism is a rationality that denies voice" to many (2010, p. 135). Even more inequitably, it will be shown in this analysis that neoliberalism is a rationality that denies listening to many.

This occurs because competition is a fundamental underpinning principle of market logic and capitalism in general. Kenneth Burke (1969) referred to the "wrangle of the marketplace", also calling it a "scramble". Economists argue that this wrangle ensures that the best ideas, products, services, and organizations survive and prosper, while also claiming that it is equitable because of the 'trickle down' of wealth and prosperity and also because the wrangle is largely self-regulating through open competition and forces such as supply and demand that create equilibrium (Debreu, 1959). However, problems inevitably occur because those involved in the wrangle have greatly varying weight and strength. The wrangle of the marketplace is a bit like a sumo wrestler jostling with a jockey. Drawing on Burke, some contemporary rhetorical scholars see the public sphere as a 'marketplace of ideas' in which there is a "robust contest of ideas" through discussion and debate (Heath, 1992, p. 20). But whose ideas gain prominence and acceptance is a matter of who gets to speak and, even more important, who is listened to. (*Author note: Saying who is 'heard' would avoid ending the preceding sentence and others like it with a preposition, a practice that grammatical purists object to! But hearing and being heard are significantly different concepts than listening and being listened to, as will be explained in this chapter.*)[4]

Increasingly, as noted in economics literature, markets are becoming globalized and Philip Bobbitt (2003) argues that the nation state has been superseded by the 'market state', as world markets are increasingly formed on supra-national lines. This is further distancing the voices of citizens in localized communities from large and megalithic organizations, rendering them but whispers unheard and unheeded by centres of decision making such as New York; London; Washington, DC; and Brussels.

In neoliberal capitalist societies, it is imperative to look not only at public communication between governments and citizens, but also at public communication between corporations and their stakeholders and publics. The public communication practices of the market conceptualized as part of *marketing* and related functions such as market research, advertising, customer relations, public relations, and corporate and organizational communication, as well as political communication, will be examined in detail in Chapters 2 and 3.

Civil Society

In addition to the realm of the state (government and the legislature) and the market (business and the economy), civil society is an important 'third sector' of most societies. This is the "sphere of social interaction between economy and state ... composed ... of the sphere of associations (especially voluntary associations), social movements, and forms of public communication" (Cohen & Arato, 1994, p. ix). While the public sphere is interpreted broadly by some to denote all of the physical and virtual spaces in which citizens, their representatives, and various types of organizations communicate and negotiate about matters of common interest, it is more correct and useful to refer to this third sector as civil society to differentiate it from the activities of traditional political actors and institutional politics such as party campaigning, elections, and the proceedings of parliaments, congresses, and senates, as well as the marketplace. While noting that civil society is a complex concept with multiple forms, Michael Walzer emphasizes that civil society is "the space of uncoerced human association and also the set of relational networks" that are formed to protect and advance the interests of those involved (1992, p. 89). Mark Lyons (2001) refers to civil society as "a lively, vibrant space, full of argument and disputation about matters of greatest import to its citizens" (p. 207) and further notes that the concept broadly denotes the promotion of citizens' political engagement and development. For a detailed discussion of civil society, see Edwards (2009, 2014).

While some seek to colonize civil society as part of the market economy or subsume it within politics or specific NGO agendas, and others dismiss the concept as Leftist naïveté, it is relevant to note that, despite intellectual debate, civil society continues to be seen as an important part of society alongside and overlapping with the state, the market, and private individuals and families. Habermas, who developed the prevailing concept of the public sphere, acknowledged civil society as something separate. In stating that citizens need various resources to enhance deliberation and public debate to enable them to participate in the public sphere, Habermas identified four key resources: (1) a regulated mass media system that serves the interests of the public (not simply advertisers and corporate interests); (2) a network of autonomous civil society associations engaged in facilitating communicative reasoning and public opinion formation; (3) a liberal-egalitarian political culture; and (4) social rights such as freedom of speech and freedom to congregate (1996, p. 488).

Civil society has expanded enormously in the past half-century, particularly in terms of NGOs, as noted by John Keane (2009a, 2009b) in his discussions of 'monitory democracy'. In an analysis of civil society, Michael Edwards (2014) reported that there are more than 80,000 NGOs worldwide, although he is careful to note that civil society is broader than NGOs. This estimate refers to major NGOs only, as the United Nations (2014) reports that there are around 35,000 NGOs operating internationally—4,000 with formal consultative status with the United Nations Economic and Social Council (ECOSOC) and a further 31,000 working with the UN in some way—while the NGO Web site lists around 40,000 international NGOs (NGO, 2010). In addition, because of broad definitions of the term 'NGO', there are millions of NGOs operating nationally. For instance, the US Department of State (2012) reports that there are an estimated 1.5 million NGOs operating in the US alone, and India had around 3.3 million NGOs in 2010, according to the sustainable development and human rights Web site OneWorld South Asia (2010). NGOs range from major human rights groups such as Amnesty International and global aid and health organizations to community-based education, health, and environmental groups, as well as a range of 'think tanks', institutes, foundations, committees, councils, and associations.

Institutions such as churches and the academy, trade unions, the wide range of charities and other types of non-profit organizations that exist and play an important role in most societies, as well as social movements such as anti-nuclear, gay rights, and animal rights groups also are seen to form civil society. In addition, there are new kinds of volunteer organizations utilizing the public space of the Internet such as MoveOn.org, which offers free membership for concerned citizens to collectively campaign on various issues.

The key characteristics of civil society are volunteerism and commitment to the general social good rather than representation of specific interests, as discussed by Sidney Verba and colleagues in their civic volunteerism model of participation (Verba, Scholzman, & Brady, 1995). Some civil society organizations engage in politics, but in most cases their role is broader. Robert Putnam and others argue that non-political organizations in civil society are vital for democracy because they build social capital and shared values, which are prerequisites for participation and creation of a viable representative democracy and an equitable society. In *The Life and Death of Democracy* (Keane, 2009a), and in his extensive writing on what he calls *monitory democracy*, John Keane notes that a proliferating range of "extra parliamentary, power scrutinizing mechanisms" has evolved in the past 50–60 years to help counterbalance some of the power inequities of big political parties, big government, and big business and give a voice to minorities left out of official politics (2009b, n.p.). An active civil society is "the chicken soup of the social sciences" that will help ailing democracies recover from their malaise of citizen disengagement, lack of participation, and lack of trust, according to Michael Edwards (2009, p. 3). American writer Jeremy Rifkin calls civil society "our last, best hope" (as cited in Edwards, 2014, p. 3).

While the market views and treats people as *consumers*, within the public sphere and civil society people are seen as citizens, and *citizenship* entails certain rights as well as responsibilities. "Active citizenship" is widely identified in research as preferable to "passive citizenship" in terms of citizen engagement and participation in politics and civil society, which in turn create government legitimacy (Kane, 2000, pp. 223–224; Turner, 1994, 2001). Kane (2000) links active citizenship with the notion of "thick community", whereas passive citizenship results in "thin community" (pp. 224–225). Active citizenship requires not only voice in the sense of a right and opportunity to speak, but also the right and opportunity to be listened to.

Bryan Turner (1994) argues that there needs to be a refocussing on citizenship because the collective focus on states is under challenge by globalization and increasing numbers of people who suffer statelessness, such as refugees. Turner proposes a broader notion of citizenship than conventional concepts that denote an entitlement to resources within the borders of a nation state. He calls for recognition of *cultural citizenship*, which he says "can be described as cultural empowerment, namely the capacity to participate effectively, creatively, and successfully within a national culture" (2001, p. 12)—wherever that may be located. Wayne Hudson (2000) similarly calls for disarticulating the notion of citizenship from what he sees as the nostalgic idea of the nation-state. This suggests that many organizations need not only to listen locally and nationally, but also to expand their capabilities to listening across borders.

While civil society is based on volunteerism and cooperation, communication also lies at its core. Volunteerism largely depends on public communication that rallies public support and issues calls to action. The messages of NGOs, institutions, charities, and industry, professional, and community organizations are propelled into the public sphere and contribute to meaning making and the construction of reality through public communication.

Communication is a vast and diverse field of study and practice that has evolved since the seventeenth century (Mattelart, 2007), ranging from interpersonal communication and speech communication to mass communication and, more recently, into the broad field of communication studies (Craig, 1999), as well as numerous disciplinary fields such as political communication, marketing communication, corporate communication, organizational communication, and public relations. One would think that communication would be well covered by now—that there would be no substantial gaps in our knowledge and practices. It is almost universal practice for job applicants to write 'good communicator' on their curricula vitae and applications. The senior vice president of corporate affairs for the UK and northern Europe of one of the world's best-known multinational brands described his company as "a listening organization", but was not available to be interviewed for this study (personal communication, September 15, 2014). Such assumptions and claims are shown to be mostly wrong by the research findings and critical analysis presented in the following chapters, which indicate that there are communication problems in all of the three domains discussed in the previous sections. Specifically, there is a deficit of listening, which renders voice valueless for many and ultimately denies representation and recognition. It is argued that this devaluing and denial are highly destructive for governments, political parties, businesses, as well as many other institutions and organizations, and ultimately society for the reasons outlined in the following discussion.

The Central Role of Organizations in Contemporary Societies

While studies of interpersonal communication and citizen participation in democracy such as those of Coleman (2013a, 2013b), Couldry (2010, 2012), Crawford (2009), Dreher (2009, 2012), Penman and Turnbull (2012a, 2012b), and others have recognized listening as an essential part of communication and affording voice that matters, examinations of listening have

rarely turned their attention to organizations. The few exceptions are confined to specialist disciplinary studies of internal organizational communication between management and employees, analyses of entities that function
specifically as representative organizations, and some nascent attention paid
to listening in public relations (e.g., Burnside-Lawry, 2011). This is a significant gap because in industrialized societies with institutionalized politics and
social systems (Chadwick, 2006), or what Couldry calls "complex societies"
(2010, p. 100), citizens not only work in and are represented through organizations, but they need to interact with an array of organizations on a daily
basis in accessing goods and services, complying with laws and regulations,
and living as agentic social actors. These include government departments
and agencies, corporations, various NGOs, institutions such as police, hospitals, libraries, schools, universities, museums, associations, clubs, foundations,
local businesses, councils, and so on. Along with the key role of government
even in so-called de-regulated states, James Muldoon (2004) describes how
multinational corporations are "active participants in global political and economic affairs" (p. 341).

In their book *Collective Action in Organizations: Interaction and Engagement in an Era of Technological Change*, Bruce Bimber, Andrew Flanagin, and
Cynthia Stohl (2012) identify the traditional and continuing central role of
organizations in contemporary civil societies and usefully explore how individuals today engage with organizations using an increasing array of media
and communication technologies. However, as the title indicates, they focus
on specialist 'collective action' organizations and their acts of representation. Similarly, Couldry discusses organizations in the sense that they serve
as "mechanisms of representation" providing "distributed forms of voice" for
individuals whom they represent (2010, p. 101). While providing valuable
contributions to discussion of voice and listening, particularly in relation to
democratic politics, these analyses do not examine how the policies, cultures,
structures, and systems of organizations broadly, across various sectors of government, business, industry, the professions, and society, facilitate or hinder
interaction, engagement, participation, and social equity.

It is significant and pertinent to this analysis that organizations today
deploy a range of specialist staff, agencies, and resources ostensibly for public
communication as well as specifically for consultation with stakeholders and
publics (Macnamara, 2012a). These investments include:

- Advertising campaigns (often multimillion-dollar/pound/euro
  investments);

- Market research and marketing communication such as direct mail and e-marketing;
- Public relations, estimated to be growing by 10 per cent a year in major Western markets (Sorrell, 2008) and up to 23 per cent a year in some fast developing countries such as Brazil (ICCO, 2011);
- Burgeoning departments, units, and agencies employed for customer relations, employee relations, investor relations, and community relations;
- Web sites; and
- Mechanisms, tools, and systems purportedly for engagement, dialogue, and consultation such as interactive social media sites, feedback forums, 'listening posts', inquiries, reviews, and so on.

A number of studies of advertising, public relations, election campaigns, organizational and corporate communication, and even some reviews of public consultations reveal that these so-called mechanisms and practices of 'communication' are often predominantly focussed on disseminating information—that is, *speaking* to express and amplify the voice of an organization (e.g., Bennett, Wells, & Freelon, 2011; Foreman-Wernet & Dervin, 2006; Macnamara, 2010, 2013; Sriramesh, Rivera-Sánchez, & Soriano, 2011).

Even in the age of interactive social media which offer explicit and much-vaunted affordances of two-way interaction and dialogue, Kate Crawford has noted that "'speaking up' has become the dominant metaphor for participation in online spaces" and "listening is not a common metaphor for online activity" (2009, p. 526). Despite much being made of the Obama online campaigns, use of Web 2.0–based social media for one-way information transmission (i.e., speaking) by politicians, political parties, and organizations, and a corresponding lack of dialogue and listening, have been widely reported (Gibson, Williamson, & Ward, 2010; Macnamara & Kenning, 2011, 2014; Macnamara & Zerfass, 2012; McAllister-Spooner, 2009; Rosenstiel & Mitchell, 2012; Vergeer, 2013; Wright & Hinson, 2012). This one-way focus will be further discussed in Chapter 2 and explored in detail in Chapters 3 and 4, which report and analyze new empirical research specifically looking at listening.

In her analysis of voice in multicultural communities and marginalized groups, Tanja Dreher (2009) pointed to the need to shift focus and responsibility from individuals and communities 'speaking up' to "the institutions and conventions which enable and constrain receptivity and response" (p. 456).

But her identification of a need for research into this broader context of organizational listening has so far not been taken up, other than in her and Jo Taachi's work on digital storytelling in a social theory context (Dreher, 2012; Taachi, 2009).

While the personally attentive, intimate approaches of interpersonal listening cannot be applied to the large-scale interactions of organizations with thousands, hundreds of thousands, or even millions of stakeholders—what Andrew Dobson calls the problem of "scaling up" (2014, pp. 75, 124)—some level of listening by organizations is essential to maintain a healthy democracy, for organizations to maintain staff motivation and loyalty, for businesses to maintain relationships with customers, and for social justice and equity. While Nick Couldry (2010) refers to the need for large-scale voice in what he calls complex societies (i.e., industrialized, corporatized, and highly organized), little if any attention has been given to large-scale listening.

It is not only a matter of big corporations or governments not listening. Studies as early as 1915 by Michels found that voluntary organizations are "susceptible to non-democratic tendencies"—or what they termed the "iron law of oligarchy" because ruling elites or leaders curtail democracy in an attempt to maintain power (Michels, 1915, as cited in Bimber et al., 2012, p. 20). William Gamson and Emilie Schmeidler (1984) and Mayer Zald and David McCarthy (1987) report that oligarchic structures often result in disengagement of members in voluntary membership organizations because their opportunities for participation become curtailed. Significantly, none of these studies specifically looked at listening, focussing more on the broader concepts of participation and voice. But it is implicitly clear that the non-democratic tendencies of organizations and members' concerns about lack of participation are linked to listening. In their analysis of organizations, Bimber et al. go on to propose two levels of participation that are important for members of organizations. The first is the level of personal interaction that members have with one another. The second dimension is *engagement*, which they define as "how much people perceive that they are able to shape the agenda and the direction of their organization" (2012, p. 32). In today's globalized world in which organizations often operate across national borders and online, personal interaction is increasingly less likely. This places greater emphasis of other forms of engagement as the glue that binds members of organizations together and, ultimately, binds societies. As will be argued throughout this book, engagement is impossible without listening—although one would not get this impression from the extensive discussion of engagement in political, marketing, and public relations literature that rarely mentions listening.

Based on the work of Bimber et al. and others who have studied organizations, this analysis looked at a range of organizations including government, corporate, non-government, and non-profit organizations. This study recognizes that there are new types of social movements that are not based on traditional organizational structures—what Bimber et al. call "organization-less groups" involved in "organization-less organizing" (2012, p. 4). For example, Occupy arranged major protests in cities around the world following the global financial crisis of 2007–2009 without a headquarters, management structure, or even a single leader. Some of the citizen uprisings in the Middle East described as the 'Arab Spring' also occurred without a formal organizational structure. Lance Bennett and Alexandra Segerberg (2012) examined several such groups in detail and concluded that they are based on a *logic of connective action* facilitated through personalized information sharing and networking using new technologies, rather than the traditional *logic of collective action* that relies on assembling high levels of organizational resources and formation of collective identity. These groups and coalitions are beyond the scope of this study, but are increasingly recognized as part of civil society, and it would be interesting to examine how and how well they listen as well as speak. Even though they appear to enable an expansion of voice, at this stage there is no evidence that they listen or facilitate listening any better than traditional organizations.

The Valorization of Voice and Speaking

Human communication is widely conflated with voice and speaking, particularly in relation to public communication and the public sphere. Voice and speaking, including public speaking, have been studied since the early Western civilizations of ancient Greece and Rome where rhetoric—the art of speaking persuasively—became recognized as one of the foundational liberal arts based on the writings and oratory of Plato, Aristotle, Cicero, and Quintilian (Atwill, 1998; Kennedy, 1994). Rhetoric was also studied and developed as early as 500 BCE in Islamic societies of North Africa (Bernal, 1987), and in China (Lu, 1998).

In Book 1 of his *Politics*, Aristotle wrote that "nature … has endowed man alone among the animals with the power of speech" and identified speaking as a key attribute that defines humans (as cited in Haworth, 2004, p. 43).

Aristotle differentiated speaking from voice in its basic physiological form, noting that animals have a voice that can express sounds to signal fear, hunger, pain, and so on. But humans alone acquire the power of language that they can express in spoken, written, or visual forms. It is this symbolic expression in spoken, written, and visual forms that we metaphorically refer to as voice in the context of politics and civil society.

Franz Kafka's ape, in endeavouring to convince its captors of its worth as a being, learned to drink alcohol "making no grimace, like an expert drinker" as part of emulating them and then, in a climactic scene, reported:

> … because I had to, because my senses were roaring, I cried out a short and good "Hello!" breaking out into human sounds. And with this cry I sprang into the community of human beings, and I felt its echo—"Just listen. He's talking!" (Kafka, 1917, p. 6)

Kafka's ape knew that, even more than being social with humans and joining in their merriment, the single most convincing thing that it could do to demonstrate 'humanness' was to speak. Through speaking, Kafka's ape is transformed into a new life in which it ultimately gives an address to the "esteemed gentlemen of the academy".

Renaissance political philosopher Thomas Hobbes echoed Aristotle's trope saying "the most noble and profitable invention of all others was that of speech" (1651/1946, p. 18).

Rhetoric with its focus on speaking remains one of the major traditions of human communication scholarship and practice identified by Robert Craig (1999) and expounded in a number of communication studies texts (e.g., Craig & Muller, 2007; Griffin, 2009; Littlejohn & Foss, 2008). In fact, for much of the twentieth century and even into the twenty-first century, human communication has been widely studied as *speech* communication, particularly in North America (Cohen, 1994; Chaffee & Rogers, 1997; Rogers & Chafee, 2006).

Democracy is founded on the principle of *vox populi*—the voice of the people (Fishkin, 1995). In democratic societies, citizens and stakeholders are regularly urged to find their voice, speak up, and have their say. For instance, a Google search of the term 'have your say' in early 2015 yielded 620 million Web links ranging from local, state, and national government sites in Australia, New Zealand, the UK, and the US, to airport authorities, universities, the BBC program called *Have Your Say*, and the TuneIn *World Have Your Say* site. Similarly, a search of the term 'speak up' yielded 121 million Web links to sites such as 'speak up to stop bullying' to the 'speak up' initiative of Project

Tomorrow, a non-profit education organization in the US. As Gideon Calder observed, in most discussions "agency is located on the side of the speaker rather than the listener" (2011, p. 129).

When citizens experience a lack or loss of voice, a number of scholars point to significant social, cultural, and political problems. For instance, Charles Husband (2000) and others have drawn attention to the lack of voice in any meaningful sense afforded to ethnic minorities and argue that this constitutes inequity and injustice. Feminist scholarship similarly has identified lack of voice available to many women as a social inequity negatively impacting the status and identity of women in many societies, which has added to the tradition of debate focussed on speaking, voice, and representation (e.g., Butler, 1999; Tuchman, 1978; Weatherall, 2002).

Tanja Dreher, who has particularly examined the plight of marginalized groups, has noted that "in much research and advocacy, there is a strong emphasis on voice, representation, speaking up and talking" as enablers of democracy and social equity (2009, p. 446). We are told that "voice matters", not only for interpersonal communication, but also for participation in society, identity, and social equity (Couldry, 2010, 2012). Kate Lacey (2013) refers to the "fetish of participation as 'finding a voice'" (p. 188). Meanwhile, in much scholarly and professional literature there is an implicit assumption, particularly in free speech democratic societies, that political and social leaders, elected officials, civil servants, and organizations are disposed, if not eagerly waiting, to listen to citizens who exercise their voice.

It needs to be recognized that, while the traditional view of politics is based on a vocal metaphor (i.e., voice), the power of visual media and the "age of spectatorship" have spawned an alternative ocular view that claims the power of the people is exercised through watching, which affords "supervision, inspection, examination and scrutiny" (Green, 2010, p. 128). However, while some such as Jeffrey Green argue that "the people's gaze" is a form of power and influence in what he and some others term *plebiscitary democracy* (2010, p. 128), the reality is that, beyond monitoring, any meaningful request, direction, comment, or censure requires enunciation in spoken or written language. In other words, while 'watching' undertaken by what Michael Schudson (2003) calls monitorial citizens may contribute to what John Keane (2009a, 2009b) calls monitory democracy, communication through language remains essential for democratic politics and civil society. Others also criticize watching, which is mostly done through media, because "it turns citizens into spectators rather than actors" (Coleman, 2013a, p. 212).

Despite a modernist obsession with systems theory and scientific models that led to thinking of communication as *transmission* of messages and information (e.g., Berlo, 1960; Shannon & Weaver, 1949), communication and voice are more accurately conceptualized as *dialogic*, informed by the work of Mikhail Bakhtin (1981, 1963/1984, 1979/1986), Martin Buber (1923/1958, 1947/2002), and Hans Georg Gadamer's (1960/1989) concept of openness to the other. Gadamer's contribution is important, as it highlights the fundamental principle that dialogue is not simply turn-taking at speaking. Gadamer's discussion of openness and responsiveness to others is examined in more detail later in this chapter in defining listening.

In his "first philosophy" that focusses on self-other relations, Bakhtin rejects the rationalist notion of humans as autonomous subjects independently and objectively observing the world and coming to understand it and themselves. Bakhtin emphasized that "people do not have access to a coherent image of themselves as objects in the world" (Cooren & Sandler, 2014, p. 227). Instead, he argued that humans are fundamentally dependent on other people. He said: "Everything that pertains to me enters my consciousness, beginning with my name, from the external world through the mouths of others" (Bakhtin, 1979/1986, p. 138). One might add, in the context of this analysis, that our consciousness is also informed by the ears and receptive senses of others. When we are listened to, we feel recognized and valued. When others do not listen to us, we feel devalued and marginalized. As François Cooren and Sergeiy Sandler (2014) note in their analysis of Bakhtin's concepts of polyphony and ventriloquism that will be examined later, each of us is present in the world as an actor and perceiver. Human subjects, their identity and their *lifeworld*, are constituted by dialogic relations with others. Influenced by the work of Martin Buber, Bakhtin argued that any form of communication, to be communication, must be dialogic—not monologic.

Similarly, James Carey (1989) draws on Burke, Heidegger, and Dewey in his classic work *Communication as Culture* to focus attention to the importance of *conversation* in human society. Communication theorists such as Craig and Muller (2007) and Littlejohn and Foss (2008) emphasize two-way *transactional* understandings of communication over one-way transmissional views, with a focus on meaning rather than messages.

Leslie Baxter (2011) identifies that relationships are necessarily dialogical encounters, and fields of applied public communication such as public relations lay claim to a two-way dialogic approach and even *symmetry* between organizations and their publics (J. Grunig, L. Grunig, & Dozier, 2006;

L. Grunig, J. Grunig, & Dozier, 2002; Kent & Taylor, 2002), as will be discussed further in Chapter 2.

Nevertheless, John Durham Peters refers to communication theory as "the natural history of our talkative species" (1999, p. 9). His reference to speaking as a central focus in human communication is telling (pun intended), and deeply concerning. As Joseph Conrad said in *Under Western Eyes* through his characters Councillor Mikulin and philosophy student Razumov:

> "Listening is a great art," observed Mikulin parenthetically.
> "And getting people to talk is another," mumbled Razumov.
> "Well, no—that is not very difficult," Mikulin said innocently. (Conrad, 2008, p. 68)

The Missing Corollary of Speaking—Listening

Rhetoric in its original Platonic and Aristotelian conceptualization, as well as its subsequent use in classical Greece and Rome, paid some attention to the problematic concept of audience. Donald Bryant has argued that rhetoric gives consideration to the audience (1953, p. 123). But this could be described as *audiencing* as discussed by John Fiske (1994) and Yvonna Lincoln (1997, 2001), which is principally focussed on understanding audiences in order to increase the appeal and persuasiveness of speaking so as to achieve the objectives of the speaker.

Robert Craig says that communication involves "talking and listening" (2006, p. 39) and Nick Couldry sees voice as "the implicitly linked practices of speaking and listening" (2009, p. 580). However, examination of scholarly and professional literature reveals that communication and voice are predominantly associated with speaking and that there is little attention paid in many fields of research or communication practice to the vital corollary that should "naturally accompany or parallel" speaking ("Corollary", 2015)—listening. Michael Purdy (2004) notes that there has been only a small amount of qualitative research in relation to listening *per se* and that this is primarily grounded in cognitive psychology, mostly with a therapeutic focus. Lisbeth Lipari acknowledges that listening is studied in "humanities-based communication scholarship" as well as in "social science and cognitive science literature", but that this is predominantly in the context of interpersonal listening (2010, p. 351).

In his analysis of listening in democratic politics, Andrew Dobson concludes that "the listening cupboard is very bare indeed" (2014, p. 110). Susan

Bickford (1996) was one of the first to point this out in her landmark text *The Dissonance of Democracy: Listening, Conflict and Citizenship* in which she criticized the lack of attention to listening—a cause taken up by Dobson (2010, 2014). In *Listening for Democracy*, Dobson (2014) says "honourable exceptions aside, virtually no attention has been paid to listening in mainstream political science". He adds that efforts to improve democracy have mainly focussed on "getting more people to speak" (p. 36). But, as Gideon Calder (2011) points out, the real problem in democratic politics is not being denied a voice; it is being denied an audience. Tanja Dreher makes a similar point in her analysis of marginalized communities. For instance, in discussing Muslims living in Australia, she reported that there is no shortage of articulate spokespersons and commentators within the Muslim community. The challenge faced by Muslims in this predominantly Christian country is "being heard" (2008, p. 7).

Even though understanding is commendably identified as "the beating heart" of Habermas's theory of communicative action, as Dobson notes (2014, p. 115), Habermas says "reaching understanding is the inherent telos of human *speech*" (1991, p. 287) [emphasis added]. Habermas uses 'speech' and 'communication' as if they are synonyms, and successful application of his theory of communicative action depends on what he describes as an "ideal speech situation" that is free, unconstrained, and "unsullied by strategizing, manipulation, or distortion" (Dobson, 2014, p. 115). Habermas and his supporters do not identify or see a need for an *ideal listening situation* and, overall, Habermas gives little attention to listening. John Durham Peters says "listening to others is a profound democratic act" (2006, p. 124). But listening rarely makes it onto the agenda of most discussions of democracy or politics in general. Jeffrey Green (2010) says that power and influence are predominantly understood in terms of voice in political theory. And in most contexts voice is understood as speaking and 'speaking up'. Andrew Dobson says that "much less attention has been paid to the way in which speech is received and processed" (2014, p. 17)—if indeed it is received and processed. He adds: "We normally think of empowerment as a function of the right and capacity to speak" (p. 20). Nick Couldry says that "one way of thinking about new acts of political exchange is in terms of listening", but he goes on to say "surprisingly, little attention has been given to what listening involves" (2010, p. 146) and has called for "new intensities of listening" (p. 140). Elsewhere Couldry refers to the paradox "that voice can apparently be offered, without any attention to whether it is matched by processes for listening" and describes this as "part of the banal oxymoron of neoliberal democracy" (2009, p. 581).

Bickford's and Dobson's critiques can be equally applied to other aspects of civil society beyond politics. While not specifically addressing listening, recent analyses such as those by Bimber et al. (2012), Coleman (2013a), and Couldry (2012) identify a lack of recognition felt by citizens today in organizations and in society generally, as well as in relation to political processes such as representation and voting. Similarly, in the opening line of her book *Listening Publics*, Kate Lacey notes that "listening has long been overlooked in studies of the media as well as in conceptualizations of the public sphere" (2013, p. 3). The frustrations, disillusionment, and disengagement identified by these authors are linked at least in part, if not substantially, to listening, as will be shown in this study.

Furthermore, analysis shows that there is scant attention paid to listening in business and management literature other than discussion of interpersonal listening in an intra-organizational context (e.g., human resources, employee relations, and training), as noted by Jan Flynn, Tuula Riitta Valikoski, and Jennie Grau (2008).

Even more surprisingly, in disciplinary literature specifically focussed on public communication such as public relations and corporate communication, there is a blind spot in relation to listening, as noted by Judy Burnside-Lawry (2011) and as explored in detail in Chapter 2. As will be shown, a large body of literature on political communication and election campaigns, advertising, public relations, public speaking, and many others aspects of public communication shows that we have professionalized and even industrialized speaking in contemporary free speech societies, but we have not devoted equal or even significant attention and resources to listening. The following anecdotal and scholarly comments reflect this blind spot in contemporary societies in relation to listening.

- Many countries have instigated the right to freedom of speech either constitutionally or by convention. But interestingly none has a corresponding right to be listened to.
- Public speaking has flourished as a major field of professional practice, but there is no field of practice devoted to *public listening*.
- Keynote speakers are widely sought and prized in business and industry and on the conference circuit, but it is rare to find *keynote listeners* (Dobson, 2014, p. 182). The UN Social Good Summit of 2013 featured an "inaugural class of keynote listeners" along with keynote speakers (United Nations Foundation, 2013), which was seen as a

ground-breaking initiative. Former leader of the UK Labour Party and leader of the opposition from 2010 to 2015, Ed Miliband, noted that he had never been a 'keynote listener' before being asked to act in this capacity at a Transition Network conference in London, and added "it's probably not something that politicians tend to do" (Miliband, 2009, para. 1).

- Counsellors, consultants, teachers, negotiators, bosses, partners, and others regularly say 'we need to talk', but the corresponding admonition to listen is much less common or rare.

Even though Gayatri Spivak argued two decades ago that "who should speak" is less crucial than "who will listen" (1990, p. 59), Romand Coles lamented that we have "marginalized the arts of listening" (2004, p. 687) and Les Back (2007) commented in his classic book *The Art of Listening* that listening is, in fact, in danger of becoming a lost art.

In a similar vein to Nick Couldry, Lisbeth Lipari invited a "rethink" of communication "through the lens of listening" (2010, p. 348). Also, in their 2014 review of literature related to listening Graham Bodie and Nathan Crick issued a call "to lift listening from its slumber in Western scholastic thinking and in the communication studies discipline more specifically" (2014, p. 118). This analysis adds to those general calls for greater focus on listening in studies of human communication by arguing for a review and rethink of organization-public communication conducted in the disciplinary fields of political communication, government communication, corporate communication, marketing communication including customer relations, and public relations including its constituent sub-disciplines such as employee relations and community relations.

In *Listening Publics*, Kate Lacey (2013) offers an informative historical account of the concept of listening with a particular focus on media and the importance of listening by publics as part of creating informed public opinion—to some extent the opposite focus of this study, which looks at organizations listening to publics. However, her argument that listening is "a critical activity in public life" (2013, p. 21) supports the need for both listening publics and organizational listening.

In identifying and examining the vital role of organizations in contemporary societies, Bimber et al. (2012) note the use of new media and communication technologies for engagement between organizations and citizens. Many discussions of Web 2.0 and social media are celebratory, claiming that they are creating a "democratization of media" (Siapera, 2012, p. 55) and a democratization of communication and voice (Deibert & Rohozinski, 2010). Henry Jenkins claims that blogs are "expanding the range of perspectives" that are communicated and that they mean "everyone has a chance to be heard" (2006a, p. 180f). But are they heard? Even more important, are they listened to? The distinction between these concepts, alluded to earlier, will be explored later in this chapter.

Even in the age of Web 2.0 and interactive 'social media' that hypothetically increase two-way communicative interaction, "speaking up" is the focus and listening languishes (Crawford, 2009, p. 526). For example, studies of online election campaigns and so-called *e-democracy* in the US, UK, and Australia (e.g., Gibson, Williamson, & Ward, 2010; Macnamara, 2014a; Macnamara & Kenning, 2011, 2014; Rosenstiel & Mitchell, 2012), analyses of youth engagement by Bennett, Wells, and Freelon (2011), and a recent study of public communication by more than 220 organizations in eight European and Asia Pacific countries (Macnamara & Zerfass, 2012) have all found that social media are mainly used for the transmission of information and messages (i.e., speaking), rather than listening.

For voice to matter, as Couldry (2010) quite rightly says it should, speakers and texts need to have listeners. But, returning to a literary metaphor for a moment, Oscar Wilde's frog in *The Remarkable Rocket* summarizes the relationship between speaking and listening in many situations.

> "Well, goodbye, I have enjoyed our conversation very much, I assure you." [says the Frog]
>
> "Conversation indeed!" said the Rocket. "You have talked all the time yourself, and that is not conversation."
>
> "Somebody must listen," answered the Frog, "and I like to do all the talking myself. It saves time and prevents arguments." (Wilde, 1888, p. 9)

This is not to say that some professions and organizations do not try to listen and have some success. While arguing that listening is notably absent in literature on politics and the public sphere, Andrew Dobson points out that professional fields such as nursing, counselling in areas such as psychology and psychotherapy, and education pay specific attention to listening. A body of literature in these fields attests to the importance of listening and its role in therapeutic and clinical contexts (e.g., Beatty, 1999; Fredriksson, 1999; Rice & Burbules, 2010). This analysis acknowledges the attention paid to listening in these fields. However, nursing, teaching, and counselling primarily involve interpersonal listening, often one-to-one or with small groups, and often have a therapeutic or empathetic (empathy building) rather than communicative objective. The focus of this analysis is the broader sphere of public communication and organization-public interactions, which is also critically important for the effective functioning of societies as well as organizations and for social equity and justice.

Governments also make attempts—some genuine and some not so genuine—to listen to their constituents. For instance, UK Prime Minister Tony Blair launched his 'Big Conversation' in 2003 in an attempt to reconnect with voters by showing the government was listening—unsuccessfully as it turned out. A decade later, UK Prime Minister David Cameron instituted a 'Listening Exercise' including the National Health Service (NHS) Future Forum to solicit public views on the National Health Service of Britain. However, this was described as a "sham" and widely criticized, as it came only after a stakeholder and public outcry over the government's attempt to ram a flawed Health and Social Care Bill through Parliament without public consultation (Dobson, 2014, p. 86). Such initiatives are not new in politics. In the review of public relations literature reported later in this chapter, one of the few discussions focussed on listening reviewed President Nixon's 'Listening Posts' in the US, which began in 1969 but were quietly closed down in 1971 after being deemed a failure (Lee, 2012). More recently, the US government has joined the Open Government Partnership (OGP), a worldwide coalition of 65 countries in early 2015, which aims to make their governments more open, accountable, and responsive to citizens (OGP, 2015). The Obama administration launched a range of prizes, crowdsourcing initiatives, and citizen science projects collaborating with civil societies, companies, universities, foundations, non-profits, and the public to increase government-citizen engagement (Dorgelo & Zarek, 2014).

Some will argue that democratic governments routinely gauge the mood of the electorate and respond to public opinion, which they identify through opinion polling, mass media reporting, and increasingly through social media monitoring. However, there are three limitations of such activities in terms of listening. First, they are periodic and even spasmodic. Governments tend to watch and take notice of opinion polls and respond to media reporting and editorials mostly when elections are approaching or their popularity is plummeting. Second, the voices of citizens expressed in these ways are selective, aggregated, and mediated. In the processes of sample selection for opinion

THE FUNDAMENTAL ROLE OF COMMUNICATION AND VOICE   35

polls, aggregating and averaging that occur in analyzing quantitative research (including the removal of outliers in the data), and summarizing and interpreting that occur in research reports and journalism, the voices of many citizens are reduced to faint echoes and distant cries. Third, these mechanisms of organizational listening, if they can be called that, are predominantly used for instrumental purposes—that is, they serve as tools or means to achieve the aims of the organization. While governments often abandon unpopular policies and announce initiatives (sometimes ill-thought knee-jerk reactions) in response to groundswells of public support, opinion polls and media reporting rarely if ever provide sufficient specificity to enable listening in other than a rudimentary way. The main purpose of opinion polls and monitoring of media reporting is to serve as strategic marketing tools for governments to help them target their messages so as to maintain some semblance of popularity and hold on to office for as long as possible.

One of the few areas of research and practice beyond interpersonal communication and therapeutic applications that has focussed on listening is restorative justice. In their respected work on restorative justice, Kay Pranis (2001) and John Braithwaite (2002) say that we can tell how much power a person has by how much people listen to them (e.g., see Braithwaite, 2002, p. 564).

From studies of activism in the UK, Jenny Pearce (2012) similarly reported that power is being listened to—not the right to speak. John Downing (2007) adds that there is no point in a right to free speech if no one is listening. In the same vein, Kate Lacey says that "without a listener, speech is nothing but noise in the ether" (2013, p. 166). John Dryzek goes further in saying that "the most effective and insidious way to silence others in politics is a refusal to listen" (2000, p. 149). Journalism holds as one of its key tenets 'speak truth to power',[5] but as Andrew Dobson notes, "the problem is not one of speaking truth to power, but of getting the powerful to listen" (2014, p. 92). Recognizing this somewhat surprising and concerning gap in research and professional literature, Kate Lacey recently argued that:

> The neglect of listening as a public action has … been so pervasive and so profound, that the case has to be put as strongly as possible, even if doing so runs the danger of appearing to make overblown claims for listening as the principal or most profound dimension of communication activity in the public sphere. (2013, p. 9)

This book reports research designed to explore this under-researched issue and the question crying out for investigation: 'do governments, corporations, and other types of organizations listen to their stakeholders and publics?" Even more specifically, do they "really listen", as Lisbeth Lipari challenged (2010, p. 351)? To explore those questions, we first need to have a clear understanding of what we mean by listening, particularly in an organizational context.

What Is Listening?

It is important to identify what is meant by and what can be reasonably understood as listening. If we set unrealistically high expectations, listening is bound to fall short. On the other hand, it is important to recognize that listening is more than tokenistic attention or cursory consideration. There are many forms of fake and feigned listening, as listed in Table 1.1 in this section. Ethel Glenn (1989) identified 50 different definitions of listening in a literature review in the *International Journal of Listening*. In *Listening Publics: The Politics and Experience of Listening in the Media Age*, Kate Lacey defines listening as "the active direction of the sense of hearing to discern meaning from sound" and described listening as "a *cultural practice*" (2013, p. 22) [original emphasis]. Lacey's definition is useful in drawing attention to the active nature of listening, the focus on meaning or sense making rather than simply the physical act of hearing, and the cultural dimension of listening—characteristics that will be explored in detail in this analysis. However, rather than become bogged down in multiple definitions, it is more constructive to examine the key elements that afford and collectively create listening.

The Pre-requisite of Openness

Listening is crucially informed by Hans Georg Gadamer's (1989) concept of openness to others. Lisbeth Lipari notes that listening is "focus on the other" (2010, p. 349). Gadamer specifically noted that a prerequisite for listening is that "one must want to know" what others have to say. Gadamer added that openness requires not only passive listening, but asking questions and allowing others to "say something to us", even "recognizing that I must accept some things that are against me" (as cited in Craig & Muller, 2007, pp. 219–220). Charles Husband (2000) refers to this as "courageous listening", as listeners have to push their own views into the background, at least temporarily, and be prepared for incommensurability and dissonance. Susan Bickford points out that listening entails vulnerability, as the listener is exposed to the possibility of persuasion. Referring to a political context, she says "the riskiness of listen-ing comes partly from the possibility that what we hear will require change from us" (1996, p. 149), but the same openness to persuasion, vulnerability, and riskiness apply in all organization-public communication. Lisbeth Lipari says that listening "is a profoundly difficult way of being in the world because it by necessity disrupts the sameness and familiarity of the always already known" (2009, p. 45). Others do not always feel the way we expect them to feel or say what we expect them to say. Often they say things that are surpris-ing or a shock to us, even oppositional to our views, decisions, policies, or proposals. Without openness, none of the following key elements of listening are likely to exist.

In *On Liberty*, John Stuart Mill noted that opinions expressed in public discourse were only reliable if they listened to counter-arguments, saying:

> Any person whose judgement is really deserving of confidence ... has kept his mind open to criticism on his opinion and conduct. Because it has been his practice to listen to all that could be said against him. (Mill, 1859, p. 39)

Receptivity

Nikolas Kompridis's discussion of the importance of *receptivity* can be seen as similar to Gadamer's concept of openness. Discussing politics specifically, Kompridis (2011) argues that we need to think of agency in terms other than mastery of speaking, but rather in terms of receptivity. He goes on to warn that "far from being tangential to democracy, receptivity is a condition for its renewal in that it is alert to the possibility of hitherto unheard voices" (as cited in Dobson, 2014, p. 20). Again, the principle of receptivity applies beyond political communication. It is relevant to all areas of public commu-nication as well as interpersonal communication.

Reciprocity

Reciprocity is recognized in sociology, social psychology, and anthropology as a fundamental principle for creating and maintaining human society, par-ticularly positive reciprocity (Gouldner, 1960; Regan, 1971). Reciprocity in conversation and discussion refers to the simple principle that if A speaks to B, B will respond to A in some appropriate manner (i.e., interaction should be A ↔ B). If B does not respond in an appropriate manner, it is usually the end of the interaction and A is left with the impression that either:

- B has not listened to A and, therefore, is not interested in what A has to say; or
- B does not agree with A, but does not want to discuss the matter; or
- B doesn't think that what A has to say warrants a response.

Of course, the same principles apply in relation to B → A communication. Reciprocity does not occur once in communication or in society. Ideally it is a recurring process. Dialogue and conversation, which Richard Rorty (1979) and James Carey (1989) advocated because it is even more open, broader, and more inclusive than dialogue, are characterized by reciprocity including *turn-taking* in speaking and listening and the utterance of *responses* as well as statements. While one has to be careful in narrowing human interaction to scientific principles, professor for behavioural and brain sciences at Aix-Marseilles University, Olivier Oullier (2014), notes that reciprocity is one of the essential principles of engagement.

While some argue that online discussion groups are dominated by certain loud voices and characterized by *homophily*—that is, the assembly of like-minded participants (i.e., affinity groups) and exclusion of alternative views—research has found that online discussion groups have relatively high levels of heterogeneous discussion and interactivity (Liang, 2014). One study found that online political forums have an average reciprocity ratio of 0.44 and that broader philosophical discussion groups have a reciprocity ratio of 0.53 (Himelboim, 2011). While this is far from a 1:1 equal participation ratio, these findings indicate that even in the so-called Wild West of Internet forums and social networks, around half of statements made are responded to in some way. Furthermore, research has found that, despite some 'flame wars' and some offensive online content, the majority of responses are supportive or at least polite (Liang, 2014). The research questions explored in this analysis beg the question of whether attempted public communication with major organizations, including our governments and suppliers of key services, achieves even this level of reciprocity.

Hospitality

The concepts of receptivity and reciprocity are similar to the notion of hospitality, which has been discussed at length by Roger Silverstone (2007) and offers further insights into understanding listening. Modern societies have focussed heavily on rights, but a number of sociologists and media and communication scholars are concerned about the relative neglect of duties and obligations (e.g., Hindess, 1993). Robyn Penman and Sue Turnbull (2012b) argue that in communication this bias towards rights rather than obligations is reflected in insistence on the right to speak, to be free to express opinions, and to have a voice. But, as Charles Husband (1996) says with concern, there is no reciprocal obligation to be listened to or understood.

Penman and Turnbull point out that a rights-based approach "starts from the perspective of the speaker", whereas "the obligation-based approach arising from hospitality starts from the perspective of the host, and asks how we ought to communicate with the other" (2012b, p. 76). Application of hospitality as defined by Silverstone "requires not just letting the other speak, but listening to what the other has to say" (Penman & Turnbull, 2012b, p. 77). Such an approach is more socially inclusive (Bauman, 1993), has the potential to "restore politics and culture to a more communicative space" (Gibson, 2009, p. 472), and is more ethical (Silverstone, 2007). The ethics of listening will be further discussed later in this chapter.

Engagement

The terms 'engagement' and 'disengagement' have been used a number of times in this discussion, and will be used many more times in the coming pages both in citing literature and quoting interviewees. Engagement is a term that rolls easily and frequently off the tongue in contemporary politics and it is acknowledged and criticized as "a prototypical buzzword" in marketing and other public communication practice (Satell, 2013). Brian Solis (2011) devoted a book to the subject titled *Engage* in which he said organizations need to "engage or die" (p. 2). A 2013 McKinsey survey of senior executives found that engagement with customers rated among their top 10 priorities (Brown, Sikes, & Wilmott, 2013). Governments now routinely call for and promote citizen engagement (Dorgelo & Zarek, 2014; Transform, 2010). It therefore behoves us to identify what is meant by engagement in a human sense and how it relates to listening.

Engagement is extensively discussed in psychology and organizational psychology literature where Tamara Erickson (2008) describes it as commitment involving a level of passion and investment of discretionary effort. More specifically, engagement is made up of three key elements, according to organizational psychologists:

1. A psychological bond formed through a combination of cognitive processing of information and what scholars call *affective commitment* (i.e., emotional attachment such as a sense of belonging and feeling valued);
2. *Positive affectivity*, a deeper level of positive emotional engagement beyond liking or attraction, such as absorption, enthusiasm, excitement, pride, and/or passion; and
3. *Empowerment* of those engaged, which psychologists and political scientists say is most effectively achieved through participation of some kind (Macey & Schneider, 2008; Meyer & Smith, 2000, p. 320; Rhoades, Eisenberger, & Armeli, 2001).

We have seen already that, in an intra-organizational context, Bruce Bimber et al. describe engagement as one of two participatory styles and define engagement as "how much people perceive that they are able to shape the agenda and the direction of their organization" (2012, p. 32). Drawing on Robert Heath (2006), Maureen Taylor and Michael Kent (2014) describe public engagement as:

> … a two-way, relational, give-and-take between organizations and stakeholders/ publics with the intended goal of (a) improving understanding among interactants; (b) making decisions that benefit all parties involved, not simply the organization; and (c) fostering a fully functioning society. (2014, p. 391)

However, in her useful analysis of public engagement Minjeong Kang (2014) identifies "conceptual confusion caused by marketers' use of the term engagement to describe any interaction they were having with their customers" and the tendency of marketers to "spin" using a variety of basic metrics such as clicks, visits, and downloads to claim engagement (p. 400). She also points out that measurement of engagement has been limited. Taylor and Kent (2014) note that "most of the evidence about engagement shows that it has been enacted as a form of one-way communication" [if there is such a thing]. Furthermore, most articles describe engagement "from an organizational perspective" (p. 387)—that is, organizations want people to engage with them, but there is less or little focus on organizations engaging with others who have an interest in their affairs.

It is important to look beyond superficial understandings of engagement and understand the emotional as well as cognitive dimension of engagement and, even more importantly, the role of participation. While participation can include a range of actions such as voting, becoming a member of a committee, writing letters as an advocate, or protesting, one of the most common forms of participation for most citizens is dialogue with various public and private sector organizations that form the 'superstructure' of society (Williams, 1980). As argued throughout this book, to have meaningful dialogue—and, therefore, participation and engagement—people need to be listened to as defined in the following section.

Seven Canons of Listening

The extensive review of research literature undertaken as part of this study revealed at least six key elements of listening discussed in interpersonal and organizational communication and in phenomenological, sociopsychological, sociocultural, and democratic political studies. Along with these, one further essential element is advocated in contemporary public communication practice, allowing identification of seven 'canons of listening' for organizations as follows:

1. *Recognition* of others as people or groups with legitimate rights to speak and be treated with respect (Bickford, 1996; Honneth, 2007; Husband, 2009; Young, 2000). William James (1952), the founder of American pragmatism, stated that the most "fiendish" way to deal with another person is to ignore them;

2. *Acknowledgement*, which is sometimes assumed to be part of recognition of others or seen as part of response, but quick and specific acknowledgement is an important signal to those who speak that what they say has been heard and is receiving attention (the next step or canon). In the case of organizations, acknowledgement often requires an initial communication to advise the speaker that his or her inquiry, question, or comment is being looked into—particularly when a response requires referral to a specialist department or unit, which may take some time. The 2008 Obama presidential campaign demonstrated the power of quick acknowledgement, as online and e-mail inquiries received an electronic acknowledgement within hours and sometimes minutes. While these were auto-generated using technology, the limitations as well as advantages of which will be discussed later, this at least advised citizens that their message had been received and indicated that it would receive attention;

3. Giving *attention* to others (Bickford, 1996; Honneth, 2007; Husband, 2009). Beyond an initial acknowledgement, listening to others requires

cognitive focus as well as some level of empathy (affective engagement or emotional intelligence). Both require an investment of time. Hence we often refer to attention giving as 'paying' attention. In organizations, giving or paying attention may involve referring public communication to a particular department or unit that has the specialist knowledge required to undertake the following stages;

4. *Interpreting* what others say as fairly and receptively as possible (Husband, 1996, 2000)—not glossing over, misinterpreting, or rejecting it because of prejudices or information processing barriers. These can include stereotypes; cognitive dissonance (Festinger, 1957); fundamental attribution error (Heider, 1958), which involves inappropriately apportioning cause or blame; failing to apply adequate thought—i.e., lack of central processing in terms of elaboration likelihood theory (Petty & Cacioppo, 1986); or automatically resorting to persuasion to try to 'talk the speaker out of' his or her viewpoint, position, or concern. The dominance of persuasion as an objective in mass communication and disciplines influenced by this concept such as public relations, corporate communication, and most approaches to marketing communication is revealed and critiqued in research reported in Chapter 3;

5. Trying as far as possible to achieve *understanding* of others' views, perspectives, and feelings (Bodie & Crick, 2014; Habermas, 1981/1984, 1981/1987; Husband, 1996, 2000). While it is impossible to fully understand others—and organizational communication texts and manuals recommend against telling a speaker that you know how he or she feels, as this is often perceived as "patronizing and phony" (Gibson & Hodgetts, 1991, p. 75)—Husband (2000) suggests that the right to speak should be replaced by or at least incorporate a right to be understood. He refers to the "right to communicate", often understood in terms of (a) unidirectional transmission and (b) receipt of information, as first and second generation rights and proposes the "right to be understood" as a third generation right within the tradition of human rights (2000, pp. 208–209). Stephen Covey (1989) says that to feel understood is the deepest psychological need of humans. However, in his popular book *The Seven Habits of Highly Effective People*, Covey says that even when they do listen, "most people do not listen to understand; they listen with the intent to reply. They're either speaking or preparing to speak" (1989, p. 251)—what Jacqueline Bussie calls "re-loading

our verbal gun" (2011, p. 31). Of relevance to this analysis of organizations and large-scale listening, Silverstone (2007) particularly discusses the complexity of understanding when a plurality of voices exists. The challenges of diversity and cacophony will be examined in this analysis;

6. Giving *consideration* to what others say such as in requests or proposals (Honneth, 2007; Husband, 2009). Considering the views, opinions, comments, and concerns of others is specifically listed as the sixth stage within the seven canons of organizational listening, as consideration should follow giving attention, interpreting, and gaining understanding. Considering what others say without first giving it adequate attention, interpreting what is meant, and trying to understand their position and perspective is inevitably likely to lead to miscommunication. It should be noted, however, that giving consideration does not presume or require agreement (see next point);

7. *Responding* in an appropriate way. Beyond initial acknowledgement, a more substantial response is usually required after consideration of another's expression of voice (Lundsteen, 1979; Purdy & Borisoff, 1997). As noted above, 'appropriate' does not necessarily mean agreement or acceptance of what is said or requested. There may be good reasons a request or suggestion cannot be agreed to and sometimes there are circumstances unknown to commentators, complainants, and others who speak to organizations. In such cases, an appropriate response should contain explanation of these details—although positive responses should be made when views and opinions, requests, comments, and complaints are reasonable and justified.

The third, fourth, and fifth canons—or stages if you prefer—are particularly important in organization-public communication when the speakers are less articulate than those in the organization—e.g., from low socioeconomic backgrounds, from culturally and linguistically diverse (CALD)[6] communities and non-English-speaking backgrounds (NESB), from persons with disabilities, or members of marginalized groups. In such cases, their voice may not comply with what an organization considers to be an appropriate form of address (e.g., it may contain 'bad' English, poor expression, or an emotional tone).

The importance of giving consideration and response—not just listening passively—is reinforced by practice reviews such as that of the UK Commission for Healthcare Audit and Inspection, which reported that patients who complained to the NHS expected:

- To have their complaint resolved as close as possible in place and time to the events complained about;
- To receive an explanation and an apology where warranted; and
- To ensure any necessary action is taken to prevent repetition (Commission for Healthcare Audit and Inspection, 2007, p. 4).

Listen To, Listen In, Listen Out For, Listen Up

While it seems on the surface to be a simple concept, there are multiple approaches to listening. The most common form of listening is listening *to* someone who initiates communication in some way such as through speech, an e-mail, letter, Web inquiry, or social media post, or to some thing such as a radio broadcast (Lacey, 2013)—although the latter passive form of collective listening is not the focus here.

Another form of listening, which can be impolite in the case of private conversations and problematic in some intelligence agency and security applications, but important in mass media studies and organization-public communication, is listening *in*. The most common focus of media studies and many cultural studies in relation to listening has been listening in, such as audiences listening in to radio programs (Lacey, 2013). This is a predominantly passive application, as noted above. However, listening in also can be active and ethical. An example of legitimate active listening in is social media monitoring in which an organization may follow discussions and observe comments, images, and videos posted on Twitter, Facebook, YouTube, Instagram, Sina Weibo, blogs, and other social media and networks to identify topics of interest and issues of concern. This is quite different to monitoring social media to count the number of followers of the organization and the number of likes of its own posts—an organization-centric approach focussed on identifying the scale of its own message transmission. And what is discussed here is quite distinct from spying. Social media and social networks are public sites, so there is no invasion of privacy. Other forms of listening in are attending public meetings at which the views of communities are being expressed and reading local community and specialist media.

A third and particularly important form of listening is listening *out for*. This approach to listening involves three key features or characteristics. First, listening out for involves anticipation that others may have something to say or a view to express and demonstrating readiness and preparedness to listen. Second, listening out for often requires turning down the volume of loud voices so that others may be heard. Loud voices may be outspoken individuals (e.g., the person who never stops talking at meetings) or, in an organizational context, loud voices are often institutionalized representatives such as major industry associations, unions, and powerful lobby groups. While these represent constituencies, in reality representatives are ventriloquists projecting voices that are partly their own, partly a mimicking of those they speak for or about, and partly fictional narratives of 'characters' (or caricatures) created out of consensus. They represent majorities—not necessarily the diversities that exist within their constituencies. (See more detailed discussion of ventriloquism in relation to organizational listening later in this chapter.) Also, representatives often become bureaucratized in monopolies and oligopolies distracted by their own ambitions and pursuit of power.

The third key feature of listening out for is that it often requires specific outreach activities to go beyond traditional channels of communication. Examples include researchers working with Muslim communities in Western countries whose voices have been drowned out by generalized discourses in relation to Islamic terrorism as discussed by Dreher (2009, 2010), and research among the aged and people with disabilities. For example, Cathy Treadaway, Gail Kenning, and Steven Coleman are among a number of researchers who report that elderly people, particularly those with various forms of dementia including Alzheimer's disease, are marginalized in society and argue that spaces and activities need to be specially designed for them to participate and continue to live healthy, productive lives (Kenning, 2015a; Treadaway, Kenning, & Coleman, 2014). Furthermore, Kenning (2015b) says that people with dementia have much to contribute to society and much to say—if only someone is listening. But Kenning has identified that people with dementia, a growing group in countries with ageing populations, are silenced almost immediately from the moment of diagnosis. Even in the early stages of dementia during which most people with dementia can continue as active citizens, they become 'disabled' and are *spoken for* by doctors, carers, and institutions. However well meaning these 'spokespersons' are, people with dementia join those who Nathan Dhawan says are "are illegible and unintelligible within hegemonic frameworks and thereby rendered ethically, politically and rhetorically illegitimate" (2012, p. 47).

Dobson states that dialogic democracy, which he calls for, is "as much about *listening out for* as it is about listening to" (2014, p. 34) [original emphasis]. In particular, Dobson notes the importance of "listening out for otherwise unheard voices" (2014, p. 22). Similarly, echoing Couldry's discussion of "voice that matters", Gideon Calder points out that if expressed opinions and views are to count for anything in a democracy it is "pre-conditional … that they are listened to, and listened out for" (2011, p. 128).

This applies well beyond the bounds of politics. Dreher particularly draws attention to the need for listening strategies that recognize marginalized individuals and communities. Listening out for unheard voices is important for social equity and is an important part of restorative justice, which is further discussed under 'The Ethics of Listening' later in this chapter. However, research reported in the next chapter shows that many 'ordinary' citizens in contemporary neoliberal capitalist societies—whether they are conceptualized as voters, customers, consumers, employees, members, patients, students, or in some other way—are part of a great 'unlistened to'.

A phrase that is widely used as a request or call to action in relation to listening—as well as the title of a 2004–2005 US sitcom, a 2008 music album by Hoku, the 2010 official FIFA World Cup album, a 2012 Haley Reinhart album, and a song by Oasis—is 'listen up'. The widespread use of the phrase in popular culture reflects the difficulty of getting people to listen, as it is often issued as a plea or even a command. But in spite of its instructive tone, it is often ignored. Listen up is what this book is about. It is a rallying call to trumpet the importance of listening at an organizational level; to point to the lack of listening afflicting large parts of our society; to identify the challenges in large-scale organizational settings; and to provide recommendations on how organizational listening can be effectively implemented so that listening is not just words, but meaningful, mutually beneficial interactive engagement.

Listening and Silence

Another interesting and important issue that should be addressed in a discussion of listening is silence. One form of silence has been discussed in the previous section—enforced silence created by dominant discourses, hegemony, or simply neglect. However, silence can mean many things. For instance, silence can:

1. Indicate the silent person or organization has ignored or not heard what was said;
2. Be a sign of shame and guilt. For instance, in public relations literature Roumen Dimitrov (in print) has pointed out that a 'no comment' approach by an organization in the face of media questioning is typically interpreted as tantamount to admission of wrongdoing;

3. Be a device deployed to put someone on the spot. For instance, media interviewers sometimes sit silently for several seconds (called 'dead air' in broadcast media), which often results in the interviewee filling the silence—sometimes blurting out something that he or she did not intend to say;

4. Be a productive time of thought and reflection about what was said and preparation of a suitable response.

In one of the few scholarly articles on the subject of silence within communication literature, Dimitrov (in print) identifies several key conceptualizations of silence drawn from various fields of scholarship. These include:

- Foucault's notion of *exhaustive representation*, which refers to discursive practices in which the said and the unsaid are interrelated and form a unity of discourse. Exhaustive representation is created by the loud voices referred to in the previous section and it is a repressive form of silence as it purports to have said everything on a subject and implies that there is no more to be said. In *The History of Sexuality*, Foucault (1990) gives the example of how sex could be talked about in the seventeenth century, but only in terms of carefully cleansed and purged language. What is actually meant is "no longer directly named, sex was taken charge of, tracked down as it were, by a discourse". Foucault argued that "everything that cannot be said should be scrutinized"—not only what is said (p. 20)—because through exhaustive representation discourses are created that silence those with alternative views;

- Frances Sendbuehler's concept of *profound communicative silence*, which intentionally deploys silence to convey meaning in contrast with Foucault's exhaustive representation that leaves no gaps and creates repressive silences. Sendbuehler summarizes that Foucault's exhaustive representation is "discourse that silences", while profound silence is "silence that discourses" (1994, para. 6). For instance, a refusal to talk or comment can send a strong message—a silence that talks;

- John Cage's *sound of silence*, which involves a radical departure from traditional notions of music and tonality that treats all sound other than that recognized as pleasant musical tonality as 'noise'. Cage 'composed' *Silent Piece 4' 33"* made up of 4 minutes and 33 seconds of silence to make people listen (Dimitrov, in print).

Of these concepts, silence as a productive time of thought and reflection about what has been said and preparation of a suitable response, and Sendbuehler's profound communicative silence, are the most productive notions of silence in terms of public communication. Communication must involve silence. As Lacey says, "falling silent in order to listen is not … an act of passivity, nor an act of submission, but is an active part of the communication process" (2013, p. 178). To give attention and consideration to what others say, one must be silent while others are speaking.

Listening Requires Interactivity

Ronald Pelias and James VanOosting (1987) identified *inactive, active, interactive*, and *proactive* as four increasingly intensive levels of engagement between speakers and audiences and emphasized the more intensive levels. The passive apparently pensive listener giving the occasional nod may well be thinking about his or her plans for the weekend. The organization that says it is listening and invites public comments on its Web site or social media pages may well be simply ignoring them—as the introduction to this book and research reported shows to be all too commonplace. While attentive silence, a necessary part of listening as discussed previously, is a form of interactivity, explicit forms of interaction and proactive initiatives such as asking questions are important elements of listening.

In addition, as identified in the 'seven canons' of listening, organizations will often have to send an initial acknowledgement to advise that a matter is under consideration, as well as give public inquiries and comments consideration, which may require research or referral to a specialist department or unit, and then provide a response. Just saying 'we're listening' is not enough. Listening requires a range of actions and interactions.

Listening Is Contingent

Another important point about listening is that it is *contingent* (Bodie & Crick, 2014, p. 105). That is to say, it is predicated on what others say to us. While we can plan to do listening, we cannot plan the specific interactions of listening. The processes of interpretation and trying to understand what others say and feel, and responding to them in appropriate ways, are contingent on what others have to say and how they feel. If listening is not contingent, it is rehearsed and becomes fake, pretend, or pseudo listening (see Table 1.1).

The contingency of listening was explicitly discussed by Mikhail Bakhtin, who said that in the act of speaking a speaker is:

> Actively orientated precisely toward … an actively responsive understanding [and] does not expect passive understanding that, so to speak, only duplicates his own in someone else's mind. Rather he expects response, agreement, sympathy, objection, execution, and so forth. (1979/1986, p. 69)

Listening and Hearing

Despite frequent conflation, listening is distinctly different to hearing. At a physiological level, human hearing occurs when sound waves strike the eardrum and cause vibrations that are transmitted to the brain. We can hear things, but pay no attention to them. Listening occurs when the human brain reconstructs these electrochemical impulses into intelligible sounds and we interpret some meaning from them (Adler & Rodman 2011, pp. 133–134). A metaphorical 'hearing' takes place when humans engage with texts such as documents, still images (e.g., signs and photographs), or moving images in film and video using the sensors of their eyes. In this form of engagement, listening occurs when the brain interprets meaning from impulses generated by light.

As Kate Lacey notes: "Etymologically listening comes from a root that emphasizes *attention* and *giving* to another, while hearing comes from a root that emphasizes *perception* and *sensation* of sound" (2013, p. 17) [original emphasis]. Elsewhere, she refers to the "sensory experience of listening and a political philosophy of listening" (p. 8). In this reference, the former is more correctly described as hearing, while listening does involve philosophy in the sense that it is framed by beliefs, attitudes, and values, and it involves thinking about reality—ours as well as others.

Such definitions of hearing and listening can be extrapolated into an organization-public context by understanding *organizational hearing* as the receipt of various signals such as human speaking and texts such as e-mails, letters, submissions, proposals, petitions, research reports, and mediated messages through traditional or social media. *Organizational listening* occurs when these signals and the senders are given recognition, acknowledgement, attention, interpretation, understanding, consideration, and response.

Bodie and Crick's reference to feeling is also important in understanding listening and how it differs from the physiological or physical level of hearing. Most of the literature on listening narrowly focusses on what others say. However, Graham Bodie and Nathan Crick (2014) argue that listening involves and requires hearing and *sensing*. Using a phenomenological approach, they apply Charles Sanders Peirce's *pragmaticism* and his three categories of experience, which could also be called consciousness or being. Peirce referred to these as *firstness* (quality), *secondness* (reaction), and *thirdness* (mediation). Bodie and Crick say that sensing, in which we physically or metaphorically "close our eyes" to focus and sense another and our environment is firstness; secondness involves physical reaction, which is a key part of hearing; and listening focusses on thirdness. This is a useful analysis, as it draws attention to the need in the first instance to focus all our senses and sensibilities to truly 'hear' others; followed by the need for reaction and interaction (i.e., interactivity to signal that we are paying attention and giving consideration, such as nods in interpersonal communication or e-mail acknowledgements in public communication); and finally the need for listening to mediate. By mediation, Bodie and Crick, in support of Lisbeth Lipari, mean that listening goes beyond hearing; it "connects and bridges" the parties involved (2014, p. 116; Lipari, 2012, p. 233). Elsewhere, Lipari expounds that listening is a "process of understanding" that leads to a "co-produced dialogic process undertaken by speakers and listeners together" (2010, p. 351). By identifying listening with Peirce's thirdness, Bodie and Crick distinguish listening from hearing in phenomenological terms and this understanding moves listening beyond passivity and reception towards activity and interaction. Based on their analysis, they offer the following definition of listening.

> Listening, in short, is the capacity to discern the underlying habitual character and attitudes of people with whom we communicate, including ourselves, in such a way that, at its best, brings about a sense of shared experience and mutual understanding. (Bodie & Crick, 2014, p. 106)

Lynn Cooper (1997) and Andrew Wolvin and Carolyn Coakley (1994) take a behavioural psychology approach to listening, pointing out that listening requires cognitive, affective (e.g., empathic), and behavioural responses by those whom speakers address. Such approaches align closely with engagement, as discussed previously, and focus our attention beyond receptivity and hearing to response and interaction. Individual cognition, affective response, and behavioural response are required in organizations as well as in one-to-one and small group communication.

Stephen Coleman has explored the "challenge of digital hearing" and the use of "technologies of hearing" for "listening in to the public sphere" in the context of digital democracy or what some call *e-democracy* (2013b, p. 3). But while technologies can provide tools to aid listening, such as media and Internet monitoring and text analysis software, discussion of organizational listening needs to avoid *technological determinism*. As shown in research reported in this study, organizational listening involves much more than the use of clever technologies.

Listening vs. Agreement

Having emphasized a number of elements required for genuine listening, it is also important to emphasize, as noted previously, that listening does not necessarily result in agreement. To burden listening with an expectation or requirement to achieve consensus is unrealistic and counterproductive. It is likely, in fact, that listeners will not agree with others in many situations at both an individual and an organizational level. That does not devalue or negate listening and turn it into non-listening. It is true that, in many private and public conversations, failure to agree with a speaker is described as not listening to them (Stone, Patton, & Heen, 2000). But this is often more a retaliatory response borne of frustration, or the product of unrealistic expectations. In some situations it is important to listen to viewpoints with which there is unlikely to be agreement—even listen to diametrically opposed voices. Only through this type of open listening, can diversity be understood. Otherwise, many voices remain unheard and unknown.

Psychology-based texts such as Bernard Mayer's (2000) *The Dynamics of Conflict Resolution* point out that not all listening results in resolution or agreement, and not all listening involves expectations of agreement. In fact, in many cases, speakers have relatively modest expectations, as the research reported in this book shows. Even in cases in which speakers are disappointed that agreement and support for their views are not forthcoming, research shows that they often are grateful for being heard and given consideration. Comments such as 'well thanks for listening to me anyway' are often heard at the end of conversations that involve genuine listening. As Friedrich Nietzsche said in the penultimate line of the 55th chapter of *Thus Spake Zarathustra*: "You have your way. I have my way. As for the right way, the correct way, and the only way, it does not exist" (1883/2009).

Listening Is Work

All that has been discussed so far indicates that listening is work. Susan Bickford (1996) was one of the first to note that the processes required for listening involve work. This is often overlooked in discussions of listening. Even in a one-to-one situation, listening requires effort, time, and application. When listening is translated into an organizational context, it requires considerably more than 'bending an ear' and aural senses. It requires resources such as personnel, time, and a number of other elements that will be discussed in the next section in examining organizational listening and in the following chapters. Doing the work of listening is a critically important element of communication, which all too often is focussed substantially or almost exclusively on the work of speaking.

What Is Organizational Listening?

While Jan Flynn and colleagues writing in the *International Journal of Listening* noted the absence of a widely accepted definition of organizational listening and attributed this to a lack of empirical research on the subject, Judy Burnside-Lawry attempted a definition in her study of listening competency citing Flynn et al. (2008) in which she said:

> Organizational listening is defined as a combination of an employee's listening skills and the environment in which listening occurs, which "is shaped by the organization and is then one of the characteristics of the organizational image" (Flynn et al., 2008, p. 143). (Burnside-Lawry, 2011, p. 149)

This definition incorporating Flynn et al.'s observation is somewhat useful as it draws attention to the organizational environment as well as the role of individuals in organizations who are required to operationalize listening—although the plural 'employees' is clearly preferable to the singular "employee's listening skills". The organizational environment can include its culture, policies, structure, and other elements, which will be examined closely in this study.

However, to facilitate a detailed study of organizational listening, a more precise and expansive definition is required. Drawing on the literature discussed, organizational listening is defined in this study as follows:

> Organizational listening comprises the culture, policies, structure, processes, resources, skills, technologies, and practices applied by an organization to give recognition, acknowledgement, attention, interpretation, understanding, consideration, and response to its stakeholders and publics.

Non-listening and Fake Listening

In interpersonal relations at work or with acquaintances or family members we have all experienced various types of non-listening and fake listening. One all-too-common approach is pretend listening during which the hoped for listener makes listening-looking signals (e.g., nods and even the occasional 'hmm', 'oh', or a rhetorical 'is that right'), but is actually thinking of what he or she is going to say next rather than listening attentively or mindfully. Andrew Wolvin and Carolyn Coakley call this *interruptive listening* because the so-called listener is simply waiting to jump in with his or her own point or rebuttal. As noted previously, Jacqueline Bussie eloquently refers to this as "re-loading our verbal gun with ammunition" (2011, p. 31).

Researchers warn of many pitfalls in listening and fake listening strategies including *pseudolistening, selective* listening, and *defensive* listening (Adler & Rodman, 2011, p. 136). Leonard Waks's concepts of *cataphatic* listening (a selective and only partially attentive approach that assigns what others say to prefigured categories) and *apophatic* listening (in which a listener sets aside prefigured categories and presumptions and is temporarily silent and open to what others say) also contribute to a framework in which to examine listening (Waks, 2007, 2010). These notions of listening are drawn from Aristotle's concepts of *apophasis* and *kataphasis*, which are widely applied in theology as positive and negative approaches.[7]

Even the following long list is not complete, but Table 1.1 summarizes 30 types and conceptualizations of listening based on examination of various fields of literature.

Table 1.1. Types of listening discussed in various literature.

Type of listening	Description	References
Attentive	A focussed concentrated form of listening, widely discussed in medical, psychology, and education literature incorporating empathy, acceptance, congruence, and concreteness (i.e., focussing on specifics). May hear and understand others, but does not verify it has	Eliot (2011) Gibson & Hodgetts (1991)
Inattentive	Not paying attention to what others say (see also 'Interruptive' and 'Pretend' listening)	Dobson (2014, p. 52)

Type of listening	Description	References
Active	Similar to attentive listening, but includes verification (e.g., repeating back what is heard to confirm fidelity). (See also 'Interactive')	Eliot (2011) Rogers & Farson (1987) Pelias & VanOosting (1987)
Inactive	Listening that may hear and understand others, but gives no verification or feedback (i.e., silent and unresponsive)	Pelias & VanOosting (1987)
Reflective	Similar to active listening in which the listener reflects back or mimics what the speaker says to demonstrate that what was said has been heard	Covey (1989)
Empathetic	Paying attention to another with empathy (i.e., emotional identification, compassion, feeling, and insight). This is the highest form of listening, according to Stephen Covey	Dewey (1916) Huitt (2009) Covey (1989)
Compassionate	The listener sets aside all thoughts, judge-ments, and feelings and simply offers "hospitality to another's pain" or viewpoints	Garrison (2010)
Therapeutic	Similar to compassionate listening, practiced in professional fields such as psychotherapy and counselling, but is primarily cathartic (i.e., the speaker may feel better as a result of being listened to, but the listener does no more than give attention)	Dobson (2014, p. 65)
Mindful	Attentive, careful listening that is sensitive to the other or others, similar to empathetic	Adler & Rodman (2011, p. 136)
Facilitative	Attentive listening designed to inform strat-egy such as in crisis management	James & Gilliland (2013, p. 79)
Selective	Listening to part of what is expressed and ignoring other parts, or listening to some and ignoring others—often referred to as "hearing what you want to hear"	Simon (2009) Thill (2009)
Interruptive	Anticipating what others will say and inter-rupting, or 'tuning out' and thinking about what to say next	Wolvin & Coakley (1996, p. 389)
Pretend	Mimicking listening in various ways, such as feigned interest—often while "reloading our verbal gun" when others are speaking (i.e., thinking about what we are going to say next)	Bussie (2011, p. 31)

Type of listening	Description	References
Pseudo	Pretending to listen; similar to pretend and interruptive listening	Adler & Rodman (2011, p. 136)
Defensive	Takes comments as a personal attack or criticism and focusses on mounting a defence or even counter-attack	Adler & Rodman (2011, p. 136)
Straight line	One-way, direct listening in which only one party speaks. Gives no feedback or recognition to the speaker; dialogic or transactional listening is preferred	Dewey (1972) Waks (2010)
Monologic	Effectively a refusal to listen by letting another speak without entering into any dialogue, such as clarifying or discussing points, or even giving acknowledgement (therefore similar to 'straight line' listening)	Dobson (2014, p. 67)
Dialogic	Respectful interplay between speaking and active listening	Waks (2010); Dobson (2014)
Transactional	Similar to dialogic, involves speaking and active listening; working things out in discussion	Dewey (1916, 1972)
Interactive	Similar to dialogic, involves speaking and active listening	Pelias & VanOosting (1987)
Reciprocal	Similar to transactional listening and dialogic listening, both parties listen to the other and negotiate a position of mutual understanding in a dialogic exchange	Crawford (2009)
Performative	A relational stance and dialogic performance in which listeners ethically engage in an act of learning from others across difference	McCrae (2015)
Proactive	Voluntarily seeking out opportunities to listen and offering to listen to others	Pelias & VanOosting (1987)
Indirect	Listening via mediation such as research reports, media monitoring, and through delegated listening	Baloh (1976)
Delegated	Listening that is delegated—for example to researchers and pollsters, customer relations staff, social media monitors, etc.	Crawford (2009)
Cataphatic	Interpretation through assigning what others say into categories imposed by the listener (e.g., seeing employee complaints as a result of union agitation)	Waks (2010, p. 2749)

Type of listening	Description	References
Apophatic	Listening in which the listener puts aside predetermined categories and is 'still', silent, and open to understand what the speaker says	Waks (2010, p. 2749)
Political	Susan Bickford describes politics as 'communicative engagement' and sees "listening as a central activity of citizenship"—it is "what makes politics possible"	Bickford (1996, p. 2)
Courageous	Listening in which listeners are prepared to consider incommensurability and dissonance (i.e., views contrary to and/or critical of their own)	Husband (2000)
Research	Listening is identified as a key performative element of qualitative research by Chris McCrae and this author has described evaluation research as listening to feedback and response	Macnamara (2015a) McCrae (2015)

The Ethics of Listening

As a number of scholars have identified, there are significant ethical considerations related to listening (Bodie, 2010; Bodie & Crick, 2014; Dreher, 2009, 2010; Gehrke, 2009). Tanja Dreher has drawn attention to the position of marginalized groups in societies and called for "listening across difference" (2009, 2010) as an ethical responsibility. But even in mainstream social interaction, Kate Lacey argues that there needs to be a "freedom of listening" (2013, p. 179) to correspond with the right to freedom of speech afforded in democratic societies—albeit Lacey focusses on listening by publics. As noted earlier in this analysis, this study comes from the other direction to examine how and how well organizations listen to their stakeholders and publics.

Writing in the *International Journal of Listening*, Pat Gehrke (2009) has called for a broad methodological approach drawing on phenomenology, dialogism, and relational dialectics as well as democratic political theory to understand the ethics of listening. Speech and performance scholars such as Chris McCrae (2015) take up Gehrke's call and advocate *dialogic listening* drawing on the foundational work of Mikhail Bakhtin and Martin Buber as well as ethnographer Dwight Conquergood who describes dialogue including the 'performance of listening' as a "path to genuine understanding of others" and essential for ethical engagement with others (1985, p. 9). In discussion of rhetoric and writing, Anne Surma (2005) and Cezar Ornatowski (2003) similarly identify dialogic engagement as necessary for ethical practice. However, Gehrke has noted that philosophy, ethics, and politics are "noticeably absent … in [the] list of disciplines and fields that have contributed to listening studies (2009, p. 2).

Focus on listening within politics has increased since Gehrke's criticism, such as the work of Dobson (2014) in relation to democracy and studies of marginalized groups by Dreher (2009, 2010, 2012). But as David Beard (2009) has argued, there is a need for consideration of the ethics of listening more broadly in relation to communication and media studies, cultural studies, and other disciplines.

In communication literature, Jess Alberts, Thomas Nakayama, and Judith Martin (2007, p. 28) are among the few to suggest that there is an ethical responsibility as well as a practical imperative to listen—albeit like most communication scholars they too focus on interpersonal communication. In looking beyond interpersonal communication to public communication, as is the focus of this analysis, we can find in Habermas reference to ethical considerations in the operation of the public sphere. Also Habermas's (1981/1984, 1981/1987) theory of communicative action contrasts genuine 'communicative' action with 'strategic' action designed to achieve the speaker's objectives, as noted previously. Habermas said ethical communication must include willingness among participants to try to understand others; consideration of others' as well as one's own interests; equal opportunity to express those interests; opportunity to argue against suggestions that may harm one's interest; and protection against 'closure'—i.e., shutting down discussion (Habermas, 1990). Habermas's theory of communicative action thus contributes to the theoretical framework of this analysis.

When we turn our attention to specialist fields of public communication practice such as public relations and social media use, which are theorized as interactive, two-way, dialogic, and focussed on social interaction, engagement, and relationships as discussed in more detail in the next chapter, we might expect to find detailed discussion of listening and attention to the ethical implications of listening—or not listening. However, even though PR scholars say "public relations practitioners must listen and utilize two-way communication to be ethical" (Coombs & Holladay, 2007, p, 48), analysis of PR as well as corporate communication, organizational communication, and contemporary social media use by organizations reveals these fields of public communication to be paradoxically silent on listening and alarmingly light on ethical discussion generally (Demetrious, 2013; Fawkes, 2015). The ethics of listening forms another important element of the theoretical framework of this analysis.

The Problematic Nature of Audiences

The ethics and practicalities of listening are blurred and made more challenging by traditional notions of audiences. Throughout most recorded history of literature, theatre, art, and media, there has been a privileging of the position of the speaker, the author, the artist, the producer, the journalist. Audiences have been mostly conceived as passive recipients of information and culture. For instance, modernist literary critic F. R. Leavis described the audiences of films as "unthinking" recipients of mass communication to which they "surrender, under conditions of hypnotic receptivity" (1930, p. 10).

This passive recipient view of audiences is grounded in the modernist notion of *mass society* (Durkheim, 1893/1984; Kornhauser, 1959) and *mass media* and *mass communication* theory (McQuail, 2010), which dominated thinking throughout the twentieth century, combined with related one-way transmission models of communication (Berlo, 1960; Shannon & Weaver, 1949) noted earlier in this chapter. Even with the addition of Norbert Wiener's (1950, 1954) feedback loop, thinking about communication remained predominantly one-way, with mass media including new forms of broadcasting providing a large 'pipe' for the outward flow of information from well-resourced elite organizations and a very small 'pipe' for inward flow. This transmissional broadcast notion of public communication—or what could be called a *philosophy of communication* (Arnett, 2010)—shaped popular thinking and even much scholarly opinion throughout the twentieth century and into the twenty-first century, even in the face of explicit challenges such as Roland Barthes's (1968/1977) 'Death of the Author'.

As Benedict Anderson (1983/1991) argued, audiences are largely "imagined communities" in the case of mediated communication. There is no stable mass of listeners—even for major events such as broadcasts of the Olympics and the Super Bowl; audiences are but temporary assemblies in physical or virtual space. Furthermore, and very important, even when audiences exist, contemporary analyses such as that by Nicholas Abercrombie and Brian Longhurst (1998) in *Audiences: A Sociological Theory of Performance and Imagination* and Andy Ruddock's (2007) *Investigating Audiences* show that they are not passive. Rather, "the idea of the 'active' audience" is now common currency in media and cultural studies (Lacey, 2013, p. 185). However, until recently, active audience membership has been seen as relating to actions such as selection, involvement, or resistance. Even active audiences have not been conceived as speakers as well as listeners, other than in limited ways such as during voting and occasional consultations. In such a paradigm, there is no need to listen to those conceptualized as audiences and 'consumers' in other than limited instrumental ways.

This narrow view of active audiences has come under attack in contemporary literature in relation to the Internet and social media, with terms such as the *prosumer*—the consumer who is also a producer of information (Toffler, 1970, 1980)—and the *produser* (Bruns, 2008; Picone, 2007) entering the lexicon of media studies. But to date there has not been focussed study of how, or if, the actors and elites that traditionally have dominated the ranks of speakers listen to those who New York University Professor of Journalism Jay Rosen calls "the people formerly known as the audience" (2006, para. 1).

Kate Lacey (2013) comments that "the public sits somewhere between the real and the imaginary" (p. 6) and this view and her argument in relation to 'listening publics' is a reasonable middle ground in that citizens, employees, customers, and others do make up communities and do themselves need to listen. However, she adds that when speakers speak (exercise voice), "there is a faith in the moment of address that there is a public out there and there is a faith in the act of listening that there will be some resonance with the address" (p. 7). There is considerable evidence that this faith is unjustified in many instances of public communication, as shown in this analysis.

Ventriloquism—Who Is Speaking and Who Is Being Listened To?

Ventriloquism is commonly understood as a performance that involves the making of voices (Connor, 2000). Specifically, it involves an actor, called a ventriloquist, creating multiple voices that are attributed to characters. Thus, even though they are spoken by a real person, the voices created are fake in that they do not belong to or represent any particular person. While Bakhtin did not use the term ventriloquism, one of his leading translators, Michael Holquist, applies the term in describing what Bakhtin does in his book *Marxism and the Philosophy of Language* in which the Marxist character Volosinov is manipulated to communicate meanings that are not specific to Marxism (Holquist, 1975/1981, p. 174). Holquist points out that Bakhtin illustrates how a multiplicity of voices can be heard whenever one listens to what someone is saying or reads what someone has written. This point is taken up in contemporary literature on dialogue by Francois Cooren and Sergeiy Sandler (2014) and in the context of this discussion it raises a further important question about who is speaking and who is being listened to.

While the voice of individuals may be accepted as their own in most contexts, the representations of voice by associations, councils, unions, activist groups, committees, and other collectives is a form of ventriloquism. As such, Cooren and Sandler say it raises the question of and potentially problematizes "who or even what is speaking" (2014, p. 230). This is not to suggest that the collective voices of various organizations and institutions should be ignored. But the *polyphony* present in the 'speaking for' others by organizations makes listening in and listening out for, as previously discussed, all the more important. While the capacity of organizations to represent multiple voices is one of their purposes and benefits, the processes of consensus forming means that such voices are fake in that they are not the voice of any particular person. Furthermore, power and politics result in some voices being louder and more dominant than others, and some voices may be absent altogether. Hence the ventriloquism of representative organizations and groups is a factor to consider in listening.

The Effects of Not Listening

In a clinical and therapeutic context, psychotherapists note that a major cause of psychological problems among people is a lack of being listened to. Steven Graybar and Leah Leonard say: "We frequently encounter people who have been listened to far too little in their lives. They present for therapy feeling unseen, unheard, and unknown" (2005, p. 3). This reflects Pierre Bourdieu's concern for cultural as well as social capital and his notion of *habitus* in which people "internalize their position in social space" (Bourdieu, 1990, p. 110). Stephen Coleman notes, in applying this to the subject at hand, that "people who are rarely listened to begin to think that their voices were not made to be respected" and he describes this as an injury with serious consequences (2013b, para. 30).

Socially, culturally, and politically, there are abundant signs that Nick Couldry's claimed 'crisis of voice' in contemporary societies is more accurately identified as a 'crisis of listening'. His call for "new intensities of listening" in which public bodies including governments must take account of a range of public voices remains unheeded (2010, p. 140). The results of the large-scale neglect of listening by organizations—government and the private sector—are clear in a number of studies and analyses reported in recent times as well as, increasingly, in public controversies and criticisms reported in the media.

For instance, Stephen Coleman's insightful study of *How Voters Feel* in Britain describes in disturbing terms citizens' experience of voting—one of the most formalized and significant acts of exercising one's political voice with a view to having an influence. Coleman (2013a) makes a number of alarming observations about elections. He notes that "moments of voting are remarkably fleeting". Furthermore, he reported from his study of UK citizens that the event of voting "seems curiously socially disconnected", taking place in "impersonal spaces ... devoid of ... registers of intimacy" and "acts of voting are surrounded by an eerie silence" and a "pervasive hush" (p. 3). He notes that elections and voting are predominantly understood and assessed in terms of "instrumental effectiveness" (p. 4) and concludes that democratic practice has deteriorated to "a discourse of arid proceduralism" (p. 192).

Coleman argues that "the sustainability of any cultural practice depends to a large measure on how it feels to participate in it" and adds that "the way in which politics in general, and voting in particular, are conducted is incongruent with the sensibilities of citizens as rational and emotional makers of meaning" (2013a, p. 5). In short, voting and democratic politics in general do not *affectively* engage citizens; they pay no attention to how citizens *feel*. To most citizens, Coleman says, "the rules of the political game seem too much like imposed rules and someone else's game". He concludes that there is an 'affective deficit' in contemporary democratic politics that is largely responsible for the disenchantment and disengagement, or stoic resignation at best, that characterize voting and attitudes towards politics in many democratic countries. As a result, the disposition of citizens towards traditional political engagements such as voting is "inflected by the weight of thwarted experience" (p. 3).

Perhaps this "arid proceduralism", "instrumental effectiveness", and lack of emotional engagement is why controversial figure Russell Brand publicly stated in a BBC *Newsnight* interview with Jeremy Paxman: "I've never voted, never will, as the UK's political system has created a disenfranchised, disillusioned underclass that it fails to serve" ("Russell Brand", 2013). Brand went on to comment in *The Guardian* a few days later: "I fervently believe that we deserve more from our democratic system" (2013, para. 4). Brand said the publicity created by his comments on the BBC was because he had articulated what a lot of people are thinking. "It was the expression of the knowledge that democracy is irrelevant that resonated", he said (Brand, 2013, para. 2).

Another example from the UK—but just as many examples can be found in the US—is the case of Manchester Central, an electoral ward in north-west England in which only 12 per cent of the constituents voted in a 2012 by-election—the lowest voter turn-out since 1945. A 2015 report in *The Guardian Weekly* claimed the disengagement is continuing and possibly worsening. Under a headline 'Apathy central: where people see no point in casting a vote', it stated: "Either the people of Manchester Central have given up on Westminster politics or it has given up on them" (Booth, 2015). *The Guardian Weekly* warned that "in 2014, 7.5 million Britons were unregistered to vote, with poor, black and young people least likely to be on the electoral roll" (Booth, 2015, p. 15). Furthermore, twice that number or more of registered voters do not use their vote—for example, 16 million registered UK voters failed to vote in 2010.

In the US, after a spike in voter turnout in 2008 that brought Barack Obama to the White House on a wave of popularity, more than 60 per cent of US citizens did not vote in the 2012 presidential election or the 2014 midterms, which a *Washington Post* editorial described as "pathetic" (Editorial Board, 2014). The nationwide US voter turnout of 36.4 per cent in the 2014 mid-terms was the lowest in any election cycle since World War II, according to United States Election Project data and *The Washington Post* (DelReal, 2014).

In Australia, where voting is compulsory, almost 6 per cent of voters cast informal votes[8] in 2013—the highest informal vote in 30 years (Election Watch Australia, 2013). The University of Melbourne Election Watch Web site stated that "the rising proportion of informal votes is a major democratic concern" (Election Watch Australia, 2013, para. 5). A University of Melbourne study as part of its Citizens Agenda project reported that "Australian voters are dissatisfied, distrustful and disengaged" (University of Melbourne, 2013).

The disengagement from traditional politics and civic life by young people noted with concern by a number of researchers (e.g., W. Bennett, Wells, & Freelon, 2011; Coleman, 2008, 2013a; Couldry, Livingstone, & Markham, 2007; Curran, 2011) can be seen to be substantially related to a lack of listening. For instance, a 2013 Australia Institute study of young people aged 17 to 25 found that they "don't feel as though they are being represented by politicians—they don't feel as though they are being listened to" (Lucas,

2013, p. 14). The study found young people concerned about jobs, housing, university fees, climate change, and same-sex marriage, but that these issues were not being actively addressed by politicians or government.

Charles Tilley's important study of *Trust and Rule* identified trust is a necessary condition for democracy and warned that "a significant decline in trust threatens democracy" (2005, p. 133). Coleman similarly argues that trust is a vital element of democracy and identifies two levels of trust pointing to (1) "trust between citizens so that they are confident that if they keep to their side of the bargain (e.g., paying taxes), then others will too", and (2) "citizens must have a generalized trust in the outcomes of democratic processes or they will defect from those processes" (2013a, p. 125). As shown by research literature and empirical evidence reported in this analysis, trust is directly linked to listening and much less so to who is talking most or loudest.

Beyond voter dissatisfaction and threats to democracy, lack of effective listening by organizations can have serious consequences for individual citizens. In 2014, a national inquiry was ordered into how authorities allegedly ignored systematic child abuse in some of Britain's most eminent institutions over several decades from the 1970s. The Home Office review was told that members of the government may have suppressed allegations of abuse and found that 114 potentially relevant files on child abuse were missing, destroyed or lost (Wintour, 2014). While the chief executive of the National Society for the Prevention of Cruelty to Children, Peter Wanless, who led the investigation, concluded that files had not been deliberately removed or destroyed ("Wanless Review", 2014, para. 3), clearly the government was not listening to allegations and complaints that had been made.

In Britain the National Health Service receives around 100,000 complaints a year—albeit it must be noted that the NHS provides around 380 million treatments to patients every year. However, an independent review reported that "we have become increasingly concerned about the way complaints are being managed" (Commission for Healthcare Audit and Inspection, 2007, p. 3). The Commission added:

> When people do complain, they take for granted that the NHS has a formal complaints system. However, we know that sometimes people still find it difficult to make a complaint and are often dissatisfied when they do. We know this because we have received over 23,000 requests for independent review in the past three years.

An investigation into the Mid Staffordshire NHS Foundation Trust in 2010[9] followed by a major public inquiry that concluded in 2013 found that "between

2005 and 2008 conditions of appalling care were able to flourish in the main hospital serving the people of Stafford and its surrounding area" (Stationery Office, 2013, p. 7). Media reported that 300 or more deaths had occurred in the two hospitals administered by the Mid Staffordshire NHS Foundation Trust because of poor standards shaped by cultural norms and institutional neglect of complaints (Dominiczak, 2013). A fundamental part of this culture of neglect was not listening. The final report of the Mid Staffordshire NHS Foundation Trust Public Inquiry Chaired by Robert Francis QC stated:

> Building on the report of the first inquiry, the story it tells is first and foremost of appalling suffering of many patients. This was primarily caused by a serious failure on the part of a provider Trust Board. It did not listen sufficiently to its patients and staff or ensure the correction of deficiencies brought to the Trust's attention. Above all, it failed to tackle an insidious negative culture involving a tolerance of poor standards and a disengagement from managerial and leadership responsibilities. (Stationery Office, 2013, p. 3)

The 'Francis Report' made 290 recommendations in relation to the Mid Staffordshire hospitals and the UK health system generally and the Mid Staffordshire Trust's licence was revoked on November 1, 2014 (Gov.UK, 2015).

More recently, research in the UK led by Tom Reader and Alex Gillespie from the London School of Economics and Political Science has found continuing alarming evidence of citizens' complaints to hospitals being inadequately considered or even ignored entirely. After identifying wider symbolic, material, and relational aspects of care as important factors in avoiding patient neglect and "care scandals", and calling for a broader approach than focus on regulations and training (see Reader, Gillespie, & Mannell, 2014), Reader, Gillespie, and Jane Roberts (2014) synthesized data from 59 studies reporting 88,069 patient complaints to develop a coding taxonomy for patient complaints. They noted that "methodologies used to analyze patient complaints are inconsistent or do not provide an optimal level of depth" (p. 10)—in short, current methods of processing and analyzing complaints from patients in the health care system do not yield consistent useful insights. Reader, Gillespie, and Roberts argue that "the systematic collation of data on patient complaints potentially provides a mechanism through which the standard of healthcare can be monitored and system-level interventions developed" (p. 10). This research will be revisited in Chapter 4, as it informs the design of some elements of an 'architecture of listening' that is outlined in that chapter. In their most recent research, Reader and Gillespie coded a random sample of

1,000 patient complaints from the 100,000 received each year by UK hospitals into three categories—clinical issues (safety and quality); relationship issues (communication, listening, and rights); and institutional issues (environment and administration). Each category is coded into three levels of severity. While this work was ongoing at the time of writing, Reader and Gillespie report that complaints about safety, quality, and listening are a leading indicator of mortality in the subsequent year. The listening category was defined as "trying to give information to the staff but not being heard" (Alex Gillespie, personal communication, March 19, 2015). This finding supports the claim made in the introduction of this book—that a lack of listening can even lead to death in some cases.

In the US, a chilling report in 2014 alleged that black Americans are more afraid of the police than they are of criminals. This dangerous plummeting of public trust in government agencies was inflamed by the controversial death of Eric Garner, a 43-year-old father of six during his arrest for selling 'loosies' (single cigarettes sold illegally to avoid tax) on Staten Island, New York, which caused anger and mass protests after video showed that police restrained Garner in a 'grappling hold', also referred to as a chokehold (Helmore, 2014). Medical examiners concluded that Garner was killed by "compression of neck (choke hold), compression of chest and prone positioning during physical restraint by police" and ruled Garner's death a homicide (Nathan, 2014), although that does not constitute murder under law. On December 3, 2014, a grand jury decided not to indict the police officers involved, which sparked widespread disbelief and outrage. The police and the courts were seen as not listening to widespread public concern.

The Guardian reported a worldwide review at the end of 2014 titled 'The Year the People Stood Up', noting that "civil societies are standing up to entrenched establishments and asking for accountability" in a number of countries. The Guardian review pointed to popular uprisings in Brazil and Turkey in 2014, the Occupy Central movement in Hong Kong, protests in the main square of Kiev, the Euromaidan movement in Ukraine which has demanded open, non-corrupt government, and argued that "it is neither romantic nor naïve to suggest that people power is on the march globally" (Noughayrède, 2014, p. 24). The Guardian also warned that rising citizen discontent in a number of countries has become a breeding ground for populist parties such as Marine Le Pen's Front National in France, and Geert Wilders's Party for Freedom in the Netherlands, as well as disenfranchised youth joining terrorist organizations (p. 25).

Corporations came under public criticism in the UK in 2014 when an independent report described the big six energy companies' customer service as "awful". A survey by the British energy regulator Ofgem found that more than 33 per cent of customers of British Gas, EDF, E.on, npower, Scottish-Power, and SSE as well as a number of small energy suppliers were "very dissatisfied" with the way complaints were handled. Only one-third felt their complaints and inquiries had been treated fairly (Karim, 2014).

A 2009 study of chief executive officers (CEOs) in the US by the Arthur Page Society (2009) found that they perceived their most pressing issue to be lack of trust among their key stakeholders and publics. In the same year, an Ipsos-MORI survey exploring public trust in politicians, government, and the professions in the UK found that all categories of leaders and representatives registered their worst net trust score (the percentage of people who trust them minus those who do not) since the study began in 1983 (Campbell, 2009).

Things were even worse at the time of the Ipsos-MORI (2015) survey.[10] The study found that just 16 per cent of Britons trust politicians to tell the truth. While 'politician bashing' has been something of a public sport in some democratic countries for many decades, trust in civil servants, which was already less than 50 per cent in 2009, also alarmingly declined to just 44 per cent in 2015—albeit this is higher than in the 1980s. Many other important organizations and institutions also have experienced continuing falls in public trust, including the police (down from 65 per cent to 60 per cent in one year from 2014 to 2015), and clergy and priests (down from 85 per cent in 1983 to 71 per cent in 2015). Perhaps an explanation of popularity of social media is that only 22 per cent of Britons trust journalists to tell the truth, according to Ipsos-MORI (2015).

The Edelman Trust Barometer, an annual industry survey of 33,000 people (27,000 members of the 'general public' and 6,000 'informed public respondents')[11] in 27 markets carried out by the leading PR firm Edelman, also has consistently found low levels of trust by citizens in government and corporations (e.g., Edelman, 2013, 2014). The 2014 Edelman Trust Barometer reported that 44 per cent of citizens trust government (the same figure reported by Ipsos-MORI, 2015), which was lower than trust in media (52 per cent) and business (58 per cent). NGOs were the most trusted type of organization (64 per cent). These were the percentages of people expressing *any* level of trust on the Edelman scale. In terms of 'trust a great deal', only 16 per cent of people trust business or media to this extent, and just 15 per cent trust government a great deal.

Even more alarmingly, trust in major institutions and organizations in most countries is falling further, according to the Edelman Trust Barometer (Edelman, 2015a). In its 2015 global overview Edelman reported:

> In the last year, trust has declined for three of the four institutions measured. NGOs continue to be the most trusted institution, but trust in NGOs declined from 66 to 63 per cent. Sixty per cent of countries now distrust media. Trust in government increased slightly, driven by big gains in India, Russia and Indonesia but government is still distrusted in 19 of the 27 markets surveyed. And trust in business is below 50 per cent in half of those markets. (para. 1)

Friends and family are now the most trusted sources of information, followed by academics and 'experts'. CEOs and government leaders and officials remain at the bottom of the list for both 'informed' and 'general publics', with extremely low trust levels. Only one in four members of the 'general public' trust business leaders to correct problems and mistakes and only one in five trust them to tell the truth and make ethical and moral decisions (Edelman, 2014, 2015a).

Of course, it would be wrong and illogical to attribute the loss of trust in government, corporations, and institutions solely to a lack of listening. Clearly the behaviour of organizations has a lot to do with public perceptions of them. However, Stacy Ulbig has reported research showing that affordance of voice does not create trust or satisfaction among those who get to speak—in fact, she concluded that "a voice that is not perceived to have an influence can be more detrimental than not having a voice at all" (2002, para. 1). Based on a survey of public attitudes towards municipal government in the US, she found:

> Neither political trust nor policy satisfaction respond to increased voice alone. Believing that one's voice, loud or quiet, has an influence is important. Feelings of policy satisfaction were increased only when citizens believed they had both increased voice and influence, and feelings of political trust were diminished when only a loud voice was present. (2002, para.1)

While Ulbig did not use the term listening, her finding that perceived influence is a key factor leading to trust and satisfaction, which is supported by Bimber et al.'s finding that meaningful engagement including a capacity to "shape the agenda" is a determinant of trust in and support for organizations generally (2012, p. 32), clearly shows that listening is a mandatory requirement for governments and all types of organizations to maintain public trust and support. One cannot influence someone else or a policy or decision unless those involved are listening.

In a recent critical analysis of ethics in public relations, Johanna Fawkes (2015) warns against the common response to problems such as loss of public trust or crises that advocates "better communication might be the solution" (p. 37). In particular, her warning relates to notions of communication as distributing information and campaigns aimed at persuasion—what a cynical view might see as propaganda designed to veneer problems and sway public opinion towards positive perspectives. While organization-public communication is the central focus of this analysis, Fawkes rightly argues that professions and organizations need to "reflect more deeply on what changes they need to make", suggesting that "ethics not communication is the key" (p. 37). This analysis takes it as a given and a starting point that organizations need to act ethically and accepts that the low level of public trust in businesses and other organizations is, at least in part, a result of poor behaviour. Notwithstanding, listening is intricately bound up with ethical behaviour and resolution of a number of problems in society in at least two ways. First, listening in itself is an ethical requirement, as previously noted. Second, only through listening can organizations know and understand the concerns, anxieties, frustrations, disillusionment, and disenchantment of their stakeholders and publics, as well as their needs, expectations, and hopes.

Theoretical Frameworks for Organizational Listening

A number of concepts and theoretical frameworks for examining voice, speaking, and listening have been noted in this chapter, drawn from interpersonal communication and disciplinary fields in which listening has been addressed to some extent, such as studies of the public sphere and democratic politics. It can be seen that, beyond the interpersonal realm, listening is widely overshadowed by discussion of voice and speaking. It is mostly assumed, or overlooked altogether. Despite the central role of organizations of various types in industrialized and post-industrial complex societies, listening by organizations is particularly lacking attention. Furthermore, as will be shown in the next chapter, which extends this literature review and examines specific fields of public communication practice, listening is little researched and largely untheorized in marketing communication, corporate communication, and public relations including its various sub-fields such as employee relations and community relations.

Graham Bodie and Nathan Crick (2014) call for an integrated approach to investigate listening, rather than examination within one of the various "camps" (Purdy, 2000, p. 49). While such an approach requires an expansive review, this analysis argues that, for the importance and methods of organizational listening to be understood and appreciated, it needs to be examined within a multidisciplinary theoretical framework. The following concepts and theories will not be explained in detail, as some have been summarized already in this chapter and are all well documented elsewhere, as noted in citations. Key bodies of knowledge that inform both critical analysis and analysis of empirical data in this study include:

- *Human communication theory* drawn from the field of communication studies, particularly rhetorical, sociopsychological, phenomenological, and sociocultural perspectives as outlined in the 'seven traditions' of communication scholarship identified by Robert Craig (1999) and elaborated by Craig and Heidi Muller (2007) and Stephen Littlejohn and Karen Foss (2008);
- *Communication ethics* (see Carter, 2001; Hudson & Kane, 2000; Johannesen, 2001; and others), although this field is largely focussed on interpersonal communication;
- *Listening theory*, which while mainly focussed on interpersonal listening, provides definitions and identifies the importance, role, and key components of listening (Bentley, 2010; Bodie, 2011; Bodie & Crick, 2014; Covey, 1989; Glenn, 1989; Honneth, 2007; Husband, 2009; Purdy, 2000, 2004; Purdy & Borisoff, 1997; Waks, 2007, 2010). Listening theory also draws attention to the *ethics of listening* (Beard, 2009; Bodie, 2010; Dreher, 2009, 2010; Fiumara, 1990; Gehrke, 2009; Lipari, 2009, 2014; Silverstone, 2007) and *listening competency* (Burnside-Lawry, 2011, 2012; Cooper, 1997; Cooper & Husband, 1993; Wolvin & Coakley, 1996);
- *Dialogue, dialogism,* and *dialogic theory of relationships* (Bakhtin, 1981, 1963/1984, 1979/1986; Baxter, 2011; Buber, 1923/1958, 1947/2002);
- *Democratic political theory* in relation to voice, participation, and representation (Bickford, 1996; Calder, 2011; Carpentier, 2007, 2011; Coleman, 2013a; Couldry, 2010, 2012; Curran, 2011; Dahlberg, 2014; Dobson, 2010, 2014; Fraser, 1990, 1992; Schudson, 1997, 2003);
- The *public sphere* (Castells, 2010; Habermas, 1962/1989, 2006; Held, 2006);

- *Theory of communicative action* (i.e., strategic vs. communicative action), as proposed and elaborated by Habermas (1981/1984, 1981/1987, 1990);
- *Social theory*, particularly in relation to power and social structure, civil society, and issues such as *social equity* (Couldry, 2010, 2012; Dreher, 2009), *social capital* (Putnam, 1995, 2000, 2004), *cultural capital* (Bourdieu, 1990), and the important role of *social interaction* (Argyle, 1969/2009);
- *Citizenship theory* (Carter, 2001; Hudson, 2000; Hudson & Kane, 2000; Kane, 2000; Marshall, 1950; Turner, 1994, 2001); and
- *Restorative justice theory* (Bazemore & Schiff, 2001; Braithwaite, 2002; Pranis, 2001), although this specialist field is largely focussed on redressing harm caused to victims of crime. However, it does emphasize dialogue between offenders and victims including listening to understand the perspective of the other, and offers particular insight in relation to listening to marginalized groups.

In addition, this analysis is informed by theories, models, and concepts in specialist disciplinary fields of public communication, which will be outlined in the next chapter to set the scene and framework for analyzing research data. Disciplinary fields and practices most directly involved in organization-public communication include:

- *Marketing communication*, particularly *relationship marketing* and *customer relations*;
- *Political communication*;
- *Government communication*;
- *Organizational communication*;
- *Corporate communication*;
- *Public relations*; and specialist fields of public communication such as
- *Public consultation*.

Notes

1. As noted in the Introduction, many scholars see the singular notion of 'the public' as a "rhetorical fiction" (Lacey, 2013, p. 5). Social scientist Nina Eliasoph (2004) and public relations scholars Jim Grunig and Todd Hunt (1984) advocate the term 'publics' (plural) to refer to groups of people with whom interaction is desirable or necessary to recognize social plurality and diversity. 'Stakeholders' is a term proposed by R. Edward Freeman

(1984) in his book *Strategic Management: A Stakeholder Approach* denoting individuals and groups that can affect or are affected by the activities of an organization and which have a legitimate interest in the operations of the organization.

2. The *agora*, an open place of assembly in ancient Greek city states where citizens gathered to hear statements from rulers and discuss public issues, is idealized in revisionist history and some political discourse. However, it is often not acknowledged that the agora such as the famed Agora of Athens was open only to freeborn male citizens. Women and slaves could not attend or participate.

3. It should be noted that researchers broadly agree that young people are disengaging from politics as it is traditionally practiced (e.g., through political parties, which claim to represent citizens). However, it is not considered accurate to say young people are disengaged from politics per se. A number of studies such as Loader, Vromen, and Xenos (2014) point out that young people are seeking to engage in politics in new ways relevant to their everyday lived experience and their concerns.

4. Use of the term 'different than' also raises objections from some grammatical purists, but the *Oxford Dictionaries* state that different *from*, different *to*, and different *than* are all acceptable phrases (see http://blog.oxforddictionaries.com/2014/01/different-from-than-to).

5. The phrase 'speak truth to power' originates from the title of a pamphlet produced by the American Friends Service Committee (Quakers) in 1955, written by a number of authors including Bayard Rustin who was excluded from recognition but later reinstated as an author (see AFSC & Rustin, 1955).

6. Some governments and organizations prefer alternative terms to CALD (culturally and linguistically diverse), such as culturally and/or ethnically diverse (CAOED).

7. While *apophasis* is referred to as a negative approach in theology because it denotes the practice of perceiving and describing something by stating characteristics that it does not have (e.g., we do not know what God is), this implies openness to various possibilities, whereas *kataphasis* (a positive approach in theology) denotes the practice of perceiving and describing something in specific terms that are limiting.

8. Informal votes include ballot papers not filled in or marked inappropriately, such as defacing or writing comments on ballot papers.

9. The first inquiry in the Mid Staffordshire NHS Foundation Trust was established in Parliament in 2009 and commenced in 2010.

10. The 2014 Ipsos-MORI Veracity Index survey interviewed a representative sample of 1,116 adults aged 15+ across Great Britain. Interviews were conducted by telephone December 5–19, 2014.

11. The 'general public' sample refers to randomly selected citizens, while the 'informed public' sample is composed of university-educated professionals.

· 2 ·

HOW ORGANIZATIONS SAY
THEY COMMUNICATE

Public and private sector organizations engage in public communication through a range of practices. As this is not a text on specific disciplinary practices of public communication, these will not be examined in detail. However, a broad overview and general understanding of the ways in which various types of organizations—government, corporate, NGO, institutions, and non-profits—purport to communicate with their publics is necessary in order to identify where and how listening might occur, and then examine those sites to identify the extent to which and how well organizations listen.

Research

One of the most substantive ways that organizations and industries potentially listen is through research. Research is conducted for a number of reasons and purposes including:

- *Social research,* such as social attitudes studies conducted by governments, institutions, and industry and professional organizations to identify citizens' awareness, perceptions, concerns, and interests in relation to various issues. These can range from satisfaction with public transport and health services to controversial topics such as migration. An example is the British Social Attitudes Survey, which has been conducted annually since 1983;

- *Market research*, which is designed to support marketing through identification of customer needs and preferences in relation to products and services and often informs the development of new products and services;
- *Customer satisfaction* studies, which specifically examine levels of customer satisfaction with existing products and services;
- *Employee satisfaction* studies, which canvass the views of employees on matters such as job satisfaction, organizational culture, pay and conditions, internal communication, and so on;
- *Reputation* studies, which solicit stakeholders' perceptions of organizations, often relative to competitors in the same sector; and
- *Opinion polling* such as studies conducted during political election campaigns to identify the popularity of parties, candidates, and policies.

Scientific and technical research conducted as part of product development, such as laboratory testing of new drugs or safety tests of motor vehicles, are not included as potential sites of organizational listening as, while very important, those fields of research are not related to communication.

All of the types of research listed can potentially involve effective listening. For instance, market research typically involves surveys, focus groups, interviews, and other research methods to collect and process the views, concerns, and opinions of 'consumers'. However, in most cases market research is *administrative* in research terms and instrumental—that is, it is conducted to solve specific practical problems for the organization and serve the organization's interests. Such research is designed and framed to find out what the organization needs to know to more effectively market its products or services. It is rarely open-ended research in which those studied can raise any issue they wish and express their views on matters of concern to them. Furthermore, much market research is quantitative, composed of mostly closed-end questions. In many such studies, participants can do little more than tick boxes under multiple choice questions. When qualitative market research is conducted, such as focus groups, the discussion is usually concentrated on specific issues that the organization wants to know about. The views, opinions, and concerns of people outside the research brief are considered 'off topic' and usually ignored. Thus, administrative research tends to involve selective listening (see Table 1.1).

Sometimes organizations including government departments and agencies and corporations partner with universities and independent research institutes to conduct research, which brings scholarly rigour to the research processes. But even in such cases, the presence of an independent research specialist cannot ensure the findings receive serious *consideration*, create *understanding*, and receive an appropriate *response*, which are three of the seven canons of listening proposed in Chapter 1. While research is potentially a major method of organizational listening, its efficacy from a stakeholder and public perspective depends on the purpose of the research, the research questions asked, the openness of the methodology, and what is done with the findings—noting that organizations can simply 'bury' findings that are unfavourable to their interests and highlight and use findings that suit their purposes. Several types of research and specific examples of research undertaken by organizations in relation to public communication are examined in Chapter 3.

Marketing Communication

Market research usually precedes and is undertaken to inform a number of communication activities related to marketing, which is a multibillion-dollar field in capitalist societies focussed on generating sales of products and services. What is called *marketing communication* to differentiate it from other marketing activities such as distribution arrangements (also called 'channel' management) is composed of a number of well-known and widely deployed practices including:

- *Advertising* (press, radio, TV, outdoor, and online);
- *Sales promotion* such as competitions, special offers, and in-store displays;
- *Direct marketing* including direct mail and e-marketing; and
- *Sponsorships*.

Advertising has been the dominant form of marketing communication throughout the twentieth century and early twenty-first century, although there has been a significant shift away from traditional mass media advertising such as 30-second TV and radio commercials in the past decade due to a number of influences. These notably include *audience fragmentation* (Anderson, 2006, p. 181; Jenkins, 2006b, pp. 238, 243) in the era of proliferating digital information sources and increasingly popular social media (Macnamara, 2014a), the rise of 'ad blocking' technologies such as TiVo, and growing resistance to advertising because of *persuasion knowledge*—recognition by consumers of content as intentional persuasion, which reduces attention and impact (Friestad & Wright, 1994). While advertising is deservedly the focus of much research, it is not included in this study as, notwithstanding recent developments in interactive advertising, advertising is predominantly and unashamedly about transmitting persuasive messages to potential consumers of products and services. The specialist field of *corporate advertising* involves distribution of persuasive messages about organizations and issues, but is equally a one-way transmissional practice.

It is significant to note that, even though market research and pre-testing that precede and inform advertising involve some listening, the largest field of organizational public communication practice valued at more than US$500 billion a year worldwide (Magna Global, 2014) involves little if any listening as defined in this analysis (see Table 2.1).

Table 2.1. Global spending on advertising in 2014.

Advertising	Spend in 2014 ($US)
Global TV advertising	$174 billion
Global Internet advertising	$117 billion
Global newspaper advertising	$100 billion
Global magazine advertising	$50 billion
Global outdoor advertising (billboards, bus sides, etc.)	$36 billion
Global radio advertising	$35 billion
Miscellaneous (e.g., merchandise)	$10 billion
Total global advertising	$520 billion

Sources: PWC (2014); Statista (2014).

Some new forms of advertising such as *user-generated advertising* have incorporated receptivity and interactivity, but this is strictly limited to themes and messages set by the advertiser. User content is selectively adopted based on how closely it matches the advertiser's objectives. Despite a variety of innovative techniques, other new forms of advertising also remain almost exclusively one-way transmission of organizations' messages including:

- *Search advertising*, which involves the placement of relevant advertising into the search results based on keywords (e.g., Google Ads);
- *Rich media advertising* such as promotional content in videos and animations;

- *Social media advertising* such as ads appearing in Facebook; and
- So-called *native advertising*, which involves the embedding of advertising content into many forms of media content from interviews to drama shows (Macnamara, 2014a; Macnamara & Dessaix, 2014).

Similarly, sales promotions and direct marketing involve organizations sending promotional messages to consumers, with audience response limited to choosing between products and services or opting out of various interactions such as promotional e-mail. The deluge of promotional e-mail ('spam') has become such that some information technology leaders are predicting that e-mail use will decline in the next decade and may even be abandoned altogether. Sponsorships typically involve organizations branding events and materials to gain exposure and are another form of one-way promotional communication.

The definition of marketing communication published by the American Marketing Association (AMA) puts emphasis on relationships, which have been a significant focus in marketing over the past few decades (Palmatier, 2008). In contrast with previous *transaction marketing* approaches that had a short-term focus on achieving sales, *relationship marketing* purportedly shifts focus to creating relationships with customers over time. Leonard Berry (1983) is attributed with being the first to propose relationship marketing and his and subsequent studies identify three key elements or principles that allegedly distinguish this type of marketing:

1. Deployment of engagement activities throughout all stages of the relationship life cycle, which are described as (a) identifying, (b) developing, (c) maintaining, and (d) terminating. The types of engagement differ at each stage;
2. Recognition of the multiple relationships that are important in marketing. As well as the central role of customers, important relationships include those with suppliers, distributors of products and services (often called 'channel partners'), and other partners such as market research firms and marketing and promotion agencies;
3. Pursuit of mutual benefits for customers and partners as well as the organization (Palmatier, 2008, pp. 1–2).

These principles, particularly the third one, sound altruistic. A more pragmatic view is that relationship marketing is a response to the widely acknowledged adage in marketing that it is easier and less expensive to sell to an existing customer than it is to acquire a new customer. Some marketing studies indicate that it costs between 4 and 10 times more to acquire a new customer than it does to keep an existing customer (Chartered Institute of Marketing, 2010). Therefore, ongoing relationships are sought with customers so that repeat sales can be gained and 'upselling' can occur (i.e., selling other higher value products and services). For example, banks routinely deploy relationship marketing, which typically involves appointing 'relationship managers' to make regular contact with customers, particularly 'high net worth' customers. While engaging in a rhetoric of relationships, the real role of these relationship 'managers' (an interesting term in itself) is to turn trading account customers into investment accounts and also sell them insurance, superannuation, and various other products that the bank offers.

Despite claims of mutual benefits and interactivity between organizations and customers, Robert Palmatier says in his book *Relationship Marketing*: "Relationship marketing is the process of identifying, developing, maintaining, and terminating relational exchanges with the purpose of enhancing performance (2008, p. 3). A similar definition was derived from a synthesis of 26 different definitions by Michael Harker, who concluded that relationship marketing is "an organization actively engaged in proactively creating, developing and maintaining committed, interactive and profitable exchanges" (1999, p. 16). These descriptions clearly identify the real objectives of relationship marketing and suggest that listening is likely to be limited and selectively undertaken in ways that help achieve organizational performance.

Customer relations, which is increasingly conceptualized and practiced as customer relationship management (CRM), is sometimes included as part of marketing communication. For instance, the AMA has defined marketing as "a set of processes for creating, communicating, and delivering value to customers and for *managing customer relationships* in ways that benefit the organization and its stakeholders" (Palmatier, 2008, p. 1) [original emphasis]. However, customer relations/CRM has evolved to be a separate department in most organizations and, because of its specific focus on engaging with customers and its substantial potential for listening, it is examined as a specialist practice in this study.

Customer Relations

As noted in the previous section, customer relations is a specific area of marketing communication that ostensibly should involve a considerable amount of listening. Whereas most marketing communication is focussed on generating sales and is therefore promotional and mostly outbound, customer relations is the practice of responding to and supporting customers post-purchase. Organizations have a vested interest in maintaining the support of their customers, who are described as the lifeblood of commercial organizations, and in many cases they have legal obligations to listen and respond to customers. This field of practice is also referred to as *customer service, customer care, customer engagement* and, more recently, as *customer relationship management* (CRM). While customer service is sometimes narrowly conceptualized as providing service to customers when they request it (e.g., repairing or replacing broken products under warranty or providing information on services), customer relations, CRM, and customer engagement increasingly denote proactive and ongoing interaction between an organization and its customers. These practices are delivered in a number of ways including through:

- *Call centres*, which manage customer helplines, 'info' lines, inquiry centres, and so on. Traditionally these have been telephone centres, but are increasingly expanding to include e-mail communication and even social media monitoring and response;
- *Physical offices* for product returns, service, and customer inquiries. These may be in headquarters, country or regional offices, and/or in local offices, stores, and service centres;
- *Field staff* who interact with and sometimes visit customers; and
- *Relationship managers* who are specialist staff dedicated to building and maintaining relationships with customers, as discussed in the previous section.

The above mechanisms for customer relations mostly involve one-to-one communication, so unlike many other forms of interaction between organizations and their stakeholders and publics, they involve substantial *interpersonal* communication. In addition, though, customer relations and engagement include mediated public communication such as direct mail, newsletters, and sometimes events (e.g., previews of new products such as new model cars). What is collectively called customer relations here for short is a major part of many organizations' communication with a key public and, because some and often most customer relations involves responding to customers' inquiries, complaints, and requests, it should be a major site of organizational listening.

However, research suggests that there are disconnects between organizations and their customers. For example, in a 2012 survey of more than 1,400 corporate executives McKinsey researchers found that companies "talk past" their customers—that is, what they talk about is not what customers want to hear and talk about. The McKinsey study found that leading global companies mainly talked about (1) roles and models of corporate social responsibility; (2) practicing sustainability; (3) their global reach; (4) their power to influence and shape the market; and (5) innovation. Their customers most wanted to hear about and discuss (1) caring for and having open and honest dialogue with customers and society; (2) acting responsibly along the full length of its supply chain (i.e., across its whole business operations including with partners); (3) having the right level of specialist expertise; (4) fitting with the values and beliefs of its customers; and (5) being a leader in the field. Significantly, at least three of the top five things that customers want to discuss are not addressed by organizations, and four of the top five things that organizations talk about are of little or no interest to customers (Freundt, Hillenbrand, & Lehmann, 2013).

It is also questionable whether customers want to be 'managed'. A generous interpretation of CRM sees it as a professionalized and systematic approach to supporting customers. However, it can also be interpreted as a strategic form of management designed to manipulate and exploit customers. The era of 'big data' in which information on customers' purchases across multiple sectors, personal interests, income level, family members, and so on makes such management potentially more manipulative than ever. The senior vice president of Google, Lorraine Twohill, said in 2015 that "it's definitely the golden age for marketing", pointing to the fact that marketers now "know far more about their consumers than ever before". While she commendably stated that "you have to think about the consumer as a human being", Twohill spoke of Google's excitement about "the automation of media planning and buying through the use of data and algorithms—what's known as 'programmatic'" marketing and media planning (as cited in McKinsey, 2015, paras. 9–10). In an interview published in McKinsey's *Insights* newsletter, she went on to talk about listening. However, it was an interesting take on listening. When asked specifically about whether organizations such as Google were getting better at listening through new technologies, Twohill responded in the affirmative giving the example that "we can put products in front of people and get consumer insights back almost in real time … you can more quickly get user insights, and reach more people" (para. 22). Further, in her only explicit mention of listening, Twohill emphasized storytelling by marketers and said "we tell real-life stories. We say, 'listen, your life will change because our product will do this'" (para. 15). In short: (1) the company tells 'consumers' to listen to it and

(2) the company listens, but only to gain insights that help it reach more people to sell more products.

Another instructive article on customer relations published by McKinsey emphasized customer engagement and said: "Engagement goes beyond managing the experience at touch points to include all the ways companies motivate customers to invest in an ongoing relationship with a product or brand" (French, LaBerge, & Magill, 2012, para. 6). This illustrates the focus on motivating customers to invest in a company's products and brands, but makes no mention of a company doing anything to engage with customers other than selling them products and services.

Academic literature also paints a largely one-way and exploitive picture of customer relations and CRM. For example, in an introduction to customer relationship management, Injazz Chen and Karen Popovich say: "Customer relationship management (CRM) is a combination of people, processes and technology that seeks to understand a company's customers. It is an integrated approach to managing relationships by focussing on customer retention and relationship development" (2003, p. 672). Most significantly, they add: "A CRM business strategy leverages marketing, operations, sales, customer service, human resources, R&D and finance, as well as information technology and the Internet to maximize profitability of customer interactions" (2003, p. 673). The last phrase makes the purposes of customer relations and CRM in a corporate context quite clear—to maximize profitability of businesses. Customer engagement is a one-way street in the words of most industry, professional, and academic literature.

However, noting that customer relations is also practiced by government, particularly in what are called arm's length bodies (ALBs) involved in service delivery, management, or consultation functions on behalf of governments, and noting that customer relations is a major site of direct organization-public interaction, this study paid close attention to customer relations.

Political Communication

Political communication is defined by Pippa Norris in the *International Encyclopaedia of The Social and Behavioural Sciences* as "an interactive process concerning the transmission of information among politicians, the news media and the public". She adds that "the process operates downwards from governing institutions towards citizens, horizontally in linkages among political actors, and also upwards from public opinion towards authorities" (2001,

p. 11631). More specifically, political communication is understood as the public communication practices of politicians and other political actors such as political parties and other types of political organizations such as lobby groups, 'think tanks', activists, and interest groups in relation to policy and public affairs. Political communication makes up a substantial proportion of communication in the public sphere in democratic societies (Habermas, 1962/1989, 2006).

However, while Norris says political communication flows upwards from public opinion to political leaders and authorities, research shows that it more commonly flows downwards to citizens. Political communication is widely implemented as advocacy undertaken for the purpose of persuasion to win office and gain support for policies. Election campaigns are the most visible and high profile form of political communication, and exert an increasing influence on this field of practice. While election campaigns were once conducted in a period of one or two months immediately prior to elections every three or four years in most democratic countries, a troubling development for many social and political scientists is the "permanent election campaign" (Canel & Sanders, 2012, p. 87; McChesney, 2008). This refers to elected governments remaining in campaigning mode after they are elected, instead of settling down to focus on good management of the nation's economy, infrastructure, and social systems, and even acting in a bipartisan way on issues of universal importance. Governments in permanent campaign mode are more focussed on scoring victories over their opposition parties and working to ensure re-election than they are on governing.

In permanent campaign mode, and in an effort to avoid potential criticism in independent media, many politicians and other political actors have flocked to social media, but they mostly use these channels for talking, not listening, as reported in numerous studies noted in Chapter 1 (e.g., see R. Gibson & Cantijoch, 2011; Gibson, Williamson, & Ward, 2010; Macnamara, 2011, 2014a; Macnamara & Kenning, 2011, 2014; Rosenstiel & Mitchell, 2012).

Furthermore, even though politicians may listen through meetings with constituents and being out 'on the hustings', research indicates that when they do listen they mostly give recognition, acknowledgement, attention, interpretation, understanding, consideration, and response to a select few, predominantly elites and loud voices. For example, a study in the US by Martin Gilens and Benjamin Page (2014) reported that "economic elites and organized groups representing business interests have substantial independent impacts on US government policy, while average citizens and mass-based interest groups have little or no independent influence" (p. 564). Couldry (2012), Coleman (2013a), and others have made similar observations in relation to politics in the UK.

While political communication is conducted by organizations in some cases, such as political parties, much of it is initiated and maintained by individual political actors such as elected representatives (i.e., politicians), advocates, journalists, and 'spin doctors'. This places much political communication outside the scope of this study, which focusses on organization-public communication. The role of representatives such as elected politicians has been extensively studied (e.g., Shapiro, Stokes, Wood, & Kirshner, 2009). Also, the partisan, increasingly celebrity-orientated, and often propagandist public communication of political leaders and their apparatchiks has been extensively examined elsewhere (e.g., Louw, 2010; Macnamara, 2014b; Smith, 2010; Street, 2004; Welch, 2013). Listening conducted by individual political representatives is noted, but was not a focus of this study. However, some organizational aspects of political communication were examined.

Of more direct relevance to day-to-day organization-public communication is the closely related field of *government communication*, which is discussed next. Citizens require and rely on factual, non-partisan information on a wide range of issues in accessing government services, understanding and complying with laws and regulations, and exercising their democratic right, and they expect civil servants in government, who are effectively paid by taxpayers, to be responsive to them. The broad field of government communication was given major attention in this study.

Some researchers note and express concern about the blurring and overlap of political communication and government communication (Sanders & Canel, 2014; Turnbull, 2007), and various studies and inquiries have recognized and reinforced a need for distinction. For example, the Phillis Review of government communication in the UK in 2004, which found "a three-way breakdown in trust between government and politicians, the public, and the media" and reported that this had led to "increasing disillusionment amongst parts of society", recommended that:

> Modern government communication should be based on openness, not secrecy, and on more direct, unmediated communications to the public. It stressed that there needs to be genuine engagement as part of policy development, and positive presentation rather than spin. It recommended … coordinated communications which reinforce the Civil Service's political neutrality rather than a blurring of government and party communications. (Turnbull, 2007, pp. 128–129)

Government Communication

The term 'government communication' has traditionally been associated with top-level executive communication within governments (e.g., between department heads and officials). However, in contemporary use government communication also refers to communication by "institutions established by governments to do its work at national, regional and local levels" (Canel & Sanders, 2012, p. 85). In this broader "multilayered reality", government communication is defined as follows:

> Government communication refers to the aims, role and practice of communication implemented by *executive* politicians and officials of public institutions in the service of a political rationale, and that are themselves constituted on the basis of the people's indirect or direct consent and are charged to enact their will [original emphasis]. (Canel & Sanders, 2011)

This definition is recited because it helps distinguish the close but nuanced difference between political communication and government communication and draws our attention away from the beguiling spectacle of major national political events to everyday state and local government affairs, and because it reminds us that government communication should be carried out with the direct or at least indirect consent of the people, and in their interests. Also, government communication adheres, in theory at least, with the 'neutral competence' model of government in which the civil service offers impartial advice to ministers and interfaces in a non-partisan way with citizens (Diamond, 2014). Doris Graber, who has provided some of the most comprehensive analyses of communication in the public sector, quotes Joseph Viteritti, saying "meaningful communication between government and the people is not merely a management practicality. It is a political, albeit moral, obligation that originates from the basic covenant that exists between the government and the people" (Graber, 2003, p. 226; Viteritti, 1997, p. 82).

A number of other analyses similarly argue that the existence of citizens informed about government actions is fundamental to a successful democracy and that this requires government information to be open and accessible to citizens (e.g., Fairbanks, Plowman, & Rawlins, 2007). Government communication includes providing citizens with information about public goods and services such as health and education, social security, travel visas, and so on. Governments use the full gamut of communication media to inform citizens including media publicity, Web sites, newsletters, reports, brochures, and other publications (increasingly in digital form), events, and increasingly social media. Sally Young (2007) edited an extensive volume on *Government Communication in Australia* that identifies communication between citizens and their governments as a key measure of the health of any democracy, but highlights criticisms of excessive government use of public relations and marketing to create a 'PR state' (Deacon & Golding, 1994; Ward, 2003). This term originated from a study of taxation and representation by David Deacon and Peter Golding (1994) that identified extensive use of public relations by governments not only to promote policy and provide information to citizens, but also to outmanoeuvre opponents. They also expressed concern about the institutionalization of public relations within government. The validity of such concern depends on how public relations is conceptualized and practiced—issues that will be examined in a following section of this chapter and are very relevant to understanding organization-public relationships and interaction.

Significant also in government communication is that communication between citizens and their governments is described in contemporary political and communication speak as G2C—government *to* citizens (Garson & Khosrow-Pour, 2008)—emulating the buzzwords of B2C (business to consumer) and B2B (business to business). Sometimes G2C is used as an acronym for 'government to consumer' (Khosrow-Pour, 2008), affirming the neoliberal logic that Nick Couldry (2012) says has permeated government as well as the commercial sector in contemporary capitalist societies. 'C2G'—citizens to government—is not discussed in this field of literature although, to be fair, most discussion of G2C is focussed on delivery of services to citizens and e-governance. Nevertheless, the focus on delivery, transmission, providing or sending information, and speaking is clear.

The responsibilities of government communication also include public consultation on major issues and responding to inquiries from citizens. Organizational listening is central to public consultation—a specialist field of communication that will be discussed further later in this chapter.

Corporate Communication

Corporate communication, also referred to as *corporate relations* and *corporate public relations* (CPR) despite some differences in interpretation, began as a small specialty field of study and practice in schools of management and communication. Originally, the term was used to differentiate communication about an organization and its environment from communication about products and services, which is described as marketing communication (Argenti, 2003; Hallahan et al., 2007). In the US, the term has increasingly become associated with the public communication of large public companies (i.e., corporations). However, in Europe some authors have used the term more broadly, based on its Latin root *corpus*, which means body. In this context, corporate communication is used to describe communication in relation to any corporate body, not only commercial companies (e.g., Van Riel, 1995). Still others use the term as an umbrella description to refer to all internal and external communication of organizations—corporate, organizational, and marketing communication. In their analysis, Paul Argenti and Janis Forman (2002) define corporate communication as "the corporation's voice and the images it projects of itself on a world stage populated by its various audiences" (p. 4). In reviewing the literature, Hallahan et al. (2007) summarize four main types or uses of corporate communication as follows:

- The communication of commercial, mostly publicly listed corporations (Argenti, 2003);
- The communication of organizations (Van Riel, 1995);
- Holistic communication in a corporate environment (Goodman, 1994); and
- Holistic communication in an organizational environment (Oliver, 1997).

In his widely used texts on corporate communication, Joep Cornelissen argues that corporate communication is the appropriate term and function for a holistic overview and coordination of an organization's communication. He says there is evidence that organizations are increasingly seeking to integrate their communication and argues that they are doing this "primarily through the lens of corporate communications instead of IC [integrated communication] or IMC [integrated marketing communication]" (2004, p. 46). However, even though Cornelissen sees corporate communication as an umbrella term and function incorporating both organizational and marketing communication, his definition and description of corporate communication shows that it is very similar to public relations as conceptualized in the US and to some extent in Europe, referring to it as a "management function" involving communication with "stakeholder groups" to establish and maintain organizational "reputation" (see 'Public Relations' later in this chapter). In the second edition of his text, Cornelissen (2008) modified his earlier views somewhat, identifying corporate public relations (CPR) and marketing public relations

(MPR) as two branches, with CPR engaged in a number of corporate communication functions. He also dropped the 'S' from communication, as adopted in this analysis. However, he continued to maintain that "corporate communication is the management framework to guide and coordinate marketing communication and public relations" (p. 30). He reiterated this view in the third edition of *Corporate Communication: A Guide to Theory and Practice*, saying that "corporate communication is a management function that offers a framework for the effective coordination of all internal and external communication" between organizations and their stakeholders and publics (Cornelissen, 2011, p. 5).

Corporate communication activities include providing advice on communication to corporate management, production of annual reports and environmental and sustainability reports, speech writing, corporate publicity (e.g., releasing financial results for public companies), and producing and managing corporate Web sites, corporate blogs, and social media sites. Sometimes internal communication with employees—also called employee communication—is included as part of corporate communication to help differentiate it from marketing communication. More commonly, however, internal communication in organizations is described as organizational communication.

Organizational Communication

Organizational communication is a field of practice that recognizes communication is fundamental to the operations and functioning of organizations. In practice and in much scholarship organizational communication is focussed primarily on *internal* communication within organizations, such as employee communication (also referred to as employee relations and staff relations). Thus, it could be more correctly termed *intra-organizational* communication. More recently the field has expanded to include *inter-organizational* communication, such as that between national, state, and local levels of government, between branches and country offices of corporations and between government departments, and even internationally such as between government bodies of various countries (Crossman, Bordia, & Mills, 2011, p. 87). Despite its focus on communication inside organizations, it is a form of public communication because employees are a public by the definition applied in the cognate fields of organizational communication, public relations, and corporate communication (Canel & Sanders, 2012).

Focus on organizational communication originated in the US in the 1930s and 1940s, with the field of practice initially theorized and studied within the rhetorical tradition of communication and derivatives such as the specialty field of *speech communication* (L'Etang, 2008, p. 189). This heritage led to a focus on the methods of rhetoric, argument, and debate that are used in superior-subordinate relations and the technical structures of formal and informal channels of communication within organizations. More recently, organizational communication has been heavily influenced by the social sciences, particularly psychology, and has sought to develop *communication science* that explains communication within small groups and large organizations (Hallahan et al., 2007, p. 19).

Stanley Deetz (2001) identifies several ways of looking at organizational communication. One approach is to look at specific departments or units and how communication influences what they do and how they operate. Another way of studying organizational communication is to look at the forms and types of communication that flow within and across organizations. However, both of these approaches become limiting, with one focussing on the work and processes of particular departments and the other examining communication activities and materials, without seeing the broader picture of why organizations communicate. Deetz says "a third way to approach the issue is to think of communication as a way to describe and explain organizations" (p. 5). In other words, organizations *are* communication. Even though they exist as legal entities and have physical and human resources, it could be said that organizations are discursive accomplishments, as it is only when people come together and think and interact to achieve common goals that organizations become what they are. Without effective internal and external communication, organizations are non-functioning or dysfunctional structures. Also, the reputation and brands of organizations that exist externally are largely the stories that people such as staff, customers, and other stakeholders tell. In their text *Key Issues in Organizational Communication*, Dennis Tourish and Owen Hargie (2004) say "communication is central to the study of what managers do, and to the effectiveness or otherwise of organizations" (p. 6).

Organizational communication specialists recognize changing understandings of human communication, influenced initially by the positivist philosophies and theories of modernism and, more recently, by relativist interpretivist theories of postmodernism. Pamela Shockley-Zalabak (1994) identified four major approaches to organizational communication as:

- The *mechanistic approach* based on views of an organization as a "well-oiled machine operating with quality precision" in planning, design, and maintenance of organizational structures and processes (p. 3);
- The *human relations approach*, which shifts emphasis from structure and work and process design to the interactions of individuals, their motivations, and their influence on the organization. This approach, which evolved into the *human resources* approach, recognizes that work is accomplished by people and focusses on cooperation, participation, satisfaction, and interpersonal skills. The main focus of communication in this approach remains on interpersonal relations and small group interactions;
- The *systems-interaction approach*, which recognizes the importance of organizational structures, systems, and people inside the organization interacting, but expands thinking to explore how "people, technologies, and environments integrate to influence goal-directed behaviour" (p. 5). This approach continues to have a strong grounding in systems theory, but incorporates a recognition of the influence of the external environment on organizations;
- The *interpretative-symbolic-culture approach*, which draws on humanist and poststructuralist theories to identify how organizational behaviour, is shaped by meaning-making among organization members who are engaged in subjective interpretation and influenced by cultures internally and externally. Human communication theories such as *adaptive structuration* (Giddens, 1984; Poole, Seibold, & McPhee, 1985) and *symbolic convergence* (Bormann, 1982) inform an interpretative-symbolic-culture approach to understanding organizations.

Gibson Burrell and Gareth Morgan (1979) developed a similar model of organizational communication that also identified four perspectives, which they described as *functionalism, interpretivism, radical structuralism,* and *radical humanism*. However, in the *Handbook of Organizational Communication* W. Charles Redding and Phil Tompkins (1988) argue that there is not a major difference between radical structuralism and radical humanism, as both draw on critical theories and propose three perspectives, which they describe as *modernist, naturalistic,* and *critical*. Their modernist approach is similar to Shockley-Zalabak's mechanistic approach and Burrell and Morgan's functionalist approach as well as elements of the human relations approach, while the naturalistic approach is similar to the interpretative-symbolic-culture and interpretivist approaches. Other useful contemporary discussions of organizational communication include Charles Conrad and Marshall Scott Poole's (2012) *Strategic Organizational Communication in a Global Economy* and Keith Miller's (2009) *Organizational Communication: Approaches and Processes*.

William Kennan and Vince Hazelton (2006) argue for recognition of what they call "internal public relations", which they define as the processes of creating understanding between management and employees (p. 332). This shows the close relationship between organizational communication and public relations, which is discussed next.

Public Relations

One of the first challenges that confront anyone trying to understand public relations is defining and describing the practice. In a review of the field, Rex Harlow (1976) identified 472 different definitions of public relations ranging from an 87-word definition produced by Harlow himself to a parsimonious 10-word definition provided by Jim Grunig and Todd Hunt (1984). For simplicity, just three of the many definitions of PR found in PR texts and journals are cited below. The first is listed because it is the only one that mentions listening, collaborative decision making, and responding to publics; the second because it is one of the most widely used; and the third because it is one of the simplest. The second definition below also mentions goodwill and understanding between organizations and their publics.

> The management function that entails planning, research, publicity, promotion, and collaborative decision making to help organizations … listen to, appreciate, and respond appropriately to those persons and groups whose mutually beneficial relationships the organization needs to foster as it strives to achieve its mission and vision. (Heath & Coombs, 2006, p. 7)

> Public relations is the planned and sustained effort to establish and maintain goodwill and mutual understanding between an organization and its publics. (Institute of Public Relations, UK, 1991, as cited in Kitchen, 1997, p. 25)

> The management of communication between an organization and its publics. (Grunig & Hunt, 1984, p. 6)

From an analysis of PR literature, Bruce Berger (2007) concluded that "public relations is characterized by historical dissensus in the field about what the practice is, who it serves, and what its roles and responsibilities are" (p. 228).

There are several reasons for lack of clear definition of the practice of public relations. First, some societies do not use the term 'public relations' to describe public communication practices identified under this label in US-dominant models and literature. For example, a study conducted in 25 European countries found that the term 'public relations' is not widely used in Europe (van Ruler, Verčič, Bütschi, & Flodin, 2001) where similar practices are referred to as *strategic communication* (Aarts, 2009; Aarts & Van Woerkum, 2008), *communication management* (van Ruler & Verčič, 2005), *corporate communication* (Cornelissen, 2011; Van Riel, 1995; Van Riel & Fombrun, 2007; Zerfass, 2008), or simply as communication (with and without an 's'). Krishnmurthy Sriramesh reports that many Asian languages do not have an equivalent term for public relations (2004, p. 328). Second, even in the US, UK, Australia, New Zealand, and other countries that use the term 'public relations' or 'PR', practitioners performing similar roles also operate under titles such as *public affairs, corporate communication, corporate relations*, and *public information* (Broom, 2009, p. 23; Macnamara, 2005, pp. 22–23).

While some studies claim that the practices of public relations date back to the earliest civilizations of Egypt, Iraq, Greece, Rome, and China (e.g., Broom, 2009; Heath, 2005; Sriramesh, 2004; Wilcox & Cameron, 2010), the term 'public relations' was created and the practices given focus in the US in the late nineteenth century, and the field of practice gained prominence in the twentieth century (Broom, 2009, p. 91; Hiebert, 1966, p. 87). American histories of PR identify "pioneers" of public relations as Ivy Lee who set up business in New York in 1904 as a 'publicity counsellor' and provider of 'public information'; George Creel who headed the Committee on Public Information, which spearheaded US propaganda efforts during World War I; and particularly Edward Bernays whose 1923 book *Crystallising Public Opinion* claimed to "set down the broad principles that govern the new profession of public relations counsel" (Wilcox & Cameron, 2010, p. 52). The term 'public relations' reportedly first appeared in the 1897 *Yearbook of Railway Literature* published in Chicago reporting on major promotions by railroad companies to attract settlers to the American Midwest (Cameron, Wilcox, Reber, & Shin, 2008, p. 66; Campbell, 2004, para. 4)—although there are other claims dating back to 1807.[1] However, Edward Bernays is credited with coining the term 'public relations counsel' and is widely cited as the "father of public relations" (Guth & Marsh, 2007, p. 70).

Alistair Campbell, former director of communication and strategy for British Prime Minister Tony Blair from 1997 to 2003, commented on the ubiquity of public communication and public relations, saying:

There has always been 'comms'. There has always been public affairs. There has always been PR. There has always been spin. Read the bible for heaven's sake. (Campbell, 2013, para. 11)

In 1984, Jim Grunig, the eminent US professor of public relations, co-authored a landmark book with Todd Hunt that outlined four models of PR, which he described as (1) *press agentry/publicity*; (2) *public information*; (3) *two-way asymmetrical* PR; and (4) *two-way symmetrical* PR. The four models provided a historical perspective (nineteenth century press agentry) as well as both a *positive* theory in social science terms (a description and explanation of actual practice) and a *normative* theory (a description and explanation of what ideally ought to be)—although later iterations of Grunig's theory became criticized as normative and not practical.

While media publicity is still the focus of many PR campaigns, Grunig and his various co-authors including Todd Hunt and his scholar wife, Larissa Grunig, have argued for several decades that two-way symmetrical public relations is the only truly ethical method of practicing PR, as well as the most effective method, and actively promoted the two-way symmetrical concept of PR worldwide. They say that this approach, which incorporates Jim Grunig's *situational theory of publics* (Grunig, 1966, 1997) and *co-orientation* theory advocated by Glen Broom (1977) and Broom and David Dozier (1990), balances the interests of an organization and its publics and leads to mutual benefits and mutual achievement of objectives.

During the 1990s and early 2000s, a number of variants of these models were developed, including a *mixed motive* model proposed by Priscilla Murphy (1991), which argued that a mix of asymmetry and symmetry was required in practice (e.g., public education campaigns on road safety may be one-way persuasion) and a *contingency* model proposed by US PR academic Glen Cameron and his colleagues (Wilcox & Cameron, 2010, pp. 59, 251–252), which argued that the direction and balance of information flow was contingent on circumstances.

Following a major study involving an extensive literature review; a survey of 327 organizations in the US, Canada, and the UK; and 25 in-depth qualitative interviews with senior management in the most and least excellent[2] PR departments identified in the survey (known as The Excellence Study); these and a number of other theories coalesced into *Excellence theory of PR* reported and expounded in three books (Dozier, L. Grunig, & J. Grunig, 1995; Grunig, 1992; Grunig et al., 2002). The Excellence Study identified 14 communication attributes that correlated with organizational excellence including the following principles:

1. The senior public relations executive has influence within the *dominant coalition*—the senior management group of the organization;
2. The public relations function is *separate to marketing*;
3. A *two-way symmetrical* model of public relations is practiced;
4. The senior public relations practitioner has *knowledge and professionalism*, including relevant academic qualifications and training in ethics;
5. Public relations is managed *strategically* in that it is focussed on achieving goals and objectives, which are ideally measured and evaluated (Grunig et al., 2002, pp. 12–17).

Excellence theory of PR has become the dominant paradigm of PR globally (L'Etang, 2008; Pieczka, 1996, 2006; Spicer, 2007). However, it has a growing band of critics. Alternative theories and approaches to public relations include the following.

- *Relationships management* (RM) approach—Jim Grunig and his co-authors argued since the early 1980s that PR is fundamentally about creating and maintaining relationships with key stakeholders and publics (e.g., Grunig & Hunt, 1984; Hon & Grunig, 1999). Relationships between organizations and their stakeholders were particularly emphasized by Mary Ann Ferguson (1984) and relationship management has been developed as a specialized focus in PR by John Ledingham and Stephen Bruning (Ledingham, 2006; Ledingham & Bruning, 1998, 2000). Interestingly, listening is not discussed in any detail in relationship management approaches to PR, but focus on relationships should logically put listening at the centre of PR.
- *Rhetorical theory* of PR—Eminent US PR scholar Robert Heath (1992, 2001, 2006, 2007, 2009) has championed rhetorical thinking in public relations for several decades emphasizing its core principle of dialogue—not the pejorative popular interpretation of rhetoric as empty promises and 'spin'. Heath (2006) notes that rhetoric can be categorized as *manipulative* or *invitational* and, like communication scholars Sonja Foss and Cindy Griffin (1995), he advocates an invitational approach that he says is ethical and ultimately more effective than one-way attempts at persuasion. Heath acknowledges that rhetoric includes advocacy, but states that "advocacy is a two-way street" in the rhetorical tradition (2007, p. 47), allowing and even inviting "counter-advocacy" (p. 51). Rhetors must be open to alternative and oppositional views and engage in *dialogue*.

- *Advocacy* approach—Critical PR thinkers such as Johanna Fawkes (2010, 2015) say that the rhetorical approach to PR, with its acceptance of persuasion, and a large part of PR practice reflects an advocacy approach and she and a number of writers see this as the dominant form of practice. Taking a Jungian approach to examining public relations, Fawkes argues that propaganda and persuasion are the "core shadow material" of PR (2015, p. 195). She says that Excellence theory approaches with their emphasis on symmetry "minimize persuasion in order to overstate the idealized versions of the field" and she adds that "this impoverishes professional ethics by disregarding the reality of practice" (p. 105). Patricia Curtin and T. Kenneth Gaither (2005) say "the dominant normative paradigm has removed propaganda and persuasion from the ranks of legitimate public relations practices", but they argue that their 'circuit of culture' model "demonstrates the need to recognize them as part of the repertoire of legitimate practices" (p. 109). Fawkes pinpoints persuasion as the "site of struggle to define PR" (p. 105) and PR ethics scholar Shannon Bowen (2008) agrees, seeing the PR function as that of advocate, paid to promote the interests of the employer, not other publics or society as a whole. Management scholar Lance Porter is in no doubt, saying "public relations professionals are paid to advocate ideas and to influence behaviour" (2010, p. 132).

- *Dialogic theory* of PR—This body of theory developed largely by Michael Kent and Maureen Taylor (2002), which draws on the foundational communication theories of Bakhtin (1981, 1963/1984), Buber (1923/1958, 1947/2002), and Gadamer (1989), proposes that dialogic thinking and dialogue are central to PR. Kent and Taylor identify six characteristics of dialogic PR: (1) orientation (i.e., towards the other), (2) mutuality; (3) propinquity (i.e., publics are consulted on matters that affect them); (4) empathy; (5) acceptance of risk; and (6) commitment (2002, p. 26). An important point made by Taylor and Kent (2014) is that dialogue and being *dialogic* are not the same thing. They point out that, while dialogue refers to a specific instance of a two-way discussion, being dialogic is a broader philosophical stance informing a procedural approach to create an open interactive communication environment in which the views and interests of others are recognized and respected. They say dialogic thinking precedes actual dialogue and should permeate public relations work (p. 390). Recently, Craig

Maier (2015) has gone further and called for Richard Rorty's notion of *humane conversation* to be applied in PR as it is "much broader and spans numerous types of direct and indirect encounters" (p. 30).

- *Engagement* approach—In 2014 Kim Johnston noted that "engagement has been heralded as a new paradigm for public relations in the 21st century" (2014, p. 381) and a special issue of *Journal of Public Relations Research* was devoted to 'public relations and engagement' (Vol. 26, No. 5). In this, Maureen Taylor and Michael Kent (2014) reviewed their dialogic theory of PR and Bree Devin and Anne Lane (2014) argued that organizations enact engagement through corporate social responsibility (CSR) initiatives to support organizational claims to legitimacy and mutual benefit. However, Devin and Lane acknowledged that "engagement remains under-theorized". They added: "Although stakeholder engagement is widely acknowledged as important, there is no shared understanding of what the concept means or what its characteristics are" (p. 437)—a concern supported by business ethics writer Michelle Greenwood (2007). Global PR firm Edelman has made strong claims to creating engagement for its clients with its chairman Richard Edelman talking about engagement in global tours and publication of a glossy booklet titled *Public Engagement in the Conversation Age*, which states that "listening is more important than ever before" (Edelman, 2009, p. 4).
- *Critical theory* of PR—What Jacquie L'Etang (2009) calls "radical PR" thinking began to emerge from the late 1990s in books such as L'Etang and Magda Pieczka's (1996) *Critical Perspectives in Public Relations*. Also, a landmark special issue of the *Australian Journal of Communication* edited by Shirley Leitch and Gael Walker (1997) thematically titled 'Public Relations at the Edge' presented a range of European, Australian, and New Zealand perspectives that differed substantially from dominant functionalist models. These examined issues such as power differentials between organizations and their publics, access to media, ethics, and societal interests. Rethinking of PR and non-US perspectives started to enter the mainstream of PR literature in texts such as *Handbook of Public Relations* edited by Robert Heath (2001) and a decade later UK critical PR scholar Lee Edwards noted that "much of the research presented in the 2010 SAGE *Handbook of Public Relations* (Heath, 2010) contests functional PR theory" (Edwards, 2012, p. 11). More recently, the launch of *Public Relations Inquiry* in 2012

as a journal devoted to critical PR scholarship and publication of *The Routledge Handbook of Critical Public Relations* devoted to alternative perspectives (L'Etang, McKie, Snow, & Xifra, 2015) reflect a growing concern about some aspects of PR. For a summary of critical PR thinking see these publications, as well as Edwards and Hodges (2011) and Fawkes (2015). Johanna Fawkes says that public relations in Western capitalist societies "has become aligned with a kind of liberal management theory where concern for publics is designed to facilitate alignment with management goals" (Fawkes, 2015, p. 205). In this context, she says PR is "falsely claiming to serve social rather than corporate or shareholder interests" (p. 28).

- *'The sociocultural turn'*—In the past decade, critical PR scholars have cited and advocated a 'sociocultural turn' in PR (Edwards & Hodges, 2011). Lee Edwards and Caroline Hodges argue that increasing focus on sociological and cultural factors "constitutes a 'turn' in PR theory that shifts the ontological and epistemological focus of the field" (p. 3) from its location in strategic organization management in the service of elites to a sociological and cultural context, and from functionalism and behaviourism to social interaction and more humanistic understandings of the world based on social theory. However, despite useful insights in Patricia Curtin and Kenneth Gaither's (2005) 'circuit of culture' model of PR based on the *circuit of culture* developed by Paul du Gay and colleagues (du Gay, 1997; du Gay, Hall, James, Mackay, & Negus, 1997; Nixon & du Gay, 2002), there is no working model of sociocultural public relations at this stage.

Nevertheless, with the exception of the advocacy approach, this overview shows that most conceptualizations of PR make claims for two-way communication, relationships, dialogue, engagement, and social interaction in which listening should, in theory, be a key part of practice. Discussion of ethics in PR also implies concern for and consideration of others including listening. For instance, two critical voices within the dominant US literature on PR, Timothy Coombs and Sherry Holladay, say of ethics in PR:

> There is no magical code of conduct that will solve all ethical concerns experienced by public relations professionals .... The best advice is that public relations practitioners must listen and utilize two-way communication to be ethical. Two-way communication sets the stage for mutual influence. You cannot be influenced by a group if you never hear it. (2007, p. 48)

Public Consultation

Public consultation is expected and sometimes a requirement for both governments and corporations in democratic countries in a number of situations. This development has been driven by a shift in politics in which "citizens are no longer perceived as the passive recipient of public benefits but rather as an active part of a common solution to social problems, bringing experiential expertise and local knowledge" (Durose, Justice, & Skelcher, 2015, p. 139). Bodies such as the Organization for Economic Cooperation and Development (OECD) and the National Collaborating Centre for Methods and Tools (NCCMT) differentiate consultation from communication and participation. Interestingly, in relation to government the NCCMT (2011) states that in public communication "information is disseminated *from* the government *to* the public" [emphasis added]. This perpetuates the misunderstanding that communication equates to transmitting information and reinforces one-way approaches. The Centre does add that in consultation "government asks for public input on a specific policy issue" and defines public participation as the exchange of information between publics and government involving dialogue in a range of forums such as citizen juries and panels and consensus conferences (p. 1).

The OECD, more accurately in communication theory terms, describes three forms of interaction between organizations and publics as (1) notification; (2) consultation; and (3) participation (Rodrigo & Amo, 2006, p. 1). Within consultation, the OECD identifies a number of levels or types including:

- *Informal public consultation*—This involves discretionary, ad hoc, and non-standardized contacts between government or other organizations and their stakeholders and publics. This may occur in telephone calls, letters, e-mails, and informal meetings. There are differing views on the merits and ethics of informal public consultation. These informal contacts are common and encouraged in a number of countries such as the UK and Australia, but they are viewed suspiciously in the US because they are seen to violate norms of openness and equal access (Rodrigo & Amo, 2006, p. 3). Critics argue that governments and organizations selectively seek input to support and justify their preferred position through informal, non-regulated public consultation. On the other hand, some see informal consultation as more flexible,

dynamic, and accessible, being free of the fixed schedule and structure
of formal consultation;

- *Circulation for comment processes*—The first level of formal public consultation involves circulation of draft policies or proposals to those
affected or likely to have an interest. This approach is more systematic, structured, and often has some basis in law, regulations, or policy
within jurisdictions (i.e., it can be a legal requirement for some policymaking processes or projects). However, this process is seen as insufficiently open and transparent because the organizer maintains control
over who is invited to comment;
- *Public notice and call for comment*—This second level of formal public
consultation is more open, transparent, and even-handed as it involves
issuance of a public notice, usually through mass media, inviting all
interested parties to comment. Such measures were adopted in the US
as early as 1946 and a 'public notice and comment' system continues
today. By 1998 some 19 OECD countries had requirements for public
notice and comment in relation to all new regulatory proposals and
many other initiatives such as major development projects (Rodrigo &
Amo, 2006, p. 3);
- *Public hearings*—A third level of formal public consultation is the conduct of public hearings, which are widely advertised and open to all,
and which involve contributors presenting their submissions in person.
A benefit of public hearings is that all presentations and submissions
are available to be seen and read by others at the time of presentation,
allowing response and second-round submissions if required.

Notwithstanding the openness of public notice and comment consultations and public hearings, levels of participation are low in most countries
(Rodrigo & Amo, 2006, p. 4). Some suggest that this is because of lack of
interest and complacency. However, it is also a practical reality that contributions to public consultations take time and sometimes considerable skills
in research and submission writing—particularly in the case of formal public
consultations. Normative theories of democracy call for *citizen engagement*,
which is defined as:

> ... involvement characterized by interactive and iterative processes of deliberation
> among citizens (and sometimes organizations), and between citizens and government
> officials ... to contribute in meaningful ways to specific public policy decisions in a
> transparent and accountable manner. (Phillips & Orsini, 2002, p. 3)

However, such engagement may well be beyond the will or capabilities of many citizens. This is an important consideration in deciding on methods and tools for public consultation. Those that are most accessible as well as most effective need to be considered—a factor that informs analysis undertaken in this study and reported in Chapter 3. Methods and tools commonly used for public consultation include:

- Advisory bodies;
- Public meetings;
- Citizen juries and panels;
- Deliberative polling (a specialized form of polling that incorporates deliberation);
- Focus groups;
- Surveys;
- Consensus building exercises such as 'consensus conferences' and 'dialogues'; and
- Referenda (Abelson et al., 2001; Rodrigo & Amo, 2006).

While all of these provide opportunities for stakeholders and publics to have their say and make an input to decision making, they all suffer from a number of limitations. Advisory bodies are often composed of leaders and representatives of major groups in a field and can thus be the 'usual suspects' with which governments and organizations deal regularly, and they are often elites. Also, as an analysis by Abelson et al. (2001) observes, all except public meetings and referenda involve selection of members or samples, which can mean a lack of representativeness and exclusion of minority and marginalized views. Furthermore, governments and organizations can ignore all of these methods by which stakeholders and publics express their voice—i.e., the effectiveness of all depends on organizational listening.

Consultation and citizen engagement as defined previously are closely related to *public participation*, although public consultation has much more explicit policy and regulatory support and more widespread implementation at an informal and formal level. This is interesting because, as noted earlier, the OECD lists participation as the third level of organization-citizen interaction above consultation. Also, Sherry Arnstein's (1969) widely used 'ladder of participation' model locates consultation as only slightly higher than "informing" and categorizes it as "tokenism" along with "placation". She argues that "partnership" and "delegated power" are required for true participation, with the ultimate participation being "citizen control" (see Figure 2.1).

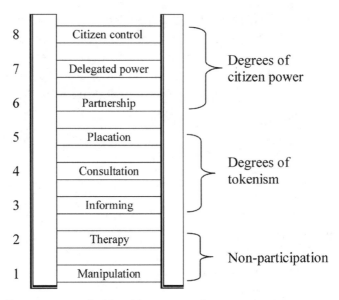

Figure 2.1. Sherry Arnstein's Ladder of Participation.[3]

It is questionable whether the higher rungs in Arnstein's ladder are realistic, especially in relation to highly technical infrastructure projects and matters such as climate change that involves scientific research. Nevertheless, the gap between consultation and participation is worthy of close attention and is explored in this study. A recent examination of public consultation in relation to the proposed high speed rail network (HS2) in the UK claimed that "public participation has increasingly contributed to policy decision making" (Crompton, 2015, p. 27), but did not present evidence that the HS2 project has involved true public participation or whether the mostly traditional formal public consultation undertaken has influenced policy.

The International Association for Public Participation (IAP2) Public Participation Spectrum broadly reflects Arnstein's model, as it lists five key stages or levels of participation as follows:

- *Inform* (to provide the public with balanced and objective information);
- *Consult* (to obtain public feedback);
- *Involve* (to work directly with the public throughout the process);
- *Collaborate* (to partner with the public in each aspect of the decision); and
- *Empower* (to place final decision making in the hands of the public) (IAP2, 2015).

In the IAP2 Public Participation Spectrum, consultation is not seen to be as open and participatory as involvement and collaboration, or what Arnstein calls partnership. Nico Carpentier and Benjamin De Cleen (2008) observe that "participation is a complex and contested notion, covering a wide variety of meanings" and they reject any conceptual stability of the term, referring to it as "a floating signifier, overloaded with meaning" (p. 1). This fluidity in definitions; the normative and often idealized human expectations in relation to communication as noted by John Durham Peters (1999); the limitations of public consultation cited; along with the calls for higher levels of partnership, involvement, collaboration, and empowerment, all need to be taken into consideration and frame and inform analysis of organizational listening reported in the next chapter.

Social Media

In the past decade, new opportunities for organization-public communication have emerged in the form of what are called social media or digital media—although the latter term is increasingly non-distinguishing given that all media and content are becoming digital. In this discussion, the term social media is used to denote Web 2.0–based media and networks such as Facebook, Twitter, YouTube, LinkedIn, Pinterest, Instagram, Google+, Tumblr, Flickr, Vine, and other emerging interactive online platforms.

This is not the place to examine social media in detail—for detailed analysis see Curran (2012), Flew (2014), Fuchs (2014), Macnamara (2014a), Papacharissi (2011), or Siapera (2012). However, social media need to be given special attention in an analysis of listening because of their potential to facilitate two-way communication and dialogue. It could be argued that in the era of mass media, organizations had limited communication channels that facilitated listening, as mass media such as press, radio, and television were predominantly one-way transmissional channels, and other organizational communication media such as newsletters, annual reports, direct mail, et cetera were similarly one-way.

Andreas Kaplan and Michael Haenlein define social media as "a group of Internet-based applications that build on the ideological and technological foundations of Web 2.0 and that allow the creation and exchange of user generated content" (2010, p. 61). Their definition is useful in that it draws attention to the ideological as well as the technological dimensions of social media. Compared with early uses of the Web that featured static content and one-way information transmission, referred to as Web 1.0 (Vergeer, 2013), the ideological foundations of Web 2.0 are openness for interactivity, participation, and collaboration (Boler, 2008, p. 39; O'Reilly, 2005). In his popular text, *Convergence Culture*, Henry Jenkins emphasized that Web 2.0 is about culture more than technology and, in particular, "participatory culture" (2006b, p. 243). Similarly, Michael Xenos, Ariadne Vromen, and Brian Loader claim that "Web 2.0 functionalities" and "the unique properties of social media" overcome key limitations of Web 1.0 and facilitate participation (2014, p. 154). José Van Dijck says:

> The very word 'social' associated with media implies that platforms are user centred and that they facilitate communal activities ... indeed social media can be seen as online facilitators or enhancers of human networks—webs of people that promote connectedness as a social value. (2013, p. 11)

The public relations industry has been particularly welcoming and celebratory of social media. For instance, Vince Hazelton, Harrison-Rexrode, and Keenan claim that public relations is "undergoing a revolution" because of social media (2008, p. 91). In the foreword to Deirdre Breakenridge's (2008) book *PR 2.0: New Media, New Tools, New Audiences*, social media advocate Brian Solis effuses: "Welcome to what just may be the greatest evolution in the history of PR" (Solis, 2008, p. xvii). He claims that with the shift to social media, "monologue has given way to dialogue" (p. xviii). In the title of another book, Solis and Breakenridge (2009) claim that Web 2.0 is "putting the public back in public relations". Similarly, in the third edition of *Corporate Communication: A Guide to Theory and Practice*, Joep Cornelissen states that social media "create new ways of reaching and engaging with stakeholders". He adds that the development of new media "provides an organization with the opportunity to engage in conversations and to tell and elaborate its story or key message to stakeholders or the general public in an interactive way" (2011, p. 154).

The opportunity, yes. But most of the independent research to date indicates that social media are being used for one-way transmission of organizations' messages. In his critical introduction to social media, Christian Fuchs rejects ambit claims such as those above and points out that "alternative online media can easily become commodified and transformed into capitalist businesses" (2014, p. 63). A number of other scholars report empirical studies that show the potentiality of social media are not necessarily realized in practice—particularly when used by government and corporations intent on 'getting their messages across'. For instance, Tina McCorkindale reported that "most companies in the Fortune 50 were taking advantage of the opportunities of Facebook, but were not utilizing this medium to its fullest extent" (2010, p. 12). A study of private and public sector organizations in four European countries and four Asia Pacific countries found that most used social media for 'strategic' organizational goals and most monitored social media spasmodically (Macnamara & Zerfass, 2012). As noted in Chapter 1, studies of election campaigns in the US, UK, Australia, and a number of other countries have found overwhelming use of social media for sending messages (i.e., speaking) with little listening (e.g., Adams & McCorkindale, 2013; Gibson & Cantijoch, 2011; Gibson, Williamson, & Ward, 2010; Macnamara, 2011, 2014a; Macnamara & Kenning, 2011, 2014; Rosenstiel & Mitchell, 2012; Vergeer, 2013). A longitudinal study of social media use by PR practitioners from 2006 to 2012 by Don Wright and Michelle Hinson in the US reported a focus on one-way dissemination of messages (Wright & Hinson, 2012, p. 1). Michael Kent, who co-developed dialogic theory of PR has reported: "If we look at the use of social media by most large corporations, we see that the communication tools that were invented for 'sociality' are typically used in a one-way fashion to push messages out to publics" (2013, p. 342). More recently, in a review of dialogic theory of PR, Maureen Taylor and Michael Kent concluded that "most social media engagement articles find engagement via social media to be a one-way communication process from an organization to followers or friends, rather than constituting any sort of participatory or interactive engagement" (2014, p. 386).

This suggests that the rhetoric of dialogue, interaction, engagement, and listening are not being realized even in social media. However, social media are still referred to as 'new media' by many researchers and practitioners (Flew, 2014; Siapera, 2012). Hence it is important to closely examine organizational practices for signs of change and adaptation to new forms of interactive media that facilitate two-way communication, dialogue, and engagement.

Correspondence, 'Contact Us' Links, 'Info' Lines, and Help Lines

Organizations also communicate and claim to listen through a range of other channels such as letters, e-mail, Web site queries or questions (e.g., 'contact us' sections), and telephone information lines and help lines. Many government departments and agencies have large units responsible for correspondence with citizens, as reported in Chapter 3. Despite the era of digital communication, many citizens still write letters—and they expect a hearing and a response. At the other end of the scale, people increasingly voice their concerns through social media such as Twitter. As a result, organizations—public and private—are having to adapt to new practices of public communication.

The Missing Link in Public Communication

Despite the widespread rhetoric of two-way interaction, dialogue, conversation, engagement, and relationships in human communication theory generally and in various disciplinary fields of public communication theory and practice, a search of relevant literature reveals that discussion of listening—an essential corollary of speaking—is strikingly absent from most articles, research monographs, and textbooks. Within communication texts, only a few discuss listening (e.g., Adler, Rodman, & du Pré, 2013; Alberts, Nakayama, & Martin, 2007; McCrae, 2015) and even fewer have chapters or sections focussed on listening (e.g., Trenholm, 2008; Wolvin, 2010). Listening is not mentioned or mentioned only in passing in many major communication texts such as Craig and Muller (2007), Littlejohn and Foss (2008), and Severin and Tankard (2001). Those who do discuss listening exclusively focus on interpersonal listening at an individual and small group level (e.g., Griffin, 2009). Alberts et al. (2007, p. 28) are among the few to suggest that there is an ethical responsibility as well as a practical imperative to listen—albeit they too focus on interpersonal communication. It is argued here that this ethical responsibility accrues at an organizational as well as interpersonal level.

Within disciplinary fields that focus specifically on public communication by organizations such as organizational communication, corporate communication, and public relations, as well as specialist sub-fields such as employee relations and community relations, it is particularly troubling that organizational listening is little studied or discussed. For instance, a number of specialist books on organizational communication, even multi-edition texts by respected authors, do not mention listening (e.g., Daniels & Spiker, 1994; Kreps, 1990; Pace & Faules, 1994; Shockley-Zalabak, 1994). While it could be argued that some of these books are dated, the seventh edition of *Strategic Organizational Communication in a Global Economy* by Charles Conrad and Marshall Scott Poole (2012) devotes just a few paragraphs to listening by managers to elicit information from employees in face-to-face conversations

(p. 260) and a single paragraph stating that listening skills are among the skills required of supervisors (p. 136).

Public relations literature fares even worse in terms of focus on listening, despite claims that *two-way* interaction, *dialogue, engagement, relationships,* and even *symmetrical* communication are core concepts in these fields of applied public communication (Grunig & Hunt, 1984; Grunig et al., 2002; Kent & Taylor, 2002; Ledingham & Bruning, 2000). A search of articles published in *Public Relations Review* and *Journal of Public Relations Research,* identified as the two most representative PR journals globally (Kim, Choi, Reber, & Kim, 2014), found that listening is mostly mentioned within discussion of dialogue (e.g., Kent & Taylor, 2002; Sommerfelt, Kent, & Taylor, 2012) and relationships (e.g., Waymer, 2013), along with a few mentions in relation to values in PR (e.g., Spicer, 2000; Gregory, in print) and leadership (e.g., Grunig, 1993). However, a recent analysis in public relations literature concluded that, despite much attention to dialogue, "there is very little research on dialogic communication principles" other than the pioneering work of Kent and Taylor (Lee & Desai, 2014, p. 83).

This research confirmed this gap. A keyword search of *Public Relations Review* articles published between 1976 and 2014 found only 217 that mention listening anywhere in their text. However, only two articles focus specifically on listening—an analysis of President Nixon's 'Listening Posts', which began in 1969 but were quietly closed down in 1971 after being deemed a failure (Lee, 2012), and an analysis of audience research by arts institutions (Foreman-Wernet & Dervin, 2006). Listening is mostly referred to in passing with no examination of what listening entails at an organization-public level. For instance, in an article titled 'Revisiting the Concept of Dialogue in Public Relations', Petra Theunissen and Wan Noordin (2012, p. 10) cite Robert Heath who suggests that "listening and speaking" are key elements of dialogue, but provide no further discussion of listening. In an analysis of Twitter use by US presidential candidates, Amelia Adams and Tina McCorkindale say that "retweeting, when done appropriately, can show that candidates are listening to their constituents" (2013, p. 359). While retweeting involves some level of attention, recognition, and response, resending 140-character tweets does not in any way meet the definitions of listening advanced in the literature cited. On the few occasions that methods of listening are discussed in PR literature, listening is mostly equated with monitoring and environmental scanning (e.g., Sonnenfeld, 1982, p. 6). A search of *Journal of Public Relations Research* identified 132 articles that mention the word 'listening', but even fewer articles in this journal examine how listening is operationalized in organization-public relationships and none focuses specifically on listening.

The most detailed discussion of listening in public relations to date emerged in the 'Melbourne Mandate', an advocacy paper developed in 2012 by the Global Alliance for Public Relations and Communication Management (Global Alliance, 2014), and a subsequent article elaborating on these principles, which identifies "the ability of the organization to listen" as one of three spheres of PR value adding (Gregory, in print). Anne Gregory lists seven requirements outlined in the Melbourne Mandate to build a culture of listening in an organization, as follows:

1. Develop research methodologies to measure an organization's capacity to *listen*, and apply these metrics before and after the pursuit of strategy and during any major action;
2. Identify and activate channels to enable organizational *listening*;
3. Identify all stakeholder groups that affect the pursuit of the organization's strategy, both now and in the future;
4. Identify these stakeholder groups' expectations and consider them both in the organization's strategy and before taking any action;
5. Ensure sound reasons are communicated to stakeholders in cases where their expectations cannot be met;
6. Prove that the organization is genuinely *listening* as it takes actions in pursuit of its strategy;
7. Evaluate the effectiveness of the organization's *listening*. (Gregory, in print) [emphasis added]

Listening is discussed in a book by Italian PR and knowledge management consultant Toni Muzi Falconi written in association with US PR scholar Jim Grunig, Emilio Zugaro, and Joao Duarte (Falconi, Grunig, Zugaro, & Duarte, 2014). In the first chapter, Falconi commendably says that "a listening culture is necessary" in organizations (2014, p. 2) and the book includes a chapter by Emilio Zugaro (2014) that proposes six steps for "stakeholder relationships listening". However, the book contains no referencing or primary research and Zugaro's chapter, which he describes as "musings", contains only brief details about listening (2014, p. 84). While the authors are well qualified and the book includes some useful insights from professional practice along with a summary of Jim Grunig's widely circulated relationships theory of PR, it is more polemical than analytical. Nevertheless, it contains advice that is highly supportive of this analysis with Falconi stating: "We take listening for granted. Within business- and communication-related campuses or in lifelong learning professional programs there are very few, if any, courses dedicated to listening" (2014, p. 33). He goes on to argue that listening "is an inherent and integrated part" of the communicative process and supports Jim Grunig's concept of "listening to stakeholders not only to change them, but also to change myself", as opposed to Edward Bernays's scientific-persuasion approach that is based on listening to improve the persuasiveness of the organization's communication (as cited in Falconi, 2014, p. 34).

Listening also receives little attention in PR research books and textbooks. For instance, 'listening' is not listed in the index of the main 'PR Excellence' text, which is widely recognized as representing the dominant paradigm of public relations (Grunig et al., 2002), or in the index or contents of a dozen other international PR and corporate communication texts examined (e.g., Botan & Hazelton, 2006; Cornelissen, 2011; Tench & Yeomans, 2009; Wilcox & Cameron, 2010). On the few occasions that listening is discussed in public relations literature, it is with an organization-centric focus on effectiveness— that is, listening only insofar as it helps an organization achieve its objectives. For example, after stating that "effective public relations starts with listening", the widely used textbook *Cutlip & Center's Effective Public Relations* goes on to describe listening as part of "systematic" and "scientific research" associated with achieving the organization's goals (Broom, 2009, pp. 271–272). While mentioning listening several times in the context of rhetorical theory, *Today's Public Relations: An Introduction* by Heath and Coombs (2006) similarly positions it as part of research to help practitioners strategically target publics,[4] as shown in the following quotation. Heath and Coombs say "today's public relations practitioner gives voice to organizations" and, to their credit, add that "this process requires the ability to listen". However, they go on to narrowly configure listening by saying "listening gives a foundation for knowing what to say and thinking strategically of the best ways to frame and present appealing messages" (2006, p. 346). This is a clear example of what John Fiske (1994) and Yvonna Lincoln (1997, 2001) call *audiencing*—a process of constructing others as objects of study or for targeting—and is a far cry from listening as defined in the literature.

In an influential widely republished article, Cezar Ornatowski drew critical attention to the organizational centricity that permeates many organizations and renders listening little more than intelligence gathering to plan their next move, saying:

> Effectiveness and efficiency, understood in terms of usefulness to employers, as the basic premises for communicative action appear to leave the communicator no provision, at least in theory, for action that does not 'efficiently' further the goals of the institution or interests she serves. (2003, p. 174)

Organization-centricity is also demonstrated in many practice-based discussions of engagement. For instance, the University College London says on its Web site that its Public Engagement Unit supports UCL staff and students in a range of activities and lists the first one as "*telling* public groups about our work" (UCL, 2014) [emphasis added]. To be fair, the college does define engagement further down the Web page in more detail, noting that it is a "two-way process involving interaction and listening". But, as Taylor and Kent say: "Most evidence about engagement shows that it has been enacted as a form of one-way communication. Second, most articles describe engagement from an organizational perspective" (2014, p. 387).

In public diplomacy, particularly what is termed the *new public diplomacy* (Melissen, 2005; Nye, 2010a; Riordan, 2003; Snow, 2009), in which direct public communication as well as government-to-government communication is central (Kochhar & Molleda, 2015, p. 52), claims are made for listening. For instance, Sarabdeep Kochhar and Juan-Carlos Molleda say that public diplomacy on behalf of a country "can be thought of as a process of national listening and understanding the needs of other countries and communicating its viewpoint to eventually build relationships" (2015, p. 53). Echoing early descriptions of PR (Goldman, 1948), J. Gregory Payne says "effective public diplomacy is a two-way street" (2009, p. 582). In a recent review of public diplomacy, Michael Schneider (2015) cites a 2009 US Department of Defense report to Congress that "stressed the importance of 'active listening' and sustained engagement with relevant stakeholders" (p. 19). Similarly, in the same edited volume, Bruce Dayton and Dennis Kinsey say:

> Effective communication in public diplomacy depends on a solid understanding of the point of view of the people with whom you are communicating. There, one of the first steps in a strategic approach to public diplomacy is to determine the perceptions of the people you are trying to reach ... adhering to a principle of two-way communication, or what we think of as dialogue, helps to open doors of communication .... If you aren't listening ... then your communication is fundamentally one-way. One-way communication is not generally effective for building positive relationships. (2014, p. 267)

However, in his review Schneider identifies a need for "ongoing consideration" of "messaging versus dialogue" and "tactics versus strategy" (p. 33).

Nancy Snow reports a 2003 review of US public diplomacy that stated "…
the State Department, which oversees most efforts, seems to view public
diplomacy not as dialogue but as a one-sided exercise … America speaking
to the world" (as cited in Snow, 2015, p. 80). In proposing an "ethical vision"
for public diplomacy, Hua Jiang (2015, p. 176) observes that "scholars have
called for a shift of public diplomacy's focus from *information dissemination*
(one-way communication) and *control of* [the] *communication environment*
(one-way communication) to *network* approaches and *engagement* (two-way
communication) [original parentheses and emphasis]. Snow's long-term study
of the field affirms that public diplomacy—even the so-called new public
diplomacy—is "primarily an asymmetric information model" that distributes
political information. It is also evident in Snow's and others' analyses that
public diplomacy as practiced by countries such as the USA have alienated
rather than built relationships with other countries and contributed to distrust and even hate and jihad.

Drawing on the concept of listening competency developed by Wolvin and
Coakley (1994) and expounded by Cooper (1997) and Cooper and Husband
(1993), Judy Burnside-Lawry (2012) has called for *organization-stakeholder listening competency* as one way to bridge this debilitating and damaging gap.
Drawing on the work of Cooper and Wolvin and Coakley, Burnside-Lawry
defines listening competency as:

> … the presence of affective, cognitive, and behavioural attributes that contribute to
> 'accuracy', the perception that the listener has accurately received and understood
> the message sent, and 'effectiveness', where the listener demonstrates supportive
> behaviour to enhance the relationship between speaker and listener. (2012, p. 104)

While the latter part of the above definition is useful in suggesting that listening competency should lead to behaviour that enhances the relationship
between speaker and listener, this concept falls short in a number of respects.
First, reference to "the *perception* that the listener has accurately received and
understood the message sent" [emphasis added] suggests that organizations
can get away with tokenism and pretend listening. They may receive and
understand messages sent, but still ignore them. Second, competency is too
often associated with attributes and skills and ignores other important factors
such as structural, political, technological, and resource dimensions of large-
scale listening, which apply in most cases of organization-public communication. Indeed, the Qualities of a Competent Listening Organization (QCL)
taxonomy presented by Burnside-Lawry (2012, pp. 113–114), while making

a useful contribution to the sparse literature in the field, focusses mainly on 'qualities' as the name suggests (e.g., open-minded, willing to listen, establishes eye contact, is patient, cares, is approachable). Thus, it too is derivative of interpersonal listening models and fails to identify how organizations can address the not inconsiderable challenges of listening to substantial numbers of stakeholders and members of publics who often hold diverse and sometimes conflicting views.

It seems incongruous that in the sizeable body of literature on organizational communication, corporate communication, public relations, and public diplomacy that discusses dialogue, relationships, two-way interaction, and symmetry, there is scant research and little by way of descriptions or models of organizational listening. While a lack of listening might be expected in advertising that, by nature, is primarily composed of speaking (or spruiking) to promote brands, products, services, and messages, it is also concerning that the literature on major marketing communication practices such as market and consumer research, relationship marketing, and customer relations also ignores listening other than in limited and highly selective, self-serving forms. This gap and the limitations of listening evident in these fields of practice are further exposed in research reported in the next chapter.

Information vs. Communication

While the broad field of human communication and most of the public communication practices identified in this chapter have been theorized as two-way interaction and transactional, there is considerable evidence that human communication has been overrun by an informational logic. Under the heady influence of modernism, human communication has been likened to telecommunications and described in a number of models as the transmission of information. As well as being reflected in the early communication models of Claude Shannon and Warren Weaver (1949), David Berlo (1960), and others, it is not uncommon to read in mid-twentieth century literature statements such as "communication [is] the transmission of information" (Berelson & Steiner, 1964, p. 254) and see communication described in terms of a 'sender' and a 'receiver' of messages. Such concepts of communication see these roles as static. They give little or no attention to reciprocity.

In the twenty-first century, the phrase 'content is king' has become a mantra in Internet marketing and communication, implying that creating information and entertainment is the locus of communication ("Content Is

King", 2014; Gates, 1996).[5] In an article outlining five strategies for "superior customer engagement", McKinsey recommends appointment of a chief content officer in organizations, describing the role as responsible for "delivering compelling content that forges stronger emotional bonds with consumers" (French et al., 2012, para. 15). Preoccupation with content, as well as 'storytelling' on behalf of organizations and brands that has become another buzzword in marketing (DeMers, 2014), maintains focus on production and transmission—that is, on voice and speaking. It is intriguing that McKinsey believes that content (i.e., information) can create strong emotional bonds with people. Research in psychology, sociology, and communication studies suggests otherwise. Furthermore, it is most often the voices of elites such as government officials, politicians, big business leaders, journalists, and professional advocates and lobby groups that speak through media and public communication content. Scholarly and professional literature suggests that public communication is *done to* people in most cases.

The dominance of a one-way transmissional notion of communication has been noted in a range of sociological, media studies, cultural studies, organizational communication, and public relations literature, such as the following.

> The transmission view of communication is the commonest in our culture. (Carey, 2009, p. 12)

> Our basic orientation to communication remains grounded, at the deepest roots of our thinking, in the idea of transmission. (Carey, 2009, p. 13)

> Until late in the 20th century, the transmission model served as the basis for conceptualizing communications activities by organizations. (Hallahan et al., 2007, p. 20)

> Contemporary theorists have criticized the current dominance of a transmission (sender-receiver) model of communication in everyday thinking. (Craig & Muller, 2007, p. 1)

A significant personal experience during the research project reported in this book brought home the common misunderstanding of information as synonymous with communication. In early 2014 I was appointed adviser and expert witness on public communication to the Hazelwood Mine Fire Inquiry in the Australian state of Victoria (Hazelwood Mine Fire Inquiry, 2014, p. 414). Early in that year, a bushfire ignited brown coal in an open cut mine near the town of Morwell in the Latrobe Valley around 150 kilometres east of Melbourne. Brown coal ignites much more easily than black coal and can be very difficult to extinguish, particularly when the fire enters underground coal seams, which can smoulder for months or even years. In the US, the Centralia coal mine has been burning since 1962 (O'Carroll, 2010). The Hazelwood coal mine burned for 45 days before the fire was extinguished, spreading thick smoke and ash over the town of Morwell, which is located immediately adjacent to the mine. As well as causing health concerns for residents with respiratory problems and the elderly and causing damage such as pollution of rain water tanks, burning brown coal can emit toxic fumes and mercury into the atmosphere, as well as carbon dioxide, making it hazardous to human health and the environment when emissions reach high levels or occur over an extended period of time.

The town of Morwell is a tight-knit community composed largely of mine workers and their families, along with people involved in support services and agriculture in the surrounding area. While being what many colloquially call 'salt of the earth' folk, Morwell's population is largely low socioeconomic status (SES) owing to relatively low education levels and low incomes, the population has an above average proportion of elderly, and Internet connectivity and use is much lower than Australia's high online rate of 94 per cent (Internet World Statistics, 2014). These statistics were known to government authorities including the Victorian Department of Health, the state Environmental Protection Authority (EPA), and the Department of Human Services (DHS) responsible for community support and welfare and are important in evaluating the public communication that followed the outbreak of the Hazelwood mine fire.

Research and critical analysis undertaken as part of the adviser and expert witness role, presented to the inquiry in a 60-page report (Macnamara, 2014c), revealed that the key government departments and authorities referred to above provided information to the local community mainly via their official Web sites. Furthermore, much of the information was technical or semi-technical in nature, such as reporting "particulate monitoring" of PM10 and PM2.5 and presenting tables of data on chemicals such as chloromethane, carbon disulphide, butadiene, ethylbenzene, and dichlorodifluoromethane (Macnamara, 2014c, p. 38). To be fair, the government bodies also distributed simplified fact sheets, although most of these had to be downloaded from the Web. Public meetings were held, but the first was not convened until a week after the coal mine fire started when resident concern and anxiety were already running high. The Country Fire Authority (CFA) provided more direct communication to the increasingly fearful Morwell community because of their 'on the ground' presence fighting the fire. But, overall, most information was posted online and neither the Department of Health nor the coal mine company attended the first public meeting. In fact, the coal mine company did not attend any of the public meetings held during the crisis (Macnamara, 2014c, p. 42).

In the inquiry's public hearings, legal counsel appearing on behalf of the Victorian government and the coal mine company retaliated against my report's conclusion of inadequate public communication by pointing out that more than 150 'communications' were issued by government organizations during the period of the crisis. I repeatedly clarified that they were referring to *information*, while I was examining *communication*. Two and a half hours of argument, supported by evidence of lack of community understanding, resident anxiety, fear for their health and safety, and confusion over whether or not they should evacuate the town, did not convince the silver-haired and silver-tongued legal counsel that communication is very different to disseminating information. But perhaps the inquiry's report, which contained 18 recommendations including some calling for improved communication, will shake the government organizations as well as companies into rethinking their misguided adoption of the problematic paradigm of communication as information dissemination and message transmission—what is often referred to as the 'SOS approach' (sending out stuff).

The final report of the Hazelwood Mine Fire Inquiry noted: "Throughout the 45 days that the fire burned, members of affected communities felt they were not listened to and were not given appropriate and timely information and advice that reflected the crisis at hand and addressed their needs". It added: "Government departments and agencies did not engage to any significant extent in listening to, or partnering with local residents and community groups (Hazelwood Mine Fire Inquiry, 2014, p. 28). In mid-2015, the state government of Victoria re-opened the Hazelwood mine fire inquiry to investigate claims of premature deaths caused by smoke from the 45-day coal mine fire (Hazelwood Mine Fire Inquiry, 2015). Again, this shows that a lack of listening can have serious consequences.

Chapters 1 and 2 have theorized, conceptualized, and defined listening and shown a neglect of listening in a wide range of literature as well as examples of failures to listen in public communication practice. This sets the scene and provides the framework for empirical research to examine how a number of major public and private sector organizations go about public communication through marketing, customer relations, organizational communication, government communication, corporate communication, public relations, social media, public consultation, correspondence, and various 'info' lines and help lines.

Notes

1. Newsom, Turk, and Kruckeberg (2007) report that some historians credit Thomas Jefferson with first combining the words 'public' and 'relations' into 'public relations' in 1807, while others say the term was coined by lawyer Dorman Eaton in an address to the Yale graduating class of 1882.
2. In the Excellence Study, Jim Grunig and his co-researchers used definitions of 'excellent' companies based on the research of McKinsey consultants Tom Peters and Robert Waterman (1982) published in their popular book *In Search of Excellence*.
3. Sherry Arnstein's Ladder of Participation and her original article are available online at http://lithgow-schmidt.dk/sherry-arnstein/ladder-of-citizen-participation.html
4. Public relations practice widely uses the terms 'targeting', 'target publics', and 'target audiences' reflecting a transmissional approach to communication and conceptualization of various groups of people as recipients of messages and not as senders of messages or dialogic participants. Marketing similarly uses terms such as 'target markets' and 'consumers'.
5. Bill Gates reportedly first coined the phrase 'content is king' in an essay of that title published on the Microsoft Web site on January 3, 1996 ("Content Is King", 2014). The original essay is available on WayBack Machine at http://web.archive.org/web/20010126005200/ http://www.microsoft.com/billgates/columns/1996essay/essay960103.asp

THE CRISIS OF LISTENING IN ORGANIZATIONS AND SOCIETY

Informed by the critical review of literature summarized in the previous chapters and concern expressed by a number of writers such as Couldry (2010), Coleman (2013a), Dobson (2014), Dreher (2009), and others in relation to specific areas of organization-public interaction, a research project was launched in 2013 that involved a two-year exploration of how, and the extent to which, organizations listen to their stakeholders and publics.

The Organizational Listening Project

The Organizational Listening Project was prompted in part by The Listening Project (www.thelisteningproject.net), a research collaboration involving Australian and international media and cultural studies scholars that focussed attention to the importance of listening for social equity and representation of diversity in a series of events and publications produced between 2008 and 2011—albeit this project did not investigate organizational listening. More specifically, this research grew out of a 2012 study of how organizations are using social media. This found that the interactive features of Web 2.0–based social media are not being used in most cases and that, instead, most are using social media primarily for information transmission—a finding confirmed by many other studies before and since (Gibson & Cantijoch, 2011; Gibson, Williamson, & Ward, 2010; Macnamara, 2010, 2011, 2014a; Macnamara & Kenning, 2011, 2014; Macnamara & Zerfass, 2012; McCorkindale, 2010; Rosenstiel & Mitchell, 2012; Wright & Hinson, 2012). The research particularly looked at social media use for engagement and public consultation (e-consultation) and found a lack of two-way interaction as well as a potential for online discussion involving many participants to dissolve into cacophony and confusion unless there are structure and systems facilitating participation. This led to the first speculation on the need for an 'architecture of listening' (Macnamara, 2013).

Subsequently, a literature review and a pilot study were undertaken in 2013, and findings of the pilot study were reported, reviewed, and debated (Macnamara, 2014d, 2014e, 2015b), which provided useful feedback and suggestions. The primary research reported in this chapter was conducted in 2014 and early 2015. After the initial pilot study in Australia, in-depth qualitative research was undertaken in three countries—the US, the UK, and Australia—so, while the findings cannot be generalized, they are relevant to major markets and likely have transferability to a number of organizations and a number of contemporary Western democracies. As discussed under 'Methodology', the research involved intensive examination of organization-public communication by 36 organizations involving interviews with more than 100 senior executives responsible for communication and/or public consultation and engagement, and content analysis of more than 400 key documents such as communication plans, reports, and other key records.

Aims and Objectives

The aim of this project was to explore organization-public communication and, in particular, to examine the practices, resources, effort, and time committed by organizations to speaking—such as through government and corporate communication, public relations, customer communication, employee communication, and so on—and compare that with the practices, resources, effort, and time committed by the same organizations to listening to their various stakeholders and publics. Secondly, noting the likelihood of a significant disparity in speaking versus listening based on the literature and the findings of the pilot study, the project sought to identify the major internal and external factors that influence organization-public communication as well as tools, systems, technologies, resources, and practices that could facilitate increased dialogue and engagement.

Research Questions

The overarching research question explored in this research was 'how, and how well, do organizations listen to their stakeholders and publics?', noting that listening is a fundamental corollary of speaking to achieve two-way communication, dialogue, conversations, engagement, and relationships as identified in communication literature.

In operationalizing the study, the following 10 specific research questions were investigated to gain a more comprehensive and holistic understanding of organization-public communication than that presented in normative theories and practical texts focussed largely on information transmission and promotion, as shown in previous chapters. Furthermore, the study was designed to move beyond identifying the problem to examine key contributing factors and investigate alternative approaches and relevant systems, processes, tools, technologies, and practices to facilitate organizational listening. This required exploration of the following questions.

1. Why do organizations engage in organization-public communication—i.e., what are the main goals and objectives of organization-public communication?
2. What are the main ways (methods, practices, and channels) in which organizations attempt to communicate with stakeholders and publics?
3. To what extent is organization-public communication two-way transactional and dialogic?
4. What are the main media and methods used by organizations for speaking (i.e., to express and disseminate the organization's voice), including the scale, frequency, and intensity of their use?
5. What are the main media and methods used by organizations for listening to stakeholders and publics, including the scale, frequency, and intensity of their use?
6. What barriers, obstacles, and challenges inhibit listening in and by organizations?
7. What tools, technologies, systems, and methods best facilitate scalable organizational speaking?
8. What tools, technologies, systems, and methods best facilitate scalable organizational listening?
9. What other factors—cultural, structural, political, resources, time, etc.—impact organization-public communication in terms of both speaking and listening?

10. What are the benefits of two-way transactional communication involving listening as well as speaking between organizations and their stakeholders and publics?

Methodology

The most appropriate way to study organizational listening is by examining case studies of organizations at work going about their typical public interactions. As far as possible, a naturalistic approach is preferable. A scientific instrument is not readily available to test organizational listening in the way an audiometer can test human hearing. Scientific approaches such as experiments create artificial situations, which may not reflect actual practices. Also, despite their alleged scientific rigour because of their capacity to produce statistically reliable and generalizable findings, methods such as surveys rely on self-reporting, which in this case would be highly subjective and involve unsubstantiated claims.

Therefore, while a large amount of empirical data was collected, this research was interpretative as it required analysis of claims, observed behaviours, activities such as research projects and consultations, and documents such as plans and reports, and it was qualitative as the purpose was to explore how, and how well, organizations listen. This was not simply a study of how many inquiries organizations respond to or how many consultations they conduct, but how they listen in terms of giving recognition, acknowledgement, attention, interpretation, consideration, understanding, and response to others as defined in the literature. Hence, the study was conducted using qualitative case study methodology (Stake, 2008; Yin, 2009) within a naturalistic interpretive approach, which is able to generate rich, detailed information. Nevertheless, the researcher was mindful of the challenges and limitations of the interpretative approach and qualitative methods, and paid careful attention to the design of the research, as will be explained in the following.

While an inductive approach to exploring issues, phenomena, and practices, and applying interpretative analysis to a relatively small number of cases to generate conclusions and theory lack the statistical generalizability of 'scientific' quantitative research methods, qualitative research is required to have *credibility, dependability, confirmability*, and some level of *transferability*, which contribute to the overall *trustworthiness* of the research, as noted by Lincoln and Guba (1985), Silverman (2000), Shenton (2004), and others. These were established through careful design of the research, transparency in relation to how the research was done (e.g., the sample and how it was selected), and rigorous conduct of the research such as recording interviews and observations (e.g., with digital audio or video), and doing systematic analysis of transcripts and video recordings. The methodological processes applied in this study are outlined in some detail before presenting findings to illustrate the scope and trustworthiness of the research.

Sample

The study was particularly interested in how organizations with substantial numbers of stakeholders and publics listen (i.e., large-scale listening rather than interpersonal, dyadic, or small group listening). Also, while it was not designed to be statistically representative or generalizable, the study was conducted with the intention of identifying common practices in different types of organizations in a range of industries and sectors and in a number of geographic regions to ensure the maximum relevance and transferability of findings. Therefore, a *purposive* sampling method was used in which selection of units or cases is "based on a specific purpose rather than randomly" (Tashakkori & Teddlie, 2003, p. 713). As Miles and Huberman (1994) note, defined case (purposive) sampling for qualitative studies is informed by the conceptual question, not a concern for "representativeness" (p. 29). Bryman (1988) and others note that well-selected defined cases produce findings that have a broad generalizability to particular contexts, or what Lincoln and Guba (1985), Silverman (2000), and Shenton (2004) prefer to call transferability.

The sampling frame employed Miles and Huberman's three-stage approach for qualitative research sampling by (1) selecting some "exceptional" or exemplary cases; (2) selecting some "discrepant", "negative", or "disconfirming" examples; and (3) selecting some apparently typical examples (1994, p. 34). In simple terms, this can be described as selecting some cases at each end of the spectrum and some in the middle. Exceptional and exemplary examples were identified from academic articles, media reports, and announcements of specific initiatives in organizational listening, such as the MasterCard Conversation Suite (MasterCard, 2014; Weiner, 2012) and the 'global listening tool' used and much-touted by another multinational corporation. Discrepant negative examples were identified from media and public criticisms of organizations for lack of listening and engagement with stakeholders and citizens, such as criticism of the UK Government and its Department of Health in relation to complaints that led to the Mid Staffordshire hospitals crisis and the 2013 Francis Inquiry (Dominiczak, 2013; Stationery Office, 2013); severe criticism of the UK Government for lack of listening and consultation in development of its Health and Social Care Bill 2012;[1] and reports of customer complaints about energy, finance, telecommunications, and other companies (e.g., FTC, 2015; Karim, 2014). Identifying typical examples of organizations was more difficult to do in a neutral way, but in line with the objectives of the study and the overall conceptual question sampling included:

1. A mixture of government, corporate, non-government (NGO), and non-profit organizations, although most focus was on the two largest sectors of government and corporate organizations;

2. Organizations in each of the above categories in three countries—the UK, the US, and Australia—to gain findings relevant to major developed democratic countries where listening to citizens is most specifically defined and normatively theorized;

3. Organizations with a substantial number of stakeholders and publics and with resources committed to public communication (i.e., primarily large organizations);

4. Organizations that are leaders or 'top three' in their sector, as these are likely to be representative of practices in the sector.

This sampling approach also reflected purposive sampling strategies summarized by Teddlie and Yu (2007) based on the methodological advice of Glaser and Strauss (1967), LeCompte and Preissle (1993), Patton (2002), and others, including *typical case* sampling, *extreme* or *deviant case* sampling (also known as outlier sampling), *maximum variation* sampling, *revelatory case* sampling, and *critical case* sampling. As Teddlie and Yu say, "many QUAL studies reported in the literature utilize more than one purposive sampling technique due to the complexities of the issues being examined" (2007, p. 83) and they note that "comparisons and contrasts are the very core of QUAL data analysis" (p. 81) [original emphasis].

Accessing a purposive sample to provide a comprehensive picture of organizational listening and achieve findings with credibility, dependability, confirmability, and transferability—what the researchers previously cited collectively refer to as trustworthiness—posed some challenges. Even though all organizations and individuals participating in the study were de-identified other than some who specifically agreed to be cited, the study had the potential to expose management and staff to embarrassment internally and also to reveal flaws in organization systems (e.g., lack of response to inquiries). Participation was encouraged by identifying the study's findings as a learning exercise from which participating organizations could benefit, including receiving a free pre-publication copy of a research report (Macnamara, 2015a). This served as an incentive for some. In addition, introductions were gained through senior third parties well known to selected organization representatives (see 'Acknowledgements'). However, a number of organizations declined to participate. Thus, the sample also contained an element of *convenience* sampling because it accessed only organizations that were willing to participate (see 'Limitations'). Notwithstanding, the study is based on a substantial sample of major organizations in the UK, the US, and Australia, as outlined in the following.

A pilot study undertaken in late 2012 and early 2013 examined three organizations in Australia: a large national information technology company; a multinational service provider enterprise; and a large public sector institution with an active communication program with its stakeholders. The major portion of the Organizational Listening Project reported in this chapter involved in-depth analysis of public communication activities within a further 33 public and private sector organizations during 2014 and early 2015.

The objective of sampling was to examine a relatively even balance of organizations in the two major categories—government and corporate—with a proportionally smaller sample of NGOs and non-profits, and also to gain an approximately proportional sample in the three countries. This was largely achieved, although greater cooperation and openness among government organizations, particularly in the UK, resulted in a higher proportion of public sector cases than corporations (see 'Limitations'). Examination of government-public communication was boosted by a decision of the executive director of government communication for the UK government to grant largely unfettered access to senior communication staff in the UK Cabinet Office, Whitehall, and a range of UK government departments and agencies. In total, 14 UK government departments and agencies selected by the researcher were studied and the public communication of seven was analyzed in detail (see 'Research Methods'). US government departments and agencies were much more reluctant to participate and therefore fewer were studied. However, in addition to two departments studied specifically, including one mega-department, a senior spokesperson for the US administration with a 30-plus year career in public communication in the US civil service agreed to provide an overview of US government to citizen (G2C) and OpenGov initiatives.

Within government, both departments and agencies, which are referred to as arm's length bodies (ALBs) in the UK, were examined due to their different roles and environments. Departments and ministries are heavily involved in development of policy and closely aligned with and affected by political decision making by ministers, members of Congress, the White House, or Whitehall. Government agencies are mostly involved in implementation of policies, regulation, and service delivery to citizens, and are more public facing as a result. This study was cognizant of the 'democratic deficit' perspective of ALBs because "the main characteristic of these bodies is their relative autonomy from elected politicians in the way they exercise their functions" (Durose, Justice, & Skelcher, 2015, p. 138). Some argue that authority and legitimacy should "flow out from elected politicians, reciprocated by a singular line of accountability back to them", as is the case with government departments and ministries (Durose et al., 2015, p. 137). However, this is seen as creating politicization of the civil service by some. In contrast with the 'democracy eroding' view of arm's length bodies including QUANGOs (quasi-autonomous government organizations), the alternative 'democracy enhancing' view is that they provide a positive pluralism and polycentrism that afford multiple forms of accountability and provide "a means of reducing the privatism of elite partisan bargaining" (Durose et al., 2015, p. 138). It is argued that through this they protect the rights of actors who otherwise are likely to be marginalized (Bellamy, 2010). Some US scholars refer to independent regulatory agencies, for example, as the "fourth branch" of government, operating alongside the legislature, executive, and judiciary (Yackee, 2006). So it was considered important to conduct research inside both types of government bodies and eight of the 18 government organizations studied—almost half—were ALBs/agencies (see Table 3.1).

More corporations were accessed in the US than in the UK. While the total US sample was smaller due to a number of 'no responses' and some refusals, the 11 case studies examined in the US, as shown in Table 3.1, made up a substantial sample for qualitative research, particularly given the size and extent of operations of the companies and government bodies participating. US corporations studied included a number of Fortune 500 companies including two Fortune Top 50s and several of the world's leading brands—e.g., MasterCard was one that agreed to be named.

Table 3.1. Sample breakdown of the Organizational Listening Project.

Organization type	Australia	UK	US	Total
Government	2	14	2	18
Corporate	3	3	8	14
NGO/non-profit	2	1	1	4
Totals	7	18	11	36

Given the sampling frame (i.e., large corporations, government departments and agencies, NGOs, and non-profit organizations), the study was conducted in the main business centre of each of the countries—namely, New York, London, and Sydney—as well as two additional cities in each country to gain some broader perspectives, including national capitols such as Washington, DC, and some major regional cities. Regional locations are not named because this could reveal the identity of some major corporations and government departments or agencies that are well-known in those locales.

After multiple requests, numerous no-responses, and several declines, as well as practical limitations presented by availability of key executives in the period of the study, the sample was constructed as shown in Table 3.1. Despite some skews in the sample caused by factors beyond the researcher's control, this represents a large study in qualitative terms. *Redundancy criterion*—also referred to as *information saturation, information redundancy, thematic redundancy,* and *diversity exhaustion* (Glaser & Strauss, 1967; Morrison, Haley, Sheehan, & Taylor, 2002, p. 118; Strauss & Corbin, 1990; Teddlie & Yu, 2007)—was achieved halfway through the study (i.e., after 18 case studies). The additional case studies were undertaken for *confirmability* and to balance the sample geographically and by organization type as far as possible.

Ethics

The research project presented a number of ethical challenges and the research design went through several revisions based on experiences gained in the pilot study. Even after the first few cases were examined, the methodology was refined based on experience, as explained in the following.

Ethics approval was sought and gained through the author's university prior to beginning the study, as is the normal procedure for scholarly research involving human interaction. This provided that (1) interviews proceeded only after written consent, with a right to withdraw at any time without explanation or justification; (2) de-identification of interviewees and organizations participating in the study; and (3) protection of any confidential information gained as part of the research. However, beyond Human Research Ethics Committee approval, a number of other quite challenging ethical dilemmas confronted the researcher. These are briefly explained to demonstrate validity in the findings as well as ethical conduct of the research. Three issues in particular emerged in designing the research and testing stages, which had to be addressed.

- *Pre-empting and priming participants versus hidden objectives and possible deception*—From the outset, introducing and explaining the research posed the dilemma that explicitly stating that the study was examining organizational listening primed participants to highlight their listening activities and even over-emphasize them, rather than talk honestly about their most common communication strategies and activities (i.e., it could create *response generation*). On the other hand, not telling participants that the study was specifically interested in listening within the context of organization-public communication could mislead them and trick them into talking about public communication broadly, which could result in them inadvertently omitting to mention some listening activities. To overcome this dilemma, interviews were conducted in two parts. The first part asked questions about the organization's public communication generally, without alluding to or explicitly discussing listening. This helped identify participants' main objectives, strategies, and priorities in public communication and revealed whether listening activities were spontaneously mentioned. Then, in the second part of interviews, participants were specifically asked about how they listened to stakeholders and publics. As well as open-ended questions, interviewees were asked a series of specific probing questions about a wide range of possible listening activities (e.g., does your organization do research; does your organization do social media monitoring, and if so how; does your organization do public consultation?). This ensured that the topic was extensively explored.
- *Biased data through self-reporting*—Along with surveys, interviews also involved self-reporting, which can contain exaggeration and even misrepresentation. It had to be expected that many senior communication managers would claim that their organizations listen, so interviews alone could not provide reliable data. To overcome this problem,

triangulation of data was used (see 'Research Methods'), as well as probing questions as outlined above.

- *Incomplete data caused by interviewee selection*—A third factor that emerged during the pilot study is that listening is often widely dispersed in organizations being potentially undertaken by many staff and departments, units, or even service providers. These were identified from the literature, experience in the field, and the pilot study to include customer relations, research or insights, correspondence units, policy and public consultation teams, and operational field staff, as well as roles, functions, and units specifically responsible for public communication such as corporate communication, public relations, and community relations. Therefore, multiple interviews were conducted in each organization with executives responsible for these functions. Furthermore, a number of service providers were included in the sample such as research and social media monitoring and analysis firms engaged by major corporations or government bodies (see explanation in the next section). This helped ensure that the study examined all key sites of organizational listening.

Research Methods

Noting that self-reporting by organization staff had the potential to overstate listening and that some organizations were likely to be reluctant to make admissions that indicated a lack of listening, the project used a triangulation approach to draw data from three sources.

1. *In-depth interviews*—A primary research method deployed was in-depth interviews with senior staff in communication-related roles using a semi-structured approach. This employed an interview question guide in two parts as discussed previously to ensure exploration of all key issues, but contained predominantly open-ended questions. The interview question guide is provided in Appendix 1. The starting point for interviews was the senior communication managers in organizations, who were considered best placed to report on communication activities of their organization. These typically have titles such as director, executive director, or head of communication, 'communications',[2] or corporate communication; communication manager; corporate communication manager; or public relations manager. Some multinational

organizations have positions such as head of global communication or chief communication officer (CCO)—a relatively new title that reflects a rise of communication to the 'C suite' of executive management along with the CEO, chief financial officer (CFO), chief marketing officer (CMO), chief information officer (CIO), and so on. Some marketing managers were also interviewed in cases in which their focus was on marketing communication and/or relationship marketing. In addition, recognizing the multi-sited nature of listening in organizations as reported in the following, interviews were also conducted with senior staff in specialist functions such as customer relations/customer relationship management (CRM), research (often referred to as insights), public consultation, social media monitoring and analysis, and internal/employee communication. Up to seven interviews were conducted in some organizations, while in others the head of communication preferred to provide all comment, soliciting information from colleagues as required. Furthermore, during the study it became apparent that a number of organizations outsource some organization-public communication that potentially or explicitly involves listening, such as social media analysis, to specialist research firms and agencies. On the recommendation of the organizations studied, a number of these specialist research firms were added to the sample as they have first-hand knowledge of these practices. A total of 104 interviews were conducted, an average of 2.89 (almost three) interviews per organization. All interviews were face-to-face and all except two were conducted by the author. The author's background working in the public communication field for almost 30 years afforded understanding of the domain under study and helped establish "empathy" and rapport with interviewees, which researchers such as Arthur Berger (2000, p. 124) note is important for gaining trust and insightful findings. Two interviews were conducted by research associates because of their specialized expertise and access to a local area healthcare organization. Interviews ranged from 1.25 hours to three hours.

2. *Document analysis*—To help validate data gained in interviews, the study also collected a range of documents that contain evidence of organization-public communication activities. These included 'strategic communication' plans; reports of communication programs and activities; evaluation reports including tracking of key performance indicators (KPIs) on the basis that organizations usually evaluate what

is most important to them; research reports; records of public consultations; and even job descriptions. While some organizations declined to supply such documents, most did on the condition that the specific contents were not revealed. In addition, a range of documents relating to public consultation, engagement, and open government were downloaded from government Web sites such as www.gov.uk and corporate sites to access information about relevant initiatives such as the MasterCard Conversation Suite (http://newsroom.mastercard.com). While job/position descriptions do not comprehensively describe what activities are done in practice, and roles can change over time, these do identify key responsibilities, priorities, and tasks. These were sourced from an executive recruitment firm specializing in the corporate and marketing communication field, which provided 95 typical job/position descriptions of senior communication-related roles. In total, more than 400 relevant documents were obtained and analyzed for evidence of organizational listening.

3. *Field tests (experiments)*—Thirdly, field tests were conducted as mini-experiments in which the author and research associates submitted 'real life' inquiries, questions, complaints, and comments warranting a response via e-mail or to the Web sites and social media sites of organizations studied. The organizations were not notified of this research method and it was not considered necessary to do so, as the inquiries were all genuine. This method provided independent empirical evidence of how organizations listen and respond to stakeholders and publics. During the period of the research 25 inquiries, requests for information, complaints, or comments warranting a response were submitted to the online sites of organizations, and responses were monitored and recorded.

Data Capture and Analysis

All formal interviews were digitally recorded and transcribed verbatim to facilitate textual analysis and retrieval of participants' statements, which are quoted extensively in this chapter to allow them to speak in their own words as far as is practicable. In longer discussions and conversations, some of which took place over a whole day and during multiple visits to organizations in some cases, detailed note taking was undertaken drawing on anthropological and ethnographic techniques. Notes were also taken during interviews to record key points that interviewees emphasized and to describe observations such as computer screen presentations of information when documents were not provided. Notes were digitally captured directly on a notebook computer, or handwritten notes were keyboarded into a digital document within 48 hours to maintain maximum literal and contextual accuracy (i.e., while the information and experiences were still fresh).

Transcriptions of interviews were analyzed in the first stage of data processing using NVivo 10 to inductively identify key issues, topics, and concepts discussed by participants in line with qualitative textual and content analysis procedures (Neuman, 2006; Punch, 1998; Shoemaker & Reese, 1996). Almost 1,000 pages of transcripts were analyzed in NVivo to produce lists and 'word clouds' showing the most frequently occurring terms, concepts, and phrases. After initial *open* coding focussed on identifying key terms and topics in the texts, NVivo was used to undertake some second-level *axial* and *pattern* coding to group terms and concepts into categories (Glaser, 1978; Glaser & Strauss, 1967; Punch, 1998, pp. 205, 210–221). These were derived from a mixture of inductive and deductive analysis. For instance, terms were categorized as 'listening-orientated' and 'speaking-orientated' where possible based on grouping synonyms and derivative words in the texts (inductive), while *a priori* categories were used to deductively categorize terms into specific fields of practice such as customer relations, public consultation, and so on. The latter categorization affords disciplinary insights to inform further research and teaching in those fields of practice.

While bringing a systematic approach to data analysis and mitigating subjectivity by the researcher, this somewhat mechanistic analysis told only part of the story, however. An important part of interpretative analysis was comparing transcripts of interviewees' statements with interviewer notes, from which additional information was obtained, emphasis identified, and references to key documents accessed. In the second stage of data analysis, more than 200 pages of researcher notes and more than 400 relevant documents collected as part of the study were reviewed and the content compared with the statements and claims of interviewees. For instance, if an interviewee claimed public consultation was undertaken, a report of the consultation was requested and examined to confirm or disconfirm claims made. Concurrently, results of field tests (experiments) were tabulated to identify the rate and types of responses received.

These intensive second and third stages of interpretative analysis used a mixed inductive/deductive approach drawing on *grounded theory* to move back and forth between data sets and between analysis and theorizing (Glaser & Strauss, 1967; Strauss & Corbin, 1990). During these stages, data from interview transcripts, documents, and researcher notes were used to identify thematic categories such as culture, policies, structure, resources, skills, and technologies.

This painstaking and laborious three-stage process of data analysis using textual analysis, constant comparative method (Frey, Botan, & Kreps, 2000, p. 281) across the three data sets, and critical interpretative analysis as recommended by Stanley Deetz (1982),[3] was undertaken over a period of two months in the second quarter of 2015 primarily by the author who conducted all but two of the interviews and reviewed all documents. This afforded deep immersion "in the world of the message pool", a methodological strength noted by content analysis specialist Kimberley Neuendorf (2002, pp. 102–103). To provide a check on subjectivity and assist interpretive fidelity, a research associate conducted the NVivo analysis and reviewed approximately 10 per cent of the interview transcripts and notes to compare them against draft findings and conclusions. Some minor revisions were made based on this 'intercoder' analysis.[4] Furthermore, as noted earlier, draft findings were shared with participants in a pre-publication research report (Macnamara, 2015a), allowing for review as well as a period of reflexivity and reflection by the researcher and participants. A summary of the scope and methodology of the study is provided in Table 3.2.

Table 3.2. Summary of methodology of the Organizational Listening Project.

THE ORGANIZATIONAL LISTENING PROJECT		
Organizations studied	36	Government departments and agencies, large corporations, medium to large NGOs, and non-profits
Interviews conducted	104	Face-to-face, in-depth semi-structured, 1.25–3 hours
Interviews per organization	1–7	Conducted with senior communication-related executives such as corporate communication, marketing communication, public relations, consultation, research/insights, and customer relations (CRM)
Average number of interviews per organization	2.89	

Documents analyzed	412		Communication plans, evaluation reports and 'dashboards', consultation reports, research reports, and job descriptions of senior communication-related roles
Field tests/experiment (*n*)	25		Inquiries, questions, and comments needing a response submitted via letters, e-mail, organization Web sites, or in social media to organizations
Data capture and analysis	Recording of interviews Note taking Transcription of interviews Textual analysis of interviews Interpretative analysis of NVivo data, notes, and documents		Digital audio 200 pages by interviewer Pacific Transcription Solutions NVivo 10 Applying triangulation, hermeneutics, and reflectivity, research associate conducted NVivo analysis; participants given draft findings to review

Limitations

Limitations of the study have been noted already to some extent. These pertain mainly to the extent to which the study accessed a convenience sample due to a number of organizations declining to participate (non-response bias) and the potential for 'response generation' when organizations were informed that the study was examining their listening practices, combined with the potential for exaggeration and even false claims in self-reporting research methods such as interviews.

As noted previously, another feature of organizational listening that became apparent during the study is that some organizations outsource activities that involve listening, such as media monitoring and particularly social media monitoring and analysis. In relation to the latter in particular, organizations often do not have the skills or tools to track the vast volume of social media comment, and therefore engage specialist research firms or consultancies to undertake this role. This limitation was addressed by including interviews and detailed observations within three international service providers, including two in which noteworthy listening initiatives were being conducted (the MasterCard 'Conversation Suite' and another multinational corporation's 'global listening tool').

Notwithstanding, this study did not include all potential organizational listeners and sites of listening. For example, it did not examine the work and practices of field staff, which in some organizations number many thousands and who engage with citizens, customers, members, and others every day. It also did not examine the listening activities of politicians in the context of political listening and representation. As argued by a senior UK government spokesperson in the next section, government departments are mostly charged with implementing policies and political decisions; it is largely the responsibility of politicians to listen to voters in a democracy. However, this overlooks the responsibility of government departments and agencies to conduct public consultation, respond to public inquiries, and provide customer service in some cases.

As in all qualitative research, pre-conceptions and subjectivity are also potential limitations and factors for constant vigilance and address. However, in addition to the explanations and initiatives noted previously, it is felt that the limitations faced were substantially addressed by:

- The size of the sample (36 case studies);
- The seniority of interviewees (placing them in positions of knowledge);
- The leadership position of organizations studied (mostly large government departments and agencies, Fortune 500 companies, and large NGOs or non-profits), which have substantial public communication programs;
- De-identification that enabled organization staff to speak freely and answer questions honestly (even if cautiously, given organization loyalty and fear of making admissions that reflect negatively on themselves);
- The triangulation methodology that provided a substantial level of validation and verification of participants' claims; and
- The data analysis methodology and the period spent checking findings with participants and reflection before publication.

This study did not canvass the views of stakeholders and publics, which might appear to be an obvious perspective for inclusion. However, considerable data already exist indicating widespread disengagement and dissatisfaction among various types of stakeholders and publics (e.g., Coleman, 2013a). Furthermore, those external to organizations can only provide their *perceptions* of organizational listening—or non-listening. Organizational attitudes, processes, tools, systems, breakdowns, and failures, as well as effective organizational listening, can only be explored inside organizations, which is where this study focussed.

The focus on large organizations did create one further limitation of this study, however. While the sample ensured findings related to leaders and well-resourced enterprises, it is likely that small organizations, such as small businesses and local government offices and local non-profit associations, are more engaged with their stakeholders and publics because of proximity and social integration (i.e., those who work in these organizations also usually live in the adjoining community). This would be an interesting area for further study in relation to organizational listening.

Despite some inevitable limitations, this study gained a quite thorough and comprehensive understanding of how and how well organizations listen, as well as why they don't. As noted, up to seven interviews were conducted in some organizations to access various departments and units involved in organization-public communication, ranging from public relations and corporate communication to customer relations and public consultation. Return visits were made to a number of organizations for second-round interviews to ask follow-up questions and probe issues. The researcher was taken 'inside' the workings of government and business in a number of cases, including spending several hours physically sitting at workstations in one of the largest call centres in the UK listening first-hand to organization-public communication through headphones and observing staff responding to public inquiries and complaints via e-mail and even on Twitter. Visits to specialist agencies and consultancies conducting monitoring and analysis of online discussion on behalf of organizations afforded the opportunity to observe systems and their content in real time and talk to the developers and operators about the back-end databases, software, and processes used. A number of interviews and discussions were conducted at the highest level, culminating in confidential briefings by senior government officials in Washington, DC, and an invitation to Number 10 Downing Street to observe the operations of the 'press office' and talk with the head of communication for the British prime minister. Researchers are not always so fortunate, or so laden with responsibility.

How Organizations Really Communicate, or Don't: Research Findings

Non-response

The first finding of this study emerged even before analysis of the mountain of data collected in interview transcripts and documents began. One-fifth

(20 per cent) of organizations contacted with a request for information and/ or an interview did not respond in any way. Researchers recognize the right of any individual or organization to decline to participate in a study. It is also recognized that refusal to participate can be based on legitimate and reasonable grounds, such as being too busy, short-staffed, having key staff on leave, and so on. The Human Research Ethics Committee (HREC) approval for this study specifically provided for organizations to decline to participate and even to withdraw from the study after initial agreement without having to explain or justify their decision. No prejudicial meaning was placed on decisions by organizations to not participate. But a lack of any reply to requests constitutes data relevant to this research. It suggests a lack of listening as defined in this study. Specifically, it explicitly demonstrates a lack of acknowledgement and a lack of an appropriate response, and it implicitly suggests a lack of recognition, a lack of attention, and a lack of consideration.

This interpretation of non-response is not based on naïve expectations following a single request that may have been overlooked in an overloaded e-mail in-box, or ignored as unwelcome 'cold calling', as contacts by unknown persons are termed in sales and marketing. All requests for interviews with communication executives not personally known to the researcher (the vast majority) were made through introductions by a senior third party who was well known to the organization representative contacted. Acknowledgements in the front of this book list some of the senior office-bearers in professional organizations, companies, and government who provided introductions. In addition, at least two approaches were made to each organization selected— and sometimes three. A further relevant factor is that all inquiries and requests were submitted to staff members responsible for the organization's *public communication* or staff members listed on the organization's Web site as available for public comment. In short, it is their job to respond to public inquiries— even if that is to say no.

The heads of communication for a number of major corporations such as pharmaceutical giant Merck simply did not reply—not even to multiple e-mail messages following a supportive introduction sent by a third party well known to the senior communication executive. Even worse, the world's largest PR firm, Edelman (World PR Report, 2014), did not respond despite four attempts to make contact on three continents—two in the UK, one in the US, and one in Australia. This case is particularly interesting because, even though PR firms were not part of the sample, Edelman was approached because the company's CEO Richard Edelman declared in 2008 that public engagement is the future of public relations (Ovaitt, 2008). Furthermore, the company published a report in 2009 titled *Public Engagement in the Conversation Age* (Edelman, 2009) and has continued to advocate engagement since (Edelman, 2015b). Further still, as a PR firm the company ostensibly specializes in public communication. It failed to do so on this occasion. The national communication and marketing staff of Deloitte in one country also failed to respond to multiple e-mail requests for an interview despite a preliminary discussion not long before.

In addition, no response was received from a number of airlines (including two national flag carriers), telecommunications companies, banks, energy suppliers, and consumer products manufacturers and retailers contacted. Some of these were related to requests for interviews and, even worse, some were genuine inquiries, requests for information, or complaints submitted by the researcher or research associates. These 'no shows' in public communication are named because their lack of response of any kind means that they are not covered under the confidentiality and de-identification provisions of the research project's ethics approval. It is well understood that senior executives of big organizations are very busy and may not have time or a desire to participate in research. A simple "sorry we cannot participate" or "we can't meet right now" would have been sufficient to gain protection under the ethics guidelines applying to this research and to demonstrate responsiveness and goodwill.

A number of other organizations could also be 'named and shamed'. The purpose however is not to single out individual organizations for criticism, but rather to show that even market leaders fail to get past first base in the seven canons of listening, and to set a context for exploring factors that affect organizations' capacity to listen to stakeholders and publics including barriers and obstacles as well as issues such as resources, time, systems, and technologies. While the failure of a substantial number of organizations to respond in any way—even to say "no"—is a concerning finding, it begs questions such as whether organizations simply ignore some communications, or whether institutional procedures and systems stifle response in some way. These concerns are explored in the following sections that examine various aspects of organizational listening.

Multiple Modes of Listening

From an early stage of the research it was clear that organizational listening can occur in many ways—most of which are not called 'listening'. This study identified at least 10 major ways in which organizations potentially listen. This is not to report that they do listen through these modes, but listening can occur through:

1. Formal representations (e.g., by members of a parliament or a congress on behalf of their constituents);
2. Direct face-to-face interaction by public-facing staff such as sales personnel, front counter staff in offices, and field staff;
3. Formative and evaluative research such as surveys, interviews, focus groups, and ethnographic studies;
4. Formal public consultation (offline and online) involving submissions, presentations, meetings, and structured comment;
5. Informal public consultation such as 'town hall' meetings, discussion forums (online and offline), citizen juries, and feedback mechanisms such as suggestion boxes (usually electronic these days);
6. Web site inquiries such as to 'contact us' and complaints sections;
7. Media monitoring and analysis;
8. Social media monitoring and analysis;
9. Telephone calls and e-mail to customer relations departments or units (and increasingly tweets and posts on social media); and
10. Letters.

Executive director of government communication for the UK Government, Alex Aiken, argues that in many situations it is not the job of government departments to listen to citizens. He says that is the role of political representatives. "The politicians are expected to listen to their constituents and take citizens' views into account in making policy. Once policy has been decided, then government departments are charged with implementing that policy", he argues (Aiken, personal communication, September 29, 2014).

However, Bimber et al., present a number of qualifications and some counter arguments. They point out that "many of the policy decisions that governments need to make are neither discussed nor contested during election campaigns" (2012, p. 226). Also, they argue that politicians respond to median voters and often do not pay attention to voters "at either end of a range of preferences". Similarly, governments seeking to stay in power and maintain popular support are more likely to follow opinion polls, many of which suffer from a number of severe limitations as a democratic instrument. For instance, (1) they are based on small samples of voters; (2) they aggregate citizens' voices into a hypothetical 'average' voter; and (3) they tend to focus on major issues of concern to governments and often ignore issues that citizens are concerned about. Bimber et al. acknowledge that "it would be wrong to conclude … that voters do not influence policymaking" through their elected political representatives (2012, p. 227). Responsive, electorally active politicians spend considerable time in their electorates and employ electoral staff to keep in touch with the views of their constituents. Aiken's point that government departments often have no choice but to implement policies that they are told to implement is also a valid one that must be taken into consideration in examining the listening activities of government departments. Nevertheless, it has to be recognized that the separation between politics and government is not well defined or consistent. Also, it has to be recognized that politicians sometimes get things wrong, or push personal agendas, or are forced to 'toe the party line'. One senior government executive involved in public consultation and research talked about the importance of collecting reliable data and said "often what people are talking about and concerned about is completely different to what ministers are talking about … sometimes what people are concerned about is not on politicians' radar" (personal communication, February 3, 2015).

In democratic societies, all organizations including government departments and agencies are expected to undertake at least some of the methods of listening outlined in the previous pages. Some methods such as media monitoring are proxy forms of listening, and others such as appointment of PR firms and consultation experts involve delegated listening. An inclusive view of listening needs to be applied in the case of organizations given that they are required to undertake large-scale interaction with stakeholders and publics and this was the approach taken in this study.

Multiple Sites of Listening

Flowing out of identification of multiple modes of listening is recognition that listening can be done at multiple sites within organizational systems. As noted previously, many government communication professionals interviewed in this study argued that elected members of parliament (MPs), members of Congress (MC), and senators have a primary responsibility for listening to publics and stakeholders. Equally, a number of organizations argued that sales staff, personnel in regional and local offices, and various field staff who interface directly with customers and potential customers are the principal 'ears' of an organization. There is some validity in these claims. Nevertheless, the professional fields of practice that specifically claim to implement communication—whether it is called corporate communication, marketing communication, government communication, or organizational communication—and those purporting to be involved in public consultation, customer relations, public relations, and engagement have an explicit commitment to two-way interaction and dialogue that requires listening as well as speaking on behalf of the organization. These practices and sites were a particular focus of this study.

While this study did not produce generalizable statistically representative data as noted, statements about capacity and focus in interviews and analysis of a range of documents indicated that the most active and sustained sites of organizational listening are, in order:

1. Customer relations and customer service departments and units, including complaints-handling teams, many of which process huge volumes of interactions on a daily basis;
2. Research and 'insights' departments, units, and contracted research companies;
3. Social media staff and agencies;
4. Public consultation teams and units (sometimes located in policy departments or units);
5. Government communication units and staff located in department and agencies;
6. Organizational communication, particularly in relation to internal/ employee communication;
7. Political organizations such as political parties (but noting that listening by individual politicians was not examined given the focus of this study on organizations);
8. Marketing communication departments, largely because of their focus on market research, customer relations, and relationship marketing, but with the qualification that much of this involves instrumental, sales-orientated listening, as will be critically examined;
9. Corporate communication staff; and
10. Public relations departments, units, and agencies.

Organizational listening practices overall as well as listening at each of these sites will be examined in the following analysis of case studies. In addition, one further site at which listening is required in all organizations to connect listening to decision making and policy making is discussed.

Overall Patterns, Themes, and Narratives

Overall patterns and themes in the views and self-reported behaviours of participants (i.e., narratives of what they do) were identified from NVivo analysis of transcripts. The 'top 100' communication-related terms mentioned by interviewees are listed in Appendix 2. This shows a wide variety of terms, topics, and issues discussed, and needs further breakdown and analysis for sense making. For instance, discussion included very frequent mentions of terms such as media, communication, digital, and social, which is unsurprising given that the research was focussed on public communication. Also, unsurprisingly given that it is a buzzword in marketing and public communication as noted in Chapter 1, engagement was mentioned frequently. Furthermore, because specific questions were asked about listening, this term appeared near the top of the list of issues discussed (see Appendix 2 for a detailed breakdown of most mentioned terms and concepts). For a simpler visual overview, Figure 3.1 presents a 'word cloud' of the main communication-related terms discussed by interviewees scaled by relative frequency.

Figure 3.1. The main communication-related terms discussed by interviewees.

Figure 3.2 presents an overview of the main topics and contexts discussed by interviewees. This shows extensive discussion in relation to government, policy, issues, management, organizations, the public, groups, and employees, along with frequent mentions of a number of social media platforms. (Note the names of organizations mentioned have been deleted from this 'word cloud' to comply with the de-identification commitment given to participants.)

Figure 3.2. The main topics and contexts of communication discussed by interviewees.

In the second round of NVivo analysis involving axial and pattern coding undertaken to group terms by descriptive categories, the most frequently used terms were coded into two broad categories of 'listening-orientated' terms and 'speaking-orientated' terms. Figure 3.3 shows an overview of the main ways through which interviewees say they undertake listening. Reportedly, organizational listening mainly occurs through engagement activities and consultations, with frequent mentions of direct listening and some discussion of audiences (e.g., their interests and needs) as well as interactivity.

consultations
engagement
listening

Figure 3.3. The main terms and topics discussed by interviewees in relation to listening.

In comparison, Figure 3.4 shows the main concepts related to speaking on behalf of the organization that were discussed by interviewees. This shows a primary focus in public communication on making stakeholders and publics informed. Information is seen to a large extent as a panacea for addressing communication problems. If stakeholders and publics do not support or are in conflict with an organization and its policies and actions, public communication practitioners see this most often as a result of those groups and individuals not being informed. A common assumption is 'if they are informed they will think as we do and do what we want'. Figure 3.4 also shows a focus on talking, producing content, messages, speaking, broadcasting, and voice.

Figure 3.4. The main terms and topics discussed by interviewees in relation to speaking.

The most widely discussed concepts related to listening and speaking that are overviewed in Figures 3.3 and 3.4 are listed by frequency of mention in Table 3.3.

Table 3.3. The most frequently used terms related to listening and speaking.

Term	Mentions	Weighted %	Similar words included
Informed	398	19.02	Inform, informal, information, informational, informing, informs
Engagement	365	17.45	Engage, engages, engaged, engagements, engaging
Listening	312	14.91	Listen, listened, listens
Talk	291	13.91	Talks, talked, talking
Consultation	230	10.99	Consultations, consult, consulted, consulting, consultancy, consultancies, consultant, consultants
Content	87	4.16	Contents
Message	73	3.49	Messages, messaged, messaging
Audience	64	3.06	Audiences
Speak	64	3.06	Speaks, speaking, spoken
Broadcast	47	2.25	Broadcasts, broadcasting
Interactive	40	1.90	Interact, interaction, interactions, interactivity
Hear	35	1.67	Hears, heard, hearing
Collaboration	29	1.39	Collaborate, collaborating, collaborative, collaboratively
Voice	28	1.34	Voices
Advocacy	17	0.82	Advocate, advocates, advocated, advocating
Distribution	10	0.48	Distribute, distributed, distributing
Disseminate	2	0.10	Disseminate, disseminated, disseminating
	2,092	100.00	

Table 3.4 brings these data further into context by comparing the most commonly used 'listening-orientated' and 'speaking-orientated' terms. This shows that, based on the *volume* of what interviewees talked about, their organizations engage in a near even balance of listening and speaking. In fact, this suggests that they do slightly more listening through engagement, consultation, collaboration, and other ways than speaking in various forms such as producing content, distributing messages, and advocacy. However, closer analysis presents a different picture.

Table 3.4. A comparison of listening-orientated and speaking-orientated terms used by interviewees.

Listening-orientated terms	Mentions	Speaking-orientated terms	Mentions
Engagement	365	Informed	398
Listening	312	Talk	291
Consultation	230	Content	87
Audience	64	Message	73
Interactive	40	Speak	64
Hear	35	Broadcast	47
Collaboration	29	Voice	28
		Advocacy	17
		Distribution	10
		Disseminate	2
TOTALS	**1,075**		**1,017**
%	51%		49%

Despite frequent claims of listening, even the most upbeat listening claimants were circumspect when it came to specifics and giving an overall rating to their organization's listening. The final question posed to all interviewees asked them to make an overall estimate, in approximate terms, of the proportion of their budget, time, and resources that are spent on speaking-related activities and the proportion of their budget, time, and resources that are spent on listening-related activities. The customer relations departments of two organizations rated their work as primarily listening, suggesting ratios of 60:40 and 70:30 listening versus speaking, respectively. One public engagement and consultation team also rated its work as 70 per cent listening versus 30 per cent distributing information. However, beyond customer relations, consultation, and research staff, the majority of interviewees were reflexive and self-critical, with many claiming a 70:30 speaking versus listening ratio. Around one-third of interviewees characterize their public communication activities as between 80:20 and 90:10 speaking versus listening. One rated his organization's speaking to listening ratio as 95:5. Even when high claims are made for organizational listening, interviewees suggest that there is "a split" between listening-intensive specialist functions such as research/insights, customer relations, and public consultation, compared with other broader public communication functions such as marketing communication, corporate communication, and public relations. Furthermore, they acknowledge that some of the key listening activities such as research and consultation occur only occasionally—sometimes only once a year or even once every few years— whereas marketing communication, corporate communication, and PR are perennial. While these are not statistically reliable quantitative ratings, averaging responses from interviewees indicates that, overall, the public communication of most organizations is around 80:20 speaking versus listening. Given that these are self-assessments, claims in relation to time and resources spent on listening are more likely to be generous rather than minimalist.

Because they are self-assessments and are fairly arbitrary indications, deeper interpretative analysis is required to understand what organizations do on a daily basis with the objective of organization-public communication. The following sections discuss how organizations listen in the various disciplinary fields and functions studied. These are discussed in the order of functions identified previously as major sites of listening based on the focus of participating organizations as reflected in interviewees' statements about capacity and activity, as well as analysis of documents such as communication plans and reports.

Listening in Customer Relations

The most direct and explicit location of listening in most of the organizations studied is their customer relations function. As noted previously, this function has a range of different names including customer service, customer relations, customer care, and customer relationship management (CRM). The last term, which dominates contemporary customer relations literature, gives a sense of the primary focus of this function and of the inherent tension in the interactions between organizations and their customers. While *management* of customers might be highly desirable in an organization focussed on systems, efficiency, and profit maximization, there is no evidence that customers want to be managed in the way that CRM is described (Chen & Popovich, 2003; Palmatier, 2008).

Discussions with two large telecommunications companies, one in the US and one in Australia, revealed a high priority placed on customer relations and customer communication. Both spoke of being "customer centric". The head of corporate communication in each of the companies unequivocally stated that identifying and understanding customers' needs and engaging customers were collectively their highest priority in public communication. However, a field test conducted with one of the 'telcos' involving a request to upgrade a broadband account to get higher Internet speed resulted in mixed responses. To be fair, the company did ultimately offer a package to upgrade the service including a new (unrequested) free router. But it took numerous phone calls and several return calls from different personnel in the company's customer service department, none of whom knew of their colleagues' actions, and several of whom provided conflicting information (personal communication, April 8–9, 2015). Customer service, while ultimately delivered in a way that exceeded expectations, was a confusing, often chaotic scramble among staff members who appeared to be working on commission, or at least a bonus scheme for 'shifting product', rather than listening to and engaging with customers.

An even less satisfactory case study involved an insurance company that makes much of its customer focus in TV advertising. Reality failed to live up to advertising rhetoric when an insurance claim was submitted following a burglary that occurred coincidentally during the period of this study.[5] Despite a police report confirming theft of some jewellery, and provision of photographs of most of the missing items, the insurance company took two weeks and numerous phone calls to decide whether it would pay out. Then, when it did approve the claim, it advised that it would provide credit to the value of the stolen items at nominated jewellery stores. When this offer was refused on the basis that it was contrary to the terms of the policy, the insurance company eventually paid out the relatively modest amount of cash. However, the most significant part of the company's customer service as far as this study is concerned is its customer communication following the transaction. Within days of the payout the company sent an e-mail requesting customer feedback. The e-mail listed only one question with a five-point Likert scale offering a choice of "awesome, good, acceptable, bad, very bad" (personal communication, April 11, 2015). It is debatable whether 'acceptable' is the mid-point in this scale, as the first three ratings could be classified as meeting expectations,

with only two below standard. But, the most significant aspect of this interaction was that the online link for 'feedback' provided no opportunity to
enter comments—only a single choice to click one of the options on the five-
point scale. Also, despite having dealt with several staff during the claim process, there was no opportunity to rate anyone other than the initial contact
whose name was pre-entered in the feedback form. This is hardly listening
to customers. All customer engagement was framed within tightly scripted or
rehearsed statements and limited choices. When three attempts were made
to break these shackles and 'speak' to the company directly, things became
even worse. First, a reply e-mail sent in response to the company's e-mail
message asking for feedback 'bounced'. Second, an attempt was made to send
a message to the insurance company via the 'Wall' on its Web site that has
a menu tab specifically titled 'Feedback', which invitingly states "Have your
say—we're listening". When the 'submit' button was clicked after entering
information, the Web site repeatedly reported "Sorry, an error occurred". A
last-ditch attempt was made to submit comments on the company's Web
site 'Contact us' page. However, here too the 'submit' button produced an
error message (personal communication, April 13, 2015). The company's
systems and processes ensured, either intentionally or unintentionally, that
it heard what it wanted to hear—and nothing else. The company may have
been having technical problems, but this was more than a case of an organization having a bad day. The issues described occurred over several days
and the overall customer relations experience in this case was one of non-
communication and a complete failure to listen. UK professor of corporate
communication Anne Gregory makes an important point that not only is
there a problem of organizations not listening; just as problematic is "being
dishonest about their capacity and capability to listen" (personal communication, June 2, 2015).

Interestingly, a number of government agencies and even a few departments spoke about their 'customers' and these were not organizations responsible for delivery of services such as transport. Even some government bodies
involved in collecting taxation, licensing, and dealing with industry conceptualize the key organizations and individuals that they deal with as customers. The director of corporate communication of one large UK government
department said: "We treat ourselves as if we are a major corporation"
(personal communication, September 24, 2014). This indicates that Nick
Couldry's (2012) concern about neoliberalism permeating government as well
as business is well grounded, and the implications of neoliberal thinking and

the commodification of citizens as customers is explored in this analysis. In Australia, the Department of Premier and Cabinet in the state of New South Wales appointed a Customer Service Commissioner for the state in 2012—the first such appointment in Australia.

Despite some examples of poor customer service, close study of customer relations across a range of organizations revealed many dedicated compassionate staff and highly committed managers. A visit to one of the largest government call centres in the UK was particularly insightful. More than 1,000 customer advisers work in large, open-plan office spaces handling more than 12 million customer contacts a year—1 million a month. An additional 8 million customer contacts are processed through the centre's automated voice-activated system, adding up to a total of 20 million customer contacts a year—although it should be noted that another UK government department handles 70 million phone calls a year through its call centre (personal communication, September 24, 2014). Historically the call centre visited in this study handled telephone calls only, but it now accepts and responds to e-mails from customers and the agency's e-mail address for customer contact is publicly listed on the central Gov.UK Web site (https://www.gov.uk). The agency received 600,000 e-mails from customers in 2014. Furthermore, the agency started responding to tweets on Twitter in 2014 and has a small but growing team delivering customer service via social media and cross-training other call centre staff in social media interaction with customers. The manager of the centre says the agency's aim is to have an integrated team of customer advisers all able to respond via telephone, e-mail, or on social media (personal communication, February 5, 2015). This approach in itself indicates listening by the organization, as it is responding to a customer trend to express complaints in social media rather than wait in telephone switchboard queues. In addition, several hours spent sitting with headphones on listening to phone calls and observing advisers responding by e-mail and on Twitter revealed a high level of training among advisers as well as a surprisingly personalized approach. For instance, one young male customer adviser demonstrated the suite of e-mail templates prepared by the agency for responding to common customer inquiries and requests. However, he commented that he rarely used the standard template without some modification. He explained:

> I stick to the basic information. I don't change the facts or the policy statements. But you put a few personal phrases in, such as 'thanks for your inquiry' and you add things like 'I hope you find this helpful'. You also try to make the language simple and friendly. (personal communication, February 5, 2015)

This approach took longer than using the template e-mail responses, but observation of a number of complimentary return e-mails from citizens indicated that recipients appreciated the personal friendly style and directness of e-mail. The young man was still able to 'make his quota' of customer contacts, aided by fast keyboard skills. Observation of the nascent social media team revealed an even more customized and personalized approach. Tweets were responded to in casual conversational tones—even the occasional 'smiley'. Links were provided to official policies, rather than trying to summarize complex rules and regulations in 140 characters. Interestingly, another UK government agency with a high volume of customer contact is also embracing Twitter and does not share the concern of some organizations that social media 'opens the floodgates' and creates unmanageable workloads. The director of communication acknowledged that response time expectations are more demanding in social media, but said:

> I'm having this discussion with my helpline team and trying to explain that for each tweet that comes in, that's a letter that didn't. It doesn't stop people wanting answers, it's just a change of channels. It's not additional work—just a new way of doing it. (personal communication, September 26, 2014)

At the government agency with one of the UK's largest call centres, a mature-age woman adviser spoke calmly and reassuringly to a number of confused customers and one slightly irate man who called the agency's telephone hotline, supported by a computer-assisted telephone interviewing (CATI) system. It was clear from her pauses during which callers spoke (sometimes rambled for several minutes) and then hearing the customer adviser's response that she was listening to them with attention and empathy. She acknowledged their concerns, afforded recognition—at no stage being dismissive or patronizing—and provided appropriate responses to the best of her ability within the agency's policies. The agency's customer relations and customer service appears to be having some success as, despite operating in an environment of regulations, taxes, and not infrequent penalties such as fines, only 0.05 per cent of customer contacts escalate to formal complaints (personal communication, February 5, 2015).

The head of corporate communication at the same government agency was one of the interviewees who claimed a 70:30 listening to speaking ratio in its public communication. This appears to be somewhat justified by the substantial proportion of its work focussed on customer relations, including the operations of its large national call centre. In some other respects, however, she was more cautious. For instance, when asked about letters from members of the public, she acknowledged that the agency received a lot of letters and admitted that many of the responses "are not particularly customer friendly". She said some of the agency's standard letters "have been in existence for many a year and are not drafted in a user friendly way". Specifically, she pointed to a need for more "plain English" communication. She also reported that the agency had no media monitoring or media analysis facility at the time of the interview other than monitoring done manually by the "press office". Interestingly, the term 'press office' is used by a number of UK government departments and agencies, even though their media relations role includes radio and television (i.e., broadcasting) and their total public communication function includes responsibilities well beyond traditional media. The agency's corporate communication head said "getting in things like Sprout Social to track social media took two attempts …. [W]e [sic] are a huge organization and it's about moving the boat slowly" (personal communication, September 23, 2014).

Companies also use various methods and new technologies to 'keep in touch' with customers and ostensibly to 'build relationships' with them. But as discussed under 'Marketing Communication' and 'Customer Relations' in Chapter 2, simply responding to and meeting customers' needs and concerns is not the primary purpose of customer relations. Commercial organizations live or die based on sales, and keeping customers and acquiring new customers are their overriding concerns. These goals are pursued in increasingly profession-alized practices for *managing* customers. Observation of CRM practices in one large commercial organization revealed that practices are largely proactive rather than reactive and undertaken to (1) gain repeat sales; (2) 'upsell' cus-tomers to other products or services offered by the organization; and (3) moti-vate satisfied customers to become advocates for a brand or organization. The fourth purpose of customer relations—resolving problems and complaints—is undertaken as required to avoid criticism, which can damage a brand and an organization's reputation if it is spread by word of mouth or, worse, becomes public through media reporting or social media comment. But three out of the four objectives of customer relations are about selling.

Increasingly this is given effect in CRM through capturing more and more data about customers to build profiles of them. Hence there is wide-spread excitement in business about 'big data'. Vast amounts of data can be 'harvested' because of the digital trails people leave—the books they buy on Amazon, the flights they book, the hotels they stay in, even the comments they leave in social media. A happy birthday wish or a 'get well' message sent by a grandchild can add to a customer profile and generate direct marketing messages about superannuation schemes, new holiday destinations, or some new health treatment. Every commercial organization wants frequent flyers, platinum card holders, gold members, club floor guests, and high net-worth account holders. In this sense, customers are a resource to be managed and exploited. This is not to imply a sinister exploitation in all cases, but this reflection is necessary to contextualize customer relations. Organizational listening to customers in commercial organizations is as much or more about self-interest as it is about serving the interests of customers. This type of listening could be called *strategic listening* to add to the list shown in Table 1.1.

One government agency involved in controversial environmental issues reported a very different story. Its 'customer contact' staff who are involved predominantly in reactive public communication find interaction with members of the public "challenging", particularly when dealing with upset and angry people. In an extreme case, communication and engagement executives reported that staff operating telephone contact lines had even received death threats. The head of stakeholder engagement explained that "most of our calls are from people who are unhappy. They don't contact us when they are happy with things". She said a number of staff had been on stress leave and that the agency was concerned about the mental health of staff dealing frequently with irate citizens (personal communication, November 19, 2014). However, no other government organization or corporation raised similar concerns even when asked specifically about this worrying implication of customer engagement, including a similar environmental regulatory agency in another country. The head of the large UK customer call centre interviewed cited continual training and operating in shifts with regular breaks as important strategies to avoid damaging levels of staff stress. Nevertheless, this finding needs to be noted by managers of customer relations functions and by advocates of increased stakeholder and public engagement. While listening to citizens is an important element of democratic participation and social equity, a practical reality is that some people are not nice. Customer relations and call centre staff report that some are rude, aggressive, nasty, and even abusive. This raises the point that stakeholders and publics have responsibilities in relation to their behaviour if they want to be listened to, and organizations need to have strategies in place to support and protect staff when they are addressed by unacceptable methods of public speaking.

Listening in Research

Every organization studied undertakes some form of research and most do research on a regular basis. Many of the organizations studied, particularly corporations, conduct market research to inform product and service development and marketing strategy, but this was outside the scope of this study because of its very specific instrumental focus. However, four common types of research undertaken within the public communication functions of organizations that warrant close study are customer satisfaction research, employee research, stakeholder research, and reputation research, all of which may be undertaken for formative or evaluative purposes, or a combination of both. Another major focus of research in the public communication field is specialist measurement and evaluation studies. These and several other approaches to research were examined in this study.

- *Customer satisfaction studies* are undertaken by most commercial organizations and increasingly by government departments and agencies. In this study, all but one of the corporations examined undertake 'customer sat' research, as it is referred to, along with almost half of the government case studies. This research is mostly undertaken using surveys and these are predominantly commissioned by marketing departments and units in organizations. Customer satisfaction surveys are primarily evaluative, although they are formative in the sense that findings inform organization strategies to improve customer satisfaction and efforts to better meet customers' needs. While it is argued that research such as customer satisfaction studies involve listening, the predominance of quantitative methods such as surveys confines listening within predetermined frameworks. Also, like a number of other research practices in organizations, this type of research is *administrative* and *instrumental*—that is, it is carried out to help resolve particular practical questions and problems and serve the interests of the organization such as identifying ways to operate more effectively and efficiently.[6] Thus, it is organization-centric. Nevertheless, it has to be acknowledged that organizational listening does occur through such studies and some organizations go beyond tokenistic efforts. For instance, the UK government agency with the large call centre referred to under 'Customer Relations' conducts an annual customer satisfaction survey, focus groups, and in-depth interviews with key stakeholders; collects feedback from its customer service advisers; subscribes to the UK government's RepTrak reputation survey; and undertakes its own bespoke reputation survey annually. In addition, it has established a sizeable 'customer insights' team. This specialist research approach is discussed separately in the following pages.

- *Employee surveys* are undertaken by all the organizations studied. These are mostly designed to identify levels of employee satisfaction and morale, as well as gain insights into specific issues such as employees' awareness of various matters such as organization vision, values, and particular policies or plans.

- *Stakeholder studies* are most typically surveys undertaken to canvass the views, attitudes, concerns, and interests of key external stakeholders and publics on specific issues or topics, although some involve interviews to gain qualitative insights. However, quantitative research is the predominant approach. In the case studies examined, this involved mainly 'tick a box' questions with limited opportunity for participants to comment in response to open-ended questions and limited scope to express their views beyond the bounded context of the survey questions. However, almost all organizations studied—both public and private sector—conducted some form of stakeholder study, usually on an annual basis. Along with the predominant closed-end quantitative approach, a further limitation observed in the case studies examined is that most organizations focus on their key stakeholders and define these quite narrowly. Stakeholders listened to are usually limited to close partners; major business, industry, and professional representative organizations; official bodies such as local government authorities and councils; and direct affiliates and dependencies such as retailers, branch offices, or distributors. Recognized stakeholders are most often elites and the 'usual suspects'. Many who might consider themselves stakeholders on a moral, intellectual, or human rights basis, or at least stakeseekers, live in a shadow land on the fringes of the corporate world and representative politics.

- *Reputation studies* are similar to stakeholder studies and customer satisfaction research, but are focussed more broadly on canvassing overall perceptions of an organization among key stakeholders such as customers, partners, investors, industry organizations, and key community groups. A number of omnibus reputation studies are offered such as the RepTrak study undertaken by The Reputation Institute for a number of clients including corporations and government bodies. For instance, in the UK most government departments and agencies subscribe to an annual Reputation Survey of the UK Public Sector. Many corporations also commission bespoke RepTrak studies or subscribe to the company's standard annual studies such as the Global RepTrak 100, which identifies the world's top 100 brands. In addition to stakeholder and reputation studies that are typically conducted annually, a number of organizations conduct what many refer to as 'pulse' studies. These involve smaller samples and often scaled-down questionnaires to gain findings on a more frequent basis, such as quarterly.

- *Measurement and evaluation* have been collectively identified as the 'Achilles' heel' of public relations (Macnamara, 1992, 1999) and as lacking in corporate communication and organizational communication as well as PR even today (Watson, 2012; Wright, Gaunt, Leggetter, Daniels, & Zerfass, 2009; Zerfass, Verčič, Verhoeven, Moreno, & Tench, 2012). The PR and corporate communication industry has been accused of focussing on outputs—putting out information— rather than working to achieve outcomes. For instance, a survey of 2,200 practitioners in 42 European countries, reported that 75 per cent of European practitioners acknowledged an inability "to prove the impact of communication activities" (Zerfass et al., 2012, p. 36).

The public relations industry has mostly pursued a basic and largely automated approach to evaluation, particularly focussed on evaluation of media coverage using online search tools and content analysis software programs. Many are quantitative only, reporting the volume of mentions, audience reach, and counts of key messages, while some use algorithms to calculate what is referred to as tone, sentiment, or favourability. The terms themselves reveal some of the limitations of PR research for evaluation. For instance, sentiment is "an attitude, opinion, or feeling" in humans ("Sentiment", 2015). While it can be reflected to some extent in media content such as social media posts, in general sentiment does not reside in texts. Tone is a more appropriate term to denote the qualitative dimensions of texts, although tone is largely subjective as it is determined by an organization or its agents from the perspective of the organization. Favourability is a more honest qualitative measure as it openly identifies media content as favourable or unfavourable to the interests of the organization, rather than making some generalized qualitative claim about texts.

Mark Weiner, CEO (North America) of Prime Research, says the PR metrics market is emerging from an era of basic automated solutions that often use 'black box' methodologies and secret algorithms to an approach that "combines technology and talent" (personal communication, January 12, 2015). The Association for Measurement and Evaluation of Communication (AMEC) in Europe and the Institute for Public Relations (IPR) in the US have spearheaded a project to develop international standards for measurement and evaluation of PR and corporate communication since 2011, following the Barcelona declaration of measurement principles (IPR, 2010). Weiner strongly advocates standards as well as a combined human and machine approach. He says automated data collection and classification can go so far, and machine learning systems are extending that capability. But Weiner argues:

> Automated coding is fast, but really stupid. Data on its own is [sic] dumb. Real time data processing gives information, not insights. Humans are needed to interpret data and write reports that summarize what it means. Humans make decisions and judgements. And only humans can give advice and make recommendations. (personal communication, January 12, 2015)

The head of communication for one major company studied agrees with this approach and also argues for the need to look beyond simple metrics. His organization is increasingly accessing 'big data', producing analytics, reporting via 'dashboards',[7] and uses the Net Promoter Score (NPS). This is a measurement method introduced by Paul Reichheld in a 2003 *Harvard Business Review* article titled 'One Number You Need to Grow' that asks customers to score an organization on a 0–10 scale for one question: 'How likely is it that you would recommend [organization name] to a friend or colleague?' Scores of 9–10 are rated 'loyal enthusiasts' or advocates; scores of 7–8 are classified as 'unenthusiastic customers' who are seen as vulnerable to competitive offerings; and scores of 0–6 are considered to be 'unhappy customers' who can damage a brand through negative word of mouth or *word of mouse* online (Net Promoter Community, 2015). However, while supporting ongoing data collection and analysis, the head of communication said:

> There is a need to step back occasionally from the data and reflect to see the trends. You can't just watch the 'worm' going up and down on dashboards and charts. You can get too close to metrics and not see the wood for the trees. (personal communication, November 11, 2014)

While evaluation is traditionally focussed on identifying effectiveness, and this is most typically done from an organizational perspective, evaluation potentially facilitates listening in two respects. First, it utilizes a range of research methods such as surveys, focus groups, and interviews to collect and analyze the views and perceptions of stakeholders and publics. Second, it can and should incorporate evaluation of organizational responses to the requests, needs, interests, and concerns of stakeholders and publics (Macnamara, 2015a). In this sense, evaluation is important to 'close the listening loop' by identifying how well an organization relates to and adapts to its stakeholders and publics. However, evaluation rarely includes critical self-evaluation and, while it seeks feedback, it very often fails to give feedback to others—an issue that will be further explored later in this chapter under 'Listening in Management'.

UK government departments and agencies have been implementing substantially increased evaluation of their public communication activities under the leadership and advocacy of executive director of communication, Alex Aiken, who established an Evaluation Council composed of industry and academic experts able to advise the Government Communication Service (GCS)[8] and implemented an ongoing training and mentoring program in UK government departments and agencies (Government Communication Service, 2014a, p. 8). Aiken introduced a 'Mandatory Evaluation Project' (MEP) and seconded a senior departmental communicator, Paul Njoku, to coordinate the project, which had developed 'evaluation champions' in 30 departments and ALBs by the end of 2014 (Njoku, 2014). Analysis of evaluation reports and dashboards of 14 UK government organizations combined with interviews conducted in this study revealed a newfound commitment to evaluation. Focus as of early 2015 remained predominantly on quantitative measurements, but a number of qualitative methods are being gradually introduced and a noteworthy observation that emerged from this analysis is the presence of what this study calls the *evaluation factor*. This is a significant influence that affects all planning and implementation of communication activities when evaluation is built into work processes. It exerts its effects quite simply: when practitioners know that their work and activities will be rigorously evaluated, they pay much more attention to formative research to understand audiences and identify what is likely to be most effective, as well as to careful planning. They are much less likely to undertake activities with low likelihood of success, so wastage and failures are reduced even before evaluation is undertaken. The evaluation factor may have deleterious effects in some circumstances, such as creating reluctance to take risks, but overall it is a positive influence.

While most evaluation of communication is based on quantitative output metrics such as reach, impressions, sentiment or tone of messages, click through rates (CTR), cost per thousand (CPM), and cost per click (CPC), a few of the UK government departments and agencies studied are using highly advanced research methods for evaluation. One presented evaluation dashboards based on longitudinal studies, structural equation modelling, and CHI-squared Automatic Interaction Detection (CHAID) analysis, which is used for prediction in a similar fashion to regression analysis. Also, some innovative research is being used in UK government departments for formative research, as outlined in the following. No corporations studied used any of these advanced research methods. Despite claims that government often lags the private sector in innovation, effectiveness, and efficiency, a conclusion of this study is that government is well ahead of the private sector in evaluation and use of research generally, particularly in the UK. (See details of further research innovation in the next bullet point.) However, overall, research for measurement and evaluation is rudimentary in most of the organizations studied.

- *Behavioural insights* are an emerging focus in research in the public communication field. While the influences on human behaviour have long been studied in behavioural psychology, the study of behavioural insights has broadened to incorporate social anthropology, behavioural economics, and some aspects of neuroscience, and has only relatively recently been applied in public communication and what is referred to as *nudge marketing*. Even then, behavioural insights research, sometimes referred to as 'behavioural economics', is usually conducted by specialist teams and units outside of the practices of marketing communication, corporate communication, and public relations.

Drawing on the research of Richard Thaler and Cass Sunstein (2008) as espoused in their book *Nudge: Improving Decisions About Health, Wealth, and Happiness*, the UK government has been an innovator in this area, setting up a behavioural insights team, also known as the Nudge Unit, in 2010. Number 10 Downing Street subsequently divested the unit in 2014 as a 'social purpose company' jointly owned by the Cabinet Office, employees, and Nesta, which describes itself as an "innovation charity" (http://www.behaviouralinsights .co.uk). Behavioural Insights Limited, as it is now called, is headed by British psychologist David Halpern.

Other countries are also turning to behavioural insights to inform policy making and influence citizens' behaviour. In the US, Harvard University's John F. Kennedy School of Government has established the Behavioral

Insights Group (BIG), and the White House set up a Nudge Unit in 2014 (Nesterak, 2014). In Australia the state government of New South Wales has established a Behavioural Insights Community of Practice (http://bi.dpc.nsw .gov.au) to share knowledge across departments and agencies.

Behavioural insights, or nudge techniques, focus on understanding the social, cognitive, and emotional triggers of human behaviour and identify subtle changes to the way messages are presented and decisions are framed that can have a significant impact on behaviour. From one perspective, behavioural insights are gained to assist in persuasion of stakeholders and publics (i.e., one way to serve the organization). But behavioural insights can also lead to changes in an organization. Two examples were revealed in this study, one of which involves civil servants working in partnership with academics. In the first (Hallsworth et al., 2015), researchers identified that 5.5 million hospital outpatient appointments were missed in 2012–2013 (NHS England, 2014), a 'did not attend' (DNA) rate of 9.3 per cent of total health and medical appointments in the year. That may sound unimportant and understandable in a busy world. But missed appointments cause inefficient use of staff (e.g., doctors and other health professionals being paid to attend facilities unnecessarily) and cost British taxpayers £225 million a year (National Audit Office, 2014).

Two randomized controlled trials (RCTs) were conducted in 2013–2014 to test various forms of reminders and the content of reminder messages. These found that SMS (short message service) text messages performed better than other reminder methods such as telephone calls or e-mail. Four different SMS text messages, as listed below, were tested with 10,000 patients in the 'nudge' trial to identify the most effective wording of reminders.

1. Appt at <clinic> on <date> at <time>. To cancel or rearrange call the number on your appointment letter.
2. Appt at <clinic> on <date> at <time>. To cancel or rearrange call <NUMBER>.
3. We are expecting you at <clinic> on <date> at <time>. Nine out of ten people attend. Please call <NUMBER> if you need to cancel or rearrange.
4. We are expecting you at <clinic> on <date> at <time>. Not attending costs NHS £160 on average, so call <NUMBER> if you need to cancel or rearrange. (Berry, 2014).

The trials found that adding a conformity message (most others keep their appointments) as in the third SMS text increased attendance. Furthermore, the research identified three characteristics for the most effective communication (SMS text 4): (1) using personalized language including directly addressing recipients as 'you'; (2) identifying the cost to the NHS of each missed appointment; and (3) listing the phone number to call for cancellations. Use of this form of reminder reduced missed appointments from 11.7 per cent in the control group to 8.3 per cent, saving millions of pounds a year (Hallsworth, Berry, & Sallis, 2014; Hallsworth et al., 2015). The involvement of academics working with government communication staff has afforded rigour and credibility for the research, and led to published articles and a number of forthcoming articles in academic journals.

In the second 'nudge' project examined, also in the health area, 1 million people were exposed to eight variants of messages designed to prompt organ donation (more than 135,000 exposures of each)—one of the largest randomized controlled trials ever conducted in the UK. Adoption of the best performing message was estimated to generate 96,000 additional registrations of organ donors a year (Harper, 2013).

At the time of this study another major UK government department was preparing to test its communication "products" including letters, standard e-mail messages, leaflets, and brochures after appointing two behavioural insights specialists to its staff. The behavioural insights staff reported that they were working to produce communication standards for the department based on plain English approaches and research showing what language, terminology, and phraseology works best (personal communication, February 6, 2015). The director of communication for the department said:

> I'm really encouraged by the small team of people who look at the sorts of communication we're sending out. They're terrible. They're badly written. Official, complex and I have to say, look I'm a graduate and I can't understand them. (personal communication, September 30, 2014)

Notwithstanding its successes and considerable adoption in government communication in the UK, the US, and Australia, behavioural insights or 'nudge' research is not widely adopted in major fields of public communication practice. Given that advertising agencies, public relations firms, corporate communicators, and internal organizational communication teams spend much of their time crafting messages and producing content, it seems short sighted that they have not adopted these techniques to improve their effectiveness through better understanding of the needs, interests, and preferences of their stakeholders and publics.

- *Academic research*, while mostly produced for scholars, can offer rigorously derived insights to inform practice and is often freely available in the public domain. However, only two organizations mentioned academic research—both government bodies in the UK. One was the government body working to reduce missed medical appointments, which jointly conducts studies and publishes its findings. Another government agency noted that it frequently draws on academic studies and occasionally partners with universities to gain credible, reliable research. Given that many universities seek partners and are increasingly focussed on the social, professional, or industry impact of their research, this seems to be an opportunity going begging in many government and commercial organizations.

In his 2015 book *Performative Listening: Hearing Others in Qualitative Research*, Chris McCrae describes research as listening, specifically calling for the application of *performative listening* in qualitative, narrative, and arts-based approaches to research and inquiry. He says performative listening is a relational stance and performance in which listeners ethically engage in an act of learning from others across difference (McCrae, 2015). Measurement and evaluation have been described as "listening to feedback and response" and then "contingent on what is learned, responding in a way that takes account of the views of others" (Macnamara, 2015a, p. 10). Thus, research is a key site of organizational listening—although it is often under-used or used in narrow, instrumental ways to gain answers to questions that organizations want to ask and nothing more.

Some organizations describe social media as an environment for "real time research" through monitoring comments about various issues, products, or organizations. However, social media comprise a large and growing network of channels for various types of interaction. While research is one use of social media, this is mostly informal and the broader interactive applications of social media warrant separate discussion.

Listening in Social Media

Social media are viewed with great enthusiasm in most communication-orientated functions within organizations and appear to be rapidly closing in on customer relations as the primary form of organization-public interaction, and also challenging formal methods of research as the primary means of gaining feedback, insights, and intelligence. Indeed, as noted in the previous sections, social media are increasingly being used for customer relations and research. Some interviewees described social media as "free real time research".

This study examined several major social media initiatives that are allegedly focussed on listening including the MasterCard Conversation Suite and a 'global listening tool' created by another multinational corporation. The MasterCard Conversation Suite has received considerable attention and publicity—hence the company was prepared to be identified in this research. Senior vice president for corporate and external communication at Master-Card, Andrew Bowins, has publicly declared that the company's "global corporate communication function is evolving from a broadcast model reliant on intermediaries to a direct, real-time communication ecosystem" (as cited in Weiner, 2012, p. 8). In a 2012 interview in *Kommunikations Manager* he said: "We have established platforms and a global framework to listen to and engage consumers, merchants and influencers across online, social and traditional media". Bowins added that the company's social media activity "begins with real-time social media listening and analysis" (as cited in Weiner, 2012, p. 8). It does this through a custom-built online monitoring system that tracks 6,000 keywords in 26 languages across traditional and social media globally 24/7—what the company refers to as an integrated media analysis system. The system includes content from Facebook, Twitter, YouTube, Pinterest, Tumblr, and Sina Weibo, as well as major traditional media online news sites. As of early 2015, the system was annually identifying 36,000 traditional media articles and more than 3 million social media items such as blog posts, tweets, and videos that refer to MasterCard or issues of interest to the company, according to one of the digital specialists operating the system (personal communication, January 15, 2015).

The MasterCard Conversation Suite is outsourced to Prime Research, a specialist research company charged with building the system and overseeing all monitoring and analysis. This relationship has been publicly reported by Bowins (Chapman, 2013; Weiner, 2012, p. 9). An important feature of this system is that, unlike some other media monitoring services, responses to comments or inquiries are not written by social media specialists or PR staff. An authorized Prime Research spokesperson for MasterCard said "MasterCard management in various regions and business units makes the decisions on whether to respond or not, and how to respond" (personal communication, January 15, 2015). The contracted operators of the MasterCard Conversation Suite sometimes identify posts that they assess as warranting a response and refer these to a relevant MasterCard executive or unit. But all responses and comments made on behalf of the company are posted by an appropriate MasterCard executive. This is an important part of the process in terms of authenticity. Some other systems involve a 'PR-izing' of organizational responses and comments.

Physically, the MasterCard Conversation Suite is made up of massive LED displays at the company's Purchase, New York, headquarters and in its offices in Miami, Mexico, and Brazil, as well as interfaces on the PCs of key staff worldwide. These present graphical dashboards showing the volume of articles and mentions of relevant issues; the audience reach of those items; the volume of reposts such as retweets; and the percentage that are favourable, unfavourable, and neutral; as well as real-time feeds of the content of the most relevant articles and social media posts. The system "sucks in" data to an IBM-based 'back end' from a number of data suppliers and services and then analyzes the content using proprietary applications to produce the dashboard showing charts and content such as tweets ranked by topic and relevance, according to the senior digital specialist responsible. For instance, MasterCard tracks safety and security, travel, innovation, small business, and a range of financial issues, as well as mentions of its name and related products such as its PayPass Wallet.

An impressive feature of the MasterCard Conversation Suite is that the company's staff can respond to comments and messages on various platforms from within the Conversation Suite. For example, they can select a tweet in a feed, type a response, and their response is sent as a direct message or broadcast tweet over the Twitter network. "MasterCard executives don't have to leave the Conversation Suite and go to Twitter or Facebook to interact—they just click and type", the spokesperson said. Also, the MasterCard Conversation Suite can translate into English and from English into other languages using Google Translate that it integrated into the system (personal communication, January 15, 2015).

In addition to the automated dashboards presented on screens, the MasterCard Conversation Suite has two further levels of analysis. Advanced analytics are available via menus that allow Boolean searches of all data in the system—for example, to examine conversations about certain issues in particular regions in particular time frames. The processing of advanced analytics is fully automated, but this function requires entry of search terms by the user. Prime Research provides training for MasterCard executives on an ongoing basis. For instance, the spokesperson said that in July 2014 after some significant upgrades were made to the system, 250 MasterCard staff were trained either face-to-face or via WebEx (personal communication, January 15, 2015).

The third level of analysis is really an add-on to the Conversation Suite. This involves bespoke reports produced by applying human interpretation to the data collected. Specialist content and data analysts at Prime Research produce monthly or quarterly written reports by region, quarterly corporate reports overviewing issues globally, and what they call insights reports based on "deep dive" analysis. These reports are produced using a combination of automated machine analysis and human analysis. For example, all coding of the 36,000 traditional media articles a year selected on the basis of relevance is done by humans (personal communication, January 15, 2015).

There can be little argument that the MasterCard Conversation Suite involves listening by the company. It is one of the most sophisticated listening systems identified in this research and deserves acknowledgement. However, two qualifications need to be made in the context of this study of how organizations listen. First, the MasterCard Conversation Suite is a substantial investment. Neither MasterCard nor Prime Research would reveal the cost of building and operating the system, but it is clearly many hundreds of thousands of dollars annually, and possibly several million dollars in total including data feeds, proprietary software design, hardware, and staffing by specialist researchers, social media analysts, and data analysts. While providing an exemplar of how scale can be achieved in organizational listening, such a system is beyond the means of many if not most organizations. Second, discussions revealed a commercial strategy underlying the company's commitment to listening that oscillates between authentic engagement for mutual customer-corporation benefit and exploitation of customers through the harvesting and clever analysis of data. A senior social media manager involved in supporting the Conversation Suite explained that there are "two types of social media listening". She described these as (1) *engagement* to hear what people are saying and what they are concerned about to respond to and interact with them, which often leads to multiple exchanges (conversation); and (2) *intelligence* based on collectively using what people are saying to inform strategy and tactics, often not acknowledging or responding to them (personal communication, January 12, 2015).

Several senior US communication and research practitioners argued that listening for intelligence is authentic ethical listening and posited intelligence as the primary form of organizational listening (personal communication,

April 27, 2015). While it may be legal and even ethical in some cases, intelligence cannot be considered open active listening as defined in listening and communication literature. Listening for intelligence is selective, indirect, monologic, cataphatic, and self-serving. It is not active, mindful, dialogic, transactional, or apophatic (see Table 1.1). While interpersonal rather than organizational, a simple litmus test is to gauge the reaction of a family member or friend to being told that you are listening to them to gain intelligence. This is not to say that organizations cannot legitimately listen to gain intelligence, but open ethical listening requires more than gathering intelligence, which is described as information of strategic or competitive benefit (Nasri, 2012).

The intelligence gathering purpose of social media monitoring and analysis is often conducted to identify *influencers* as well as issues to be 'managed' as part of the PR and corporate communication practice of *issue management* (Heath, 1997). Influencers are usually engaged—or 'targeted' in marketing and PR speak—because of their capacity to persuade others as credible intermediaries. MasterCard's Andrew Bowins told the PR industry journal *The Holmes Report* that "influencer relations" is the greatest opportunity for marketing and PR to innovate ("Innovator 25", 2014). Identifying and engaging influencers for the strategic benefit that this affords the organization is a key objective of the MasterCard Conversation Suite, according to the digital specialist interviewed. Influencers are identified using a scoring system that takes into account factors such as the number of posts they make online, the number of followers or fans they have, and other data such as their Klout score (personal communication, January 15, 2015). While it would be naïve to expect that companies should not derive commercial and competitive benefit from social media monitoring, noting that their commercial objectives are legitimate and their success is often important to the economy and employment as well as shareholders, the balance between listening for engagement and listening for intelligence is a delicate one. The MasterCard Conversation Suite appears to involve both—and therefore could be considered mutually beneficial for the organization and its stakeholders and publics. The company's online newsroom is called The Engagement Bureau (http://newsroom .mastercard.com)—although a link to this could not be found on the main MasterCard corporate Web site (http://www.mastercard.us), not even using the site search tool.

Another major investment in social media listening that was examined is the global listening tool of a US-headquartered multinational corporation. The company is demonstrably innovative in terms of communication, having brought in an anthropologist to help management better understand what motivates employees and engage with them. As with the MasterCard Conversation Suite, the development and operation of the global listening tool have been outsourced to a specialist research firm. The system features a custom-designed portal for the organization to view statistical and graphical data such as charts and 'word clouds' as well as the text of relevant traditional media articles and social media posts. High-quality dashboards present summaries of key data such as the volume, reach (audience size), tone, and share of voice of articles and posts relevant to the company and competitors tracked. According to a spokesperson, the underlying technology is a Cognos database with automated feeds from media content suppliers, from which query tools import selected data into proprietary applications for analysis and reporting.

The project manager in charge of the tool at the research firm says the proprietary global listening tool of the corporation tracks content relevant to the organization and five of its key competitors in 650 priority media worldwide as well as across a wide range of social media. The system is largely automated, using neuro-linguistic programming (NLP) with learning capabilities to filter relevant content. At the time of viewing the global listening tool, there were 6,300 traditional media articles in the system as well as a large volume of social media content. As with the MasterCard Conversation Suite, decisions in relation to responding to posts and comments are made by the corporation's executives, not the research firm's media or data analysts, although this is often based on the advice of the project manager responsible for the system. The project manager agrees that tracking and analysis cannot be fully automated. He said "the system depends on entering keywords to track" and "humans are needed to make decisions on whether to respond". He also explained that the research firm went beyond providing automated dashboards. SPSS (statistical package for the social sciences) is used to conduct additional statistical analysis, and bespoke reports are produced by the research firm to provide insights and recommendations to the client (personal communication, January 12, 2015).

A third highly sophisticated social media monitoring and analysis site examined is operated internally by a leading computer company. The company has established a digital and social media centre, which includes the company's global analytics hub. The head of global corporate communication and public affairs said "social media is [sic] a key tool for listening as well as speaking". However, in an interview he reported that the company does not conduct any regular formative research and he talked predominantly about the system in terms of "getting our message out" (personal communication, January 13, 2015).

One of the world's leading airlines and the largest government customer service centre in the UK use social media for monitoring and responding to customer inquiries and comments about their products and services. As of early 2015 the airline was receiving 200–300 customer contacts a day via Twitter and reported that this is growing rapidly, as many customers seek to avoid often lengthy periods on hold when contacting telephone-based CRM systems. The airline also accepts and responds to customers via Facebook, e-mail, and its Web site as well as telephone. This company was one of those tested with an online query and its response was moderately good, with a reply received within four days. In addition to using social media for customer communication, the airline has adopted a policy of using social media as its first response channel in a crisis. A spokesperson explained that the airline has three social media strategies, which she described as:

- Customer service;
- Crisis communication first response; and
- Promotional campaigns.

The airline has used Saleforce's Radian6 social media monitoring and analysis software for a number of years, but changed in 2014 to a small start-up specializing in "behavioural forensics" and online CRM (Lexer, 2015). In 2014 the company also incorporated Local Measure into its social media monitoring and analysis strategy, which provides geo-location information. This allows the airline to track social media posts to a particular airport and even to airline lounges. The airline's manager of digital communication told the story of a frequent flyer who received 'happy birthday' tweets from family and friends while in one of the airline's lounges. The airline's social media team quickly sent a message to the lounge manager who arranged a small cake and a greeting for the passenger. Welcome to customer service in the twenty-first century! Is such customer engagement a good thing, or is it an invasion of privacy and 'big brother' sugar-coated and disguised to look benign and friendly? Such questions deserve debate, as neoliberal societies rush headlong into CRM aided by 'big data', satellite-linked geo-location services, and Web 3.0 in which you don't have to find things—they find you!

The same company has run into major criticism for some of its promotional efforts in social media and the manager of digital communication admitted that "none of the airline's senior management engage professionally in social media" (personal communication, March 3, 2015). So it is reasonable to conclude that many of these initiatives are pioneering efforts and it will be some time before interactive social media engagement is embedded in corporate culture.

A different approach is taken by some other corporations. One of the world's largest IT&T companies with a quarter of a million employees (see further discussion under 'Listening in Organizational Communication') has moved in the past few years to 24/7 monitoring of social media and all monitoring is done internally. The VP of corporate communication said that communication staff members are rostered on shifts including over weekends to monitor key social media platforms. These staff members send alerts to relevant managers and departments in the company when they identify posts requiring a response. The VP explained:

> If you see somebody tweet or post on Facebook about a service problem they're having, you immediately flag the customer care team who are also standing by on the weekend so they can jump in right there and then. (personal communication, January 14, 2015)

Furthermore, the telecommunications company authorizes a large number of its staff to post stories, comment, and respond on social media, and allocates responsibility for monitoring related responses to the authors. "It's the author's responsibility to monitor for 24 hours after they post a story or comment. If it looks like something is really hot, then they have to keep monitoring until it's over", the VP of corporate communication said (personal communication, January 14, 2015).

During the period of this study the director of Lenovo's Digital and Social Media Centre of Excellence in Singapore, Rob Strother, delivered a keynote address to the International Summit on Measurement hosted by the Association for Measurement and Evaluation of Communication (AMEC) in Amsterdam—a public forum. In this, he declared that "Lenovo is social at heart" and outlined how the company conducts "always on listening" through social media. However, while emphasizing listening in the title and content of his slide deck, Strother described Lenovo's objectives in social media as "to talk with" customers and stakeholders, "to humanize the brand", and "to engage the audience" and create "fans" so as to "ignite a movement of evangelists to influence the perception, opinion and ultimately the buying decisions of consumers" (Strother, 2014). While gaining customers is a legitimate activity of commercial organizations as acknowledged already in this analysis, this description illustrates a continuing focus on talking and seeking engagement primarily or only to create evangelists for promoting a company and persuading people to buy its products.

Another market leader corporation has appointed a 'chief social officer' to head one of five units in its communication division along with corporate communication, product communication, employee communication, and executive support such as writing speeches. The company uses Yammer internally among its 43,500 staff, around 40 per cent of whom (approximately 18,000 staff) are active on the online collaboration platform, making it one of the largest Yammer sites in the world. Internal communication and collaboration on Yammer are coordinated by three Yammer community managers, according to the head of "employee engagement communication" (personal communication, October 21, 2014). The CEO also publishes a regular blog and the company uses proprietary social media sites to engage with retailers, investors, and customers, as well as public platforms including Twitter, Facebook, YouTube, Google+, Google Hangouts, Instagram, Tumblr, Vine, LinkedIn, Pinterest, and Snapshot. The company also uses Lithium for customer relationship management and was experimenting with Evernote as a collaboration tool at the time of this research. This rather heavy commitment to social media is managed by "12 to 15 communication staff including six social media managers responsible for supporting regions". The head of communication said "collaboration is where it is at". He pointed to two types of collaboration online: (1) document sharing at a basic level and (2) conversations. He said collaboration could help with problem solving, such as customers "chipping in with ideas to help other customers" (i.e., crowdsourcing customer support), as well as idea generation in general. Furthermore, he said practical benefits of online collaboration included a reduction in meeting time and reduced e-mail (personal communication, November 11, 2014).

The range of social media used by this company is interesting and the head of communication was probed on this issue. He reported that the company did not believe that there is a single 'killer app' for collaboration and social media engagement. He said "our policy is to experiment. We believe in fail fast and move on. Learn from testing. Be agile". However, he was frank about the challenges. He said "it's really, really hard" referring to the demands of 24/7 operation that is increasingly expected online. But he sees a limit to the "speeding up". He said "the good news is that we will reach terminal velocity because there comes a point when people cannot process any more information, or more quickly. Once you reach 24/7 and real-time response, that's terminal velocity" (personal communication, November 11, 2014). Whether or not he is correct, only time will tell! However, his advice on how to cope with the demands of social media was common to a number of case studies. He said:

> We have to be structured for that. The changes brought on by social media are trans-formational in terms of the shift from 'one to many' to 'many to one' and 'many to many'. That means working weekend shifts. Working Monday to Friday is going out the window. Staff now need to work flexible hours. That doesn't suit everybody, but increasingly workers welcome the flexibility to work from home sometimes, to work remotely, to have flexible hours. In [company name] we are adopting a policy of all roles flex. (personal communication, November 11, 2014)

He said that "Generation Y—the so-called Millennials [Strauss & Howe, 2000]—are more flexible in their approach to work, so this will result in changes in the workplace".[9] However, despite this progressive attitude expressed by the head of communication, and despite a "relaxed policy" on social media use by staff supported by regular training, only 15–20 per cent of the company's employees have social media engagement in their role. "We want this to be 100 per cent in future", the head of communication said.

Many of the government departments and agencies studied are also using social media increasingly. In the UK this is aligned with the national govern-ment's 'digital by default' strategy (Cabinet Office, 2013), as discussed specifi-cally under 'Listening in Government Communication'. Government reports and plans reveal that communicators recognize the limitations of one-way broadcast approaches to public communication and have an awareness of and commitment to two-way dialogic approaches. For instance, one of the largest UK government departments with annual spending of around £160 billion, the Department of Work and Pension (DWP), recognizes that "TV and radio are consumed by more people than any other media channel", but says in its published 'Communications Strategy 2014/15':

> Social media has [sic] led to a major shift in the relationship between organizations and audiences. Our strategy recognizes that citizens now expect a two-way dialogue where people create and share their own content, and mistrust the old 'push' infor-mation approach. 2014/15 will see a further decisive shift away from traditional 'broadcast' digital communications towards an engagement approach, with continu-ing conversations and activity. (DWP, 2014)

However, despite *open government* and government to citizen (G2C) engage-ment policies in the UK, the US, and Australia, use of social media by government varies widely from attentive listening to pseudo listening and, in some cases, to monologue. The rhetoric of engagement and claims of listening are prolific, but promises collapse under the combined weight of habit, institutionalized practices, and pressures to achieve organizational objectives. For instance, one UK government agency reporting to a chief executive and permanent secretary with "considerable freedom" stated: "Absolutely we do more listening on social media at the moment than broadcast". However, he went on immediately to say:

> Our policy at the moment externally, for Twitter in particular, is to publish stuff that is of operational use. It's often public education … so we'll be tweeting about seminars and workshops and reminding people about key deadlines and things like that …. It's very focussed on the specific purpose of what we're doing. (personal communication, September 24, 2014)

Terms and phrases such as 'publish', 'education', 'we'll be tweeting', 'reminding', 'focussed on the specific purpose of what *we're* doing' [emphasis added] clearly indicate an orientation to speaking and distributing messages about what the organization is interested in and what it wants to achieve. When pressed specifically about listening in social media, the spokesperson checked himself and said:

> Well, I think we're trying to find—to look for a number of things really. We're looking at how things have landed, people's reaction to things. We're looking at what people are interested in. We're looking for signs of emergent issues. So that's the primary purpose of the stakeholder monitoring. (personal communication, September 24, 2014)

Interpretation using textual and conversation analysis techniques can identify hesitancy and uncertainty in this statement. It was not offered proactively when asked about the organization's objectives in using social media. It began with pauses as the spokesperson mentally searched for an appropriate response to the question—evidenced in terms such as 'well' and a long pause and starting again after the seventh word. The second and third words were 'I think'. Once the spokesperson collected his thoughts he gave some examples of listening—e.g., to monitor people's reactions and to find out what people are interested in. But this came largely as an afterthought to a number of statements referring to information, publishing, tweeting, education, and reminding people.

The director of communication for a large UK government department with a stated commitment to and flexible policies in relation to using social media found on his arrival in the role that the department's regional and local offices had 600 Twitter accounts. A more recent follow-up interview with the department's head of new media appointed in early 2015 updated this to 700 Twitter accounts that had "sprung up organically" (personal communication, February 6, 2015). While supporting a distributed model of communication (e.g., the same director encourages local offices to issue releases to local media based on centrally approved information), he was nevertheless concerned about the department's approach to social media. He reported:

> So I did an audit of what they were doing, what was actually being put out, was anyone actually talking to people and engaging through social media. No, they're not. I found they're using it as a broadcasting tool largely … it is important to me that we open it up as a two-way conversation and it's got to be a productive two-way conversation. (personal communication, September 30, 2014)

The same director of communication sees digital and social media as only part of the 'communication mix' currently, but as increasingly important channels in the future, accessed from desktops and mobile devices. He said:

> We're not picking up two-way conversations with hundreds of thousands of people. It's not happening. However, in the future in the transformation of the department between now and 2020 in which the department will have more of a digital presence, my feeling is that most people will want to transact through a Smartphone. (personal communication, September 30, 2014)

Accordingly, some government departments and agencies are employing highly skilled specialists to lead their social media activities and have implemented sophisticated online engagement strategies. For example, one large UK government health body uses social media to identify and connect with communities relevant to its objectives and campaigns. A senior member of its digital team said "we do a lot of social media listening to help us know where our communities are". An example of identifying and leveraging existing communities is further discussed in the next section, 'Listening in Public Consultation'. Then the organization conducts *influencer mapping* to identify key influencers operating within those communities. Finally, in its three-stage process, it makes direct contact with those influencers to seek their support and advocacy. The organization also encourages its policy teams to use social media such as Twitter "to understand the landscape that they're in" (personal communication, February 2, 2015).

Social media have resulted in changing expectations in relation to response time, which is creating additional pressures on resources and systems in many organizations. Prior to social media, most of the government departments and agencies studied operated on the basis of 20-day turnaround for correspondence such as letters and e-mails. All agreed that this policy is no longer acceptable to most people. A number of government organizations as well as companies are moving to 24-hour response times via social media. The director of communication for a UK government agency involved in regulation and standards said "we respond to phone calls within 24 hours". He added: "We don't have a KPI for tweets, but I think same day response is acceptable" (personal communication, September 26, 2014). The assistant director of communication of a government agency involved in health services said:

> When someone can tweet and get the same questions answered within an hour, we can't continue to take three weeks to provide a response by letter. We need to be bringing our response rate targets for customer letters in line with social media. We're not resourced to do it. But I think we'll start to see this happening. We've had to flex our teams to develop the capability for quicker response—our staff work flexible hours. (personal communication, September 25, 2014)

The deputy director of media and communication for a government agency involved in protecting the public from major hazards and during emergencies said "our people have a very deep commitment ... in an incident like that, colleagues stay on the line. We will roster 24/7 for up to three months". She said that during such incidents "every night of the week we have 10 people on duty through the night for social media and press predominantly" (personal communication, September 24, 2014).

Interestingly, in terms of responding to complex inquiries requiring research or referral to specialist staff, few interviewees reported that they send an initial acknowledgement—one of the 'seven canons of listening' (see Chapter 1)—while a detailed response is prepared. A two-step process of quick acknowledgement followed by detailed response some time later seems to offer a practical approach for organizations struggling with the demands of 24/7 digital communication.

A controversial issue in relation to social media is who manages the function in organizations. According to several studies, most commercial organizations manage social media through their marketing department (e.g., King, 2015; Owyang, 2010). The head of corporate communication for a leading automotive manufacturer expressed concern at this approach saying "part of the problem is that social media is owned by marketing. They use it primarily for promoting brands and products" (personal communication, January 30, 2015). The social media director of the agency managing the MasterCard Conversation Suite expressed similar concern saying "marketing staff cannot help giving in to the urge to sell". She said social media should be a broad corporate or government communication responsibility where the focus is two-way communication rather than promotion and selling (personal communication, January 15, 2015).

This section has focussed on the activities of specialist digital and social media units and staff where these exist in organizations as well as the work of specialist digital and social media agencies employed by organizations. Social media use that is integrated within other functions such as corporate communication and public relations is further discussed in sections of this chapter reporting on those functions. While most interviewees in this study agreed that social media communication needs special focus in the short-term because of its relative newness, most feel that, ultimately, social media should be democratized channels for organization-public interaction open to all in an organization, working within a governance framework provided by staff training and guidelines. The head of communication in one public sector health organization said having a head of social media is "like having a head of faxes" (personal communication, September 25, 2014).

Another potentially controversial issue and a warning for organizations wanting to increase their interaction and engagement through social media is that the range and frequency of *cyberhate* offences are growing, as reported and discussed by Whitney Phillips and colleagues (Phillips, 2015; Phillips & Milner, forthcoming). Along with cyberbullying and hacking, a number of online malpractices can affect organizations as well as individuals, including:

- *Trolling*—Internet users, referred to as trolls, who create discord on the Internet by posting inflammatory content that creates outrage (Fuller, McCrea, & Wilson, 2013);
- *Doxxing*—distributing documents (docs or dox) revealing the identity and confidential or sensitive information about a person or organization (Quodling, 2015);
- *Swatting*—making false reports to police and security forces with the intention of having a heavily armed response team sent to the target's home or office (Quodling, 2015); and
- *Digilantism*—online vigilantes who take justice into their own hands (Coldewey, 2013).

None of the organizations that were studied mentioned these as potential risks to manage, and none had strategies in place to address such problems should they arise. This raises further doubt on the capacity of many organizations to facilitate and maintain effective large-scale dialogue and engagement online.

A wide range of social media monitoring and analysis tools and services were mentioned by interviewees or noted in documents reporting on their organizations' activities. The most used by the organizations studied for day-to-day social media monitoring, management, and analysis are Google Analytics, Hootsuite, Tweetdeck, Netvibes, and Brandwatch. Radian6 was praised, but described as expensive. The most used online consultation tool in the sample studied is Citizen Space. At the higher level of bespoke and customized media and communication research, Prime Research and Social Bakers are used by several exemplar case studies, while the most used CRM tools among the organizations studied are Salesforce's Marketing Cloud, Brandwatch, and Sysomos, with two using Lithium. The most used media analysis service provider among the organizations studied is Gorkana, but this is most likely skewed by the slightly higher UK sample size. The range of tools and services used or mentioned is shown in Table 3.5. A number of these have functionality across several categories, but as far as possible they have been grouped by type and core function.

Table 3.5. Popular media monitoring and analysis tools and services.[10]

Category	Product/Service	Details
Media monitoring *(basic tools):*	Google Alerts	https://www.google.com/alerts
	Mention	https://en.mention.com
Media monitoring *(services):*	Cision	http://www.cision.com
	BurrellesLuce	http://www.burrellesluce.com
	Gorkana	http://gorkana.com/pr-products/ media-monitoring (owned by Cision)
	Kantar Media	http://www.kantarmedia.com
	iSentia	http://www.isentia.com (formerly Media Monitors)
	Meltwater	http://www.meltwater.com
	CyberAlert	http://cyberalert.com

Category	Product/Service	Details
Media analytics *(vendor supplied):*	Google Analytics	http://www.google.com/analytics
	Tweetdeck	https://tweetdeck.twitter.com
	Twitter Analytics	https://analytics.twitter.com/about
	Twitter for Business	https://business.twitter.com
	Facebook Insights	https://www.facebook.com/insights
	Pinterest Analytics	https://analytics.pinterest.com
Media analysis tools *(basic, free or low cost):*	Hootsuite	https://hootsuite.com
	Netvibes	http://www.netvibes.com
	Sprout Social	http://sproutsocial.com
	Social Mention	http://socialmention.com
	Tableau	http://tableau.com
	Klout	https://klout.com
	Traackr	http://traackr.com
	Trackur	http://www.trackur.com
	Coosto	http://www.coosto.com
	Topsy	http://topsy.com
	Lexer	http://lexer.com.au
	Local Measure	http://www.getlocalmeasure.com
	Pulsar TRAC	http://www.pulsarplatform.com
	Simply Measured	http://simplymeasured.com
	Buffer	https://bufferapp.com
	Kiss Metrics	https://www.kissmetrics.com
	BuzzNumbers	http://www.buzznumbershq.com (owned by iSentia)
	Twitalzyer	http://www.twitalyzer.com
	Moz Pro	https://moz.com/pro
	Quintly	https://www.quintly.com
Media analysis *(proprietary, advanced tools, mostly automated)*	Radian6	http://www.exacttarget.com/au/products/social-media-marketing (now owned by Salesforce)
	Brandwatch	http://www.brandwatch.com
	Gorkana	http://www.gorkana.com (Gorkana Group incorporates Gorkana, Durrants, and Metrica; owned by Cision)

Category	Product/Service	Details
	Visible Technologies	http://www.cision.com/us (now owned by Cision)
	SR7	http://www.sr7.com.au (now owned by KPMG)
	Cymfony	http://www.cymfony.com (purchased by Visible Technologies 2012, which is now owned by Cision)
	Buzzlogic	http://www.twelvefold.com (now owned by Twelvefold)
	Infegy Atlas	https://infegy.com
	SAS Analytics	http://www.sas.com/social
	SocialSignin	http://socialsignin.co.uk
	Vizie	http://www.csiro.au/en/Research/ DPF/Areas/The-digital-economy/ Digital-service-delivery/Vizie
Media analysis (*service providers*):	Gorkana	http://www.gorkana.com
	Prime Research	http://www.prime-research.com
	Salience Insight	http://www.salienceinsight.com
	Cision	http://www.cision.com (owns Delahaye, MediaMap, Vocus, Visible Technologies & Gorkana)
	Ketchum	https://www.ketchum.com/ research-analytics
	CARMA International	http://www.carma.com (CARMA US owned by Salience Insight; CARMA Asia Pacific owned by iSentia)
	Kantar Media	http://www.kantarmedia.com
	MediaTrack	http://www.mediatrack.com
	Precise	http://www.precise.co.uk (a Kantar Media company)
	We Are Social	http://wearesocial.com
	Meltwater	http://www.meltwater.com
E-consultation & *collaboration:*	Citizen Space	www.citizenspace.com
	Yammer	https://www.yammer.com
	CrowdAround	A planned replacement for Yammer (https://prezi.com/qujtzn_zxqyj/ crowdaround)

Category	Product/Service	Details
	SocialText	http://www.socialtext.com
	eNgageSpace	https://www.engagespace.co.uk
	Evernote	https://evernote.com
	Objective	http://www.objective.com
	Dialogue by Design	http://www.dialoguebydesign.co.uk
	IdeaScale	https://ideascale.com
Reputation:	Alva	http://www.alva-group.com
	Brandseye	http://www.brandseye.com
CRM:	Salesforce	http://www.salesforce.com/au/marketing-cloud
	Brandwatch	http://www.brandwatch.com
	Sysomos	https://www.sysomos.com
	Lithium	http://www.lithium.com
	Nielsen Buzzmetrics	http://www.nielsen-online.com/products_buzz.jsp?section=pro_buzz#1
	IBM Watson Analytics	http://www.ibm.com/analytics/watson-analytics
	Simplify 360	http://simplify360.com
	Alterian	http://www.sdl.com/cxc/digital-experience/alterian.html (now owned by SDL)
	Foresee	http://www.foresee.com
	Epicor Clientele	http://www.evron.com/crm/clientele.asp
	Marketo	http://au.marketo.com
	Eloqua	http://www.eloqua.com
	Hubspot	http://www.hubspot.com
Data suppliers/ feeds:	GNIP	https://gnip.com
	LexisNexis	http://www.lexisnexis.com
	Moreover Technologies	http://www.moreover.com (purchased by LexisNexis in 2014)
	Datasift	http://datasift.com
	Spredfast	https://www.spredfast.com
	Sprinklr	https://www.sprinklr.com
	Oracle Social Cloud	http://www.oracle.com/us/solutions/social/overview/index.html
	ListenLogic	http://www.listenlogic.com

Listening in Public Consultation

Another proactive and purposeful method of direct listening to stakeholders and publics is the practice of public consultation. As noted in Chapter 2, consultation is a legal requirement of government and sometimes corporations in many countries, particularly in the case of major policy initiatives and major infrastructure projects. All government departments and most of the government agencies studied undertake regular public consultation. At the departmental level, public consultation is mostly focussed on gaining input to policy making, whereas at the agency level it is more often conducted to inform implementation and day-to-day operations.

In the US, a substantial number of public consultations are under way at any one time on a wide range of issues. Information about most of these can be viewed online at Regulations.gov (http://www.regulations.gov), a Web portal that provides information on physical forums as well as the opportunity to enter comments directly online. For example, at the time of this research a national 'public notice and comment' was under way on the operation and certification of small, unmanned aircraft systems (i.e., drones). The home page of the Regulation.gov Web site displays a list of all consultations under way and one click takes visitors to a dialogue box where they can comment (see Figure 3.5). In addition, an important feature of the site is that near the top of the comment box is a link to open a 'docket folder'. This opens a folder that contains useful information about the issue under consultation such as reports, fact sheets, results of inquiries, research data, and so on—although a simpler name than 'docket folder' would be helpful. Also, at the top right of the comment box is a link to 'alternate ways to comment'. This provides users with information on how to e-mail or even send written comments through the postal system. The provision for citizens' input by post, e-mail, online, or face-to-face at meetings does afford quite open and flexible access.

US corporations interviewed did not have experience in public consultation other than informal consultation with stakeholders such as business partners and employees. The way these were discussed indicated that they were more exercises in gaining 'buy in' rather than genuine consultations to canvass and consider the views of others. However, US government agencies reported several large public consultations following disasters and crises. These consultations were convened to canvass views on what went wrong, what was done right, and how processes could be improved. A US government spokesperson reflected on one major consultation saying "we faced an

Figure 3.5. The online public consultation interface of the US government site Regulation.gov.

angry mob in some of these discussions. But we had to have them" (personal communication, January 19, 2015). Given a number of changes in agency structure and even legislation that followed some of these consultations, it has to be concluded that at least in some cases organizations listen in public consultation and take meaningful action as a result.

In recent years, the UK has seen a number of major national public consultations, including the belated public consultation on the Health and Social Care Bill introduced by Andrew Lansley that eventually, after much controversy, became the Health and Social Care Act 2012 (Dobson, 2014, p. 86; Timmins, 2012). More successful in terms of gaining high levels of public engagement were the public consultations on the UK Marriage (Same Sex Couples) Act 2013, which drew a record 500,000 responses (Gov.UK, 2013), and the Northern Futures consultation led by the then Deputy Prime Minister Nick Clegg that concluded in November 2014 ("Northern Futures", 2014). A more recent example examined in this study involved a very large national infrastructure project that started as a research project in 2009 before a decision was taken to go ahead in 2010—although the project did not have Royal Assent (final approval) at the time of this study. Therefore, there was still an opportunity for interested parties to make their views known. Because of the nature and scale of this project, it has been presented to the UK Parliament as a Hybrid Bill, a form of proposed legislation that combines both a public bill for matters in the national interest and private bill for matters that affect individuals.

The UK government is bound by the Aarhus Convention[11] to consult and is also subject to the European Commission's Environmental Impact Assessment (EIA). As the project involves the compulsory acquisition of private property, construction on urban and rural landscapes, and operations that will create noise, there are many issues of concern for residents living near the project, environmentalists, local communities, and farmers. The project, when complete, will offer benefits to citizens. However, the main benefits arguably will accrue to businesses. Therefore, most business and industry organizations want the project to proceed. Such a situation presents a test for consultation and an interesting case study to examine, as it is involves multiple diverse interests with varying levels of influence and power and some conflicts of interest (e.g., environmentalists and residents negatively impacted by the project versus the commercial interests of businesses and the project builder).

The corporate plan of the company established by the UK government to develop and manage the project lists among its themes and goals "engaging with all our stakeholders fairly", "respect for the communities, wildlife and places affected" and "working in partnership with Britain's city regions". Also, under its statement of values, it says: "We listen to people without prejudgement" (De-identified company, 2014a, pp. 13–14).[12] In line with these principles and to comply with the Aarhus Convention and EIA, the company has conducted extensive public consultation during phase one of the project (pre-build). One of the early public consultations in 2011 received 55,000 responses, some of which were 100 pages long. The project team uses an independent research company to analyze response when it reaches such levels—in this case Ipsos-MORI.

As well as a number of formal consultations on issues such as compensation packages for compulsory land acquisition, which was active at the time of this research, the head of community and stakeholder engagement, the community stakeholder manager, the head of consultations, and a member of the 'public response team' emphasized that engagement was ongoing. One said:

"You simply would not be doing your job if you were just doing formal consultations. It would be a very narrow set of responses you'd be getting" (personal communication September 29, 2014). The communication and stakeholder engagement team of the company prefer the term 'engagement' to consultation and listed a range of methods employed by the company. These include face-to-face discussions. The head of community and stakeholder engagement said: "I mean, you're on the ground out there talking to people. That's part of the job" (personal communication September 29, 2014). As well, the company uses events such as public meetings, Web sites, and increasingly social media. In addition, the company commissions surveys to gauge public opinion and also has conducted focus groups with key stakeholders and members of the "general public". Consultation has extended to door knocking, but only on a limited scale within the metropolitan area of London. These activities are delivered by a multi-disciplinary team incorporating staff from stakeholder engagement, public response, and communication including media publicity, events management, and social media specialists. This case study demonstrates an important structural and operational requirement that several government departments and agencies referred to—the necessity for a number of functions to work closely together rather than in siloes, particularly policy, consultation/engagement, communication, and research staff.

The primary online site and official record of UK government public consultation is the Gov.UK Web site. However, the head of communication for the national transport infrastructure project company said "Gov.UK is a very vanilla approach. You're not always able to put the context around a consultation that will help guide people through it" (personal communication, September 29, 2014). In one respect, her comments echo criticisms of the Gov. UK site reported in the next section under 'Listening in Government Communication'. But, in another sense, putting context around a consultation could be interpreted as framing it in such a way that certain issues are highlighted, while others are downplayed, which can be problematic. For instance, attention can be deviated from issues that an organization does not want to subject to scrutiny. The company responsible for this major infrastructure project has experimented with Citizen Space as an online consultation tool offering greater flexibility and begun to use a range of social media. It uses Tweetdeck and Hootsuite to monitor comments in social media and was "looking at using Google Analytics" at the time of interview. A spokesperson said:

> We listen on social media much more than we actually promote or publish information. We study. We have a full-time social media officer who is monitoring the

main channels every day. We have a daily report on what people are talking about. (personal communication, September 29, 2014)

An impressive aspect of the project's public consultation approach is that the company's staff do an *equality impact assessment screening* at the start of all consultations. The head of consultations explained:

> We look at the population. We get some data about the demographics of the target groups. All our consultations are national, but we target certain groups through our publicity, so we look at the demographics, broadband access, income levels, language, and so on …. Then we tailor our approaches to those groups. (personal communication, September 29, 2014)

Some of the more innovative approaches to consultation in relation to the project include appointment of a residents' commissioner in 2015 and planning for 'pop-up' information centres in towns and villages, as well as 'drop in' events in addition to scheduled town hall meetings. The company's head of community and stakeholder engagement cited limitations to traditional town hall meetings, saying:

> I think town hall meetings are rarely the best way of getting information across …. [A]ctually the people who are turning up don't always get the best level of service out of that or the best information because actually it's quite difficult to get information across in that kind of format. (personal communication, September 29, 2014)

The preceding paragraphs illustrate some important techniques for public consultation, including placing emphasis on understanding those to be consulted (e.g., their socioeconomic status, cultural background, language, media access, and literacy), tailoring consultation methods to them, and *outreach* activities, which will be discussed further in the following cases. However, close analysis reveals some other symbolic elements in this discussion that reflect limitations in this otherwise substantial commitment to public consultation. While raising reservations about town hall meetings, the company's head of community and stakeholder engagement referred to "getting information across" twice in one statement. Other statements in the same context indicate that the organization is not so much concerned about participants in the consultation getting their information across, but rather the organization getting its information and messages across.

Furthermore, in the most recent discussions with this organization, staff referred frequently to meetings and discussions with local councils, local MPs, regional airport operators, local chambers of commerce, industry groups, various action groups, supply chain partners, and, by the admission of one staff member, "the captains of industry" (personal communication, January 27, 2015). While such meetings are a necessary part of consultation, there are two problems in relation to the selection of whom to consult. First, many consultations gravitate to the 'usual suspects'. Representative organizations, which are assumed to speak for their constituencies (see a challenge to this view later), are usually the prime participants in consultations. But who are left out? Who are not represented? Often there are many who are not represented by the groups selected for consultation. Second, the force of power relations lurks beneath the surface like a timeless ocean current. Business groups, industry, organized action groups, councils, and so on are invariably better resourced and more skilled in making representations than most individual citizens and small communities. What may appear to be simple matters for professional staff in organizations, such as writing a submission, standing up to speak in public, and doing research to mount a strong argument are not within the skill set or experience of many residents in suburban and rural communities. That is not to say that such people are unskilled—indeed they may have high levels of skill and experience in various trades, agriculture, the arts, crafts, caregiving, community management, and so on, and they have local knowledge that can be valuable in many projects. But even if they do seek to participate in consultations, they are often at a major disadvantage or their voice is dismissed because they do not speak the language of consultation, often couched in legalese and policy-politico speak.

A 2014 report by the company managing the project discusses how people and enterprises in the north of England can have their views and interests represented under a heading 'A voice for the north'. This highlights a further limitation in traditional public consultation methods. While commendably reaching out to voices beyond the power centre of London, the report says that the authority of northern representation "would be determined by its ability to speak with one voice" (De-identified company, 2014b, p. 37).[13] As discussed in Chapter 1 under 'The Public Sphere', this places emphasis on consensus and homogeneity, which are criticized foci of deliberative democracy (Bickford, 1996; Fraser, 1990; Mouffe, 1999, 2005). It is highly unlikely that a region as diverse as northern England will speak with one voice. Furthermore, it is highly likely that so-called representative groups do *not* present the views of many of those within their area or sphere of interest. This point is recognized by the consultation and engagement team of the UK infrastructure project studied, with a spokesperson saying:

Most places ... have some kind of action group associated with them who have been set up in response to ourselves. These tend to be not necessarily very representative of the community and it may actually be pushing a particular single issue. If they become the focus of engagement, actually we get a very narrow view of what locals want. (personal communication, September 29, 2014)

While much of the focus of public consultation is placed on those who speak up, another interesting point raised by consultation and stakeholder relations staff working with this national infrastructure project is that a large number of those in the vicinity of or potentially affected by the project are *disengaged*. A substantial number of disengaged people is a common characteristic of projects with a long lead time, highly technical issues, or matters in which people feel they have no say or no power to influence decisions. As this infrastructure project entered phase two and nears construction, one of the leaders of engagement commented that "the group we are really concerned about is the disengaged" (personal communication, January 27, 2015). The dilemma of the disengaged also has been identified by a national scientific organization in Australia, which released research during the period of this study showing that "as many as 40 per cent of the Australian public were unengaged, disinterested or wary of science". It concluded that doing more of the same science communication is not the answer, as it is 'preaching to the converted' and called for different approaches (Searle & Cormick, 2015). In some cases the disengaged may not be a concern because they may be unaffected. On the other hand, the disengaged are often a sizeable group that can be left out and left behind in fast-moving, highly organized consultations, only to surface later as disgruntled and alienated citizens. It is problematic that public consultations often interpret silence as consent.

The ultimate test of public consultation is to ask whether anything changed as a result. While this may be an unfair question in some cases (e.g., consultation may reveal original plans to be the most acceptable), the consultation team for the major UK infrastructure project was asked "has the project been changed from the form in which it was originally proposed?" The answer: "No, not really" (personal communication, January 27, 2015).

Some of the issues raised in the major infrastructure project consultation have been recognized and addressed at least to some extent in other public consultations studied. One in particular stood out and warrants discussion for the positive way it dealt with the shift to *e-consultation* (i.e., digital forms such as e-mail and online), a high volume of public comment, and the skew caused by organized interest groups. In late 2013 and through early 2014, the UK government conducted a public consultation on part-time and casual employment contracts. A particularly controversial part of the regulations in force at the time was an exclusivity clause that precluded contracted part-time employees from working with another employer even when no work was available from the contracting organization. In 2014 the government department coordinating the public consultation found itself faced with 38,000 submissions, compared with the 1,000–2,000 responses received in most public consultations. One of the senior executives who was interviewed reflected that:

> The traditional way of government consultation and listening to people involved writing a consultation document, publishing it, and giving a two- or three-month time period for responses such as written submissions .... The next stage is to have seminars or workshops ... in which you try to get people to comment in person. (personal communication, January 28, 2015)

A newly appointed executive in the department compared the consultation with traditional public consultation methods and commented:

> What's happened here has been a revelation to me. People have been listening to what's happening and what's being said on the Internet and using things that I have never heard of before such as using Netvibes to pick up chatter and themes that are emerging and then to either engage in debate or to relay to ministers that this is an emerging issue. (personal communication, January 28, 2015)

So what was such a revelation? Three things distinguish this public consultation. First, it went well beyond the requirements of formal public consultation in its active promotion of public engagement. Rather than simply posting details of the consultation on Gov.UK, the consultation team reached out to groups such as Mumsnet (www.mumsnet.com), an online community of parents attracting 70 million page views and over 14 million visits per month, and Saga (www.saga.co.uk), an online site for the over 50s, and asked them to encourage their members to submit comments. This extended the consultation beyond the 'usual suspects' of employer groups and trade unions to people with an interest in flexible part-time and casual work. Second, the team conducted some insightful data analysis. Using keyword searches, a team of policy and communication staff, commendably working together, identified that "it wasn't a case of 38,000 people who were interested and wrote a response". Filtering e-mails and documents that contained the same titles and key messages revealed thousands of slightly varying versions of the same submission. "What we had was an organized campaign that was skewing the data", one of the team leaders reported (personal communication, January 28, 2015). Within a short time, the team identified that the campaign was organized by the action group 38 Degrees (www.38degrees.org.uk). The team leader said:

> 38 Degrees picked it up and just went bananas. What they did was actually quite clever, because with most campaigns people will just send you stock text. They'd formulated five separate responses that covered the five things that they thought were most terrible about the … contracts. (personal communication, January 28, 2015)

She added: "By the end we had something like 36,800 responses just from members and supporters of 38 Degrees". The next thing the department's consultation team did was also noteworthy. The lead of the consultation reported:

> After we started to get all these thousands of similar e-mails we actually contacted 38 Degrees. They came in to see us and brought some workers with them who told their story. We tried to head them off, but it didn't work. But we did invite them in. I have to say there were a lot of people who were a bit surprised by that, that we were actually engaging with the campaign group directly. (personal communication, January 28, 2015)

Two further initiatives by the department are useful indicators of how public consultation can be made meaningful and socially equitable. The lead of the project reported that "our wonderful social researchers set up some coding sheets for the more formal consultation responses and then circulated these across the team and everybody donated time to code them". A relatively small team of seven or eight staff did deductive content analysis of thousands of submissions using the coding framework provided. A number of the department's staff worked through weekends. The project leader confessed that the data analysis "was quite basic" and that the team already knew "what they'd said in the main"—particularly in the case of the submissions influenced by 38 Degrees. But she explained that "it was finding out what else they'd said that could be of value", as well as paying particular attention to the other 1,200 submissions that were independently produced.

The final initiative taken by the department was the circulation of a questionnaire on the basis that even those who did not want to write a submission, letter, or e-mail might fill out a simple questionnaire. Many did and, tellingly, 80 per cent of respondents supported part-time and casual employment contracts without specified hours of work because of the flexibility they offered to parents with children, carers, and the elderly. While the survey did not use probability sampling, it provided a counterbalance to the organized campaigning and demonstrated the importance of outreach in consultation to access otherwise unheard voices. The consultation led to some policy changes including prohibiting exclusivity clauses, but maintained the provision for flexible contracts. This consultation identifies some best practice principles and steps for others to follow, although it must be noted that much of the success stemmed from individual dedication including staff working overtime and on their own time.

Not all government consultations are as open and as effective. Another government department involved in closing almost 300 regional inquiry centres that had been in operation since the 1950s recognized that, while technological and social change provided a rationale for the closures, local communities and citizens were likely to be concerned. The department undertook public consultation on its plans to replace local inquiry centres with online information and telephone 'info' lines and help lines. However, its description of the consultation was intriguing in two respects: who was consulted and how were they consulted? A spokesperson said:

> There has been negative feedback from the unions and from a small number of politicians .... But we *told* them we were doing it, we *told* them why we were doing it, we *gave* them *facts*, we *wrote* to every single politician ... and *explained* why we were doing what we were doing and when .... We *wrote* to the local governments as well to *tell* them what we were doing and why and when and how. We had the minister *write* to members of Parliament and significant members of government whose constituencies were affected by this, as well as voluntary organizations. (personal communication, September 24, 2014) [emphasis added]

In a following statement, the spokesman said: "We are seeking to *inform* them about things that are happening". Italics have been added to these verbatim quotes, from which only repetitive phrases and sentence fragments have been deleted, to highlight the actions that were involved in the so-called consultation. The statements are rife with the terms 'told', 'tell', 'wrote', 'write', 'explained', 'gave', and 'inform'. Furthermore, the description makes it clear that the department was 'doing it' (closing the inquiry centres) and that it had already decided when. What the department's spokespersons described was not consultation. It was simply another public information campaign. These statements reveal the loquaciousness of some organizations and their overwhelming compulsion to tell and inform, even when supposedly consulting. A further limitation of this approach to consultation is that the focus was primarily on local politicians. The department was questioned on whether it had consulted directly with members of the public. The response was: "No, not to the public. We did that via the media, so our press office would do that". Again, the term 'press office' was used and a focus on media relations was revealed as central to much government communication and public relations. Illustrating that the above statements were not isolated examples selectively quoted, the discussion of public consultation with this department ended with this summary:

> If there's a new policy that is controversial, that people misunderstand, we will *write* and *explain* what's going on. It could be things that are not new, but we just feel there needs to be more *information* …. [W]e're trying to *persuade* and *influence* people with *information*, as well as simply provide *information*. (personal communication, September 24, 2014) [emphasis added]

To be fair, the same department does run conferences involving stakeholders twice a year that "give people a voice and an opportunity to discuss and give us general feedback" and "to ask completely unscripted questions". Also, the communication staff record videos at what they call 'customer closeness events' and present these unedited to departmental management. The videos sometimes contain frank critical comments from 'customers' (personal communication, September 24, 2014). One government regulatory and standards agency also reported video recording stakeholder and public comments and presenting these to their senior management and board of directors. The director of communication commented: "The board can see a selection of what people have actually said, which we find quite powerful" (personal communication, September 26, 2014). Notwithstanding, the aforementioned national government department's communication team maintains a predominantly transmissional view of communication, saying "we can reduce the areas of disagreement by improving the flow of information" (personal communication, September 24, 2014). And it is a flow of information from the organization to stakeholders and publics to which he is referring.

A leading university, a non-profit organization in the sample studied, reported a number of consultations during the months immediately prior to this research in relation to closing one of its campuses and moving staff and students to a central location, as well as during construction of several new buildings. The construction program was disruptive to staff and students, although it subsequently resulted in improved facilities. Staff members were consulted through a series of meetings. However, interviews with staff indicated that these were primarily informational. "There was little if any opportunity for staff to suggest changes to plans or get management to do things differently", one said (personal communication, November 7, 2014). Staff members were mainly *informed* about the building program through a series of electronic newsletters.

In a more open approach to consultation the same university engaged a professional public consultation agency to assist in negotiations in relation to closing one of its campuses. The campus move consultation included 'town hall' meetings with affected staff and with residents and community representatives in the area. Also, consultation included extensive discussion with local government authorities in relation to the redevelopment of the facilities undertaken in preparation for the move. Redevelopment included the closure of campus car parks, which resulted in hundreds of students and staff members parking their cars in neighbouring streets while work was undertaken—an issue that caused resident angst and letters of complaint to the local council. As a result of consultation, the university negotiated with the council for additional public transport to reduce traffic congestion in the area and consultation specialists 'door knocked' residents to assure them that the university was listening and responding. Staff members were also engaged in planning the move. This case study illustrates both ends of the public consultation spectrum—genuine listening, responding, and negotiating to find a mutually satisfactory middle ground in some cases, along with information transmission and persuasion dressed up as consultation in other cases.

Much public consultation takes a static 'sit and wait' approach in which an organization invites public submissions or comments and then simply accepts what it receives. It is clear from talking to organizations with extensive experience in various types of public consultation that this approach mainly collects the views of the 'usual suspects', and the voices of many others are not heard. This occurs because the rules of the game are stacked against some (e.g., requirements for formal submissions, good writing skills, and public presentations skills); because elites and professionalized groups are better resourced with specialist staff and time to do research and make submissions; because of lack of opportunity (e.g., meetings and forums are often conducted only in certain locations); and because some people simply do not believe that their voice matters.

Only a few of the organizations studied undertake *outreach* in public consultation, such as visiting relevant communities and specifically asking for comment from a range of groups and individuals. This is more time consuming than standardized consultation formats. However, greater use of outreach methods of consultation and communication is an imperative for socially equitable and truly representative listening. As well as going into specific areas and communities to seek their views and setting up specific forums offline or online, outreach can be effectively accomplished and communication greatly expanded by leveraging existing communities and partnering with other organizations. For example, like the part-time contracts consultation that engaged Mumsnet in spreading the word and soliciting input about employment contracts, a health-related public consultation on issues affecting men teamed up with PistonHeads (http://www.pistonheads.com), the UK's largest online motoring forum (personal communication, September 29, 2014). What has an online site frequented by car lovers and 'petrol heads' or 'rev heads' got to do with health? It is visited by more than 2.5 million men a month, that's what. Taking consultation on men's health to PistonHeads, as well as other non-health sites such as Money Saving Expert (http://www.moneysavingexpert .com), are examples of innovation in public consultation and public communication. Another government health organization reached out to Twitter groups such as @WeNurses, an online conversation among health care professionals, particularly nurses, scheduled every Thursday evening at the time of this study (#weNurses). But only three of the 36 organizations studied showed evidence of doing what could be called proactive outreach in consultation. Outreach provides opportunities for those missed in institutionalized consultation processes, thus affording broader and more balanced representation and social equity. Also, well-planned outreach benefits organizations by allowing them to apply the marketing aphorism 'fish where the fish are' (Owyang, 2009). The health department spokesperson commented: "The WeNurses is a great one for us because it is an organically created community and there's tens of thousands of people who are on their lists" (personal communication, February 2, 2015).

Listening in Government Communication

While government communication is a long-established field—perhaps as old as government itself—in the past few decades, governments in many democratic countries have conducted reviews and introduced initiatives with the aim of increasing transparency and creating more open government. They are also increasingly focussed on engaging citizens to regain participation in democracy and trust in the face of sharp and alarming declines in both, as outlined in Chapter 2. Increasingly these objectives have been pursued in digital environments because an increasing number of citizens use the Internet for sourcing information and services and also because of the reduced costs of digital service delivery and communication compared with traditional methods (e.g., production costs of brochures and forms).

The UK government's major commitment to digital/online engagement with citizens had its genesis in the *Digital Dialogues Report* (Miller & Williamson, 2008), the *Power of Information* review by Ed Mayo and Tom Steinberg (2007) and the following Power of Information Task Force review (Cabinet Office, 2009) under the leadership of Richard Allan (former British member of Parliament, now Baron Allan of Hallam, and director of policy for Facebook Europe at the time of this study). The final report of the Power of Information Task Force review recommended a substantial reduction in the thousands of government Web sites and their replacement with a single online portal for citizens to access government information and services. The focus remained on information and service delivery in a special report by Martha Fox (Baroness Lane-Fox of Soho) to the former Minister for the Cabinet Office Francis Maude in 2010. Fox stated:

> Directgov as an organization does two different things. It provides access to online transactional services such as student loans, car tax and Jobseekers' Allowance, and it publishes government information for citizens in one place on the Web. (Fox, 2010, p. 1)

However, a shift occurred following the UK Directgov Strategic Review carried out in 2010, which recommended that the Directgov.UK Web site launched in 2004 continue as a primary portal for UK government information and services in 2004, and that it be expanded to include citizen engagement, policy consultation, and e-democracy initiatives (Transform, 2010), as shown in Figure 3.6.

Directgov brand/domain				
Consumer	**Business**	**Departments**	**News**	**Engage**
Utility focused transactions Key information & guidance	Information and transactions for Businesses	Specialist content for more niche and professional audiences	Press releases and news for media outlets and interested public	E-democracy, policy consultation, & citizen engagement
Delivered by **Directgov** team	Delivered by **BusinessLink team**	Delivered by **Departmental teams**	Delivered by **Central Newsroom (CO/No10)**	Delivered by **Digital Engagement teams**
Shared web services				

Figure 3.6. The expanded role of the Directgov.UK Web portal to include citizen engagement, consultation, and e-democracy.

The UK's 2012–2013 *Government Digital Strategy* required that "corporate publishing activities of all 24 ministerial departments move onto Gov.UK by March 2013, with agency and arm's length bodies' online publishing to follow by March 2014" for projected savings of £1.7 to £1.8 billion a year (Cabinet Office, 2013, pp. 2–3). In early 2015, it was reported that the UK government's 'digital by default' strategy and establishment of a single government Web portal had saved £11 billion (Rigg, 2015, para. 3)—an increased efficiency gain on what was predicted. The decision by the UK government to integrate all major government department and agency information and services through one Web portal (https://.gov.uk) has put the UK ahead of most countries in terms of digital access and simplicity.

While the US government has a central official Web site (http://www.usa.gov), a spokesperson for the US administration in Washington, DC, said the US was "well behind at this stage" in providing a single portal for government information and services (personal communication, January 19, 2015). The US Department of State (2015) lists more than a dozen US government Web sites in addition to www.usa.gov as sites of important information on matters such as benefits, disaster assistance, grants, and regulations. Recent initiatives such as the US health care portal (https://www.healthcare.gov) are separate Web sites and "cost a bomb" according to a US government spokesperson (personal communication, January 19, 2015). Looking ahead, the US government is seeking efficiencies as well as improved effectiveness in its public communication.

Australia has followed the UK example, launching MyGov in 2013 (https://mygov.au) to replace its previous federal government Web portal (www.australia.gov.au) and, like other countries, this is as much to do with cost savings as it is with services and citizen engagement. Governments face a catch-22 in some respects in relation to communication. For instance, in response to media criticism over government spending on media monitoring and PR, Australian minister for finance Mathias Cormann pointed out that AUD$43.3 million (US$33 million) was cut from the federal government's public affairs and communication spending in the May 2014 budget to apply over the ensuing four years. This followed media reports that the Australian federal government was spending "eye watering sums to know what the public is thinking and what the media is [sic] saying about them" (Shields, 2015, para. 1). These statements and criticisms by Fairfax Media alleging that seven Australian government departments "splashed a combined $1.2 million on market research—in many cases focus groups and polling" (Shields, 2015, para. 4) are interesting in the context of this analysis of how organizations including governments listen. They show one more of the challenges that some organizations, particularly government, face in attempting large-scale listening such as through research and traditional and social media monitoring. Listening has to be done cost effectively as well as effectively, and some methods of organizational listening can attract criticism, particularly if they are seen to be self-serving and connected to promotion, PR, and 'spin'.

In the UK, after a period of rapid growth in spending on public communication, government expenditure has been cut despite a policy of increasing citizen engagement and public communication. The number of communication staff employed by UK government departments almost doubled from 795 in 1998 to 1,376 by 2008. The 'press corps' in central Whitehall departments and Number 10 Downing Street increased from 216 in 1998 to 373 in 2008 (Gregory, 2012, p. 372). However, Anne Gregory's conclusion that this activity under the control of a permanent secretary[14] "can be seen as a high point in government communication" is questioned. Many point to substantial waste in government advertising and a focus on expensive mass media information campaigns prior to the moratorium on UK government advertising and communication spending imposed by the Cameron government in mid-2010 and subsequent cutbacks. Also, there was substantial politicization of government communication, as discussed later. Even some UK government communication heads say that cost cutting was long overdue, with £881 million—almost £1 billion—being spent on government communication including staff and media costs in 2009–2010.

National UK government spending on communication was 53 per cent lower in 2012–2013 and 2013–2014 than it was in 2009–2010. That represented savings to British taxpayers and a reduction in government communication budgets of £378 million. Total UK government spending on communication was further pruned to £289 million in 2014–2015, down almost £600 million or 67 per cent since 2009–2010 (HM Government, 2014a, p. 27). Paid media advertising by the UK government has been reduced from £589 million in 2009–2010 to £210 million in 2013–2014—a reduction of 64 per cent, or to just over one-third of what it was a few years before (Government Communication Service, 2014a, p. 2).

US government spending on communication is extremely difficult to obtain, as this information is not collected centrally. Also, definitional issues blur 'information', 'education', 'communication', 'public relations', 'diplomacy', 'aid', and even 'intelligence'. However, it appears that the US is heading in the opposite direction to that taken by more frugal states. A Congressional Research Service study in 2014 reported that US$892.5 million was spent by the US government on paid media advertising alone in 2013, based on data held in the Federal Procurement Data System (Kosar, 2014). Externally, the US government spends vast sums on 'information' and communication—or what is termed propaganda by critics. US Secretary of State John Kerry said in early 2015 that he is concerned that "the US is falling behind when it comes to putting out information" ("US spends millions on overseas propaganda", 2015, para. 2). The focus on 'putting out information' is salutary in the context of this analysis. However, the euphemistically named Broadcasting Board of Governors (BBG), which was established to "deliver accurate news and information to significant and strategic audiences overseas", had a budget of US$721 million in 2014 according to published reports. Daniel McAdams of the Ron Paul Institute said on the Russian government-owned RT network that "there's probably another $100 million in direct support to so-called 'independent news publications' overseas" and claims the BBG budget is "only the tip of the iceberg when it comes to how the US government influences media overseas" ("US spends millions on overseas propaganda", 2015, paras. 3–4). An Associated Press investigation of US Department of Defense budgets in 2009 found that spending on "winning hearts and minds at home and abroad" had increased by 63 per cent in the previous five years to US$4.7 billion and that the Pentagon employed 27,000 people for recruitment, advertising, and public relations ("Pentagon Spending Billions", 2009). Domestically, data published by the Center for Media and Democracy *PR Watch* Web site reveals that the PR firm Ketchum was paid more than US$100 million by the US government between 1997 and 2005 and PR firm Fleishman-Hillard was paid US$77 million in the same period (Farsetta, 2005)—just two indicators of the vast sums spent on so-called communication. In total, US government spending on public communication is estimated to be in the trillions of dollars and historically the bulk of this has been quite clearly focussed on informing international communities as well as American citizens. However, there are some signs that citizen engagement and dialogue are receiving increased attention, as discussed in the following case study reports.

A number of corporations including several large multinationals also reported budget cuts and/or reductions in the number of communication staff employed. No participant in this study reported imminent or likely budget increases for communication in the next few years. This indicates that in most cases any change to how public communication is enacted must be achieved with current if not reduced resources. Adding new functions and increased staff for listening are not options for most organizations in both the private and public sectors.

Many government department and agency communication executives were reflexive and frank, admitting that their organizations are "on a journey" and that they have some way to go in terms of being open and interactive. For example, the director of communication for a national government health organization described its "long-standing national stakeholder forum" as "very broadcast". He added:

> It was sort of liked because it offered a helpful update. The chief executives of major stakeholder groups could go back to their organizations and say 'I've had a conversation with the permanent secretary of the department of [name]'. But it was mainly presentational and engaged only with a limited number of stakeholder group leaders. (personal communication, September 25, 2014)

Another said:

> When I first started in this job ... we used to be completely in broadcast mode. We'd have a breakout session at forums with stakeholders, but that was just talking to people for 45 minutes, giving them loads of chapter and verse. We've tried to turn that on its head. (personal communication, February 2, 2015)

The CEO of an Australian state environmental agency said: "We used to just focus on getting information out and telling our story. Now there is a focus on engagement—including listening to the community. We are becoming more community orientated" (personal communication, November 19, 2014). The agency has appointed a director of stakeholder engagement as well as a senior stakeholder and communication officer. The CEO and his senior staff explained that the "drivers" of this shift in focus were sixfold: (1) formal requirements for public consultation applying to government bodies; (2) freedom of information (FOI) legislation; (3) media scrutiny; (4) social media, which have increased public scrutiny and afforded new channels for comment and criticism; (5) crises, which require quick public response and open communication; and (6) the lack of trust in government that is a concern to many civil servants. The deputy director of media and communication for the national environmental agency of another country said "we're a learning organization. We've moved from broadcasting information to two-way dialogic channels" (personal communication, September 24, 2014). She went further and said "we've actually moved from broadcast straight to three-way communication"—a concept that will be further discussed later in this chapter.

Despite a logical assumption that a local health authority would have close communication and engagement with its local community, the CEO of one who is a passionate advocate for quality health care reported that, on taking up his role in 2014, he found a focus on process and a centralized top-down system of management in place. Also, the government agency was subject to very restrictive policies on use of social media and all forms of communication. For instance, the CEO was required to personally sign every letter issued by the organization. Another senior staff member confirmed that the authority did "very little monitoring" of social media and had no community engagement or 'consumer' strategy (personal communication, June 4, 2015). In November 2014, the organization initiated a 'Big Conversation' with staff that involved face-to-face discussions with 850 employees in 300 different roles that generated more than 400 ideas and suggestions. The CEO also requested an analysis of the content of the organization's reports, papers, and presentations, which revealed an overwhelming focus on "finance", "money", "deficit", and management issues, with "very little content discussing patient outcomes or care" (personal communication, June 9, 2015). Second, under its new management the authority engaged in consultation with the local community under the theme 'what matters to you', rather than the previous approach of telling the community what matters. To the surprise of 'old hands' in the organization, community listening revealed that the major concerns of local citizens were vastly different to what the authority had previously prioritized. The CEO says his team is now trying to "flip health care on its head" in the 'what matters to you' approach that will inform "co-production and co-design" of services working with consumer advisory groups. The work of the new CEO is inspirational, but this government agency is at a very early stage of the journey to two-way communication, dialogue, engagement, and responsiveness to its stakeholders and publics. One could ask why this listening commenced only in 2014.

A number of companies confessed a similar position in terms of entrenched processes of one-way information transmission (e.g., see the leading automotive manufacturer case study reported under 'Corporate Communication'). Corporate 'road shows' were nominated as 'engagement exercises' by several companies, but on questioning most acknowledged that these were travelling executive presentations with a short Q&A session tacked on. But almost all interviewees were confident that practices were changing from top-down broadcasting to more interactive, consultative, and dialogic approaches. The director of communication of a major UK government department focussed on business and industry reflected on this progress, as well as the cultural iner-tia to be overcome, saying:

> It's a place I think we need to move a lot more to. Certainly I would say if I compared where we are now to where we were five years ago as an organization, we do listen. Well, we hear more and we listen a little bit more as well. But there is something engrained in our policy officials that suggests that they are experts and that they are there because they know best …. I think a lot of this is cultural. (personal communi-cation, September 29, 2014)

Another senior government communicator commented similarly about the "journey" of change and the central role of culture, saying:

> I think we're definitely on a journey. We can point to a really steep slope of improve-ments in digital. I think we'd all acknowledge that we want to be even better than we are and that, with a department of our size, it is a culture change (personal com-munication, January 28, 2015)

The most senior US government spokesperson interviewed contrasted US local and federal government responses to Hurricane Katrina that struck the New Orleans area in 2005 to Hurricane Sandy that battered New York in 2012, pointing out a number of learnings and changes to legislation that led to a very different approach. He said that, as well as giving greater authority to national emergency management agencies, the government was proactive in consulting with local authorities and community groups. He reported:

> In New York we had 148 languages. We couldn't translate information into 148 lan-guages. So we had around 2,500 people who were sent out into the community as part of external affairs to find out the names of all the community leaders and all the faith-based leaders. The last thing many people want to do is talk directly to the federal government …. [S]ome think we are going to deport them. But by working with these community leaders and asking for their help, they were able to speak to their community in their language and explain things to them …. [W]e worked very closely with a lot of very influential people who had large numbers of followers. We reached out to them and said we need your help. Can you help us get this message out? (personal communication, January 19, 2015)

While the community outreach revealed in this statement is commendable, it is interesting that discussion of engagement ultimately comes back to helping the government get its messages out. The words 'speak' and 'messages' figure prominently in this comment, despite its overall altruistic motives. It does need to be acknowledged that in an emergency such as an impending hurricane landfall in a heavily populated area, emergency management authorities need to distribute information and issue directives. But it is revealing how many comments from organizations focus on getting their messages out and getting stakeholders to do what the organization wants—rather than the reverse or mutual accommodation.

Like a number of governments, the US administration is making efforts and investing in two-way public communication. Reflecting on the election of President Obama in 2008, the US government spokesperson said that there is now an increased focus on government being open and transparent. He recalled: "The first thing Obama did was call in senior government officials to ask their opinion. What came out of those discussions were the Open Government Initiative and the Open Data Initiative [https://www.whitehouse.gov/open] as well as a US federal digital strategy" ("Digital Government", n.d.). This includes a focus on "plain English", opening up access to non-sensitive government data through making APIs (application programming interfaces) available to commercial service providers, and simplification of accessing government information. The US government spokesperson gave the example of the US Air Force that had almost 1,000 Web sites at one time. Of these, 450 were merged into a single Web site, saving US$25 million a year. In addition to simplification for users seeking information, the consolidation of Web sites dramatically reduced the number of 'back doors'[15] that hackers use, affording increased security (personal communication, January 19, 2015).

In the UK, Government Digital Services (GDS), a government unit, has built the Gov.UK portal for a reportedly modest sum, which provides a single portal for citizens to access information about government and most government services. The creation of Gov.UK involved the closure of 1,700 UK government Web sites, generating savings of more than £250 million in the two years 2012–2013 and 2013–2014 (Government Communication Service, 2014a). Through GDS the UK government also has set down policies and guidelines for civil servants on the use of social media (Cabinet Office, 2014). These are surprisingly open and flexible for a national government—and encouraging rather than restricting. In the foreword, former Minister for the Cabinet Office and now Life Peer in the House of Lords, Francis Maude, wrote:

> Digital and social media can help the civil service reach out to the people it serves. Gone forever is a world when an anonymous man in an inaccessible Whitehall office

made decisions on behalf of others—new digital technologies help civil servants across the country engage actively with the public. (Maude, 2014)

However, centralization and standardization on this one Web platform have brought some compromises. The major UK government agency operating the customer call centre visited publishes blogs on Gov.UK. It also has established a presence on Facebook, Twitter, YouTube, and LinkedIn and is able to have links to these on the Gov.UK site. But the agency is also experimenting with text messaging and Web chats and has to go elsewhere for these, as they are not supported by GDS and Gov.UK. A number of other UK government departments and agencies complained of limitations of the central Gov .UK site and the strict policies imposed by GDS. A digital media specialist working closely with the Cabinet Office said that "basically Gov.UK is an information and service delivery site. It doesn't do campaigns apart from very general information campaigns" (personal communication, September 30, 2014). A health communication specialist agreed, saying "when you want to do communication campaigns such as promoting awareness of health issues and encouraging behavioural change, you have to go to other sites" (personal communication, September 25, 2014).

Nevertheless, GDS has produced a 'Social Media Playbook', a practical guide outlining the benefits of using social media and the major types of social media and their uses, and very significantly in terms of this analysis, this includes a section headed 'Listening' which states:

> Listening to online conversations is a good place to start and can also help you refine objectives, channels, the profile of your audience, and their needs. Although this seems like the most obvious statement in the world, it's worth repeating as it's often forgotten. *Listening should always be your step one*. (Government Digital Service, n.d.) [original emphasis]

One major UK government department has established an 'open policy making' microsite where it shares case studies with other government departments and agencies to try to identify and emulate best practice. This was still in beta form at the time of completing this research, but was public and is therefore referenced (see Figure 3.7). What is significant is that listening features prominently, at least in terms of stated aspirations. The microsite features the graphic shown in Figure 3.7, which clearly positions listening at the beginning of the policy making process. However, interestingly, the model concludes with 'keep talking', with no reference to keep listening!

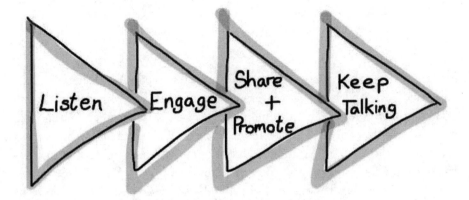

Figure 3.7. Model for engagement on the UK Department for Business Innovation and Skills 'Open Policy Making' microsite (BIS, 2015).

Even more than the limitations of Gov.UK and GDS rules and guidelines, a number of UK government departments and agencies reported that IT systems generally are a major limitation to the use of interactive digital technologies. A major Westminster government department that extensively uses Yammer internally as well as blogs complained bitterly about its intranet and access to social media. A spokesperson said "we had a big fight with the IT security dinosaurs about whether or not they would allow staff to access social media". The department has negotiated to use Citizen Space as an online consultation and collaborative tool as well as Dialogue By Design, news services such as BuzzFeed, and social media including YouTube, Facebook, and Twitter. However, staff reported that "it has been an uphill battle". The spokesperson said:

> I think for staff a big barrier is that most people are on the system that is locked down—the GSi secure intranet. It's awful and old and slow. It restricts access to social media sites. So we tend to find that we've got people running multiple browsers in parallel. (personal communication, September 26, 2014)

This department and two others reported that their version of Internet Explorer was out of date and would not download some social media content. The deputy director of a 60-member communication team in a government agency involved in health services reported that, like many other government bodies, the organization uses Yammer for internal communication and added: "But our IT people don't support it". He continued:

> We can't see moving images or have sound on our desktops. It's disabled. When I need to listen to someone on the *Today* program or see a clip, I do it on my phone ....

We put two non-networked computers in our office so staff can see and hear stuff. There is a huge challenge with our IT. (personal communication, September 25, 2014)

Similarly, the spokesperson for the Westminster department quoted previously said "we can't run video internally. Imagine that in this day and age!" (personal communication, September 26, 2014). A department promoting innovation commented: "As an organization we haven't enabled our staff to get involved in the conversation. A lot of our staff, for example, can't access Facebook on their computers" (personal communication, January 28, 2015). Another major department headquartered only a five-minute walk from Whitehall reported that "open source applications cannot be installed on departmental computers", but are necessary for some engagement activities such as e-consultation, collaboration, and crowdsourcing (personal communication, February 6, 2015).

Jannis Kallinikos, professor of information systems at London School of Economics and Political Science, says that one of the barriers to listening in large organizations is likely to be resistance to or blocking of open source and specialist software. He said government and large corporations maintain strict control of their IT systems and networks and may not allow installation or support of some of the applications necessary for organizational listening (personal communication, June 17, 2014). This raises the point that organizational listening requires the cooperation of organization IT departments and managers and possibly more flexible IT policies—albeit concerns for security as well as standardization of systems are understandable.

While governments struggle to maintain up-to-date technology to support the shift to digital communication, it is important not to overlook traditional methods of public communication that continue to function in parallel. A number of US and UK government departments report receiving from 40,000 to 70,000 letters a year. Some of these are what are termed 'ministerials' in Westminster parliamentary systems—letters sent by members of Parliament on behalf of constituents to a minister of government. These are usually referred by the minister to the department for drafting a response. However, these make up only a relatively small proportion of correspondence, with most being letters from individual citizens. Many government departments maintain correspondence units, often with 30 up to 150 staff working full-time to reply to letters.

Even though most of the organizations studied see responding to letters as an important communication activity, only one of the organizations studied conducts systematic analysis of letters. As reported by Tom Reader,

Alex Gillespie, and Jane Roberts (2014), analysis to identify the common themes and issues in letters over time can give important insights and reveal problems requiring rectification—i.e., it is a form of systematic listening. The head of public response and feedback for one UK government department described the processing of letters as being like "a military operation" and said the department's correspondence unit analyzes letters. He added: "They work with us on that. We touch base every quarter to look at any trends that are significant and any recurrent seasonal issues" (personal communication, February 3, 2015). However, while many organizations reported reallocation of resources to priority activities, systematic analysis of correspondence such as letters of complaint is not one of them in most cases. Despite hospitals and health services being a controversial sector in terms of ignoring complaints (Commission for Healthcare Audit and Inspection, 2007, 2008), a communication executive in a major government health organization that receives 50,000 letters a year on average said:

> I'd say time for me would be one of the big barriers. So those 50,000 letters—I mean I would love us to be able to analyze them, actually work out what people are saying and crunch that into useful data. But I just can't see how we are going to be able to do that. (personal communication, September 25, 2014)

Mirroring several corporate communication units studied, one major UK government department reported that it has substantially reduced the number of media releases issued in order to focus its efforts. The director of communication listed one of his priorities as "avoiding the disposable announcement", which he described as announcements that are drafted, often many times, on numerous minor matters based on habit and a predilection for distributing all information through media. Reflecting on past practices he said:

> We crafted an announcement and then moved on to the next announcement and the next announcement .... [T]he idea of getting away from the disposable announcement is recognizing that we're not getting the maximum opportunity or value out of what we put out. (personal communication, September 29, 2014)

He reported that his department had a communication staff of 170 four years before and that this was down to less than 100 at the time of the interview—a similar story to several other government departments, agencies, and even some companies that reported cuts of 30–40 per cent to communication staff levels and budget. Rather than lament this reduction in staff and budget, the director of communication described it as a positive change saying:

> Ask me whether I think the effect of losing those people was negative, I would argue the reverse. It's positive. We're definitely more efficient operationally than we were in the past and we are focussing on more important things. (personal communication, September 29, 2014)

The director was not being dismissive of employees who had left the organization. He said it has forced the communication team to become more efficient. He gave examples such as creating faster approval procedures and eliminating duplication in bureaucratic processes. He said "we tend to do things once or twice now, rather than five or six times". The shift of resources devoted to producing "disposable announcements" to other more productive activities is a further example of reallocating resources, an approach that was referred to by a number of communication 'change agents' interviewed in this study. Another senior government communicator stated bluntly: "It's about how you deploy the resources you've got and what you give your priorities to" (personal communication, February 3, 2015).

There is significant evidence that governments are trying to shift from a broadcast model of communication to engagement with and listening to citizens and some are making significant progress in this regard. However, as noted, this shift bumps headlong into technological barriers in some cases. But, mostly, goodwill and aspirations for engagement and dialogue to build trust, support, and participation collide with the inertia created by decades of 'SOS communication'—sending out stuff. Even more than technologies, practices and the social and cultural perspectives underpinning them including modernist privileging of the role of experts, transmissional notions of communication, and habit pose the greatest barriers to listening. A policy executive involved in consultation in relation to major increases in university tuition fees in the UK said of government communication on this matter:

> There was a kind of expectation that because we sent them all this information that was a job done …. [O]f course, very quickly the research confirmed that actually, not only did they not read it, they didn't understand it. They couldn't even understand half the time why we were sending them the information. (personal communication, January 28, 2015)

In her analysis of UK government public communication, Anne Gregory (2012) suggests a potential for, if not explicit, conflict between civil service communication and policy staff on one hand, who are required to be politically neutral under the Civil Service Code, and special advisers who are appointed by ministers to advise on policy and political strategy and who serve the particular party and ministers in power. However, while one UK government head of communication said special advisers can intervene and be "a challenge" at times, all other civil service interviewees reported that the blurring of political and government communication had subsided since the days of Alistair Campbell directing communication for the Blair government that led to a clamour about "the politicization of the civil service, spin, and inappropriate use of government services" and led to the 2004 review of government communication chaired by Bob Phillis (Gregory, 2012, p. 371).[16]

Nevertheless, a focus on sending out information to 'inform' and 'tell' is deeply engrained and reflected in official documents including the UK *Government Communication Service Handbook*, which guides the GCS's 3,000-plus communication professionals across national government departments and agencies. It defines the purpose of government communication as sixfold:

1. Fulfil a specific legal or statutory requirement (e.g., promote lodgement of tax returns);
2. Help the public understand the government's programs;
3. Influence attitudes and behaviours for the benefit of individuals or the wider public (e.g., discouraging drink driving and encouraging healthy eating);
4. Enable the effective operation of services to citizens (e.g., electoral registration, visa applications);
5. Inform the public in times of crisis; and
6. Enhance the reputation of the UK (e.g., promoting the UK overseas to attract investment) (Government Communication Service, 2014b, p. 10).

These purposes of government communication exclusively focus on meeting legal requirements, *creating* public understanding, *influencing* public attitudes and behaviours, *enabling* service delivery, *informing* the public, and *promoting* the image of the UK. All of them are predominantly about distributing the government's messages and information—i.e., speaking. Even though there are progressive initiatives afoot in many UK government organizations, to a quite impressive extent in many cases, there is no recognition of the need for and importance of engaging with citizens in dialogue and listening to them in this official statement that is pinned on the wall in communication units of most government departments and agencies visited.

As governments increasingly adopt *social marketing* practices, which apply marketing communication approaches to influence behaviours that benefit society as a whole, one-way informational logic is likely to prevail. While social marketing aims to contribute to the 'social good' such as through health promotion (French, Blair-Stevens, McVey, & Merritt, 2010), as opposed to commercial marketing that is conducted to produce financial benefits for the sponsoring organization, it involves strategic planning and persuasion. Listening through research is involved, but only insofar as it is necessary and beneficial in tailoring activities for maximum effectiveness. Also, a trend to *campaigns* as noted by Anne Gregory (2012, p. 373) is likely to exacerbate one-way information distribution rather than increase two-way communication and citizen engagement.

The executive director of communication for the UK government, Alex Aiken, says "the two areas of government communication where listening and engaging are an absolutely primary concern are reputation building and policy building" (personal communication, September 29, 2014). While the latter does appear to include two-way communication, engagement, dialogue, and listening in accordance with the government's open policy making commitment in a number of cases, reputation building is a predominantly promotional exercise in many executions. It is interesting that words such as 'consult the British people', 'listen to their concerns so as to address key issues in appropriate ways', and 'ensure that all voices and viewpoints are heard' do not appear in the list of purposes for government communication. This official statement of purposes and aims seems outdated and out of kilter with the policies of the UK government and the actions of many communicators including Aiken's reformist program. The same principles could not be found in US government communication policies or plans. Perhaps this continuing focus on speaking reflects a lag between officialdom and contemporary demands and expectations. But it indicates that open government and citizen engagement remain nascent developments with much more work to do.

It is recognized that not all citizens want to talk to or engage with government. Anne Gregory, who has studied government communication closely, says that all many people want is efficient delivery of services (personal communication, June 2, 2015). She points out that almost every hospital, community group, council, and so on has an advisory committee. Participation and consultation fatigue can create limitations to engagement and participation, as discussed later in this analysis. However, it is the quality of engagement and listening that is the issue and focus of this analysis, not the quantity.

Forward thinking and innovative approaches are in evidence in some government documents such as a draft discussion paper titled 'The Future of Public Service Communications—Report and Findings 1.0' produced by the Government Communication Service (HM Government, 2014b). This states: "Demographic change and a more open society means [*sic*] the top down broadcast (one-way) mode of communication is over" (p. 5). It acknowledges that "much digital communication and engagement is [*sic*] still delivered in transmit mode, following the old 'top-down' one-way broadcasting of messages rather than conducting conversations that modern communications involves" (p. 11) and that governments face three significant challenges: "trust, apathy, and negative experiences" (p. 15). The paper progressively identifies digital communication, engagement, and 'nudge' communication based on behavioural insights as key strategies to address the challenges faced. This thinking needs to filter down and the leadership and initiatives in the UK government's GCS suggest that it will. To the extent that it does, it will open up major opportunities to transform government communication, although much greater focus on the issues raised in this chapter and in the next is required.

Aiken asks rhetorically: "Can government get better at listening and engaging with communities, individuals, and businesses? Yes, it certainly can, which is part of the drive behind open policy. I would like to see more open and two-way communication". However, Aiken identifies five barriers as:

1. The sheer volume of material that government is required to disseminate and deal with;
2. The machinery of government is there to implement policy. Politicians are more responsible for listening and responding to public concerns;
3. Structurally we are set up in a way to broadcast rather than reflect;
4. Fourth, we do not make enough of the intelligence and evaluation metrics that we have; and
5. We are still moving away from a model in which government communication became quite dominated by the advertising industry. (personal communication, September 29, 2014)

Aiken noted that the UK government spent close to £500 million on advertising in 2010, compared with half that much today. He said: "Perhaps governments go into a bit of a trance and think if they advertise a scheme, a plan, an offer, it will work" (personal communication, September 29, 2014). One of the most senior digital communication specialists working with Aiken and the GCS says communication is about "two Cs"—"content and conversation" (personal communication, September 30, 2014). That view incorporates both Aiken's argument that governments have a key role in informing citizens, as well as the fundamental basis of communication as two-way interactive engagement.

As well as extensively using public consultation, a number of US government agencies and authorities are also using social media. A noteworthy example identified by several interviewees was the immediate aftermath of the 2013 Boston Marathon bombing in which the Boston Police Department not only kept the world's media up to date on Twitter, but also engaged with citizens directly during the search for the suspects. Emergency management agencies in the US also have substantially invested in two-way government-citizen communication since the widely criticized communication breakdowns following Hurricane Katrina (personal communication, January 19, 2015). However, strong overtones of information transmission remain. For instance, the official Web page of the US Army states that its public affairs function (a synonym for PR) "fulfils the Army's obligation to keep the American people and the Army informed" and adds that it also "helps to establish the conditions that lead to confidence in America's Army and its readiness to conduct operations in peacetime, conflict and war" (US Army, 2015). Significant is that the first role mentioned is keeping US citizens "informed". How it helps establish the conditions that lead to confidence in the US military is not explained, but it is significant that engaging in two-way dialogue and listening that are shown to contribute to trust are not mentioned.

Despite many refreshing examples of openness, innovation, and increasing flexibility in government communication, one state government agency in Australia demonstrated that policies of open government, transparency, and engagement still have a very long way to go in some cases. A local area health authority was approached for an interview in late 2014 as part of gaining a community-level perspective to complement, or contrast, national health department and national agency views gained from case studies in several countries. The chief executive and one other senior staff member of the local authority agreed to be interviewed and were advised that the study had university ethics approval and that this included a guarantee of de-identification of the organization and individuals interviewed. Furthermore, an information sheet provided with the request for interview made it clear that the research related to the authority's *public* communication and that no confidential information was sought. Notwithstanding, after checking with its parent department, the authority advised that state Department of Health ethics approval was also required. This involved a second detailed ethics application that took more than two months to be processed even though it was categorized as 'low to negligible risk' (LNR). But this was not the end—or not even the beginning of the case study. Further correspondence advised that a site specific assessment (SSA) had to be approved by the research governance unit of the institution and a letter of authorization was necessary from this body. This required another application form as well as copies of all ethics approvals, consent forms, and other documentation. In addition, the bureaucracy then advised that the staff to be interviewed had to provide letters confirming in writing their agreement to be interviewed—even though a consent form was already a condition of the ethics approval. A round-robin of negotiations continued until the end of May 2015—six months after the request for an interview was submitted. This request involved half a dozen forms and about 40 pages of paperwork, including a full CV of the interviewer. All to ask a taxpayer-funded government authority about how it communicates with the public! While some valuable insights were eventually obtained from this organization, the bureaucracy of this government department and authority is mind-boggling and illustrates an archaic and arcane approach to dealing with the public that lies at the heart of disenchantment and distrust of government.

Listening in Organizational Communication

As noted in Chapter 2 in overviewing the various specialist fields of public communication practice employed in and by organizations, organizational communication mostly refers to internal communication within organizations and between organizations. Internal communication is also referred to as employee communication and employee relations, but can also include communication with close affiliates in some cases such as business partners, distributors, and retailers. The relevance of two-way communication and listening in organizational communication is made clear in the findings of a 2014 US study that reported managers undertake communication "to build *trust* and *engagement* with employees" (Mishra, Boynton, & Mishra, 2014, p. 183) and rated engagement as "one of their top priorities" (p. 190). Furthermore, the study reported that executives see the primary route to building trust and engagement as *dialogue* with employees and external stakeholders (p. 192) [emphasis added].

In this study, the internal communication of one of the world's largest telecommunications companies with consolidated revenue of more than

US$100 billion and a quarter of a million employees was examined. The vice president (VP) of corporate communication and the head of internal communication were interviewed and an extensive range of communication materials were reviewed. A number of stand-out trends were observed in this organization. The most noteworthy was a fundamental shift from printed information materials to video—specifically digital video hosted internally on the company's intranet or externally on YouTube channels or other public Web sites. The company has established four video programs that are produced weekly or bi-weekly—one specifically focussed on staff matters, one covering international news, one for business partners, and one for employees to engage external audiences as advocates for the company. These programs are highly polished in terms of their presentation, with anchors introducing segments on a professional-looking set similar to TV news and talk shows. Interviews and reports from the field presented in the programs are quite often low-resolution video with signs of being shot on a handheld camera. Rather than being detrimental, this gives the reports authenticity, as they contain clear visual clues that they are not staged and that they are recorded by eye witnesses rather than professional camera crews. However, all the content is edited and curated to a high standard.

The company's shift from print to video was a result of research—or, put simply, listening to its publics and stakeholders—and it has a strong commitment to research to evaluate response to its programs. Employee surveys are conducted twice a year. For example, in 2014 an online survey was sent to 40,000 employees from among 138,000 who had watched at least one episode of the international news video program. The survey received 5,570 responses (a 14 per cent response rate), of which 93 per cent said the program was interesting and worth watching. The survey also asks employees what types of information they prefer and this informs program planning. Focus groups are also conducted regularly to gain further qualitative insights. This testing and feedback have resulted in the video program segments being two to three minutes in length. "That's the attention span for an internal video", the VP of corporate communication said (personal communication, January 14, 2015).

The CEO of the company appears regularly in videos produced for employees. While this is not unusual, a noteworthy feature of this CEO's approach is that he has an oft-expressed dislike for 'corporate speak'—that is, business buzzwords, technical terms, and managerial clichés. He advocates "simplifying how we talk", which the organizational communication team puts into practice (personal communication, January 14, 2015). This shift away from traditional corporate news presented in formal business language dotted with buzzwords and phrases such as 'fiscal performance' and 'competitive advantage' is the second significant feature of this company's organizational communication.

An example of the company's shift away from traditional corporate presentations to interesting stories is that the video programs viewed included reports of one of the company's employees rescuing a starving dog that had been thrown into one of the company's compounds and abandoned. How is such a video report relevant to organizational communication in a large corporation? This question was put to the VP of corporate communication. She said:

> It's about demonstrating the values of the company. We're showing that we are a company of caring people. We're not putting words into a corporate brochure; we're doing it. People want to work for that kind of organization. People want to do business with that kind of organization. (personal communication, January 14, 2015)

The third significant and surprising discovery in this case study was that the company's internal communication budget had been cut in the previous year and all its internal communication is coordinated by a small staff of just nine. The secret of doing new things at reduced cost is twofold, according to this communication team. First, almost everything is done internally. The company does not use an external production house to produce its video programs or even external professional comperes. The internal communication staff explained production of its video programs thus:

> We had quotes from $30,000 up to $100,000 per program. But we looked around internally and found we had people with experience in TV compering or stage work who were willing to give it a go. One of our staff had worked at a TV studio previously. The other anchor was a former beauty queen who we trained up.

> We go up to a little studio on the 24th floor of headquarters. The backdrop looks like some big fancy thing, but it's just a screen that flips. We write the script—it's usually a team effort. We put these programs out on Tuesdays and Thursdays. It's usually shot in the studios at about 7 am. Then the file gets digitally sent back to the employee communication video team in Connecticut. They add in all the B-roll stuff and come up with the final thing. Then they send it back and we post it online. It's typically posted around 2 pm or 3 pm. (personal communication, January 14, 2015)

The second secret to this company's capability to do more with less, including transitioning its internal communication from print to video as well as taking on 24/7 social media monitoring and engagement (see 'Listening in Social

Media'), is what the VP of corporate communication calls "pivoting". She said: "You have to change the structure and change the expectations. You have to clearly state the expectations and then sit back and see who rises and who doesn't". She explained that, to make the change, the company called on staff to take on new roles and develop new skills. "We provided a lot of train-ing, including in video recording and production", she said. The VP was also keen to point out that age is a not a determinant of adaptability, telling a story of one near retirement age employee who relished the chance to write in new ways for video scripts and social media after a lifetime writing formal business reports. "He became a role model and helped us change the culture", she said. 'Pivoting' has also involved changing recruitment policies and practices. The VP of corporate communication explained:

> We've put a very high premium on moving out people who do not have writing skills and bringing in people with writing skills and, beyond writing skills, we have started bringing in people with experience in TV and video. We've had to pivot in terms of internal structure and roles, training, and hiring. (personal communication, January 14, 2015)

As part of this structural and cultural change, the company has had to stop doing some of the things that it previously did and reallocate resources in order to do new things within budgets and staff levels available. Measure-ment and evaluation help in identifying less effective activities. But the VP of corporate communication acknowledged that terminating some activities such as producing newsletters or writing press releases is challenging and can meet resistance. She said as one of her final messages: "The hard question is 'what are you going to stop doing?' That is a question we're constantly asking ourselves. What represents the future? What are relics of the past that we need to stop doing?"

While a number of interesting things can be learned from this corpo-ration, the key question relevant to this study is 'to what extent does its organizational communication involve listening?' Clearly the company lis-tens through research and has responded to employees' needs and interests identified in employee surveys and focus groups. In 'pivoting' to change its communication structure, skill set, and outputs it has demonstrated listening in a general sense—e.g., to shifting media consumption patterns and social and cultural changes. The company also conducts 'town hall' meetings, both physically and via Webcasts, and the format of these one hour sessions is a maximum of 15 minutes for the CEO or other senior executives to speak, with

45 minutes reserved for questions. Hence, a significant level of engagement and listening is demonstrated in its organizational communication.

However, after several hours watching snippets of its video programs and viewing the large amounts of information on its corporate Web sites and various other sites such as YouTube, one is still left with an overwhelming sense of strategic corporate informing. The company is a behemoth, its voice is loud, and its information voluminous. It encourages employees to speak, but it provides a forum for their voices only when they echo the messages of the organization. Nevertheless, it is informative and refreshing to find a CEO and a small communication team working hard to engage with key stakeholders and going some way to listen as well as trumpet the voice of the organization.

Some government departments and agencies also demonstrated commendable innovation in their internal organizational communication, including a shift to video as well as social media. A major UK government department criticized earlier in this chapter for its narrow and talkative approach to public consultation has 176 active groups on Yammer involved in peer-to-peer communication. It also noted that the UK's Home Secretary, Theresa May, is active on departmental Yammer sites and publishes a blog. Of course, Theresa May along with the former Minister for the Cabinet Office, Francis Maude (now Life Peer in the House of Lords), have long been champions of digital communication and opening up government communication.

Despite some noteworthy examples of changing practices, most government departments and agencies spoke more about their external communication and several did not mention internal organizational communication. An April 2015 article published by the Organizational Communication Research Center of the Institute for Public Relations (IPR) in the US noted the focus on one-way, top-down transmission of an organization's messages and in the opening paragraph saw it necessary to instruct readers that:

> Employee communications is more, must be more, than simply conveying the direction and directives of management throughout an organization. Employee communication professionals must take responsibility for assisting with all communication flow within the system. This means engaging in the management of bottom up and lateral communications as well. (Smith, 2015)

Listening in Political Communication

As noted in Chapter 2, political communication conducted by individual political representatives is not the focus of this study, which examines organization-public communication. Also, discussions were held with only two senior political figures—one formally and one informally—so political communication was not assessed in detail. However, several points made in discussions with the national secretary of a major national political party and a former prime minister are noteworthy. Far from arguing that political parties listen and respond to their constituencies, both the senior political party figures expressed concern that parties and governments are losing, or have lost, legitimacy and public support because they are not listening. The national secretary of a right-wing political party said many political parties and politicians are "going through the motions of listening" and believe that they are listening. But he pointed to institutionalized practices such as tours, visits, and rallies during which the "party faithful" are organized to attend as 'cheer squads', and meetings with voters that are attended by invitation only and 'stacked' with supporters to meet and greet their representatives. He said politicians are often not listening to "real people". They are mostly hearing the loud voices of power elites and the platitudes of sycophants because party 'machines' have turned politics into highly organized, professionalized processes focussed on set-piece, highly staged events on one hand, and behind closed doors meetings on the other. The stage-managed visits to shopping malls, factories, and 'town hall' meetings are supplemented by opinion polling, which is mostly based on small samples and a narrow set of closed end questions (see 'Listening in Research'). As a result, the leaders of political parties hear only a narrow and sterilized version of citizens' views (personal communication, May 6, 2015). The former prime minister and leader of a centre-left political party, while making less explicit criticisms, agreed that major political parties are losing contact with and support of citizens, and both political leaders see this 'communication breakdown' as a key factor leading to the rise and growth of radical far-right and far-left political groups.

The political party executive's description of the political hustings reminds one of the aphorism (and Billy Connolly quip) that the Queen of the UK and Commonwealth countries believes the whole world smells of fresh paint because everywhere she goes has been painted in preparation for her visit. She rarely if ever sees the back streets and 'struggle streets' of society (Mooney, 2011, para. 11).

While limited evidence was gathered in relation to political communication in this study, what was found supports Jay Blumler and Stephen Coleman's conclusion that an "inexorable impoverishment of political communication has taken place" leading to a "crisis of public communication that is sapping the vitality of democratic political culture" (2010, p. 140).

Beyond this analysis, political communication is informed by studies of political parties' and politicians' use of social media and studies of election campaigns that have already been referred to in Chapter 1 and Chapter 2. A number of studies of the 2010 UK national election, Australian federal elections in 2007, 2010, and 2013, and even the much-acclaimed Obama presidential election campaigns in the US have reported a predominance of one-way transmission of party messages and political slogans, with little two-way interaction with citizens (Gibson, & Cantijoch, 2011; Gibson, Williamson, & Ward, 2010; Macnamara, 2011, 2014a; Macnamara & Kenning, 2011, 2014; Rosenstiel & Mitchell, 2012). While further research into public communication by political organizations such as political parties is needed to draw specific conclusions, there are indications that lack of listening is at least part of the cause of citizen disengagement from traditional politics and voter dissatisfaction that is being reflected in falling voter turnouts, 'hung' parliaments, and a rise in radical extreme right and extreme left political parties and organizations.

Listening in Marketing Communication

As noted previously in this chapter, market research involves listening, but in the very bounded sense of understanding potential consumers and then using techniques of rhetoric, psychology, and semiotics to persuade them to think and behave in accordance with an organization's objectives. Also, as noted in Chapter 2, the dominant form of marketing communication is advertising, which is overwhelmingly one-way transmission of messages—some might say bombardment with information and messages. The primary site of organizational listening in relation to marketing is customer relations, which has been discussed previously in this chapter. However, some other elements of marketing communication were examined in this study to explore listening in marketing communication as fully as possible.

The work of the marketing communication unit of a large university was studied and it provided a useful vantage point to observe contemporary marketing communication practices in the context of listening and engagement, as the university has a stated commitment to engagement with its stakeholders and a strong social conscience. It can be argued that a university should be an optimal site of interactive and relationship marketing being a non-profit organization with a range of public accountabilities, compared with commercial companies that have more narrow responsibilities as well as constant pressure to meet sales and revenue targets.

The university undertakes considerable research including a biennial RepTrak reputation study among key stakeholder groups such as employers, as well as regular student surveys, and a biennial staff survey. Quantitative surveys are followed up by focus groups in some cases to gain deeper insights into the views, needs, interests, and concerns of stakeholders including students, staff, employers, and industry and professional organizations. Engagement is a stated priority of the university evidenced in the appointment of a deputy vice chancellor (DVC) to head this role with equal status to the DVCs of teaching and research. Most faculties of the university also have appointed associate deans or directors of engagement—indeed, engagement has become a buzz-word of the university sector, as any search of university Web sites shows.

However, while the university has moved much of its information to its Web site, which was substantially upgraded in the year before this research, it maintains a relatively traditional approach to marketing communication, with its courses promoted through newspaper advertising and PR that is largely focussed on traditional media publicity and events. Furthermore, it publishes a supplement in a major newspaper in the city in which it operates, which was in printed form as recently as 2014, and still publishes a number of 'hard copy' magazines and newsletters. The university has begun to use social media, but had just 1.5 FTE (full-time equivalent) staff managing its social media presence at the time of this research, despite a student population of almost 40,000 and more than 3,000 staff. To be fair, the university is seeking to implement a "distributed model" in which academic staff and students respond to issues, answer questions, and comment on relevant content online, rather than have a central team of social media communicators. However, it still has a way to go in this regard as the institution did not have clear policies and guidelines on social media use at the time of this study (guidelines were "in development"), there was no training provided to staff or students in social media use, and monitoring and analysis were basic. The university has a presence on Facebook, Twitter, Instagram, LinkedIn, and Pinterest, but social media monitoring and analysis are limited to Buzznumbers, a predominantly quantitative tool, and automated volume and 'positive/negative/neutral' charts provided by Meltwater. The university considered Radian6, but the director of the marketing communication unit commented: "It is a market leader, but we could not afford it" (personal communication, November 3, 2014).

The director said the university's social media communication has moved through three phases, which she described as (1) "a channel to distribute messages" (transmission only); (2) "a channel to distribute messages and track our own messages, reach, and so on" (transmission with measurement of organization effectiveness); and (3) "an insights tool to monitor issues of concern, viewpoints and opinion" (transactional, but with a strategic organizational planning focus). The university has not moved to a fourth phase in which the organization actively listens and responds and she confessed that "it is still a lot of one and two" (personal communication, November 3, 2014). Nevertheless, the university has experimented with Local Measure, a geo-tracking tool (e.g., to identify social media comments and discussion that occur on campus) and engaged a professional social media consultancy to provide advice on how to better use social media for engagement. The institution is also strongly committed to consultation, which is discussed under 'Listening in Public Consultation'.

The colonization of social media by marketing departments and a resulting focus on one-way transmission of promotional messages designed to sell products and services was identified by several interviewees in this study, as reported under 'Listening in Social Media'. Most interviewees strongly argued that social media should be incorporated into corporate and organizational communication and used interactively for two-way communication and engagement with stakeholders and publics, not appropriated for marketing communication. Some such as one of the national airlines studied split social media into corporate and marketing uses. However, this results in conflicted messaging, with 'hard sell' marketing messages often backfiring and leading to criticism of the corporation as a whole. Resolving this tug-of-war among marketing, corporate/PR, and organizational/internal communication has led to many companies and government departments putting digital/social media under the management of a specialist unit or director. However, this would appear to be an interim strategy while social media are relatively new and as practices are worked out and become settled. Ultimately, social media are channels for communication and, as shown in this study and many others, they are used across all parts of organizations for a range of purposes. Integrating those uses and establishing policies for social media use seems to be a necessary part of overall public communication planning.

Listening in Corporate Communication

In some cases, corporate communication refers specifically to the public communication activities of corporations, although as noted in Chapter 2, the term 'corporate' is sometimes used to denote corporate bodies, which can include government organizations, NGOs, public utilities, and even charities. In reality, corporate communication often involves practices that are similar to or the same as public relations, but seeks to differentiate itself as a field to escape the negative implications of PR, which is often seen pejoratively as 'spin', 'flack', and hype (Johnston, Zawawi, & Brand, 2009; Macnamara, 2014b, p. 7; Wilcox & Cameron, 2010, p. 12).

One of the most striking features of the corporate communication of a leading US broadband and telecommunications company studied is that it has banned media releases, which it refers to as 'press releases', other than formal public announcements that it is legally obligated to issue. The VP of corporate communication stated:

> We're not allowed to do press releases here—other than announcements required by the stock exchange. You must think first about the audience and then the story, and then determine what is the best vehicle? That vehicle or channel is rarely press releases. (personal communication, January 16, 2015)

He explained that writing and distributing what this analysis calls media releases "was so habitual … there's no thought that goes into it. There's no thought about the audience, there's no thought about the behaviour change that you're trying to drive". The company's decision to stop issuing media releases becomes understandable upon hearing his rationale.

> I think at last count, we issued between 2,000 and 3,000 press releases a year. There's no way for that volume of activity to not cost a lot of money—all for something that you cannot prove the value of except that I can show the CEO the coverage that those X thousand press releases generated and hopefully he won't ask me to verify it in terms of impact. (personal communication, January 16, 2015)

This radical decision to stop producing media releases—a long-standing and staple corporate communication and PR activity since Ivy Lee pioneered the practice in the early 1900s (Hiebert, 1966)—is another example of the restructuring and reallocation of resources that was discussed under 'Listening in Organizational Communication' in relation to another large telecommunications company studied. Also, it echoes the decision by a major UK government department to abolish what the director of communication calls "the disposable announcement" (see 'Listening in Government Communication'). The VP of corporate communication for the US broadband and telecommunications company said that most media releases were written by an external agency and the financial savings made in agency fees freed up budget to do other things. Interestingly, he said the decision also freed up "intellectual capacity" and forced a shift in thinking away from traditional media relations.

The need to restructure the corporate communication function of the company and redeploy resources was informed by a commitment to measurement and evaluation that led to a realization. The VP of corporate communication said "there's this dirty little secret that I talk to my team about". He explained this 'dirty little secret' as follows:

> We have, for good or bad, convinced our clients, our business partners, if you will, that what we do—media clips, coverage, volume—matters. It's a dirty little secret because what we all really know is that we can't really prove that it has any meaningful impact on the business …. I think we have two choices. You can continue to close your eyes and hope that people continue to believe that clips—media coverage—mean something valuable to the business. But we know today it doesn't. We could shake a stick and get a tonne of coverage today and still turn around tomorrow and have our lunch handed to us by our competitors. Or we can use data-informed insights to engage in a way that actually has meaningful impact on brand affinity, perceptions, and the way people think about us as an organization. That's meaningful value. (personal communication, January 16, 2015)

He emphasized that the structural and cultural change to new ways of communicating is not easy, saying:

> It requires very hard decisions because, if you think about adding resources and activities, that means financial costs, and that means you have to stop something. You've got to eliminate some things … you can't just add this to what you're doing today. You've got to make a conscious decision, for instance, that 25 per cent of what you've been doing has got to cease to exist—and that impacts people, work processes, and the way we think. (personal communication, January 16, 2015)

The company has shifted substantial communication resources into research to track its brand and measure and evaluate its communication effectiveness including in social media. The VP responsible for corporate communication said the company collects data from three sources—"the voices of customers, the voices of employees, and the voices of social" (consumers and citizens generally) and integrates data from these "listening posts". In addition to surveys among its 125 million customers, the corporation somewhat bravely tabulates the results of exit interviews with departing employees and draws data from Glass Door (http://www.glassdoor.com), an independent Web site on which employees anonymously rate companies in terms of pay and conditions, culture, and behaviour. For tracking social media, the company's head of digital media said his "favourite" tool is Brandwatch, but also commented that he had used Radian6 and Buffer for social media monitoring and analysis and for "refining stories" and strategies in social media. The company also uses CrowdAround, an emerging product at the time of this research reportedly designed to replace Yammer as an internal organizational collaboration tool (Drake, 2014). The company's VP of corporate communication said "every place where our customers are allowed to engage with us we're capturing data, analyzing it, and then producing insights to inform our business". The company also calculates its Net Promoter Score (NPS) based on survey questionnaires or telephone interviews.

A 2015 measurement and evaluation report and "leadership brief" of the company's corporate communication department titled 'Insights From Customers, Influencers and Employees' that was examined presented an impressive array of quantitative and qualitative data. It reflected the company's commitment to being "data-informed", but also the VP's view that "data on its own is not enough". He said "we don't distribute them [Brandwatch reports] natively [in their original form]. We know that if we just handed those dashboards over to management there is too much of a gap, so we use them as an input to our monthly reports" (personal communication, January 14, 2015). He supported Mark Weiner, CEO of Prime Research, and other senior communication executives interviewed in arguing that, despite machine learning, interpretation and decision making by humans are vital components of monitoring and research. He said: "We found that if you rely only on a tool you get into trouble" (personal communication, January 16, 2015). One of the senior government communication executives interviewed who uses data from Gorkana Radar also warned against presenting raw automated data to management. She said that when the software showed a spike in negative discussion or a rising issue "we're very careful not to throw people into a panic .... We say, there is a spike, but this is why and this is what we're doing about it" (personal communication, February 3, 2015).

The VP of corporate communication for the US broadband and telecommunications company claimed that the organization's communication overall was 60 per cent listening compared with 40 per cent "broadcasting"— the highest overall ratio claimed by any organization in this study. The VP commented that the "pivot"—a term also used by another large corporation studied—from a traditional broadcast model to engagement and listening was "a painful, painful shift". Like several others, he pointed to a need to change the culture and structure of an organization, and to reallocate resources in order to achieve engagement and listening.

Overall, some progressive two-way engagement initiatives were observed in this company. However, despite the company's claims and progressive commitment to research and social media engagement, a number of limitations were also identified. First, it has a restrictive policy on who can represent the organization in social media. The VP said "we have a very strict policy. It is only the official spokespersons who can speak for the organization in social and that's generally defined as the corporate 'comms' team". Second, the company committed to 24/7 monitoring of social media for a time, but has discontinued this. The VP said:

> Our truth is that even if something happened, we couldn't do anything about it if it's the middle of the night. Who am I going to call? So what we do is try to be nimble and we try to get something together within six hours. (personal communication, January 16, 2015)

This may be acceptable if the company is thinking only in US time. But in a globalized business, world events and conversations on the other side of the globe can disrupt the sleep of executives in New York, New Jersey, Seattle, Michigan, California, Texas, London, Birmingham, Coventry, Sydney, or Melbourne. When the US goes to sleep, it is early morning in China, Korea, Taiwan, Japan, Malaysia, Singapore, and Australia. A US centricity was evident in several interviews with executives of US corporations including several multinationals.

A third shortfall in listening and a potential contradiction of the claim for a 60:40 listening to speaking ratio in the organization is found in the language used. For instance, in discussing the company's focus on social media in the past few years, the head of digital said it was different to traditional corporate communication, which he described as "you're either putting out fires or you're lighting fires". He said "in our function [social media], we're constantly kindling. We're always out there trying to spark something". Also, in referring to research and listening, he said "when we're speaking, we're trying to be really informed and seeing if it worked …. [W]e want to be breaking news" (personal communication, January 16, 2015).

Such statements reveal a lingering focus on speaking and preparing to speak. They show a focus on igniting discussions in social media rather than observing and listening to existing discussions. They also indicate that listening through research and social media monitoring is largely or mostly undertaken so the organization can be informed and that its reason for wanting to be informed is so it can accurately target potential customers, employees, and others with its messages. Such criticism is not to reject this case study as lacking listening. Indeed, it exhibited commendable initiatives in many respects, particularly in the use of data and generation of insights through research. But it illustrates the subconscious and often unconscious penchant for speaking that permeates public communication practices. It reveals a gravitational pull that makes most corporate, government, and organizational communication top-down and stifles bottom-up communication other than brief encounters when powerful organizations reach down to 'test the temperature' or surveil the landscape over which they reign. The force that maintains this gravity in corporate communication is capitalism with its never-ending pressure to sell products and services in order to make profits. The corporate communicators interviewed talked incessantly and often excitedly about "achieving the objectives of the business" and "creating value for the business". 'The business' is the centre point and true north of corporate communication. It is difficult to see how relationships with customers and other stakeholders and publics can be anything other than lopsided in such an environment. Perhaps corporate communication is the wrong place to look for listening. Perhaps its role is to speak for organizations. But, as other sections of this chapter show, listening is also often tokenistic and sometimes missing in other public communication practices as well.

The issue of scale has been mentioned a number of times as an important factor in organizational listening. The volumes of public communication that some organizations have to deal with are quite staggering and an example is worth noting to remind us that organizational listening is not easy. What a small business might do, or the way a local community group deals with its constituents, is generally not applicable to large-scale communication. For instance, one major corporation provided a summary of some of its public communication as shown in Table 3.6.

Table 3.6. Public communication undertaken by a large corporation.

Activity	Per day	Per month	Per annum
E-mails to CEO	15	320	3,800
Letters to CEO	10	210	2,600
Phone calls to CEO's office	0.5	7	85
Web forms	7	160	1,850

Activity	Per day	Per month	Per annum
Fax & walk-ins	0–1	7	85
Phone calls received in total	120,000	2,640,000	32,000,000
Online interactions	700,000	22,000,000	260,000,000
Store visits	110,000	3,000,000	36,000,000
Posts on social media monitored	3,500	102,000	1,224,000
Posts on organization's social media	2,250	68,000	816,000
Responses sent	1,450	43,000	516,000
Totals	940,000	29,000,000	330,000,000

Notes: Numbers are rounded and calculated based on averages in early 2015. Some numbers such as phone calls to the CEO are calculated on five working days per week; most are calculated on seven days per week as the social media team works 24/7.

Listening in Public Relations

Public relations functions such as event management, social media communication where this is managed by PR, community relations, investor relations, and formative and evaluative research could be expected to be sites of considerable listening, given the explicit focus on two-way communication, engagement, dialogue, and relationships in PR theory, as outlined in Chapter 2. However, this facet of the research was a great disappointment.

The headquarters PR function of a global automotive manufacturer was studied and was insightful both in terms of the commitment of the PR practitioner and for what it revealed about the importance of culture and structure. The PR manager was frank, saying:

> The culture here is mostly a command and control one. The senior management mostly have engineering backgrounds. That means we are very process driven and very focussed on numbers and data. But there is an awareness of the 'new world' out there. (personal communication, January 30, 2015)

Even though dialogue allegedly "has become ubiquitous in public relations writing and scholarship" (Theunissen & Noordin, 2012, p. 5), he rated the ratio of speaking to listening in his company as 90–95 per cent speaking compared with 5–10 per cent listening. He reported that the corporate PR team in the company's headquarters totalled 70 staff. In addition, its two major global brands each have their own PR teams and the corporation operates through 18 national sales companies around the world, which each have their own marketing staff. But he explained that the brand marketing teams and national sales companies are almost exclusively focussed on marketing and promotion of products. The PR manager reported that social media communication for the company is controlled by marketing, as reported under 'Listening in Social Media'. He said the company conducts social media monitoring and analysis using We Are Social and also Ogilvy's Listening Post technology platform. Like many PR agencies and some advertising agencies, Ogilvy claims to have a social media analytics capability and makes claims for listening. For instance, on its Social@Ogilvy Web site, the agency states:

> How do we create award-winning social media strategies for clients? First, we listen. From twitter to Facebook, blogs to websites, our global listening and analytics team digs deep into the millions of online conversations taking place every day about a brand, its competitors and the industry overall. We monitor social media and search behaviour to deliver actionable insights that shape the framework of effective, integrated programs .... Listening may be the first step in creating a remarkable social experience that gets people talking, but it should never stop. (Ogilvy & Mather, 2015)

However, trade journals have reported that Ogilvy has partnered with Sysomos to provide social media analysis to clients (Akhtar, 2014). This may be industry dealings unrelated to this study at one level, but it does reflect a scramble in the PR industry to provide social media services as well as measurement and evaluation and a discourse of grand claims about listening that do not appear to be grounded in reality. It seems significant that a global PR agency has not developed its own state-of-the-art capability for monitoring social media more than a decade after these media came to prominence. Furthermore, the automotive manufacturer's PR manager said "our monitoring and analysis mainly looks at quantitative metrics such as the volume of tweets and retweets and are used almost entirely for tracking mentions of the brands and their messaging". Even after several decades of intense debate in the PR industry about measurement, this allegedly "award-winning" social media analysis function remains focussed on measuring the volume of the organization's voice.

Traditional media analysis for the corporation and brands is provided by Prime Research in 21 markets globally. The manager reported that "they

analyze quantity such as volume, reach, share of voice against major competitors, and quality to some extent, such as tone. Also, they calculate a proprietary 'PR value'" (personal communication, January 30, 2015). While saying
"we don't use advertising value equivalents—management recognizes that
the old ways have become discredited", the PR manager said "there is still a
demand in management to see a dollar or pound or euro value" for communication. Calculation of a 'PR value' expressed in financial terms is controversial as it flies in the face of most social science research methodology and
is contrary to international standards being developed for PR evaluation that
dispute the validity of such metrics (IPR, 2010).

The auto manufacturer uses tracking research on brand appeal and perceptions as well as focus group research, but mostly in relation to testing new
designs and features for its products. The PR manager said "I would like to
be measuring engagement" and added "we would like to use listening tools
such as more sophisticated social media monitoring tools to track comments
and public opinion on issues. But it is a trade off on how much we can spend"
(personal communication, January 30, 2015). The company processes Web
inquiries, letters, and e-mails through its customer relations department and
also does some public consultation on local issues, such as when it is building
or expanding a plant. The PR manager said "then we go beyond the legal
requirements and talk to local schools, sponsor local sporting teams, and other
engagement activities". But it was somewhat surprising to find the headquarters PR department of a major global automotive manufacturer with such limited influence, budget, and scope. He stated frankly "we're not there yet". But,
like a number of other public communication senior executives interviewed,
he said "we're on a journey to two-way communication". In this case, the PR
manager had a vision of greater engagement. But the culture of an organization and its structure define how PR is conceived and practiced.

This is further borne out in examination of the PR function in another
industry in another country. A long-time PR practitioner, who was general
manager (GM) of corporate affairs at the time of this research with a national
wholesaler that supplies a large network of franchised stores, provided a sad
and sobering description of how some organizations do not listen. While his
title was 'corporate affairs', his role was highly media-oriented and his background includes considerable experience in public relations as well as related
practices such as public affairs. At the time of this study, the company was
involved in two major legal cases in relation to how it had treated some of its
franchised stores. Not a good start for a company that undertakes no market

research on the basis that "our franchised retailers are the eyes and ears of the company and give feedback on customers' needs and attitudes" (personal communication, March 6, 2015).

The GM of corporate affairs said "the only communication we have with our key stakeholders, our retailers, is our annual general meeting, and the CEO insists on a quarterly update newsletter which I don't think anyone reads". The company uses social media, but in "a very fragmented and broadcast way", according to the GM of corporate affairs. Social media are managed through three different units in the company—corporate affairs is responsible for its corporate Twitter and LinkedIn accounts; its marketing department uses a variety of social media for "online selling"; and a digital team has been created separately to operate the company's Facebook site. Furthermore, the digital team has been put under the control of the IT department. The GM, who is purportedly responsible for the company's overall public communication, said:

> They don't have a clue about communication. They are focussed on technology platforms and systems. We use Twitter and LinkedIn to put out announcements. There's a constant flow of little bits of information. We receive very little feedback or comment. (personal communication, March 6, 2015)

The company does do an annual staff survey conducted by an independent research firm. However, the GM of corporate affairs said there is little face-to-face communication between management and staff. "They don't go out and talk to people". He was even blunter in relation to listening, adding: "And they certainly don't listen to them" (personal communication, March 6, 2015).

So how does such a situation exist when an experienced communication professional is appointed to a senior management role in an organization? It occurs because lack of listening in the company extends to not listening to its own head of communication. The GM of corporate affairs said:

> Senior management doesn't listen to advice. They tell me that I need to develop a PR strategy to stop criticism. I tell them to stop doing what they are doing to cause the criticism, but they don't take any notice. I try to explain that they are asking me to put lipstick on a pig. In the end, it's still a pig. (personal communication, March 6, 2015)

This failure of senior management to take advice from communication specialists is an under-recognized factor in corporate communication and public relations literature, particularly critical analyses of practices such as public relations. For example, in reports of so-called PR disasters the blame is frequently attributed to the actions of, or lack of, public relations or corporate communication. But there is little analysis behind the scenes to identify what advice and recommendations were provided by PR and corporate communication staff or consultants. Public relations scholars including Bruce Berger (2005) and, more recently, Anne Gregory and Paul Willis (2013), Helen Sissons (2014), and Elspeth Tilley (2015) have noted that senior executives of organizations—referred to as the 'dominant coalition' in PR literature (Dozier et al., 1995, p. 15)—have the power to reject advice, and frequently do. In an analysis of PR ethics, Tilley identified the role of hierarchies and several types of what she calls "power silos" including the power that clients have over consultancies and power siloes inside organizations that can make it difficult for communication practitioners to get recommendations in front of decision makers (Tilley, 2015, pp. 85–86). Berger explains that this can restrict practitioners' ability to positively influence organization decision making. Similarly Gregory and Willis stress that, no matter how good the relationship between a PR practitioner and employer or client, whether senior management takes advice or not is a choice. This study found that at least in some so-called communication breakdowns, organization management had failed to take the advice of professional public communication staff. However, the cases analyzed also indicate that the thinking, language, and practices of public communication professionals are largely orientated to distributing information with the intention of informing, educating, persuading, and even propagandizing (i.e., speaking for organizations), rather than listening.

Parts of the preceding case study report are written in past tense because it is highly likely that the GM of corporate affairs will have left the organization by the time this book is published, as he was understandably very frustrated in his role and looking for alternative employment at the time of the interview.

Elsewhere, the digital and social media 'lead' (a senior vice president) and a vice president of the digital and social media team in the New York office of one of the world's leading PR firms focussed on digital and social media were blunt in discussing the use of social media and research in public relations, saying:

> The majority of what we do for clients is monitoring their own stuff—90 per cent of our clients use us for media relations. It's very media-centric. One major client issued

26 press releases in four days during a show. They considered it a success based on the volume of publicity, ... [A] lot of PR is still measured in terms of press clippings. And measurement is still mostly historical—looking back at what was done. (personal communication, January 22, 2015)

Their comments reveal strong organization-centricity and self-interest. They added: "We are monitoring and analyzing social media, but it's mostly output monitoring—that is, monitoring what the organization posts to see how much exposure it receives such as views, likes, shares, and so on". They also reported that they "track issues", but they described this in terms of identifying issues that clients could "jump on" for promotional gain. They referred to social media monitoring in this context as facilitating "news jacking" and "meme jacking" and gave an example.

For instance, if there is a story of someone famous or important taking a 'selfie' and we have a cell phone client, they can jump online and say 'hey, our cell phone can take wide-angle pics' or whatever to position their products. (personal communication, January 22, 2015)

Despite the interview taking place in the New York headquarters of the PR firm, the digital and social media team advised that they used only basic tools for social media monitoring including Google News and Factiva as well as some basic social media analysis tools such as Hootsuite, although they did note that some clients used Brandwatch and services such as Cision. The senior vice president and vice president of the PR firm were critical of some digital marketing, saying "a lot of digital marketing is e-mail spam. E-mail marketing is like drift-net fishing". They added somewhat more optimistically: "We are seeing more sophisticated uses of social media and more transactional uses. But that's a minority of organizations". This confirms findings of research by PR scholar Michel Kent, who says that, even in current best practice, "public relations professionals use social media as marketing and advertising tools" (2013, p. 340).

Media monitoring in what many UK government departments and agencies still call their 'press office' is primarily based on collecting quantitative metrics such as volume of articles and tweets (see Figure 3.8). The PR functions of NGOs and non-profit institutions, which generally have lower budgets than corporations and large government bodies, are even more basically evaluated, often with little more than counting of press clippings and broad categorization as positive, neutral, or negative (see Figure 3.9).

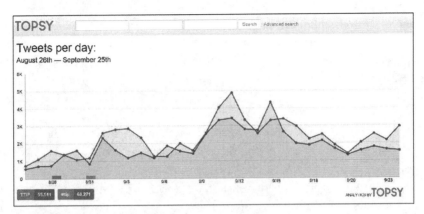

Figure 3.8. A sample of social media analysis.

Note: The organization name has been masked as part of de-identification requirements.
Source: Topsy.

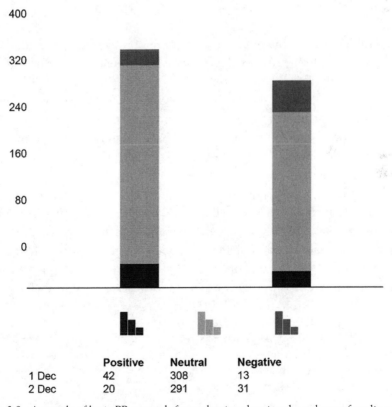

	Positive	Neutral	Negative
1 Dec	42	308	13
2 Dec	20	291	31

Figure 3.9. A sample of basic PR research for evaluation showing the volume of media coverage and the percentage of articles that are mostly positive, neutral, or negative.

Source: Meltwater.

Research by the Association for Measurement and Evaluation of Communication (AMEC) reported in 2015 confirms a number of these comments and provides a generalized picture of PR as focussed on media coverage, lacking research, and focussed on outputs. AMEC's PR industry research findings included:

- The majority of PR professionals analyze media coverage themselves;
- Advertising Value Equivalents (AVEs) are still the most used metric;
- The majority of PR practitioners do not measure outcomes, with budget cited as the main reason for not doing this. They mostly measure outputs (i.e., what they put out);
- While awareness of the existence of the Barcelona Principles (IPR, 2010) that committed the industry to rigorous measurement and evaluation using valid methods is high, knowledge of the detail is low (AMEC, 2015).

During the period of this research, Bob Jensen, a retiring senior communication executive from the US Department of Homeland Security, said in a guest lecture to public relations students that, in his experience, PR tends to focus on the "usual tactics". He listed these as "press releases, press conferences, print products such as posters, brochures and flyers, speaking at events, information on Web sites, and use of social media to push information"—and referred to traditional PR approaches as "the drumbeat of messaging" (Jensen, 2015). He said "missing tactics" in PR included "engaging influencers, real use of social media including monitoring and two-way communication, outreach to key stakeholders directly as well as through media, and developing relationships with key community leaders". He also criticized a preoccupation in PR with media publicity as a method of public communication. He reported an example of a US government PR unit proudly presenting a plan that was centred on interviews with the three leading TV networks in the US—ABC, CBS, and NBC. He told the class of PR students:

> The three major TV networks on average reach just 22 million people. That means there are 300 million people who have not been reached. Mass media reach only around 25 percent of the American public. You have to go beyond mass media to communicate with and engage communities. (Jensen, 2015)

Also, while this book was being written, the 2015 European Communication Monitor was released, a study of 2,253 communication professionals in 41

European countries, which contained questions on listening for the first time, largely at the instigation of this researcher as cited in the study. This reported that the predominant focus of PR and corporate communication practitioners is on "communication strategy", "plans", "implementation by communication departments", and "messaging", and that "listening is often neglected" (Zerfass, Verčič, Verhoeven, Moreno, & Tench, 2015, p. 54). The survey largely reflected the findings of this study in reporting that the predominant methods for organizational listening are media monitoring, social media monitoring, and stakeholder research, as well as "ad hoc listening activities" such as surveys and dialogues. This extensive survey reported that only 43 per cent of senior PR and corporate communication practitioners have any form of listening tasks in their job description and only 37.6 per cent have listening as an objective in their department (Zerfass et al., 2015, p. 61).

Mark Collinson, a partner in Compass Investor Relations in Los Angeles, who agreed to be quoted, openly acknowledges that there is a lack of listening even in specialist fields of PR such as investor relations, issue management, and crisis communication, saying:

> In the 10 years I have been listening to company conference calls I have never heard a company say, for example, 'here are some questions we have for you, our investors', or 'is there anything we have said that you find difficult to believe?' (personal communication, May 28, 2015)

He added in relation to issue management and crisis communication: "My experience is that few companies want to know what anybody thinks about a mistake, they want to tell people what they should think about the mistake" (personal communication, May 28, 2015).

Listening in Management

As reported in this study, many corporations have declared themselves to be 'customer focussed' or even 'customer centric'. Similarly, technology and design companies increasingly claim to be focussed on 'user-centred design' (Dourish, 2007) and health services providers advocate 'person-centred care' and 'person-centred environments' (Chenoweth et al., 2009, 2014). In the political domain, the views and actions of Barack Obama in the US and David Cameron's government in the UK, particularly the work of Francis Maude and Theresa May, have put open government and citizen engagement on the agenda during the early twenty-teens.

Most interviewees in this study stated that they had the support of their senior management and, despite some notable exceptions, expressed a belief that senior management took their recommendations and advice seriously. For instance, the deputy director of media and communication for a national government agency in the UK said "the amount of support we in 'comms' have had from HR and our chief executive has been second to none" (personal communication, September 24, 2014).

However, despite general statements of support and some noteworthy leadership from senior management in some organizations, the litmus test of listening in management is the extent to which the voices of stakeholders and publics are articulated to policy making and decision making. Does the organization ever change anything as a result of what it is told? That is not to say that organizations should or could do everything asked or expected of them. But for two-way communication to exist and for engagement, dialogue, and participation to matter and have any value, organizations have to (1) demonstrate listening and (2) act in response to what they hear on at least some occasions. Often—too often—one or both of these do not happen.

From the interviews conducted and from tracking the path of decisions and legislation in a number of companies and government departments, findings can be distilled into four key issues at senior management level. The first is a fear of unrealistic expectations among stakeholders and publics in relation to organizational listening. Some management and even a few senior communication executives believe that an invitation to speak to an organization with an accompanying commitment to listen will 'open the floodgates' of stakeholder and public comment and demands, which the organization will be unable to meet in terms of processing the volume or acting in a way that satisfies the interlocutors. For instance, the head of public response and feedback with one government agency said of open social media engagement:

> We don't encourage that simply because we haven't got the resources to punt back all day ... when you get a bit of a tidal wave of stuff. Once you start up an interaction, you've put your head above the parapet and somebody knows you're there, and then you get potentially deluged and you obviously can't answer it. (personal communication, February 3, 2015)

However, while some very large government departments and corporations attract high volumes of letters and customer contacts, most organizations typically hear from a vocal minority. Even large organizations often hear from only a small proportion of their stakeholders and publics. As one organization involved in a national infrastructure project potentially affecting more than 20 million people reported, *disengagement* is more common in many instances than engagement (personal communication, January 27, 2015).

A related concern is that an organization will be expected to do everything stakeholders and publics request or expect. Interestingly, other than a cantankerous few, there is evidence that most people have quite modest expectations. The senior US government communication official with more than 30 years of experience in US civil service public communication, including during major emergencies and crises, reported:

> In my experience, I find that the vast majority of people are happy just to be heard and have their opinion noted … that's part of being recognized and valued. Some of them just need to get something off their chest. (personal communication, January 19, 2015)

In cases of serious mishap or mistreatment, people expect action to be taken, as will be explored under 'Articulation of Listening to Decision Making and Policy Making' in Chapter 4. However, other research confirms that extreme and unreasonable demands are comparatively rare. For example, a review of complaints handling in the UK health system noted that, despite malpractices leading to deaths in some hospitals, "research tells us that people who make a complaint want to ensure that their concerns have been listened to and that the same thing won't happen again" (Commission for Healthcare Audit and Inspection, 2007, p. 28). The US government spokesperson acknowledged that "a small percentage of people are activists and, no matter what we do, they going to be vocal". But he reported from considerable experience that "the majority of people recognize that there's a limit to what government can do" (personal communication, January 19, 2015). Furthermore, no organization in this study reported negative feedback following genuine listening activities—that is, those that met the definitions of listening identified in this analysis. In fact, several organizations reported the opposite, such as staff at the large UK call centre who engage with citizens using personalized e-mail and social media messages as well as traditional telephone contact. They reported positive reactions even when requests could not be met, provided there was prompt considerate interaction by the organization (personal communication, February 5, 2015).

The second issue to overcome at a senior management level is selective organizational listening. The case of the insurance company reported in this chapter illustrates that some organizations listen very selectively and hear only what they want to hear. Along with the overriding importance of CEO-led organizational culture change, strategies employed by several of the organizations studied are instructive, such as video recording the comments of stakeholders and publics and presenting these directly to senior management so they can see first-hand what people are saying. Also, the use of research including regular measurement and evaluation of the attitudes, perceptions, and response of key stakeholders and publics, as implemented across UK government departments under the auspices of the Government Communication Service (GCS), is a best practice exemplar. This can be further improved by including more qualitative research and shifting from proxy measures such as social media 'sentiment' to direct audience research (e.g., focus groups, interviews, ethnography). There also remains a need to expand public consultation beyond the 'usual suspects' through *outreach* activities, as noted under 'Listening in Public Consultation'.

Senior communication executives in two organizations studied—one corporation and one government agency—reflexively noted that communication, research, and policy staff have a responsibility to persuasively present feedback to senior management and convince them of a need to listen. The director of communication of a government agency involved in regulation and standards affecting every adult in the country asked rhetorically: "We can be quite good at listening, but does that make us a listening organization ... how do we get the rest of the organization to hear what we hear?" He explained:

> We can do a fantastic citizens' forum process or research study. But of course the output is often a nice deck of slides which summarizes the methodology, the inputs, the findings. We've recognized that this isn't great for sharing with the rest of the organization. (personal communication, September 26, 2014)

What is his recommendation for getting senior management to sit up and take notice based on his experience? Like some others, he cited video clips showing customers, stakeholders, and citizens directly stating their views. He said video had more impact than written documents and slides, and the first-hand nature of recorded comments eliminated any doubts about the veracity of the information, such as concerns that 'interpretation' of the findings have exaggerated or distorted the information. Several other interviewees stressed the importance of data, particularly what they referred to as 'hard data' based on formal research and data analysis.

The third key issue that needs to be confronted in relation to senior management is that listening can be overridden by politics or other imperatives. This manifests as rejection of views, dead-ends when apparently widely supported proposals are suddenly overturned, and even, at times, broken promises. The director of communication for a UK government department described as "a £113 billion a year behemoth" with 18 ALBs connected to it noted that demonstrating listening was difficult at times. He said:

> We're a policy development organization … but you can do a huge amount of engagement and the final development of the policy can still be written over by a ministerial imperative. That then makes it look and feel like nobody's listening at all. (personal communication, September 25, 2014)

Similarly, in commercial organizations financial conditions and a number of other factors can prevent actions in response to stakeholder or public feedback and requests. To some extent, this is an inevitable practical reality. However, it does return the focus to communication. Too often when organizations cannot respond in the way stakeholders and publics expect, they fail to explain the reasons for not doing so. This leads to perceptions of *organizational deafness* even when an organization has considered the views of stakeholders and publics. Open communication, including discussion of why some requests and expectations cannot be met, is vitally important. It is part of dialogue and engagement. Closing 'the listening loop' is vitally important. If an organization is doing something as a result of listening, it should tell those involved and affected—and usually does. If it cannot, it is equally important to explain why.

An example of this common failure to close 'the listening loop' is the airline passenger survey. Selected passengers are regularly asked to fill out surveys providing feedback and comments on airline service. However, a review of two airlines' inflight magazines over the previous two years revealed there was not a single article reporting the findings of passenger surveys or reporting what the airlines had done as a result of passenger feedback. Analysis of frequent flyer newsletters of the airlines also revealed no response and a field test in which an international passenger survey was submitted, complete with passenger name and e-mail address, revealed that no personal thank you or response is sent to respondents. The impression created is that the organization is not listening. The organization may as well not distribute such surveys, as they can do more harm than good in terms of public perceptions.

While noting that organizations cannot always do what stakeholders and publics ask or expect, the fourth key issue in relation to listening in management is the articulation of the voices of stakeholders and publics to policy making and decision making in situations when there is substantial support and justification for what is sought. Stakeholders and publics need to see some resonance of their inputs. In simple terms, the voices of stakeholders and publics have to reach and be considered in the boardroom and the Cabinet Room and the party rooms and executive committee rooms. It is not enough that communication and consultation practitioners mouth dialogue and profess two-way relationships, engagement, participation, and collaboration. Noting that organizational listening is often delegated listening, particularly in large organizations, there has to be a connection from the metaphorical 'ears' of organizations (e.g., customer relations units or research teams) to their central nervous system and to their thinking brain and beating heart. Unless this articulation occurs, the voices of stakeholders and publics, even when heard, fast become fading echoes in dead-end corridors and hallways between communication staff and organization management.

This dual requirement to both demonstrate action informed by listening and explain why action cannot be taken in some cases draws attention to a confusion that commonly exists in relation to two-way communication. *Two-way* does not mean only two steps or stages—a binary of one party speaking while the other listens followed by the second party speaking while the first listens. Two-way denotes the bidirectional requirement of speaking and listening. In terms of steps or stages, communication that is effective and leads to engagement and dialogic needs to involve at least three steps, or more. For example, if an individual or group sends a message to an organization and the organization responds (two-way, two steps), but the organization does not hear further from the individual or group, the organization does not know whether the former was satisfied with the response. They may be dissatisfied, or even more concerned than before they contacted the organization. Similarly, if an organization sends a message and an individual or group responds (two-way, two steps), but does not hear further from the organization, the individual or group does not know whether the organization received, accepted, or appreciated the response.

Two of the interviewees in this study referred to "three-way communication" including the deputy director of media and communication for a national environmental agency (personal communication, September 24, 2014). Also, the concept was discussed by social psychologists Alex Gillespie and Tom Reader at the London School of Economics and Political Science in relation to analyzing complaints (personal communication, June 18, 2014, and March 19, 2015). The argument goes that two-way communication is better than one-way—the latter being information transmission and not really communication at all. Two-way ensures that others get to speak and, as argued in this analysis, both sides should listen to the other when they speak. However, dialogue, engagement, and true listening leading to understanding and relationships require more than a two-way binary 'he said, she said' process (i.e., one turn each). What these proponents are referring to is not so much three-way communication, but *three-step, two-way* communication. Three-step, or multistep, two-way communication is a requirement for dialogue and conversation that lead to engagement and relationships. (See Table 3.7 for an overview of one-step, two-step, and three/multi-step, two-way communication.)

Table 3.7. A summary of one-step, one-way communication (non-communication), two-step, two-way communication, and three-step/multistep, two-way communication.

Step	Type of communication	Comment
1.	*One-step, one-way (non-communication)* An organization distributes a message, OR An individual or group sends a message to an organization	Neither the organization nor the individual or group knows whether its message was received or, if it was, whether it was understood, appreciated, and accepted, or alternatively misunderstood, disliked, or rejected. Both sides are oblivious to the views of the other.
1. 2.	*Two-step, two-way (Type A)* An organization distributes a message The recipient responds (e.g., with a comment, like, follow, share)	The organization knows that its message was received. Second, the content and tone of the response indicates to the organization the recipient's reaction. However, the recipient does not know whether the organization received, accepted, or appreciated its response.
1. 2.	*Two-step, two-way (Type B)* An individual or group sends a message to an organization The organization responds	The individual or group knows that its message was received. The content and tone of the response indicates the organization's reaction. However, the organization does not know whether the individual or group received, accepted, or appreciated its response (e.g., are they satisfied?).

Step	Type of communication	Comment
	Three-step/multistep, two-way (Type A)	The organization knows that its message was received. Second, the content and tone of the response indicate the recipient's reaction. Third, the individual or group knows that the organization accepted and appreciated its response, or alternatively further points are raised. The exchange may continue and build mutual understanding and engagement.
1.	An organization distributes a message	
2.	The recipient responds	
3.	The organization acknowledges or comments further	
4.	The recipient comments further, etc.	
	Three-step/multistep, two-way (Type B)	The individual or group knows that its message was received. The content and tone of the response indicate the organization's reaction. Third, the organization knows that the individual or group accepted and appreciated its response, or alternatively further points are raised. The exchange may continue and build mutual understanding and engagement.
1.	An individual or group sends an organization a message	
2.	The organization responds	
3.	The individual or group acknowledges or comments further	
4.	The organization comments further, etc.	

Summary of Research Findings

This research identified a number of significant findings. The major findings derived from analysis of interviews with organization executives and relevant documents from the 36 case studies are summarized as follows, together with insights informed by comparison of these case studies with research literature reviewed in Chapter 1 and Chapter 2. Two further findings are identified in the next chapter, which examines models of public communication and consultation and the benefits of creating an architecture of listening and doing the work of listening in organizations.

Key Findings

1. Organizations including government departments and agencies, corporations, and some NGOs and major institutions spend millions and even hundreds of millions of dollars, pounds, and euros a year on

communication, both internally and particularly for public communication. This is done through media advertising, direct marketing, customer relations, political communication, public consultation, corporate communication, organizational communication, and public relations.

2. Organizations extensively 'talk the talk' of *two-way* communication, engagement, dialogue, consultation, collaboration, and relationships with their stakeholders and publics. Terms such as 'engagement' are buzzwords in marketing, corporate, government, and organizational communication literature, and a number of professional communication practices such as public relations are specifically theorized as two-way engagement and dialogue.

3. However, organization-public communication is overwhelmingly organizational *speaking* to disseminate organizations' messages using a *transmissional* or broadcast model. Analysis shows that, overall, around 80 per cent of organizational resources devoted to public communication are focussed on *speaking* (i.e., distributing the organization's information and messages). Even social media, which were developed specifically for two-way interaction, are used by organizations primarily to disseminate their messages. Some organizations acknowledge that up to 95 per cent of their so-called communication is information distribution (i.e., speaking), while best cases have a 60/40 speaking/listening ratio. It can be said that organizations construct and deploy an *architecture of speaking* composed of internal professional communication staff as well as specialist agencies and consultants using increasingly sophisticated information systems, tools, and technologies.

4. Voice is widely identified as fundamental to democracy and social equity, constitutionalized and legislated in many countries as a right to 'freedom of speech' and advocated in calls to 'speak up', 'have your say', and 'tell us what you think'. Despite assumptions and expectations that expression of voice is reciprocated with listening, voice is widely misunderstood and practiced as speaking, with little or no attention to who is listening and how listening can be effectively accomplished.

5. This is particularly the case in relation to organizations, which play a central role in industrialized and post-industrial societies (Bimber et al., 2012). Organizational listening is essential in developed contemporary societies, particularly in democratic societies, in which

citizens, customers, employees, members, shareholders, and other stakeholders and stakeseekers have to deal with public and private sector organizations every day.

6. Most organizations listen sporadically at best, often poorly, and sometimes not at all. Few 'walk the talk' of two-way communication, dialogue, conversation, engagement, consultation, collaboration, and relationships. Listening, which requires (a) *recognition* of others' rights and views; (b) *acknowledgement*; (c) paying *attention*; (d) *interpreting* what is said in order to gain (e) *understanding* of others' views; (f) giving *consideration* to what is said; and (g) an appropriate *response*, is so rare that it can be said there is a 'crisis of listening' in contemporary societies.

7. When organizational listening does occur it is mostly undertaken through (a) customer relations; (b) research; (c) social media monitoring and analysis; and (d) public consultation, as well as through representatives and field staff who directly interface with citizens, stakeholders, and members of organizations' publics.

8. However, even in these practices, listening is mostly undertaken for *instrumental* organization-centric purposes—that is, to solve particular practical problems and serve the interests of the organization. For example:

   a. Research in public communication practices is administrative, conducted to achieve organization goals such as identifying populist opinion to help win elections and understanding consumer psychology in order to sell more products and services;

   b. Customer relations involves considerable listening, but in traditional approaches this has been predominantly designed to resolve complaints, mostly through placation rather than substantive change. Contemporary approaches to customer interaction have shifted increasingly to customer relationship management (CRM) designed primarily to gain repeat sales and 'upsell' customers to higher-level products and services. Customer relations and CRM involve listening, but this is mainly involves what could be called *strategic listening*;

   c. Social media monitoring and analysis are conducted primarily for measuring the volume and amplitude of an organization's own voice, for identifying and targeting influencers who can help organizations achieve their goals, and for gaining 'intelligence' and insights to help organizations 'jump on to' issues to promote their brands, products, services, and messages. Several organizations spoke openly about "news jacking" and "meme jacking", with much less attention paid to learning and gaining feedback to inform organizational change and adaptation;

d. Despite being one of the public communication practices most explicitly orientated to listening, public consultation primarily listens to the 'usual suspects', who are elites and the loud voices of organized professional groups, with many individuals and groups ignored, silent, or disengaged. Also, many public consultations result in no change to original plans, policies, and projects.

9. Fields of practice that explicitly claim to facilitate *two-way* communication, *engagement*, *dialogue*, and create and maintain *relationships* such as public relations, corporate communication, and relationship marketing are overwhelmingly one-way information transmission representing the voice of organizations. This substantial theory-practice gap demands transformative change in specialist public communication fields such as corporate communication and public relations for them to become more ethical and socially responsible.

10. Organizational listening cannot be achieved simply by adding a listening tool or *solution*, such as automated software applications, listening posts, or a tokenistic 'have your say' page on a Web site. Organizational listening has cultural, procedural, political, structural, resource, skill, and technological dimensions. Effective organizational listening requires what has been identified in this study as an *architecture of listening* composed of a number of key elements that need to be designed into an organization and be deployed in a coherent complementary way. The elements and characteristics of an architecture of listening are discussed in detail in the next chapter.

11. Furthermore, listening is work. Once an architecture of listening is in place, organizational staff need to undertake the work of listening as well as the work of speaking—particularly staff involved in communication roles such as organizational communication, corporate communication, and public relations.

12. There is a range of technologies that can enable and support organizational listening as part of an architecture of listening. Tools, systems, and applications include simple do-it-yourself (DIY) social media tracking software through to sophisticated e-consultation

applications, 'big data' analysis, and sense making technologies. In addition to those listed in this chapter, a number of advanced tools and methods are discussed in Chapter 4.

13. A broad observation of this study, which included a substantial number of government departments and agencies, is that initiatives for greater transparency and *open government* that collectively have become a zeitgeist of contemporary Western democracies are largely interpreted and implemented as providing more and more information to citizens. This can result in information overload and hinder rather than help citizens. Open government needs to be interpreted as, first and foremost, being open to listen to citizens and shaping policies and decisions after taking account of the range of views, needs, and interests in society. Second, open government needs to involve ongoing two-way communication and engagement.

14. Engagement is mostly interpreted as engagement by stakeholders and publics with an organization, rather than a two-way street. Most organizations fail to see a need to genuinely engage with their stakeholders and publics. Engagement needs to be rethought in most organizations and recognized as a two-way process.

15. Government departments and agencies and even some NGOs are adopting the term 'customers' for citizens they serve and with whom they interact. While well intentioned in most cases, whether this leads to improved civil service and social equity is questionable, as it brings with it the principles and values of neoliberalism and capitalism including a focus on financial factors, efficiency, cost-effectiveness, and competition.

Operational Findings

16. Organizational culture is a starting point for effective organizational listening—and the most important single factor in creating an open listening culture is a progressive chief executive who is supportive of two-way communication. However, it is also important to have highly skilled, research-orientated, ethical communication professionals who act as advocates and evangelists in their organizations. Together, the two influences create a *virtuous circle* for change.

17. Public consultation needs to be wider than current formal consultation processes to be inclusive and equitable. It needs to include

proactive *outreach* to affected groups and individuals—not simply inviting and passively collecting and collating comments, feedback, and submissions, which are mostly provided by the 'usual suspects' (e.g., organized industry and professional groups such as business associations, unions, and lobbyists). Other research confirms that "there is limited understanding of public participation as an informal, or organic phenomenon whereby members of the public seek to engage in debates outside of formal mechanisms" (Crompton, 2015, p. 27).

18. Institutionalized political communication through political parties and organized political events similarly needs to be broadened to engage with the wider electorate. Current practices such as tours, visits, and rallies that are typically attended by "the party faithful", who are organized as "cheer squads", and highly staged events and meetings with official representatives, mean that politicians and parties hear the loud voices of power elites and the platitudes of sycophants, shallowly supplemented by small sample (and often misleading) polls. Thus, many political representatives and leaders gain a narrow and sterilized version of citizens' views.

19. Contrary to some claims and concerns, a commitment to organizational listening does not open the floodgates and deluge an organization with comments, requests, and expectations that it cannot process, nor create expectations that it will agree with all comments and comply with all requests. Organizations report that the greatest challenge in public communication and consultation is the *disengaged* rather than the engaged and that most people have quite modest expectations.

20. As well as undertaking effective ethical listening as defined in this study, organizations need to close 'the listening loop' by communicating (1) what was done as a result of listening, and/or (2) why some things that are requested cannot be done. When organizations do not report back to stakeholders and publics they risk "the damage that silence can create" (personal communication, September 24, 2014).

21. Closing the listening loop requires organizations and professional staff involved in public communication to recognize that two-way communication is more than two-step communication (i.e., a binary exchange). Dialogue and conversation, which lead to engagement and relationships, require *three-step or multistep, two-way* communication (i.e., party A speaks; party B responds; party A acknowledges and accepts, or raises further points; party B responds further). See Table 3.7.

22. No organization in this study reported imminent or likely increases in budget or resources for communication with their key stakeholders and publics. To the contrary, most reported recent budget cuts and reductions in communication staff, and most expect budget restraint to continue into the foreseeable future. This indicates that any change to how public communication is enacted, including creation of an *architecture of listening*, must be achieved with current or even reduced resources. However, a number of organizations are demonstrating that increased communication effectiveness can be gained through reallocation of resources and prioritization.

23. Measurement and evaluation aid the processes of prioritizing and allocating resources to the most effective and impactful activities. Without research-based measurement and evaluation, organizations are likely to spend time and resources on ineffective and unnecessary activities.

24. The interrelated processes of measurement and evaluation—a major focus in public communication practice and widely seen as lacking in scale and rigour—are themselves exercises in listening. Measurement and evaluation of the effectiveness of communication involve listening to feedback and response and then, contingent on what is learned, responding in a way that takes account of the views of others. However, measurement and evaluation, along with research generally, are often under-utilized or used in narrow, instrumental ways to gain answers to self-serving questions and tell organizations only what they want to know.

25. Mandating and formalization of evaluation in an organization creates what this study calls the 'evaluation factor'. This is a significant influence that affects all planning and implementation of communication activities when evaluation is built into work processes. It exerts its effects quite simply: when practitioners know that their work and activities will be rigorously evaluated, they pay much more attention to formative research to understand audiences and identify what is likely to be most effective, as well as to careful planning. They are much less likely to undertake activities with low likelihood of success, so wastage and failures are reduced even before evaluation is undertaken.

26. Measurement and evaluation should incorporate measurement and evaluation of an organization's responses to the requests, needs,

interests, and concerns of its stakeholders and publics—not only the response of stakeholders and publics to the organization's communication and actions. However, this rarely occurs. Measurement and evaluation are mostly conceptualized narrowly as instrumental exercises to assess an organization's impact on others.

27. Communication staff who have been successful in implementing interactive social media practices in conservative companies and government departments and agencies use a 'start small and roll out' approach. Several government departments and agencies reported training a team of 10–30 staff who then act as 'champions', 'advocates', and trainers for others. Also, several reported that providing private coaching for senior management in social media substantially changes the culture of an organization and its social media engagement.

28. Another effective strategy being adopted is using peer support and crowdsourcing to resource some functions such as customer relations— i.e., engaging other customers in answering basic customer questions and sharing information online. While closely monitoring peer-to-peer communication to avoid distribution of misinformation, some organizations are finding that crowdsourcing can answer many customer questions and resolve some problems, thereby reducing the work and resources required of the organization.

29. Flexible working hours including weekend shifts are being increasingly adopted and becoming necessary in communication and customer relations departments of organizations and their agencies such as social media monitoring and analysis firms in response to the 24/7 nature of online communication.

This chapter has reported the key insights gained from close examination of the 36 organizations studied in the UK, the US, and Australia. The purpose of this study is not simply to conduct a critique of organization-public communication with a particular focus on listening, however. Informed by the extensive range of literature reviewed in Chapters 1 and 2 as well as the findings of research reported in this chapter, the next chapter takes a further important step in the Organizational Listening Project by identifying how organizational listening can be improved and operationalized in an ethical, effective, and efficient way.

Notes

1. The bill received Royal Assent and became the Health and Social Care Act 2012 on March 27, 2012, but not before substantial amendments based on a belated 'Listening Exercise'. The controversy surrounding this policy is reported in Nicholas Timmins's (2012) book *Never Again? The Story of the Health and Social Care Act 2012: A Study in Coalition Government and Policy Making*.

2. As noted in Chapter 1, the terms 'communication' and 'communications' are used interchangeably in many organizations to denote face-to-face or mediated communication with their stakeholders and publics. The plural term is, however, widely used in relation to communication technologies and telecommunications. The singular term 'communication' is preferred in most discussions of human communication and is used in this book.

3. Stanley Deetz (1982) advocated critical interpretative research in organizational communication in a seminal journal article more than 30 years ago.

4. Full intercoder reliability assessment, a process recommended for quantitative content analysis (Neuendorf, 2002), was not carried out, as this study was qualitative.

5. This case was derived from opportunistic convenience sampling, but was included in the study because it was within the sampling frame and met the criteria for the third method of analysis—field experiments involving contact with organizations in relation to genuine inquiries, requests for information, or complaints.

6. While administrative research has been embraced by some scholars, notably Paul Lazarsfeld, it is criticized as having a narrow focus on improving processes in an organization and lacking a critical perspective (e.g., Smythe & Van Dinh, 1983).

7. Dashboards are arrangements of charts, graphs, and data on a single screen or in a brief document presenting key metrics such as the volume, tone, and trend of media coverage, public opinion, and reputation scores.

8. The Government Communication Service (GCS) replaced the UK Government Communication Network in January 2014 (HM Government, 2014a, p. 3).

9. There is research support for this contention that the generation referred to as Millennials have more flexible attitudes towards working hours. A global study by the world's largest online workspace, Elance-oDesk (2015), reported that young workers are more agile, innovative, and flexible than traditional Industrial Age workers.

10. The boundaries between software applications and vendor-supplied services are increasingly blurring. A number of these products are what are termed 'software as a service' (SaaS), which is offered online by vendors on a subscription basis. Also, some vendors offer both software tools for do-it-yourself media monitoring and analysis as well as full services.

11. The full name of the convention is 'The United Nations Economic Commission for Europe (UNECE) Convention on Access to Information, Public Participation in Decision Making and Access to Justice in Environmental Matters'. It was adopted at a meeting on June 25, 1998, in the Danish city of Aarhus.

12. This corporate plan published by the UK government department responsible for the project on behalf of the company is de-identified as part of ethics approval commitment. It is not listed in the reference list because of this requirement.

13. This major report published by the UK government department responsible for the project is de-identified as part of ethics approval commitment. It is not listed in the reference list because of this requirement.

14. Prior to 2010, UK government public communication was under the direction of a permanent secretary, the most senior civil service rank in government ministries. In other countries, the equivalent is principal secretary, deputy secretary, or departmental secretary. In December 2012, Alex Aiken was appointed as executive director to head government communication, as reported in this analysis—a lower rank than permanent secretary. However, restructuring of the UK Government Communication Service (GCS) in 2014, new strategies introduced, and a direct line of reporting to the Minister of the Cabinet Office and to Number 10 Downing Street ensure major focus and priority on UK government communication.

15. A 'back door' is an access route into computer programs that bypasses normal log-in and password requirements. These consist of default passwords and hidden parts of programs that are often left by programmers for their own use, but that can be accessed by hackers.

16. The UK Constitutional Reform and Governance Act 2010 (2010) states that the Civil Service Code requires civil servants to "carry out their duties for the assistance of the administration … whatever its political complexion" with integrity and honesty and with impartiality, whereas special advisers appointed by ministers are not required to be impartial. Other democratic countries have similar legislation.

· 4 ·

CREATING AN 'ARCHITECTURE OF LISTENING' AND DOING THE WORK OF LISTENING

The challenges of large-scale listening have been referred to several times in this analysis. These are not to be underestimated. Indeed, organizational listening could well be described as a *wicked problem*—a notion that was first outlined in management literature by C. West Churchman (1967) and defined in more detail in the context of social planning by Horst Rittel and Melvin Webber (1973). There are many characteristics of a wicked problem, but those considered key are the following: (1) there are no totally true, false, or perfect solutions; (2) wicked problems are usually unique; (3) there is no 'stopping rule' for wicked problems (i.e., a precise mechanism to know the optimal time to stop or continue a resolution process); and (4) every wicked problem is a symptom of or linked to other problems (Rittel & Webber, 1973). Furthermore, wicked problems are mostly social and humanistic, unlike scientific problems that can be resolved using systematic approaches and following precise rules such as mathematical formulae. So an overall feature of wicked problems is that they are complex and usually require multifaceted approaches.

There is often a tendency to seek simple solutions to problems, however. In the case of poor organizational listening, one such approach is to see technology as the answer. Technology, particularly digital technology, is being hailed as a panacea in many fields of politics, science, and social science, illustrated in slogans such as 'digital first' (GNM, 2011), 'mobile first', and 'cloud first' (Kundra, 2015). There is little doubt that new technologies will play a significant part in future organization-public communication and can empower customers and citizens to some extent. For instance, former chief information officer for the Obama administration, Vivek Kundra (2015), says that in future people will be able to walk into a hospital and call up data on a mobile device showing the mortality rate of that hospital. This might help address problems such as those identified in the Mid Straffordshire hospitals investigation in the UK (Stationery Office, 2013) and in the research by Tom Reader and Alex Gillespie cited in Chapter 3. However, while *organizational deafness*—the inability to hear the voices of stakeholders and publics—might be overcome through systems and technological tools, organizational listening also requires a number of other elements and characteristics.

From several hundred hours spent conducting interviews followed by several months of coding and analyzing interview transcripts, reading interview transcripts in full, comparing statements with the author's own notes and organization documents, checking information against Web sites and online documents, and then reflecting on findings in the context of the extensive literature review outlined in Chapters 1 and 2, eight key elements of an *architecture of listening* for organizations are identified. These elements are collectively referred to as an architecture of listening as they need to be designed into an organization and deployed in a coherent complementary way. They cannot be simply 'tacked on' to an organization like fake gargoyles on a building. Applying one or a few elements will not achieve effective ethical organizational listening. On the other hand, proposing an architecture of listening to facilitate large-scale organization-public communication is not intended to be prescriptive or suggest a single solution. The overall framework of an architecture of listening not only leaves room for, but encourages visionary approaches, innovation, and creativity. Like built architecture, there can be many forms and styles and infinitely varying scales. Furthermore, it is not only about creating structures, but also about creating spaces in which people can interact with organizations in mutually beneficial ways and an environment that is welcoming and inclusive. An architecture of listening counterbalances the brutalist architecture of speaking that characterizes a number of large organizations and identifies fundamental principles and elements for creating a more harmonious, productive, and equitable society.

Culture of Listening

A conclusion that became apparent early in this study is that organizational listening is grounded first and foremost in the culture of an organization. Culture manifests itself in several ways. The most debilitating is the case in which senior management simply does not want to listen—either because senior executives feel they know all they need to know or, more often, because they feel that those speaking to them have nothing worthwhile to contribute. Jacques Rancière (1998) argued that:

> The problem is knowing whether the subjects who count in the interlocution 'are' or 'are not', whether they are speaking or just making a noise. The quarrel has nothing to do with more or less transparent or opaque linguistic contents; it has to do with consideration of the speaking being as such. (p. 50)

What Rancière is saying, in the simplified yet eloquent words of Stephen Coleman, is that "the snooty dismissal of the cacophonous public is not a critique of the linguistic or semantic sophistication of their utterances, but a cultural repulse" (2013a, p. 220). It represents a refusal to accept that those ignored have a speaking part in the matter under discussion based on the view that what they have to say has no value or validity.

It is important that senior management of organizations, as well as their communication staff, recognize that various groups, constituencies, and individuals have a right to speak and to be afforded understanding and consideration. Common vulgar terms used to describe people external to formally recognized groups such as 'the great unwashed' (Bulwer-Lytton, 1830; "Great unwashed", 2015), *hoi polloi* ("Hoi polloi", 2015), the "madding crowd" (Hardy, 1874), 'punters' (Hirst & Harrison, 2007, p. 255), 'the seething masses' (Lloyd, 2012), 'the herd', 'the mob', and so on reflect an elitist culture that sees no reason to listen to such groups or their members. While the neoliberal neologism of 'customers' as a generalized term for citizens is problematic in one sense, it at least reflects a recognition of people as having some rights and power—albeit as *consumers* valued in economic terms. But those to whom organizations ought to listen include many who are not customers, or investors or shareholders, or employees. They may be local residents and communities, farmers or fishermen impacted by infrastructure projects, motorists delayed in traffic jams, commuters suffering from poor public transport, environmentalists concerned about pollution and loss of habitat, working mothers struggling to pay child care fees, young people who cannot find employment, and so on. They have rights and expectations. In a just and civil society their voices should be listened to even when they do not help a company meet next quarter's sales targets or help a politician get re-elected. Culture in this sense is similar to Stephen Coleman's identification of ideology as a barrier to listening (2013b, p. 3). In addition to altruistic reasons, there is also a strong practical argument for having an organization culture that is open and disposed to listening, as will be discussed in the final chapter.

Beyond giving recognition to others, a culture that is open to listening as defined by researchers (Bickford, 1996; Honneth, 2007; Husband, 1996, 2009; Silverstone, 2007) *acknowledges* others, pays *attention* to them, tries to *understand* their views, gives genuine *consideration* to what they say, and *responds* in an appropriate way. As noted in Chapter 3, response may be agreement and compliance, or it may be disagreement and rejection of views. In the latter circumstances, it is reasonable to expect that rejection of what an organization hears is based on good faith and good reasons and that those reasons are explained in two-way communication.

A key factor in determining the culture of organizations and their level of listening to stakeholders and publics identified in this study is the attitude and approach of the CEO. The corporations and government departments and agencies moving most from broadcast models of information transmission to engagement including listening all identified a key role played by their CEO. The Fortune 500 'telco' that has radically shifted from traditional newsletters to videos, which are largely staff-generated, identified the active role of its chairman and CEO in supporting and participating in the change. The deputy director of media and communication for an environmental agency participating in the study described the role of its CEO in "bringing in a new culture" as "huge" (personal communication, September 24, 2014). The CEO of a state environmental agency in another country asked to personally participate in interviews conducted with his communication and public consultation staff, saying engagement was among his highest priorities (personal communication, November 19, 2014).

Cultural understandings of *communication* also substantially shape organization-public interactions and specifically influence propensity to listen. Conceptualization of communication as transmitting, sending, broadcasting, distributing, and disseminating information and as telling, informing, presenting, showing, convincing, persuading, and educating is endemic in contemporary societies, as noted in this analysis. Of course, communication involves all of those things. Governments, corporations, NGOs, and non-profit organizations do sometimes need to *inform* people (one-way transmission of information), such as advising them of new policies, issuing health warnings as in the case of Ebola outbreaks, and telling people about new products and services. Sometimes they need to *persuade* people—e.g., to drive safely, eat healthily, donate to charity, register as an organ donor, as well as buy legitimate products and services. But communication is more than 'telling and selling'. There also needs to be listening. This research clearly indicates that there is too much telling and selling, and too little listening.

The legitimacy of the state in democracies, the health of civil society, and the success and sustainability of markets depend on engagement between people and between people and organizations. And engagement requires dialogue—it is rarely if ever achieved through monologue. Dialogue involves each side in any interaction having a chance to speak while the other listens, with a view to achieving understanding and acceptance, or tolerance even when agreement and consensus are not possible. As first year communication students are told (but seem to forget as soon as they leave the academy), real communication is about exchanged and shared meaning, not messages; it is an outcome, not a barrage of outputs. This fundamental misunderstanding of what communication entails is a deeply rooted cultural impediment to dialogue, engagement, and participation.

Organization centricity is a further cultural factor that creates organizational verbosity. Influenced by modernist beliefs in the superiority of experts and singular notions of truth based on rationality and scientific data, organizations believe that what they have to say is far more important and far more informed than what others have to say. In reality, many organizations chatter and gush like excited teenagers about relatively banal and mundane aspects of their products and services. And, like egocentric adolescents, most cannot stop talking and when they do talk, which is frequently or incessantly, they mostly talk about themselves.

For instance, the glossy printed Communication Strategy 2014/15 of the UK Department of Health describes its vision and purpose in its foreword as "show how the department continues to play a fundamental role at the heart of a successful health and care system" (Department of Health, 2014, p. 5) [emphasis added]. On the next page, it introduces the four sections of the document: "Our offer"; "our policy programmes", "our priorities", "our corporate programmes" (p. 6). The department is front and centre. The people it serves are somewhere 'out there'. The communication strategy does state "understand audiences" as one of its objectives, but this conceptualization of people such as workers in the health care system and patients is semantically significant. Their part in any interaction is confined to the role of audiences—generally understood as reception and listening, usually in silence. Furthermore, the purpose of understanding audiences is explained as "we will map out key stakeholder and digital influencers so that we can identify and prioritize the people who will make the biggest difference to audience opinion" (p. 17). This reflects the instrumental utilitarian approach to communication frequently adopted by organizations that involves listening to stakeholders and publics only insofar as it yields information that is useful to the organization in achieving its goals. It does need to be noted that an organization such as a department of health has a role in informing and persuading publics, such as campaigns to reduce obesity. It is to be expected that some or even much communication by such an organization might be one-way and persuasive. But beyond listening to gain intelligence and insights to inform the organization's campaigns, where is the voice of health care patients, their families, health care workers, and taxpayers who fund the health system?

In a digital innovation forum at the University of Technology Sydney in 2015, the then Australian minister for communications, Malcolm Turnbull, emphasized several times that transformational change requires a change of culture, not just an adoption of technology. While Turnbull, who is known as a champion of digital communications technology and architect of the Digital Transformation Office in Australia, reflected the neoliberal thinking of contemporary democratic governments in highlighting the need for organizations to become "customer focussed", his focus on culture, not just technology, is salutary (Turnbull, 2015).

Social psychologist Alex Gillespie insightfully comments that *organizational maturity* is a key factor in enabling organizations to listen (personal communication, June 18, 2014). He notes that listening inevitably requires, in the words of Hans Georg Gadamer, hearing and even "recognizing that I must accept some things that are against me" (as cited in Craig & Muller, 2007, pp. 219–220). Organizational listening also requires an ability to deal with emotional and even angry voices at times. Voice cannot be confined to reasoned rational argument and scientific facts without marginalizing much of the population. Organizations with experienced confident management are more likely to be able to deal with open dialogue and engagement than those with inexperienced and insecure management. Similarly, organizations with well-established systems, and corporations that are mature and financially stable, potentially have a greater capacity to handle diverse opinions, demands, requests, and expectations—although 'coping mechanisms' that are sensitive and mutually facilitating need to be developed.

Don Bartholomew, former vice president for digital and social media research with PR and analysis firm Ketchum in the US, proposed a *social media listening maturity model* loosely drawing on Everett Rogers's (1962) *diffusion of innovations* theory and Forrester's social maturity model (Corcoran, 2011). Bartholomew (2012) advocated a progression in social media listening through five stages from (1) reactive alerts to (2) monitoring, (3) social listening, (4) strategic listening, and, finally, (5) social intelligence. However, while usefully drawing attention to the need for organizations to progress beyond reactive alerts that notify them whenever their brand, products, or tracked issues are mentioned, this model reflects the instrumental approach critiqued in this analysis in which organizations seek to listen simply to gain strategic benefit for themselves. Bartholomew said as much in commenting: "Listening is not the goal, social intelligence is", adding "social intelligence informs actions taken by marketing or some other area of the business" (2012, para. 4).

The broader notion of organizational maturity proposed here could also be termed *organizational resilience* and some principles from resilience theory (e.g., Castro & Murray, 2010; Masten, 2001; Rutter, 1985) may be able to be productively applied to an organizational context to build capacity for more open engagement including listening—albeit this is applying the concept of resilience well outside its traditional usage in the context of governmentality and governance (Anderson, 2015; Howell, 2015). However, as Ben Anderson says in reviewing discussion in a 2014 special issue of *Politics* focussed on resilience, "there may be various types or forms of resilience" (2015, p. 60). Instead of focussing on *responsibilizing* individuals and communities, the traditional approach of resilience strategies along with high-level top-down initiatives of the state (Howell, 2015), this analysis suggests that all types of organizations need to be more responsible for discursive engagement with, as well as responsive to, their stakeholders and publics. To do so, organizations need to have the resources—cultural as well as social, technological, skills, etc.—to effectively engage with diverse interests, needs, and demands.

In the case of online listening, a number of researchers argue that changes in institutional values and practices are required for governments to be responsive. Public sector organizations are reportedly "technocratic" (Brainard, 2003), "law enforcing" (Charalabidis & Loukis, 2012), and "managerial" (Chadwick & May, 2003), as well as risk averse and hierarchal (Hepburn, 2014). This translates into what Hepburn calls a "sclerotic institutional anxiety associated with new ICTs" (p. 96) that does not fit with the open, egalitarian culture of Web 2.0 and social media. Reluctance by government to listen to and engage with citizens online is also likely to be related to the finding that the majority of online citizen participation is focussed on opposing government plans (Evans-Cowley, 2010). Also, online citizens and governments often subscribe to different models of democracy. Online citizens and communities typically seek to enact a participatory model of democracy, sometimes incorporating agonistic democracy, while most governments in Western democratic states adhere to representative or liberal models of democracy. Governments today have to contend with forms of interaction and language that are substantially different to traditional political participation (Bekkers, 2004; Charalabidis & Loukis, 2012; Saebo & Nilsen, 2004). Political scientist Ronald Deibert concludes that "such a profound transformation in the world political landscape raises fundamental questions about the basic structures of political participation and representation" (2000, p. 271). Much the same can be said in relation to corporate and organizational communication between big companies and institutions and their stakeholders and publics.

Nevertheless, while noting these cultural conflicts in online participation, which is an increasing mode of engagement, this research found that many government organizations and companies are adapting and undergoing considerable cultural change. This is being aided and abetted by strong leadership in some cases, such as the commitment of UK political and civil service leaders noted in this analysis, the cultural change in US politics and government instituted by Barack Obama, and the personal leadership of a sizeable number of dedicated communication practitioners. Ideally, a *virtuous circle* can be formed to foster organizational listening involving top-down inspirational leadership by senior management combined with upwards pressure from reformist and evangelical communication practitioners who understand and value communication, rather than information transmission and propaganda.

Policies for Listening

With a culture that is open to listening in place, an organization then needs to develop policies that give effect to the values and principles espoused and call for implementation of organizational listening. Ideally, policies flow directly from the CEO or equivalent in government such as a departmental secretary or even a minister. This gives them weight and importance so that they are taken seriously within the organization. The implementation of evaluation of communication under the auspices of the Government Communication Service (GCS) in the UK is a good example of clear directives coming from the top, backed up by implementation procedures and requirements for performance measurement and reporting (Government Communication Service, 2014a).

As well as being necessary for guiding internal behaviour including prioritization of activities, policies serve as invitations to those external to the organization. Unless an organization makes a clear public commitment to listening and explains how and when this occurs, stakeholders, publics, and stakeseekers are unlikely to know that their input is welcome and sought. This is particularly the case in environments in which many have already given up and become disengaged. In such cases, organizations may have a credibility problem and therefore have a job to do in regaining public trust and confidence. Hence, having policies to encourage and enable listening is not simply a matter of passing a few resolutions at meetings, publishing a statement of corporate values, or posting a glib message on a Web site claiming 'we're listening' like the insurance company case study reported in Chapter 3. Policies need to be adopted that reflect a listening culture and values of respect and consideration for others, and these need to be communicated throughout the organization and to stakeholders and publics.

One specific example is organization policies on social media use. Many organizations have very restrictive policies that preclude most employees from engaging in social media other than in a personal capacity, including some of those reported in this study. This is a missed opportunity to create organization ambassadors and a decentralized, scalable communication capability, and it conveys mistrust to employees. Some organizations do not have any policy or guidelines on social media use by employees, which comprises a lack of governance and poses risks to an organization. Organization policies on social media can justifiably and should set down guidelines on acceptable use, and specify training and monitoring, but they are also opportunities to encourage engagement and dialogue.

Beyond mere words, organizations should look for opportunities to *demonstrate* listening—not just talk about it. For example, airline passenger surveys referred to in Chapter 3 provide opportunities for airlines to report back to their passengers and potential passengers on what they have learned and how they are taking on board some suggestions to improve services. As noted under 'Listening in Management' in the previous chapter, it is highly unlikely that an airline can do everything or even most of what passengers request or suggest. But there must be something useful and practical in the thousands of passenger surveys filled out each year.

Many government bodies and corporations publish their values, vision, purposes, social responsibility statements, customer compacts, charters, and so on. Policies for effective ethical listening, as defined in this analysis, should be incorporated into all of these, along with the inevitable frequent references to informing, telling, showing, educating, sending, distributing, disseminating, transmitting, and broadcasting. But, as Anne Gregory notes, organizations need to be honest and not over-promise (personal communication, June 2, 2015). Saying the organization is listening without a culture, policies, structures, and resources in place to do so is soon discovered to be empty rhetoric that creates stakeholder and public frustration and disenchantment, which in turn can lead to lost sales, votes, support, trust, and reputation.

Politics of Listening

The politics of listening have been discussed by a number of scholars for some time (e.g., Fraser & Honneth, 2003; Honneth, 2007; Husband, 2009; Taylor, 1992), but the influence of politics has not been specifically identified in relation to organizational listening. The politics of listening occur both internally within organizations and externally in the environment in which organizations and citizens interact. Stephen Coleman discusses the "politics of voice", but he is referring to the same issue that is discussed here—the lack of attention paid to what people say and the "quality of that attention". He says factors such as class, race, gender, and age-related prejudices often "degrade the act of listening" (2013b, para. 30).

In the first instance, the politics of listening at an organizational level are played out internally in the very first stage or 'canon' of listening—giving recognition (Fraser, 1990). Those who might reasonably be expected to listen often do not recognize some others as having anything worthwhile to say, as noted under 'Culture of Listening'. This can become magnified through political influences and ideologies such as racism or sexism. Recognition is also denied because of partisanship, such as members of a political party, or a religious or ethnic group who engage in *othering* that actively discriminates against some individuals and groups (Said, 1978). For decades, even centuries, white Anglo-Saxon people in at least two of the countries in this study ignored the voices of their Indigenous people, and all three discounted and marginalized the voices of black people whose cries of indignation and pain echoed around the globe during generations of slavery and oppression. Extreme cases, one might claim. But today the voices of hard-working Muslim communities are tainted by the actions of a few and drowned out by the politics of the 'war on terror'. Many women still struggle to have their voices listened to for no reason other than gender politics.

As the presenters of the curatorial focus theme 'The Politics of Listening', at the What Now? 2015 symposium in New York noted: "The right to listen is relative, and the right not to listen, or to remain silent, is also a genuine stance" (Kellen & Kellen, 2015). Not listening is, therefore, itself an overtly political act.

Unless a culture of listening is established, organizational listening—which is largely delegated listening—can be stifled by politics inside organizations even when recognition and attention have been afforded by parts of an organization. This may be explicit, such as senior management making it clear that they are not interested in certain views or the views of certain groups that they revile or find repulsive and with which they have no interest in rapprochement. In such cases, voices fall 'on deaf ears' despite the efforts of communication staff, as occurred in the case of the general manager of corporate affairs at a national wholesaler who was reported in Chapter 3. A more insidious form of internal organizational politics, however, cuts off listening even before it gets to senior management. Indonesians have a phrase, *asal bapak senang*, that means 'as long as the boss is happy', also translated as 'never give the boss bad news'. This refers to politics inside organizations in which information that is likely to upset senior management and lead to difficult negotiations is discarded or 'buried'. Employees simply elect not to tell senior management about negative or critical views for fear that they will reflect badly on them and their colleagues, or simply because management become irritated and "things get ugly", as one customer relations executive commented (personal communication, February 3, 2015). This becomes exacerbated when senior management reacts negatively to criticism or even questioning.

Externally, neoliberalism, which imposes market values on most or all aspects of society and views citizens as *consumers*, also is a significant political influence that affects listening by governments and corporations. As Nick Couldry warns, "neoliberalism is a rationality that denies voice" to many (2010, p. 135) because that rationality is based on market logic—a view that markets self-regulate and that a successful economy translates into a successful society with benefits for all through the so-called 'trickle down' effect. In a neoliberal state, how much someone is worth financially and how much they spend largely determines their value, with the result that elites such as the wealthy, big business, banks, investment companies, ratings agencies, and share and bond markets that control capital have the most say and are listened to most (Morozov, 2014). If you are not worth much financially, your voice is not worth much. Governments need to pay more attention to the implications of allowing market logic to determine who they engage with and listen to most, and recognize that citizens have different needs to consumers. Conflating the identity and status of 'citizens' with that of 'consumers' is a wholly lamentable and ill-directed step in terms of people's roles and rights and in terms of social equity and social stability.

As Tanja Dreher (2009) and others point out, many individuals and groups are marginalized in contemporary societies, including in affluent Western countries such as those in which this study was conducted. These include Indigenous communities; low socioeconomic status (SES) groups; the poorly educated; people with disabilities; many of the aged, particularly those with diminished capacities such as people with dementia; along with those who are discriminated against and 'othered' on the basis of race, ethnicity, gender, sexuality, or physical appearance.

Perhaps the greatest contributor to the politics of listening when public communication is practiced is the power relations that exist even when organizations and their stakeholders and publics engage in dialogue. Many organizations make commitments to engagement, dialogue, and consultation—and many of those are well intended. But what many fail to adequately recognize and take account of are the significant and sometimes enormous differences in expertise and resources that exist between large organizations and their stakeholders and publics. For example, in public consultations following Hurricane Katrina that reviewed the role of local government authorities in the New Orleans area and the Federal Emergency Management Agency (FEMA), submissions were invited and received from many organizations and individuals.[1] They ranged from emergency management experts, police chiefs, and politicians to low income community members, small church groups, and charities. Some of those making representations had university degrees, years of experience and training, a bevy of lawyers in tow, specialist staff to research and write submissions, media officers to organize publicity to support their case, and full-time salaries to sustain their activities. Others had little education, no specialist expertise, no lawyers, no staff to research and write submissions, no

PR experts, and a full-time job to hold down while they tried to have their say. An equal playing field? Not by any stretch of one's imagination. Similarly, in the case of public consultation in relation to the major national infrastructure project in the UK examined in this study, the company established to develop the project has the backing of a large national UK government department, hundreds of millions of pounds, and a large team of professional communication, digital media, and PR staff, as well as legal, financial, engineering, and environmental advisers. Some of those affected by the project are small-lot farmers and residents of villages in the Midlands and northern England. The power differentials in terms of expertise, resources, time, and professionalism between organizations and many of their stakeholders and publics create inequities and afford organizations a substantial power advantage.

Stephen Coleman asks: "How many unregistered preferences, submerged opinions and stammered intentions disappear into the political vapour of democracy as it is currently institutionalized?" (2013a, p. 151). When people are consistently ignored, many eventually fall silent in what Elisabeth Noelle-Neumann (1974, 1984/1993) calls the "spiral of silence". This can be a death spiral for democracy and for corporate reputation, customer engagement, loyalty, and trust.

While the power of organizations may be deployed as *soft power* as described by Joseph Nye (2004, 2010b) in his discussions of public diplomacy, media studies scholar Kevin Howley has critically observed that "the field of public relations purposely manages public opinion in order to serve the narrow interests of government and corporate power" (2007, p. 348). PR scholars Bruce Berger and Bryan Reber (2006) and Derina Holtzhausen (2002) acknowledge that power relations exist between organizations and many of their publics. While PR is not the only expression of organizational power, the field of practice is at the leading edge of organization-public communication and relationships. The politics of listening need to be considered and addressed for effective ethical organizational listening to occur, and PR practitioners could well look to some of the principles of the *new public diplomacy* (Melissen, 2005; Nye, 2010a; Riordan, 2003; Snow, 2009) to assist in that process, such as turn-taking; one vote, one value; and the appointment of ombuds (Macnamara, 2012b, 2015b).

Another way to address and counter the politics of listening is to legislate or regulate for listening and thus institutionalize processes such as consultation. This has happened in France with the establishment in 1995 of the National Commission for Public Debate (NCPD) [*Commission Nationale du*

Débat Public]. The mixed experiences and learnings from the Commission are discussed later in this chapter under 'Models for Organizational Listening', as they are worthy of particular note.

Structures and Processes for Listening

Listening in organizations is mostly delegated to a number of specific functions, units, and even external agencies, as discussed in Chapter 3. The heads of large organizations such as presidents, prime ministers, ministers, permanent secretaries, CEOs, directors, and so on cannot personally listen to every person who wants to express a view relevant to the organization, or read every document that provides feedback, comment, suggestions, requests, proposals, and so on. Other than a limited number of letters, e-mails, and phone calls that go directly to senior management, listening is usually assigned to specialist organizational functions such as public consultation teams, customer contact units, and a range of other public communication staff and agencies as discussed in this analysis. When listening is delegated, it means that messages and meanings of those who speak to or about the organization and relevant issues need to be captured; analyzed to understand their argument as well as determine their validity and practicality; conveyed to decision makers; considered; and responded to. Criteria need to be developed for determining whether and to what extent attention and consideration will be paid to certain voices, and these need to be fair and reasonable. Developing these criteria is itself an important process to enable organizational listening. Some examples of key criteria to apply are examined under 'Articulation of Listening to Decision Making and Policy Making' later in this chapter. Furthermore, as discussed in relation to 'closing the listening loop', an organization's response needs to be communicated to relevant stakeholders and publics, and any agreed actions need to be implemented.

These steps require a number of structural elements and clearly identified processes to exist in organizations. At the most basic level, job descriptions—also referred to as position descriptions—should explicitly state that listening in various forms is a requirement of certain roles, particularly those related to communication, engagement, consultation, customer relations, research, and social media. More than simply dropping in the word 'listening', these documents that prescribe the focus, priorities, and key accountabilities of roles should specify the purpose of listening and some details of the types of listening to be undertaken. An examination of 95 job descriptions for high-level positions supplied by a leading executive recruitment agency specializing in the corporate and marketing communication sector revealed that not one used the word 'listening' in any context. A large number of the documents specified 'engagement', several mentioned 'relationships', and one listed 'collaboration'. However, none described how these interactions were to occur and most made scant reference to audiences, stakeholders, or publics other than in the context of these constituting targets for "strategic" engagement and communication. While one required its professional communication specialist to "utilize research ... to understand the perception of the brand", only one mentioned a specific listening activity. A position description for corporate affairs manager of a large national food company listed among key accountabilities: "Assistance with responses to ad hoc requests for information as required". The job descriptions highlighted "understanding the business" and "building relationships with senior management" and largely ignored understanding or building relationships with stakeholders and publics. Almost all emphasized having a "strategic" focus and approach and the context and language made it clear that this related to the traditional view of strategy as designed to achieve the organization's goals and objectives through disseminating and transmitting its information. Tasks and accountabilities listed included:

- "Refine strategies, messages and tactics to support the group's business plan";
- "Oversee development of a 'marcom'[2] strategy that drives measureable business results";
- "Design internal communication to disseminate the values, vision and mission of [company name] to all staff";
- "Manage production of annual and half-yearly reports of utilizing the media to achieve organizational objectives";
- "Develop and implement a program of events with a range of partner and stakeholder organizations to help promote [company name's] messages"; and
- "Manage the production and dissemination of written briefings on key issues".

Even in the key task that mentions "partner and stakeholder organizations", it is significant that the following words describe the objective of interaction with these groups as "to help promote [company name's] messages", with no reference to engagement or listening to the views of partners or stakeholders. These were not atypical extracts from job descriptions of senior communication roles.

An interesting finding of a doctoral research study by Howard Nothhaft (2010) at the University of Lund in Sweden who 'shadowed' the heads of communication in eight large German companies operating regionally or internationally is that they spent two-thirds of their time involved in internal interactions and only one-third involved in interaction with external stakeholders and publics. This ethnographic study excluded specialist internal communication roles such as employee relations, so it is not skewed by specialist portfolios. Nothhaft reported that most of senior communicators' time is spent in management functions such as supervising other staff, planning, monitoring, controlling, and reporting to senior management. While this partly reflects the seniority of the roles observed, it nevertheless further suggests that processes in large organizations are highly organization-centric.

Other important structural issues include clearly defined lines of reporting from listening sites in organizations to senior management decision makers, and routines for regular reporting. If there is an indirect or convoluted path from the stakeholder and public contact points in organizations to senior management, it is unlikely that the voices of stakeholders and publics will ever get through to decision makers and policy makers. Somewhere along the line a middle-level executive or administrative staff member will decide that the matter does not warrant senior executive time or that the agenda for board or management meetings is already full. Or someone will be simply 'covering their back' to avoid embarrassment or extra work. Also, if listening to feedback, comments, and sometimes criticism is a specially convened discussion in an organization, it can be a confronting exercise. Engagement and dialogue need to be ongoing and normalized in an organization, even when the views of others create tensions and conflicts to resolve.

A number of senior communication executives who were interviewed reported that structural barriers such as lines of reporting and planning procedures often stand in the way of greater engagement and listening. For example, an executive responsible for public feedback and response in one large government department reported that the communication, research/insights, and consultation staff of his organization work closely with policy teams, but described the relationship as "a challenge", explaining:

> Communication used to be seen as something you did when all the policy making and everything else was basically done ... then you thought I suppose we'd better tell somebody about it. Let's get those 'comms' guys in. By that time, of course, it's pretty difficult. (personal communication, February 3, 2015)

One other government department agreed with his assessment that communication is often not integrated into policy making and operations. The director of communication of a department involved in community services and local affairs commented in relation to social media:

> Large parts of government are still very much in the formal legalistic discharge of statutory functions kind of world …. I think people are inherently cautious about how far you can take some of the potential of social media to engage. (personal communication, September 25, 2014)

He reported that "it is getting better", however, with a wave of reform sweeping through governments in the UK and US involving a commitment to transparency and open policy making that includes engagement of citizens facilitated via digital platforms. This is beginning to flow down through the civil service with a number of departments and agencies reporting that they have adopted flexible working hours—sometimes 24/7—and that they are reallocating resources to meet changing public expectations and demands. The social media specialist with one government agency said that "one of the things that digital has done for us is that, for people outside of communication, it has helped open their eyes in terms of the damage that silence can create" (personal communication, September 24, 2014). Major corporations also are significantly restructuring their communication functions, such as the large broadband and telecommunications company that has 'banned' media releases to focus on interactive modes of communication and the Fortune 500 'telco' that has set up internal video production featuring a substantial amount of user-generated content.

There is one significant danger in government focus on transparency and *open government*, which collectively have become a zeitgeist of contemporary Western democracies. These principles are being interpreted and implemented in some cases as the provision of more and more information to citizens. This can result in information overload and hinder rather than help citizens. In a 2002 lecture series, Onora O'Neill (Baroness O'Neill of Bengarve and emeritus professor of philosophy at the University of Cambridge) said that government focus on transparency and disclosure often demonstrates a continuing informational logic. She said:

> There has never been more abundant information about the individuals and institutions whose claims we have to judge. Openness and transparency are now possible on a scale of which past ages could barely dream. We are flooded with information about government departments and government policies. (O'Neill, 2002)

Open government needs to be interpreted, first and foremost, as being open to listen to citizens and shaping policies and decisions after taking account of the range of views, needs, and interests in society. Second, open government requires ongoing two-way communication and engagement—not simply distributing information. Baroness O'Neill said "openness or transparency is now all too easy: if they can produce or restore trust, trust should surely be within our grasp" (para. 5). Elsewhere O'Neill declared: "Trust grows out of listening, not telling" (as cited in Lacey, 2013, p. 187).

In political campaigning during the 2015 Madrid mayoral elections, candidate Manuela Carmena said in an interview reported in the *Financial Times* that "to govern is to listen" (Buck, 2015, para. 5). Admittedly, the 71-year-old former judge is a veteran human rights activist and a former member of the Spanish Communist Party. But her popularity and her words send a message to major political parties and governments about listening to citizens to understand their concerns and truly represent their interests.

It also needs to be noted that some policy and communication scholars warn of 'consultation fatigue'—what the president of the French National Commission for Public Debate (NCPD), Professor Laurence Monnoyer-Smith (2015), refers to as "participation fatigue". When public consultations are held regularly they can become onerous for citizens and some groups in terms of the time and effort that are required to participate. As noted in Chapter 3, the key issue in relation to the processes of consultation and organizational listening generally is quality, not quantity. Volume of public consultation does not democracy make. Citizens need to feel and see evidence that their voices are having any effect—that their voices *matter* in Nick Couldry's (2010) terms. Organizations need to ensure that their culture, policies, and structures and processes afford genuine dialogue, including listening, rather than simply add to the volume of pointless talk.

Another function where structure and processes are vitally important is in handling large volumes of correspondence including complaints. With some government departments and large corporations having more than 50,000 letters and e-mails a year, many of which need to be referred to specialist staff or units for advice, the task of keeping track of these is significant. As noted in Chapter 3, one government department described the functioning of its customer correspondence unit as like "a military operation" with all contacts logged into a database and then tracked until they are resolved (personal communication, February 3, 2015). But most of the organizations studied operate manual systems of recording, filing, and tracking correspondence.

With correspondence increasingly in digital form, the task of logging and tracking documents is easier than in the days of handwritten and typed letters and there is no excuse for not having a central database to record and store all correspondence. This affords several benefits for both the organization and their stakeholders and publics. First, an accurate record can be kept and tracking can ensure that all correspondence is processed—preferably in a timely manner. No more ignored or forgotten letters and e-mails! When correspondence is referred to a specialist unit or person for a response, this can be recorded and tracking can ensure a response is sent. Furthermore, storing of correspondence of various kinds in a central database in digital form allows for categorization and content analysis to be undertaken to identify themes, prominent issues, and trends. If such analysis was done of complaints to UK hospitals, the Mid Staffordshire scandal may never have happened and 300 lives might have been saved and the suffering of many hundreds of others reduced (Stationery Office, 2013). Beyond such extreme cases, analysis of the hundreds of thousands of letters, e-mails, and tweets received by government departments, agencies, and corporations on a range of issues could also yield valuable insights into common concerns, interests, and views of a large number of citizens.

At a political level, the structure and processes of institutionalized politics and political communication often militate against listening despite the grand claims of democratic systems. Andrew Dobson (2014) notes that one of the key structural features of most modern parliamentary and republican democracies is party discipline and unity, which he says is deeply destructive of listening and responding. While purportedly representing their constituents, politicians are expected to 'toe the party line' on policies and decisions. Any departure is usually seen as mutiny punishable by political death. Also, as Dobson and one of the interviewees quoted in this study observe, much political communication involves set-piece events such as speeches crafted by professional speechwriters, rehearsed public statements, and stage-managed media news conferences. Unspontaneous, controlled, and inauthentic public communication is the stock-in-trade of the PR industry and political 'spin' that comprises a substantial part of political communication (Ewen, 1996; Louw, 2010). These are structural issues that are not easily addressed but remain challenges for politicians and political parties as well as political scientists and media and communication scholars.

Evgeny Morozov says that "existing infrastructure is great for fulfilling the needs of the state, not for self-organizing citizens" (2014, p. 29). In a critique of current forms of public communication and 'big data' systems specifically, as well as neoliberalism more broadly, Morozov said the focus of most systems is "results" and "effects", which "presupposes that the goal of policy is the optimization of efficiency". Instead, he argues that the preferred focus of endeavour should be on "creating ideal conditions for human flourishing" (2014, p. 29). Equally, it can be seen in the evidence presented in this study that communication is conceptualized and organized based on the principles of *efficiency* in terms of systems of transmission and *effectiveness* narrowly conceptualized in terms of an organization's perspective and interests, both of which are inimical to human communication conceived dialogically.

As noted earlier in this chapter under 'Culture of Listening', there are times when informing is a legitimate and necessary practice and, further, persuasion is not a dirty word in communication *per se*, as some hard-line critics suggest. Citizens and particular stakeholders and publics such as employees and customers need to be informed about a range of issues, and also a safe coherent society requires persuasion of its members on a number of matters, such as driving safely and eating healthily. Furthermore, persuasion of people to buy legal products is a legitimate activity that brings benefits to many. But a structure and processes need to be established in organizations to do organizational listening as well as telling and selling. Listening is unlikely to occur if it is not built into organizational structure with departments, units, and agencies tasked with listening, as well as through job descriptions, workflows, reporting procedures, and performance criteria.

Technologies for Listening

Stephen Coleman drew attention to the role of technologies for listening in the public sphere in an article that explored the "challenge of digital hearing" and the use of what he called "technologies of hearing" (2013b, p. 3). A number of other authors have written with varying degrees of excitement and optimism about *e-democracy*, *e-government*, and the potential of Web 2.0-based social media to democratize media (Siapera, 2012, p. 55) and revolutionize public communication (Gillmor, 2004; Jenkins, 2006b). Others caution against *cyberbole* (Woolgar, 2002) and technological determinism, pointing out that technologies on their own rarely determine social practices. Robin Mansell (2012) and Robert McChesney (2013) identify two 'camps' of researchers and commentators, which they call the "celebrants" and the "sceptics", while others refer to the "techno-utopians and techno-cynics" (DeLuca, Lawson, & Sun, 2012, p. 485). These discussions serve to warn, as this analysis has done, that technologies on their own will not create engagement, dialogue, conversations, participation, collaboration, or relationships. They are tools to be used—and like many tools, they can be used well or poorly, for productive purposes or counterproductively.

Having sounded those warnings, it is important to note that a wide and growing range of technologies is available to aid organizational listening as well as organizational and individual speaking. These include:

- Media monitoring applications and services (see Table 3.5);
- Social media monitoring applications and services (see Table 3.5);
- Text analysis and content analysis software programs (Krippendorff, 2003; Neuendorf, 2002). These are widely used to analyze media content, but their use can be extended to analyzing other texts such as complaints over a period, as demonstrated by Alex Gillespie, Tom Reader, and colleagues in the UK (Reader, Gillespie, & Roberts, 2014);
- Applications to analyze online consultations, sometimes referred to as *e-democracy* (OECD, 2003) and *e-consultation*, although the latter term is widely used for online medical consultation;
- Automated acknowledgement systems such as those effectively used by the Obama Online Operation during the 2008 US presidential election (Macnamara, 2014a). Such technologies, while delivering only one of the seven canons or elements of listening, can assist organizations in the challenge of replying individually to large volumes of inquiries, even with a degree of personalization;
- Specialist sense making software (Dervin, Foreman-Wernet, & Lauterbach, 2003; Foreman-Wernet, & Dervin, 2006); and
- Argumentation software and systems (de Moor & Aakhus, 2006). These last two technologies facilitate analysis and interpretation and can efficiently and effectively identify key themes and patterns even in large volumes of submissions or comment.

Social media are one of the most obvious and most accessible technologies for organizational listening. However, as reported by Tina McCorkindale (2010), Amelia Adams and McCorkindale (2013), Michael Kent (2013) and others, organizations use social media primarily for distributing their messages and promoting their brands, services, products, and events. Even in 2014, a study of complaints handling by large US companies found that "companies are not fully embracing the opportunities of social media to demonstrate their willingness to interact with and assist their stakeholders". The researchers reported that "organizational responsiveness is only moderate" (Einwiller & Steilen, 2015, p. 195).

Examples and further discussion of the application of a number of advanced technologies for large-scale organizational listening are provided under 'Models for Organizational Listening' later in this chapter.

Resources for Listening

If organizations overcome the first four barriers to listening and embrace the first four elements of an architecture of listening—that is, if they have a culture of openness and willingness to listen, policies to actively listen to key stakeholders and publics, address the politics of listening, and have structures and processes in place for large-scale listening—then the issue of resources looms large. As interviewees unanimously said in this study, organizations are highly unlikely to allocate increased budgets to public communication in the near future. Most governments are, in fact, substantially cutting expenditures in the face of public criticism for excessive spending on communication, mainly in the form of advertising and promotion. Corporations in most countries face economic pressures with lingering effects of the global financial meltdown of 2008–2009, collapsing economies in Europe, and rising competition from emerging markets, while NGOs and non-profit organizations almost always have budget constraints.

Nevertheless, several types of resources are essential for organizational listening. While some systems and tools are automated or semi-automated, listening requires the allocation of personnel to undertake listening functions such as research, social media monitoring and analysis, consultation, customer relations, and processing of correspondence. While these functions already exist in many or most organizations, they are often focussed on one-way distribution of information, as reported in this study. Extending these activities to provide greater interactivity requires resources. As well as personnel, resources required include time and budgets.

In the case of large-scale listening, the investment required can be substantial. This leads to the key question asked about organizational listening and, concomitantly, the key objection or barrier proposed. What is the benefit—the return on investment—to justify increased resources committed to organizational listening? This issue will be dealt with specifically in the final chapter of this analysis, which is devoted to examining the benefits of organizational listening. For now, it is important to point out that a key finding of this research is that none of the organizations studied increased their expenditure or staff in undertaking increased engagement, dialogue, and relationship building with stakeholders and publics. While it can be argued that all need to do better, all advised that reallocation of resources from ineffective activities allowed increased two-way communication and engagement activities to be resourced. In some cases, organizations reported doing more and getting better results with less.

The key to identifying ineffective activities and prioritizing is measurement and evaluation undertaken using rigorous qualitative as well as quantitative methods. The examples of UK government departments redeploying a relatively small amount of budget and 'head count' to gain behavioural insights that saved taxpayers tens of millions of pounds and potentially hundreds of millions of pounds are instructive. Also, the US telecommunications giant that transformed its internal communication and some of its external communication to entertaining video programs based on user-generated content and internal production is another example of the "pivoting" and step change that can transform communication without increased resources (personal communication, January 14, 2015).

Communication staff who have been successful in implementing interactive social media practices in conservative companies and government also advocate a 'start small and roll out' approach. Several government departments and agencies reported training a team ranging from 10 to 30 staff who then act as 'champions', 'advocates', and trainers for others. Also, several reported that providing private coaching for senior management in social media substantially changed the culture of the organization and led to a changed focus and reallocation of resources.

Another strategy reported is the use of peer support and crowdsourcing to resource some functions. For example, several corporate and some government customer relations units that have transitioned some or all of their customer communication online are engaging other customers in answering basic questions and sharing information. While being wary of misinformation being distributed, which they manage by closely monitoring peer-to-peer communication, they are finding that crowdsourcing can answer many customer questions and resolve some problems, thereby reducing the work and resources required.

Skills for Listening

The reallocation of resources, the shift to new processes, and adoption of new technologies noted in the previous sections have major implications for education, training, and employment in fields such as marketing communication, corporate communication, organizational communication, and public relations. The traditional list of skills and duties such as writing, editing, producing strategic plans, distributing information, liaising with journalists, and arranging events (Macnamara, 2012a; Tench & Yeomans, 2013; Wilcox & Cameron, 2010) will increasingly not be enough for organizations transitioning to true two-way engagement, dialogue, and relationship building to create stakeholder satisfaction and trust. This study found that some of the most innovative and effective communication was created by behavioural psychologists, researchers, and policy specialists committed to consultation, as well as a few pioneering social media teams in customer relations. An advertising, marketing, PR, or corporate communication executive was not to be seen at the forefront of genuine engagement, dialogue, and relationship building with stakeholders and publics, despite the rhetoric and the theorizing of these fields of practice.

As discussed in Chapter 2, listening competency is identified by a number of researchers as a key ingredient for improving interpersonal communication (Cooper, 1997; Cooper & Husband, 1993; Wolvin & Coakley, 1996). Also as noted, Judy Burnside-Lawry (2011, 2012) has taken some initial steps to apply the concept to the broader field of organization-public relationships, defining organizational listening competency as "a combination of an employee's listening skills and the environment in which listening occurs" (Burnside-Lawry, 2011, p. 149). The environment presumably refers to the organization itself, such as tools and services available to help individual employees listen (e.g., research, social media monitoring), as well as external factors such as spaces available for stakeholders and publics to speak and be listened to (e.g., consultation forums). As argued throughout this analysis, large-scale listening requires more than interpersonal listening skills and methods.

This is an area requiring further study. What can be identified immediately, however, is that skills for organizational listening almost certainly need to include knowledge of feedback mechanisms and a range of qualitative as well as quantitative research methods such as surveys, focus groups, interviews, and ethnography; operational skills in interactive digital media such as social media and e-consultation software; as well as an understanding of psychology, sociology, and anthropology. Some techniques could undoubtedly be borrowed from interpersonal communication studies of listening competency, although skills in large-scale data collection, data analytics including 'big data' analysis, data science, and knowledge management are also likely to be increasingly necessary, as well as text and content analysis.

However, in drawing attention to the need for technologies and skills in the use of various software applications and data analysis, a cautionary note needs to be sounded. Use of these tools should not reduce listening to the processing of quantitative statistical data, which is a real risk given the current fetishism for 'big data', analytics, and metrics. The complex thought processes and emotions of people cannot be represented in numbers, certainly not without being reductionist and stripping away meaning and sense in its myriad nuanced and variable forms. Organizations need to remember the hierarchy of data, information, knowledge, wisdom (DIKW)—although the definitional arguments over those terms and criticism of the implied logical progression are noted. Nor should listening tools and systems be used simply for 'intelligence' gathering that contributes to an organization's power. Communication is grounded fundamentally in humanistic as much or more than scientific and social science understanding.

Articulation of Listening to Decision Making and Policy Making

As noted in Chapter 3, the final stage of organizational listening is articulation of the voices of stakeholders and publics to decision makers and policy makers in organizations. As clearly acknowledged in Chapter 3 under 'Listening in Management', not everything that an organization 'hears' needs to be or should be referred to senior management for a decision or consideration in policy making. Some requests and proposals will be clearly impractical. Also, it is an unfortunate reality that some stakeholders and publics present extreme arguments, sometimes in extreme language. In this chapter under 'Structures and Processes for Listening' it is proposed that organizations should establish criteria for determining what feedback, comments, requests, and proposals from stakeholders and publics are presented to decision makers and policy makers. As noted, these criteria should be fair and reasonable. Abusive communication and comments that are offensive on the grounds of racism, sexism, or homophobia, or that breach other laws and regulations can be discarded quite legitimately. Beyond that, organizations need to have clear criteria and defined processes for what happens to expressions of voice by stakeholders and publics.

Criteria applied by some organizations include popularity of views or frequency of similar statements. Applying these criteria requires some form of systematic analysis of the content of submissions, proposals, petitions, letters, online comments, and other expressions of voice over time to identify common views, themes, and patterns. However, majority and common views should not be the only basis of selection of issues to address. Sometimes, minority views and even a lone voice can raise important matters. Attention should be paid to the merits of each expression of voice, the potential for the issue to escalate and cause further concern, the seriousness of the matter (such as risks to stakeholders, communities, or the organization), as well as matters such as social equity and ethics. Are some individuals or groups marginalized because they do not belong to a majority, an organized group, or a popular movement? Is it ethical to ignore some voices and what they say? These are questions that can inform the processing of information received through consultations, customer relations, research, and other channels. While one organization in the 36 studied (a US multinational corporation) employed an anthropologist to assist in employee engagement, no organizations in the sample employed or sought advice from a sociologist or ethicist in relation to their various engagements with stakeholders and publics despite many claims of *corporate social responsibility* (Heath & Ni, 2010; McWilliams & Siegel, 2001), a *social conscience* (Holtzhausen, 2000), and community engagement. These seem to be examples of expertise that could contribute to effective interpretation and articulation of the voice of stakeholders and publics to organization decision makers and policy makers. Also, risk assessment methodology, which is commonly used in business and government, can be applied. A risk assessment should weigh the likelihood and level of potential benefits and potential negative impacts of taking responsive action versus not taking responsive action.

The UK's Commission for Healthcare Audit and Inspection (2007) study of NHS complaints handling reported that "there is little evidence of trusts [divisions within the English NHS system] using complaints data to inform their decision making when commissioning services, particularly the services of independent contractors" (p. 7). As noted several times in this analysis, complaints are mostly processed individually on a case-by-case basis with no overall analysis. Periodic analysis of a sample or even all complaints could gain insights such as identification of common complaints, or complaints about a particular facility or product, that could inform proactive management action leading to a resolution before more harm is done.

Peter Dahlgren states "a blooming public sphere does not guarantee a democracy; it is a necessary but not sufficient ingredient" (2001, p. 37). What he and a number of other researchers (e.g., Baumgartner & Jones, 1993/2009) point out is that there must be a structural link between communicative spaces and the centres of decision making so that the views of and feedback from stakeholders and publics can influence agendas and decisions. In democratic politics, a central argument is that citizens should be able to influence policies that govern their lives (Held, 1996). In public companies, shareholders similarly have an expectation of being able to influence decisions, and even in private companies stakeholders and publics such as employees, customers, and local communities feel that they should be listened to and have some influence.

Nancy Fraser (1992) warned some time ago that most public spheres are 'weak' in the sense that their links to decision making are remote. Similarly, Pierre Rosanvallon argues that what contemporary democracies lack is not opportunities for citizens to express their views, but the means by which those voices can be valued within processes of policy development (2008, p. 13).

Drawing on James Bohman, Nick Couldry says that "the issue is what governments do with voice, once expressed: are they prepared to change the way they make policy?" His response is that "governments so far are a long way off acknowledging this" (2010, p. 146). This analysis suggests that corporations and even large NGOs similarly have a yawning gap between their rhetorical flourishes in relation to engagement, dialogue, conversations, participation, collaboration and relationships, and the discussions held in their boardrooms and executive suites.

This raises a question about what type and level of response is sufficient and the extent to which articulation of listening to decision making means organizations have to cave in and do what stakeholders and publics request. This is answered already to some extent in this section in recommending establishment of criteria to assess the popularity, merits, validity, risks, and ethical implications in relation to requests and demands made of an organization.

Further to this, there are frameworks guiding how far organizations need to go in response to public engagement, consultation, research findings, comments, petitions, and other expressions of voice by stakeholders and publics. For example, responsiveness is defined in some political literature as 'the congruence of collective public attitudes towards political issues with the policy preferences and actions of elected representatives" (Hobolt & Klemmensen, 2005, p. 380). This, in short, means doing what stakeholders and publics want and is referred to as an *outcome-based* conceptualization of responsiveness. An alternative and more modest view is that responsiveness can comprise an attitude and set of practices adopted by policy makers and decision makers (Aberbach & Rockman, 1994). In an *attitude-based* approach, responsiveness is defined as recognizing and considering public opinion and following a set of equitable administrative and decision making processes that may, or may not, result in change or modification. This latter approach meets the definition of listening presented in Chapter 1 and is an important contribution to the discussion because universalized expectations or requirements for policy makers and organization decision makers to always defer to stakeholders and publics are unrealistic and impractical.

Private companies cannot be expected to kowtow to the wishes of external publics, and even public companies have limited responsibilities beyond those in relation to their shareholders, employees, and the environment that are delineated in law. Too much responsiveness could prevent corporations from implementing coherent strategies and making long-term plans. Also, too much government responsiveness is seen as undesirable as it would undermine the stability and functioning of policy making by subjecting processes to whims and emotions rather than evidence. Provided open and equitable processes are in place for the voice of stakeholders and publics to be given attention, interpreted so as to be understood, and be considered by policy makers and decision makers, articulation has occurred.

However, there are indications that the bar is set far too low in terms of the extent to which policy makers and decision makers respond affirmatively to stakeholders' and publics' concerns, views, and proposals. One argument put forward for not accepting the views of stakeholders and publics is issue complexity. It is often argued that specialist expertise and knowledge are required to fully appreciate certain issues, policies, or projects. For instance, large infrastructure projects such as proposals for nuclear power stations, wind farms, and undersea drilling and mining are frequently put in this category. Allegedly, understanding the scientific and technical information involved is beyond the capacity of 'ordinary' citizens.

But Laurence Monnoyer-Smith, vice president of the *Commision Nationale du Débat Public* [National Commission for Public Debate] in France and formerly a professor at the University of Technology of Compiègne, says consideration of the views of 'lay' people can make a positive contribution on even highly technical matters. In discussing the work of the National Commission for Public Debate (NCPD), Monnoyer-Smith (2007, 2015) says the mandatory public debate process facilitated by the NCPD has brought big corporations and NGOs together to talk to each other instead of conducting a war of words through media; it has forced big companies to consider the views of people who were people previously ignored, creating greater social equity; and companies have recognized that local knowledge can often make a valuable contribution to major planning projects. In a 2015 lecture she gave the example of a company planning to upgrade a waste processing plant by knocking down an old facility with two towering smoke stacks and replacing it with a new multimillion euro 'high tech' plant. However, in public debate, it found that the local community did not want the old plant demolished as it was considered a local landmark and their real concern was not the waste processing plant, but a program to reduce waste including better collection services for recycling. The company saved money by upgrading the existing plant instead of building an entirely new plant and won community support by investing some of the savings in a better collection services for recycling and waste reduction. One could argue that the environment was also better off because of this consultative, cooperative approach. To be fair, Monnoyer-Smith (2015) also points out some negative effects of mandated public consultation and listening that are discussed under 'Models for Organizational Listening' in which the work of the NCPD is examined further.

The Work of Listening

Finally, with the eight elements of an architecture of listening in place, organizations are in a position to undertake the work of listening. Organizations should make no mistake, large-scale listening is work. Declaring a policy of transparency and openness and inviting feedback, comment, and input are only the beginning. As a UK government deputy director of communication said:

> Being open takes hard work. It's not just publishing things. It's working hard to think about and get into the spirit of the interaction …. Openness and transparency are two very different things. Transparency is like we'll give you lots of information. Openness is the other way round. It's about you talk to us. (personal communication, February 2, 2015)

The importance of not interpreting transparency and openness as simply sending out more and more information has already been identified in the findings reported in Chapter 3 and under 'Structures and Processes for Listening' in this chapter. The work of listening needs to be focussed on reception, acknowledgement, interpretation to gain understanding through analysis and other processes, consideration, and articulating the views of stakeholders and publics that are assessed as being valid and reasonable based on established criteria to decision makers and policy makers. The work of listening includes monitoring of traditional and social media to identify reported stakeholder and public concerns, views, and interests (not just tracking the organization's publicity); analyzing social media to identify and try to understand others' views (not just count the organization's 'hits', followers, and likes); conducting open-minded research and inclusive public consultations; and designing and implementing specialist listening strategies such as those discussed in the next section. Such work is quite different to the common activities of most public communication practitioners. As noted earlier, such work does not appear in the job descriptions of senior corporate and government communication roles. It seems that such work is not being done in most cases. Democracy, government, corporate reputation and relationships, and communities are the poorer because of that.

Public communication professionals mainly do the work of speaking on behalf of their organizations, or hold a megaphone to the lips of CEOs and politicians while they speak. They need to rethink their role and restructure their calendars, work plans, and job lists to do the work of listening.

Models for Organizational Listening

This analysis argues that, in addition to the ubiquitous architecture of speaking that characterizes organizations in the public, private, and third sector today, organizations need to have an architecture of listening that provides the culture, policies, political environment, structure, resources, skills, technologies, and articulations for effective engagement, dialogue, and relationships with stakeholders and publics that lead to trust, mutual support, and sustainability. Eight key elements of an architecture of listening are proposed, as outlined in the previous sections.

As noted at the beginning of this chapter, but it bears repeating, an architecture does not imply a single form or model or scale. As with the architecture of our built environment, there can be many forms and styles and infinite variety in scale. Developing scalability and testing models for organizational listening will be an important further stage of research to enable operationalization of organizational listening in various contexts and environments. However, some existing models and examples of large-scale organizational listening are available and several are briefly outlined for the insights that they provide into both the challenges and opportunities.

The National Commission for Public Debate, France

The National Commission for Public Debate (NCPD) [*Commision Nationale du Débat Public*] was established in France in 1995 and is an important model of formal public consultation to examine because it was created as an independent agency with legislated powers; it has been in operation for two decades; and as of early 2015 it had conducted 69 major public debates on national issues and 21 post-public debate consultations with some success and public acclaim.

In a public lecture at the London School of Economics and Political Science in 2015, vice president of the NCPD, Professor Laurence Monnoyer-Smith, summarized public debate and consultation in France as going through several phases, and it is worth briefly recapping the history of the commission. She described the late 1980s as a period of public unrest and protest by French citizens who felt they were not consulted on major national policies and infrastructure projects such as the building of freeways, power stations, and high-speed train services. If public consultation occurred, it was conducted by the local Prefect,[3] who is a representative of the state and therefore not neutral. As a result, an act was passed (the Barnier Law) to establish the NCPD in 1995 and the law requires that public debate is conducted in relation to all major projects and amenities of more than €300 million, facilitated through the NCPD.

There were criticisms of the first iteration of the NCPD and the French public debate process, including concerns that its charter did not provide for post-debate consultation to report back to citizens on what happened as a result of the debate, and that it could not debate the 'general interest' in relation to projects (e.g., were they necessary at all). The role of the commission initially was restricted to discussing specific matters such as the location and method of construction of proposed projects.

In response to criticism, the role of the NCPD was expanded in 1998 to include broader debate in relation to proposed projects as well as specific operational issues, and also to include post-debate feedback and consultation to advise participants on the outcomes of public debates. In 2002, the NCPD was made an independent authority.

The NCPD uses a range of methods for facilitating public debate including public meetings, consensus conferences, focus groups, Q&A sessions, online forums, and social media discussion. It appears to have some 'teeth', as around one-third of projects debated are stopped or withdrawn, around one-third are extensively modified from their original form, and only one-third proceed with minor or no modification.

However, Monnoyer-Smith sees a number of weaknesses and problems in the NCPD model. On the positive side, she acknowledges at least three benefits stemming from the compulsory public debate process facilitated by the NCPD as follows:

- It has brought big corporations and NGOs together to talk to each other, whereas they often refused to meet and fired accusations and criticisms at each other via media;
- It has forced big companies to consider the views of communities and 'lay' people, who were previously considered unable to contribute to highly technical and complex discussions and, therefore, ignored; and
- Its forums have caused big companies to recognize that local knowledge can often make a valuable contribution to major planning projects and that cooperation can be beneficial. Monnoyer-Smith gave examples, including local residents having intimate knowledge of tides that were relevant to a planned offshore wind farm and the case of local residents helping a waste processing company save money by identifying waste reduction opportunities through improved recycling services in their area.

But, beyond these positive outcomes, Monnoyer-Smith pointed out six practical and conceptual flaws in the process that institutionalizes public consultation. These are summarized in some detail as they inform large-scale organization-public listening.

- Extensive public debate has created considerable complexity and time delays in decision making. The NCPD requires four to six months to prepare for a public debate, debates usually take three to four months, and a further two months are allowed for the NCPD to issue its report. Post-debate consultation then takes another few months. So public debates take at least 18 months and are very expensive undertakings, often costing €600,000 to €800,000. The question of who pays also has become an issue and haggling over costs combined with the lengthy debate process can cause major delays and even jeopardize some important projects.

- A second, deeper philosophical concern is that, under the NCPD charter, public debate is based on "reasoned argument" (NCPD, 2015) and focussed on achieving consensus. Its Habermasian approach privileges deliberation informed by rational arguments and scientific data over people's feelings, preferences, and personal concerns. While reason and facts are important considerations, so too are the emotional and vernacular responses of citizens, such as people whose houses are going to be demolished to make way for a project or those who will find themselves living next to a proposed freeway or airport. As noted in Chapter 1, some political scientists such as Chantal Mouffe (1999, 2005) argue that true democracy needs to recognize agonistic expressions of voice and argument, and accept that consensus is an idealized state that is often unachievable. More often, diversity, plurality, and conflict are the natural states of human interaction, according to supporters of agonistic and open participatory democracy, which means that compromise rather than consensus is a more realistic goal.

- A third concern is that, despite major efforts to conduct public consultation through formalizing and institutionalizing the process, many "seek consent to already-taken decisions" (Monnoyer-Smith, 2015). In short, government or big business, or both, often have already decided on a policy or project and simply go through the motions of public consultation.

- Fourth, Monnoyer-Smith warns that institutionalized public consultation—that is, when it is made mandatory and formalized—has led to the "mobilization of opposition" and the "radicalization of opposition". Major public debates such as those conducted by the NCPD provide a national platform for NGOs and various activist groups to make headlines and build their profile—and often their membership. This is exacerbated by the fact that controversial stances make headlines more often than compromise or calm negotiation. Hence, some groups hijack agendas or "try to torpedo any and every project" because of their own politics and power struggles.

- Fifth, Monnoyer-Smith says there is a "problem of inclusion". She argues that open public debate in forums such as public meetings, while giving the appearance of consultation and democracy, is ineffective because such forums are dominated by the 'usual suspects' such as industry lobby groups, activist and advocacy groups, local politicians grandstanding to try to win votes, and loud articulate voices of the well-educated and well-to-do—an issue that has come up repeatedly in this analysis. She says the NCPD has tried to move away from public meetings to outreach activities such as mobile consultations (i.e., going to affected areas and local groups, even to individual homes).

- Sixth, Monnoyer-Smith reports that a number of communities suffer "participation fatigue"—too much consultation. As a result, some groups withdraw because of the drain on their resources and some lose interest altogether.

While institutionalized models of public consultation bring an assurance of organizational listening and report some success, the experiences of France's NCPD suggest that more dynamic and organic models may ultimately be more effective with less negative side effects. Some such models are explored in the following examples.

The 2008 and 2012 Obama US Presidential Campaigns

The 2008 and 2012 Obama presidential campaigns, particularly the former, have been widely hailed as exemplars of citizen engagement using both offline and online methods. Barack Obama was inaugurated as the forty-fourth president of the US on January 20, 2009, after a noteworthy campaign, the success of which was largely attributed to social media engagement with citizens (Qualman, 2009). Research and reports cited by Barbara Kaye (2011) claim that Obama's 2008 "online crusade" gained 1 million Facebook and MySpace friends, 112,000 Twitter followers, and 18 million views of 1,800 videos on the BarackObama.com YouTube channel (p. 209). Rachel Gibson, Marta Cantijoch, and Stephen Ward (2010) put the number Facebook supporters at 1.75 million and noted that the Obama campaign also gained 13.5 million e-mail supporters and 2 million SMS (short message service) subscribers (p. 7). In a Pew Internet and American Life Project study, Aaron Smith and Lee Rainie (2008) reported that 46 per cent of all Americans used the Internet to get news about the campaign, share their views, and mobilize others during the 2008 presidential campaign. Whereas 13 per cent of Americans said they had watched a video about the 2004 campaign online, 35 per cent reported watching at least one political video in 2008. Perhaps even more significantly, 19 per cent of Americans reported going online weekly to "do something related to the campaign", which indicates some level of engagement (p. i). A particular facet of the Obama campaigns was the use of technology such as automated acknowledgement systems. For example, all e-mails sent to Obama received an immediate reply. This was a standard template response that was auto-generated, but clever use of friendly language and insertion of the salutation 'Dear [first name]' if the sender's name was provided gave it a personalized appearance. Receipt of a fast acknowledgement assured those who sent e-mails that their message had been received and that it was getting some attention—albeit this was limited to machine reading at that point. Interestingly, perchance meetings with recipients of Obama e-mail responses during a previous research project revealed that most recognized the communication as 'form e-mails', but felt assured that an organization that went to the trouble of using technology to scan and acknowledge e-mails would also give them some further consideration (Macnamara, 2014a).

However, the first clarification that needs to be made is that the Obama campaign's use of social media was primarily for fund-raising and voter mobilization—not citizen engagement in policy making or discussion. Based on an interview with members of the Obama Online Operation referred to as 'Triple O', headed by new media director of Obama's campaign Joe Rospars, the *Washington Post* reported that the 2008 campaign raised half a billion US dollars (Vargas, 2008, para. 4). Further qualifications are made in research studies that followed the media hype. For instance, one analysis noted that, despite an extensive e-mail campaign—a reported 1 billion e-mails were sent during the campaign according to Jose Vargas (2008)—the Obama campaign team "did not reply to followers, or indicate that direct messages were being heard" during the times of heaviest use of digital technologies (Crawford, 2009, p. 530).

A Pew Research Center study titled 'Social Media and Political Engagement' found that American citizens used social media even more so during the 2012 campaign than they did in 2008, as did the candidates (Rainie, Smith, Schlozman, Brady, & Verba, 2012). By the end of the 2012 campaign, Obama had 22.7 million followers on Twitter and 32.2 million likes on Facebook, according to social media tracking company Hootsuite (Foulger, 2012, para. 4). But another Pew Research Center study examining how the US presidential candidates used social media reported that "neither campaign made much use of the social aspect of social media. Rarely did either candidate [or, by implication, his staff] reply to, comment on, or retweet something from a citizen—or anyone else outside the campaign" (Rosenstiel & Mitchell, 2012,

p. 3). The study found that campaign Web sites remained the central hub of digital political messages and these continued to be primarily one-way transmissional in nature. The sub-title of the Pew report was "Obama leads but neither candidate engages in much dialogue with voters".

While there was much to admire in the Obama presidential campaigns of 2008 and 2012 and they pioneered social media communication in some respects, they do not provide a complete model for organizational listening for several reasons. First, these campaigns had massive budgets beyond the reach of 99 per cent of organizations including major multinational corporations. Second, they gained some level of engagement, but only in a short burst and on a single issue. Therefore, they fail to demonstrate how large-scale engagement is sustainable in an organizational context (i.e., within budgets and across a wide range of operations). Third, independent research shows that they did not undertake listening as described in this analysis. They primarily involved citizens engaging with Obama in support of his objective of being elected, with only limited engagement with citizens by Obama and his team of staff, advisers, and minders.

The MIT Collaboratorium/Deliberatorium

An experimental project to test systems for ongoing online citizen engagement that has operated for a number of years is the Massachusetts Institute of Technology (MIT) online public consultation on climate change, initially called the Collaboratorium (Klein 2007) and renamed the Deliberatorium in 2008 (Iandoli, Klein, & Zolla, 2009, p. 70). The Deliberatorium, described as an MIT "collective intelligence system" (http://deliberatorium.mit.edu) and as "crowd-based innovation" ("Deliberatorium", 2015), is a 220-member user community that discusses a range of issues related to climate change.

Mark Klein, who leads the project, says on his Web site that "current collective innovation technologies fail badly when dealing with complex problems and large groups". He says the fundamental challenge in successful engagements with large numbers of people is "*super-abundance*: crowds generate so many ideas that it becomes difficult to manage the process and harvest the best ideas" ("Deliberatorium", 2015) [original emphasis]. This can lead to what this study refers to as the challenge of cacophony. Reports of the project's activities provide some useful insights into the architecture that needs to be established to process large-scale speaking and effective listening. In reporting on what was then called the Collaboratorium, Mark Klein and his co-researchers identified five key requirements for sense making in online public consultation as follows:

1. Careful design of the rules of interaction;
2. Seeding of discussions with "an initial corpus of policy options and pointers" to stimulate discussion;
3. A "committed community of contributors and expert judges";
4. Voting systems that provide citizens with simple quick ways of contributing (e.g., to support others' contributions rather than entering new comments); and
5. Tools for collating and assessing well-structured arguments (Klein, Malone, Sterman, & Quadir, 2006).

Klein warns that large-scale interactions to date through online applications such as e-mail, instant messaging, chat rooms, blogs, and wikis "have been incoherent and dispersed, contributions vary widely in quality, and there has been no clear way to converge on well-supported decisions". He cites problems in online discussion including a "low signal to noise ratio", "balkanization" as users self-assemble into groups that share the same opinions, "dysfunctional argumentation", and "hidden consensus" that is lost in the volume of comments and viewpoints (2007, n.p.). Also, "group interactions are all too easily hijacked by a narrow set of 'hot' issues or loud voices", according to Klein and Iandoli (2008, p. 1).

In a more recent paper, Luca Iandoli, Mark Klein, and Giuseppe Zolla note that "few attempts have been made to support large, diverse and geographically dispersed groups in systematically exploring and coming to decisions about complex and controversial issues" (2009, p. 69). They say that, while large-scale online organizing using low-cost technologies has achieved outstanding results in knowledge creation, sharing, and accumulation, "current technologies such as forums, wikis and blogs … appear to be less supportive of knowledge organization, use and consensus formation" (p. 70). In short, current online communication tools and approaches are effective in enabling speaking, but when issues are complex or generate widespread argument, Iandoli, Klein, and Zolla say "little progress has been made … in providing virtual communities with suitable tools and mechanisms for collective decision-making" (p. 70).

Three types of argumentation tools have been identified as important in the MIT Deliberatorium, based on the argumentation support model developed by Aldo de Moor and Mark Aakhus (2006)—*sharing, funnelling,* and *argumentation* tools. In reports of trials conducted by the Deliberatorium, Klein (2007, 2011) says that system design should include aids such as articles for users to read to become familiar with issues and for and against views before participating. Second, he says that design should provide *argument maps* to group and link ideas and arguments on a topic. Klein argues that creation and maintenance of a logical argument mapping structure requires editors with experience in argument map creation and harvesting of the best ideas from open discussion to add to argument maps. Third, he proposes that online consultation systems should provide simple tools for users to search, add comments, rate, and vote on articles and ideas, as well as post new articles. Fourth, Klein says it is essential to provide immediate feedback to users such as simple 'thank you' acknowledgements of contributions.

A challenge that besets any large-scale listening exercise is diversity of views, which can lead to cacophony and confusion, as noted. From the experiences of the MIT Deliberatorium, as well as analysis of online public consultation trials in Australia (Macnamara, 2010), some of the processes required to overcome confusion and cacophony (i.e., to help participants and the organization make sense of discussions) are schematically presented in Figure 4.1. This shows that key elements in an architecture of listening include:

1. Background reading for those unfamiliar with topics to enable them to gain understanding in order to participate in an informed way;
2. A moderation function to intervene in unacceptable communication such comments involving racism, sexism, or vilification;
3. An acknowledgement function (possibly auto-generated) to respond to speakers promptly;
4. A categorization function to group information and comments into topics or headings so they are easy to find and follow;
5. Editors' summaries to update latecomers to the conversation and condense and clarify large volumes of comments;
6. Collection of comments in a database as a secure and searchable record; and
7. Finally, and importantly, an interface with relevant policy advisers and decision makers so that majority voices and consensus can lead to action and change—what is termed *articulation* of organizational listening in this analysis.

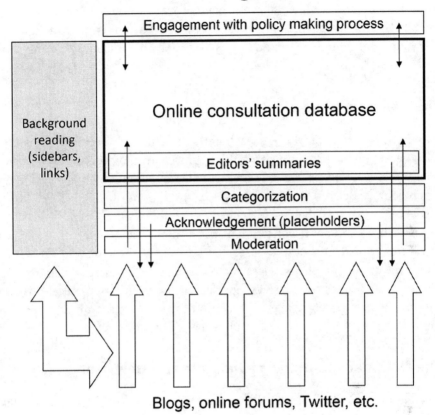

Figure 4.1. Key elements for effective large-scale online public consultation and communication (Macnamara, 2010).

This model recognizes that some who wish to participate in dialogue and debate will not know the background or lack knowledge about the issues under discussion. The provision of background reading can assist them and the overall coherence of the discussion. It also recognizes that some will join the discussion midway through or late in the day and will not be aware of what has been said already. Mechanisms such as editors' summaries can help them catch up and avoid going over old ground and endless repetition. Furthermore, it recognizes that some will have particular interests and not want to discuss some other matters. The categorization of discussion into themes or particular issues allows participants to contribute in areas in which they are interested and qualified and not have to wade through copious volumes of texts and transcripts on matters of no interest. The presence of moderators also helps maintain decorum and order and their role includes deleting content that is offensive.

The Dialogue Project at MIT

Another initiative of the Massachusetts Institute of Technology is the Dialogue Project. It takes a particular approach to promoting dialogue and public participation by drawing on the expertise of university professors in psychology, leadership, and business to lead discussions (Taylor & Kent, 2014, p. 394). The MIT Dialogue Project provides public consultation facilitation services to government, educational institutions, and business. No organizations examined in this study used the services of the Dialogue Project or any of the other specialist services and organizations discussed in this section. However, such initiatives provide specialist expertise that organizations can call on—albeit this particular approach runs the risk of too much top-down input by 'experts', which can intimidate many potential participants.

The National Coalition for Dialogue and Deliberation (NCDD)

The National Coalition for Dialogue and Deliberation (NCDD) is a network of more than 2,200 innovators who join in discussion on major issues, plan actions, and provide advice and assistance to citizens and community on civic and political participation. Headquartered in Pennsylvania, the organization describes itself as "a gathering place, a resource center, a news source, and a facilitative leader for this vital community of practice" (NCDD, 2015a). The NCDD Web site (http://ncdd.org) serves as a clearinghouse for research studies, papers, articles, and other resources such as the NCDD's 'Resource Guide on Public Engagement' and the coalition organizes conferences, forums, and seminars on issues related to engagement and public participation.

The NCDD also promotes the research of groups such as the Citizens Participation Network led by Oliver Escobar, who has published numerous articles and research reports on citizen engagement, participation, and dialogue (see Escobar, 2014; Escobar, Faulkner, & Rea, 2014), and is actively involved in public consultations such as an EU-funded study of wind farms in Scotland (Roberts & Escobar, 2014).

The Public Dialogue Consortium (PDC)

The Public Dialogue Consortium (PDC) is a non-profit organization in the US, operating mainly in California, with offices in San Jose, San Francisco, and Sonoma County. This group originally focussed on interpersonal communication, but its activities have expanded to include training and facilitation of dialogue, particularly in practices such as government-community consultation. Its approach is different to the MIT Dialogue Project, which draws expertise from academics and industry experts, in that it provides its own trained coaches to create and facilitate dialogues within groups as well as bringing different groups together to discuss community issues.

The PDC employs advanced communication techniques to support public leaders in assessing organizational and community readiness to co-design and deliver engagement processes, and provides training for organization staff, officials, and community members in communication with a focus on dialogue (http://publicdialogue.org). Even though the PDC is regionally located, it is an example of the range of specialist services and consultancies available to help organizations.

The 2003 GMNation? 'Foundation Discussion' Workshops in the UK

A series of GMNation? workshops were launched in the UK in 2003 as part of nationwide discussion and policy making in relation to genetically modified crops. These workshops have been analyzed in a number of books (e.g., Dobson, 2014, pp. 188–195) and in numerous articles, many of which are available online, so they will not be reviewed in detail here. However, these workshops are an interesting model for two key reasons. First, the GMNation? debate involved three elements: (1) a series of nine "foundation discussion workshops" coordinated by an independent steering board; (2) a review of the science led by the UK government's chief scientific adviser with a panel of academics and experts; and (3) a study of the costs and benefits of GM crops by the government's strategy unit (DEFRA, 2007). In this way, the national debate made use of independent experts, as is appropriate in highly technical matters, and involved the government's senior civil service advisers, but also allowed an open public debate—a three-tiered approach. The second key feature relates to how the public debate was structured and undertaken. Rather than setting restrictive terms of reference, as is commonly done for inquiries and reviews, the independent steering board specified some procedural guide-lines, but allowed participants to set the agenda and raise issues for discussion in the workshops (Rowe, Horlick-Jones, Walls, & Pidgeon, 2005). Andrew Dobson says the GMNation? debate was a good example of apophatic listen-ing, as discussed by Leonard Waks (2007, 2010). It suspended pre-determined parameters and categories (terms of reference) and allowed citizens to raise issues of concern to them. While having some faults, in Dobson's view, the GMNation? debate was more inclusive and more wide ranging than many so-called listening exercises.

The Restorative Gentrification Listening Project, Portland, Oregon

The Restorative Gentrification Listening Project in Portland, Oregon, is a product of the Portland Office of Neighborhood Involvement that uses restor-ative listening circles to address issues of racism and social injustice in order to build community and cultural understanding and to find ways to act together to include and value all members of a community. Portland is a growing urban area with a diverse, but mostly segregated, population. Historically the black community has been geographically located in the northeast neighbourhood, but in the past few decades, gentrification has changed the neighbourhood dramatically, displacing low-income families and small businesses. The restor-ative listening project involves forums at which the harm caused by gentrifi-cation is able to be discussed by the people affected and actions are planned to repair and redress the harm. It is based on restorative justice theory, which maintains that "only when those most impacted are heard, acknowledged, and efforts have been made to repair the harm can the community be made whole again" (Dobson, 2014, p. 137).

Critics might argue that redressing gentrification of urban areas, a trend in many growing cities, is naïve and amounts to trying to stop 'progress'. How-ever, this is a narrow view and rules out mitigation strategies such as assisting displaced residents to find alternative accommodation, funding new develop-ment projects, and promoting integration and balance. Restorative justice is a useful framework for illustrating the importance of moving beyond voice. It is the listening and acting that restore justice. Protests and pleas that fall on deaf ears amount to voice, but without listening it does not matter, in Nick Could-ry's terms. Further information on the gentrification listening project is avail-able on the Web site of the City of Portland (2015) and the NCDD (2015b).

The California Report Card

A more recent example of organized online public listening is the California Report Card (CRC), which is a mobile-optimized Web application designed to promote engagement by residents with the California state government. It was developed by Professor Ken Goldberg and the Center for Information Technology Research in the Interest of Society (CITRIS) at the University of California, Berkeley, as part of its data and democracy initiative in conjunction with California lieutenant governor Gavin Newsom. Version 1.0 was released in January 2014 (Getuiza, 2014).

The application is based on the World Bank's Citizen Report Card (World Bank, 2013), as well as a UC Berkeley online consultation application called Opinion Space, also known as the Collective Discovery Engine (UC Berkeley, 2013). On the CRC site participants are encouraged to grade the California government on a scale of A+ to F (fail) on six timely topics and to offer their own suggestions of issues that they believe need attention (Scott, 2014). While being a simple online survey in many respects, it is the open-ended nature of the site that offers the most potential for listening, with citizens able to enter comments and suggestions.

Because the data are gathered from a self-selecting sample, the creators of the project do not claim that it is a scientifically valid study. "It's more like a focus group", according to Goldberg (as cited in Scott, 2014, para. 5). In many ways, the California Report Card is a simple open online survey. But it is an example of how working with a university can tap into specialist research expertise, often at little or no cost—a strategy pursued by only two of the 36 organizations studied in this project.

The minimum level of tools and expertise required for conducting online discussion are text or content analysis applications that can use keyword searches and coding to identify themes and categorize discussion, as well as a user-friendly Web interface that is easy for users to navigate to find sections such as background reading, links to expert papers, and so on. However, a number of more sophisticated tools are available to facilitate dialogue, consultation, and analysis to interpret and summarize content, albeit these are not applied to any substantial extent in the public communication field at this stage. Some specialist applications are briefly discussed in the following section to demonstrate the potential for transdisciplinary approaches that can substantially contribute to public communication and organizational listening specifically.

Argumentation Mapping and Facilitation

Complex discussions and consultations can be assisted with the use of argument mapping, also referred to as *conversation mapping* (Sack, 2000), *discourse architecture* (Mancini & Buckingham Shum, 2006), and *computer-supported argumentation visualization* (Donath, 2002; Renton & Macintosh, 2007). Projects such as the MIT Deliberatorium draw on concepts such as the argumentation support model developed by Aldo de Moor and Mark Aakhus (2006) as noted. As well, argumentation processes are informed by the 'new rhetoric' of Chaïm Perelman (Perelman & Olbrechts-Tyteca, 1969), the informal logic and argument analysis structure of Stephen Toulmin (1959), and a number of academic models such as argument schemes proposed by Douglas Walton (1989, 2006) and the Issue Based Information System (IBIS) of Jeff Conklin (2006).

The Toulmin approach involves presenting (1) a series of key claims; (2) the grounds for each, such as supporting facts and opinions of influential people; (3) warrants that demonstrate how the grounds support the claims made; and (4) qualifiers, which are statements that limit or prescribe the validity of claims (e.g., words such as 'occasionally', 'usually', 'based on best available evidence').

Luca Iandoli, Mark Klein, and Giuseppe Zolla (2009), who applied Walton's argument schemes theory in the MIT Deliberatorium, say that it can be used by readers "to recognize and classify arguments proposed by users and check if critical questions are adequately answered, and to help authors check if their arguments are defendable with respect to the critical questions and, if not, to revise [them]" (p. 77).

The IBIS approach presents and tracks arguments by presenting (1) questions; (2) ideas that proffer possible solutions or explanations; and (3) pro/con arguments for each. The resulting framework of argument is developed and represented visually as 'tree' structures using specialist software (see Figure 4.2).

Fortunately there are software programs available to implement many of these processes without users understanding the complex concepts behind them, including free open source applications. For example, Argunet (http://www.argunet.org) is an open source argumentation mapping tool for analyzing and visualizing complex debates. It can be downloaded and used on a PC, or as a client-server application over a network to allow multiple users and sites to collaborate. The application can be used in 'sketching mode' to outline the macro-structure of a debate and also to go into specific details of each

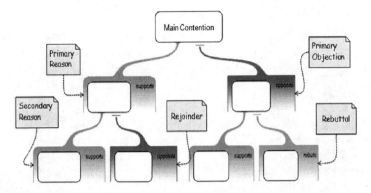

Figure 4.2. A simple example of an argument map 'tree'.

argument. The producers of the program say "this is where Argunet really shines: Every argument can be reconstructed as a logically valid premise-conclusion structure. Relations between arguments can be systematically traced back to the logical relations between the sentences used as their premises and conclusions" (Argunet, 2015). Argunet is available for Windows, Apple, and Linux.

A limitation of a number of argumentation mapping processes and argument analysis is that they are based predominantly on logic and reason. Emotional factors that inevitably arise in debates and discussions are not easily dealt with in such systems, which tend to see emotional responses as invalid. However, such systems do bring rigour and order to large-scale discussions and consultations and are examples of advanced tools available to aid organizational listening. Other examples are given by Stephen Coleman (2013b) in his article 'The Challenge of Digital Hearing'.

Sense Making Methodology

Sense making, as the term suggests, is the collection of processes by which humans derive meaning from (make sense of) experiences and data. Sense making has been studied in a number of disciplines since the 1970s. In particular, contributions have been made in human-computer interaction (e.g., Russell, Stefik, Pirolli, & Card, 1993), in information science (Dervin, 1983, 1992), and in organizational studies (Weick, 1995). Sense making methodology has been extensively used in the library and information science and technology fields (Dervin, Foreman-Wernet, & Lauterbach, 2003), but only one article could be found in research literature applying this methodology to corporate communication, organizational communication, or public relations (Foreman-Wernet & Dervin, 2006). A pioneer in developing this methodology, Brenda Dervin (1983, 1992) describes sense making methodology as follows.

> The term 'sense making' is a label for a coherent set of concepts and methods used in a now eight-year programmatic effort to study how people construct sense of their worlds and, in particular, how they construct information needs and uses for information in the process of sense making. Since sense making is central to all communicating situations, whether they be intrapersonal, interpersonal, mass, cross-cultural, societal, or international. (Dervin, 1983, para 2)

More specifically, in a communication context, sense making methodology prescribes methods of question framing, data collection, and analysis that can be used in conducting research designed to understand how people experience and make sense of the phenomenon being studied, in and on their own terms (Dervin, 1992). The final clause is important. Sense making takes us beyond the author's intentions and information transmission processes—what organizations or stakeholders might want to achieve, for example—and focusses on how recipients of information interpret that information. The processes are relatively complex, but sense making is another example of a body of knowledge that can be applied to organizational listening at an advanced level.

Knowledge Management

The field of knowledge management also has tools and processes to offer communication, consultation, and research practitioners in terms of methods for collecting and making sense of large amounts of information. Consultants such as the founder and 'chief scientific officer' of Cognitive Edge, Dave Snowden, works with governments and large corporations to apply what his company calls "a science based approach to organizations drawing on anthropology, neuroscience and complex adaptive systems theory" (Cognitive Edge, 2015). While some knowledge management (KM) tends to focus on analyzing information held inside an organization, referred to as its information assets, KM specialists such as Cognitive Edge refer to using "populations of citizens or employees to form part of a human sensor network" to collect information (i.e., listen). The company offers advanced sense making tools and methods such as its SenseMaker software (Cognitive Edge, 2015). Academic perspectives on KM are published in specialist journals such as the *Journal of Knowledge Management*. There are also professional as well as academic books on the subject, such as *Learning to Fly* written by knowledge management pioneers Chris Collison and Geoff Parcell (2001/2004), which outlines their experiences of knowledge sharing and sense making at BP in the late 1990s. Knowledge management is yet another example of the need for and opportunities available from a transdisciplinary approach to large-scale organizational listening, borrowing methods and ideas from multiple fields.

Other Listening Tools and Methods

Other less complex mechanisms that can be applied to aid organizational listening and form part of an architecture of listening include:

- *Turn-taking*, which is a feature of public diplomacy used as a way to 'level the playing field' when there are disparities of power between negotiating parties and create specific listening as well as speaking opportunities (Macnamara, 2012b);
- *Listening posts*, which can be physical locations such as 'pop up' public consultation sites (e.g., booths, temporary offices, even tents or marquees), although increasingly these are Web sites;
- *Captive Audience Meetings* (CAMs, which have attracted criticism because of their use by employers "to compel employees to listen to anti-union and other types of proselytizing" (Hartley, 2010, p. 65). Roger Hartley is one who has challenged such uses of captive audience meetings and argued for "a freedom not to listen". However, the concept of captive audience meetings can be used in a broader sense, such as using existing gatherings of citizens or members of associations and groups to discuss matters of common interest;
- *Customer engagement summits* or establishment of a permanent *customer engagement council*, which is recommended by McKinsey consultants as a way to give customers an opportunity to speak directly to management and for management to listen (French, LaBerge, & Magill, 2012);
- *Reconciliation committees*, which tend to be used mainly for major social issues such as ethnic tensions and indigenous reconciliation, but can be used to help resolve a range of conflicts;
- *Ombuds* (a non-gendered abbreviation of ombudsman), who are commonly appointed by government, but also can be established by private

sector organizations to provide an independent channel for inquiries and complaints and represent the interests of the public to an organization (Howard, 2010). If appointed in an organization, an ombud should adhere to the Standards of Practice of the International Ombudsman Association (https://www.ombudsassociation.org);

- *Citizens' juries*, which are panels of citizens who are presented with evidence and asked to decide on a number of options such as approving or opposing a project. Citizens' juries have been used to gain citizen input in relation to offshore wind farms in Scotland (Roberts & Escobar, 2014) and to decide on the development of roads through the World Heritage-listed Daintree Forest near Cairns in northern Australia (Goodin, 2008);
- *Trust networks*, which are derived from the work of Charles Tilley (2005, 2007), who described them as groups of people connected by similar ties and interests whose "collective enterprise is at risk to the malfeasance, mistakes, and failures of individual members" (Tilley, 2007, p. 82). In simple terms, trust networks have mutual dependency, or what business analysts call having 'skin in the deal', which generates a commitment to achieving mutually acceptable outcomes;
- *Study circles*, which are small groups of people who meet multiple times to discuss an issue. There is no 'teacher' or chair, but one member usually acts as facilitator. For a review of literature and examples, see Larsson and Nordvall (2010);
- *Community liaison officer* appointments for groups affected by the activities of an organization; and
- *Advisory boards and committees* with representation from all relevant stakeholders, publics, and stakeseekers—not only leaders from major groups and elites.

Two key findings further to those reported at the end of Chapter 3 emerge from the discussion and review presented in this chapter. First, this analysis suggests that institutionalized structures and processes such as the French National Commission for Public Debate, while having some benefits, are largely counterproductive, as they are shown to slow down processes, increase costs of projects, "mobilize" and "radicalize opposition" by providing a platform for vocal minorities, and even lead to "participation fatigue". Second, while this analysis is not able to comprehensively review all aids available to facilitate organizational listening, this and the previous chapters have identified a number of systems, tools, methods, structures, technologies, and models of practice that can enable and enhance organizational listening. These serve to show that large-scale listening is possible and that a body of knowledge about organizational listening is emerging, albeit it is spread across many disciplines and fields of practice and requires synthesis and further development. Hence a transdisciplinary approach is necessary, as has been taken in this analysis, with a view to disrupting entrenched practices of late modernity and making a contribution to transforming public communication for the betterment of politics, government, business, and society. The potential benefits of creating an architecture of listening and doing the work of listening in organizations are discussed in the following concluding chapter of this analysis.

Notes

1. A federal investigation was conducted by the Senate Homeland Security and Governmental Affairs Committee into the Hurricane Katrina disaster, which left at least 1,100 dead, displaced more than a million area residents, and caused hundreds of billions of dollars in damage.
2. Abbreviation for marketing communication.
3. A local area official equivalent to a mayor of a city or governor of a state.

· 5 ·

THE BENEFITS OF ORGANIZATIONAL LISTENING FOR DEMOCRATIC POLITICS, GOVERNMENT, BUSINESS, AND SOCIETY

This chapter addresses what some see as the 'elephant in the room' in the form of a number of interrelated questions about the findings reported and the recommendations presented. Collectively they pose what, in academic terms, is the ultimate question in any research project. So what? Why do organizations have to listen, including to strangers in some cases? Most specifically, what are the benefits of organizational listening? These are questions that have arisen during this research project, posed both as genuine inquiries and as veiled objections or perceived obstacles. To these I add one more: What happens if organizations don't listen to their stakeholders, publics, and concerned stakeseekers?

Based on the experiences of a number of organizations, this analysis has already argued that organizational listening does not require additional resources in the form of personnel, time, facilities, or technology. It may require *different* personnel, facilities, technologies, and skills. But successful organizations demonstrate that two-way communication including listening leading to dialogue and engagement can be accomplished through reallocation of resources from ineffective and lower priority activities. This analysis also has explained the method for identifying activities that can be scaled back or eliminated—measurement and evaluation conducted using rigorous quantitative and qualitative research.

So, in the final analysis, this is not a question of return on investment (ROI). No additional investment is proposed. This approach is taken for two reasons. First, proposing an architecture of listening and the work of listening that require additional expenditure is impractical for most organizations. Such an approach simply would not 'fly' in times of budget restraint and financial pressures. Second, the experience of a number of organizations shows that considerable wastage is occurring in public communication and that, with improved effectiveness and efficiency—characteristics desired and valued by most management—more can be done with less. The UK government, which has reduced its annual spending on communication from almost £1 billion a few years ago to around half that much, with better results in many areas, is a case in point. Also, many corporations are reducing their massive media advertising budgets and finding that equal or better results can be gained through alternative channels and methods of communication.

Nevertheless, the questions posed need to be answered. This final chapter presents some responses to two key questions: (1) what are the benefits of improved organizational listening, and (2) what happens if organizations don't listen more? These slight revisions to the questions posed at the beginning of this chapter are made simply to reflect that most organizations listen to some extent already, albeit nowhere near enough according to this analysis and the words of most stakeholders and publics. In the space available it is not possible to comprehensively answer these questions—and it has to be acknowledged that specialist expertise beyond that of this author will be required to do this. Follow-up research could productively involve specialists in management, IT, systems, and organizational development, as well as communication and social science. However, this analysis does conclude by pointing out a number of compelling reasons listening needs to be substantially improved in organizations in contemporary developed societies. It is proposed that further specific quantitative and qualitative assessment of the benefits of organizational listening should be part of exploring scalable models of organizational listening in ongoing research.

Listening to Reinvigorate Democracy and Democratic Government

Numerous studies of what is termed the 'democratic deficit' have clearly established that citizens in democracies want their governments at national, state, and local levels to listen to them more. Stephen Coleman's (2013a) research in the UK is particularly salutary—and worrying. Many UK citizens are disillusioned and disengaged. Citizens do not trust their own elected political leaders very much in any of the countries studied. Barely half trust their civil service in Britain. And 15–16 per cent trust business (Edelman, 2013, 2014; Ipsos-MORI, 2015). And it is much the same or worse in the US (see Table 5.1).

Table 5.1. The percentage of young Americans (18–29) who say they trust the listed institutions to do the right thing all or most of the time.

Source	2010	2011	2012	2013	2014
The president	44%	41%	41%	39%	32%
Congress	25%	23%	23%	18%	14%
The Supreme Court	45%	44%	45%	40%	36%
The federal government	29%	27%	27%	22%	20%
United Nations	40%	38%	38%	34%	34%
Your state government	–	28%	32%	30%	28%
Your local government	–	33%	37%	34%	33%
Wall Street	11%	–	13%	12%	12%
Mass media	17%	–	–	11%	11%

Source: Harvard University (2015).

Citizen Participation and Engagement

Political scientists, sociologists, and communication scholars unanimously see participation as fundamental to a healthy democracy, although not all agree on the level and type of participation that is desirable or achievable. For a start, it is well established that a sizeable proportion of citizens remain uninvolved and passive in politics and civil society. These are referred to *lurkers* in social media, with studies showing that as many as 90 per cent of Internet users 'lurk' in sites without making a contribution to discussion (Napoli, 2011, p. 106; Nielsen, 2006). Nevertheless, early dismissal of 'lurkers' as inactive has been replaced by an understanding that they may become informed and develop opinions through reading and viewing, which is a dimension of being active.

Beyond this qualification and limitation on participation, the decline of the *dutiful citizen*, who became informed through traditional media, possibly joined a political party or union, and voted in elections (Schudson, 1998, 2003), informs our thinking about political and government communication today. Lance Bennett and his co-researchers propose that citizens today, particularly youth, are *actualizing citizens*. While the dutiful citizen, who accepts responsibilities in relation to civic and political participation, is in decline (Bennett, Wells, & Freelon, 2011; Couldry, Livingstone, & Markham, 2007; Putnam, 2000; Schudson, 1998), researchers observe that what Bennett et al. (2011) call the actualizing citizen performing *actualizing citizenship* is on the increase. Bennett et al. say:

> This citizenship typology enables us to think about a generational shift away from taking cues as members of groups or out of regard for public authorities (opinion leaders, public officials, and journalists) and toward looser personal engagement with peer networks that pool (crowd source) information and organize civic action using social technologies that maximize individual expression. (2011, p. 839)

Nico Carpentier (2011) observes that proponents of participatory and agonistic models of democracy seek *maximalist* participation, whereas deliberative and representative forms of democracy offer *minimalist* participation. Furthermore, he says that actualizing citizens seek *multi-directional* participation including peer-to-peer discussion; *multi-sited* participation rather than "mono-sited" participation, which is a characteristic of minimalist models (e.g., voting every 3–4 years); and engage in *micro-participation* such as in small groups and movements such as Occupy (pp. 17–18). Political scientists are beginning to look past generalizing pronouncements of a decline in civic and political participation and recognize, as Bimber et al. do, "a shift from institutional-centric practices towards non-institutional ones" such as protesting and other forms of direct democracy. This reveals that the situation "is not one of decline but of altered norms of citizenship and engagement" (2012, p. 168). Such shifts in society place new demands on political and government communication. They explain why mass circulating media releases to traditional media and organizing set-piece events do not cut it as public communication with a growing number of citizens. Furthermore, the maximalist, multi-directional, multi-sited, and micro forms of participation that many citizens today seek require listening—not just information. Governments in affluent educated Western societies face a new type of citizen, and they need to adapt their public communication practices. *Mass communication* (i.e., mass transmission) models increasingly do not work.

Listening to Engage Youth

Young people in particular are disengaging from traditional politics and losing faith in government, as shown in a number of academic studies in the US, the

UK, and elsewhere (e.g., Bennett, 2008; Dalton, 2011; Levine, 2008; Saha, Print, & Edwards, 2007). The annual 'Trust in Institutions and the Political Process' study conducted by Harvard University (2015) reported that trust in the president, Congress, federal, state, and local government, and even the courts has fallen among 18- to 29-year-olds. Only 14 per cent of 18–29-year-old Americans trust the US Congress to do the right thing all or most of the time, and only 20 per cent trust the federal government in this context.

Does trust in government matter? It most definitely does, according to Marc Hetherington (2005), author of *Why Trust Matters*, Charles Tilley who has been cited already, and a number of other researchers. Kate Lacey (2013) argues that the loss of trust in politicians and government is a serious concern "because of the role that trust plays in a representative political system" (p. 187). Trust underpins legitimacy. If people do not trust a system, they are likely to defect from it, as noted by Tilley (2005) and Andrew Dobson (2014, p. 125). Either they withdraw from and ignore it, which breaks down the foundational participatory basis of democracy, or they are open to or actively seek alternative systems. The radicalization of youth in the US, the UK, and Australia, previously stable peaceful democracies, suggests that young citizens are disillusioned with institutionalized politics and government in these countries. The prevalence of 'hung' parliaments and political parties having to establish often uncomfortable coalitions with minority parties to form government in a number of democratic countries during the past decade are signs of an even broader general disillusionment among citizens with all shades of institutionalized politics.

There is evidence that loss of trust is connected to lack of listening. In the early 1990s Robert Putnam concluded that "social trust in complex modern settings" is created by "norms of reciprocity and networks of civic engagement" (1993, p. 171). The 2013 Australia Institute study cited in Chapter 1 found that young people "don't feel as though they are being listened to" and identified this as a key reason that "almost half the nation's young voters aged under-25 believe no party represents their interests" (as cited in Lucas, 2013, p. 14).

A 2014 study of the extent to which local government bodies in 10 Italian municipalities listen to citizens through social media reported that "citizens ask for a tangible and actual two-way communication with local administrations on social media" (Lovari & Parisi, 2015, p. 205). While outside the three countries included in this study, this research is cited because it is one of the few studies that asked citizens what they want from government 'communication' initiatives such as social media sites.

Evidence that dissatisfaction and disillusionment run deep and are not just the impatience of youth or the agitation of 'Leftie' radicals is the rise of what is called 'flatpack democracy' in the UK—a local level democratic reform movement created by frustrated citizens. Emboldened and empowered by the Localism Act[1] passed in Britain in 2011 (Department of Communities and Local Government, 2011), groups of citizens have begun banding together and standing independents in town council elections across Britain. For example, in Frome, Somerset, Independents for Frome (IfF) decided to contest the 17 seats on Frome's town council and in 2015 took all 17 seats. A chief proponent of the movement is 30-year resident of Frome, Peter Macfadyen, author of *Flatpack Democracy: A Guide to Creating Independent Politics* (Macfadyen, 2014). In his late 50s, Macfadyen teamed up with then 60-year-old Mel Usher to jointly found IfF in 2010. The movement seems to be spreading. For instance, Independents for Arlsey (IfA) won 14 of 15 seats on the town council of Arlsey in Bedfordshire in the May 2015 local council elections in the UK (Harris, 2015).

To rebuild trust in government and to maintain stable democracies, politicians, government departments, and agencies at all levels need to be more open to more people—not just elites and the dominant political actors such as leaders of big business and lobby groups, trade unions, major churches, powerful NGOs, and journalists. There needs to be an understanding of listening—what it requires, as well as what it does not require or promise—such as total agreement, a panacea for solving all problems, or capitulation. But there does need to be real dialogue, real conversations, real engagement—not the powdery puff that passes for them in politics and business or the one-sided talkfest to which citizens are subjected on a daily basis. Governments need to reach out to communities, including the 'poor, the downtrodden, and the weak'[2] and the "huddled masses yearning to breathe free" (Lazarus, 1883), not sit and wait for them to 'speak up' loudly enough to be heard over the din of the noisy and the narcissistic. Many are already too disillusioned, too disenfranchised, or too weak to speak up. Political parties and governments need to close the gap between their institutions and their publics, and effective ethical listening is one of the key practices to achieve that.

The costs if this does not occur almost certainly will include continuing and increasing declines in voter turnouts in elections, mid-term polls and early elections in some cases, electoral losses for traditional political parties and politicians, political tensions, the rise of new political movements, and instability of government caused by short terms and lack of continuity, which in turn lead to poor policy, and ultimately potential citizen unrest, radicalization, and social fragmentation.

The benefits of effective ethical listening can include increased trust in government, leading to political stability and increased participation in politics and civil society, which in turn lead to more equitable representation, better policy making, and reduced crises through better understanding and the early detection of concerns, problems, and changing expectations.

Of course, it would be naïve to suggest that these costs on one hand or benefits on the other will accrue from listening or lack of listening alone. It is recognized that a wide range of factors are at play in politics as well as in business and complex contemporary societies. But there can be no debate that listening is a necessary corollary of speaking and a fundamental element of voice, which is recognized as central to democracy and civil society, and also that being listened to is a deep-seated psychological need in people. Furthermore, there is strong evidence that there is a substantial and, at times, chronic lack of listening by major organizations and that the listening that is done is selective, limited, and often self-serving. There is also sufficient evidence to suggest that a crisis for democracy is in the making if trends in voter participation, trust in government and institutions, and citizen satisfaction in general continue. A logical and inevitable deduction from this evidence and projections is that action is required and that listening must be a key part of any action plan to reinvigorate democracy and democratic government.

The description of an architecture of listening and the work of listening indicates that there are no quick fixes or shortcuts and that the task is not trivial or small. A useful way to conceive of the way forward is in terms of a virtuous circle into which we can enter by beginning to listen more and better, or alternatively a vicious circle into which societies will descend if the voices of their people are devalued, ignored, or silenced.

Listening for Business Sustainability

As much as critical analysis takes issue with business on many matters, business is a legitimate and central pillar of capitalist societies. Indeed, as discussed in Chapter 1, business and market logic have permeated all areas of public and private life in neoliberal societies. Large and small businesses dominate the economies of all of the world's developed countries and play a key role in developing countries. It is important therefore that the performance of listening is examined in relation to business.

Listening for Successful Strategy

Businesses fail or thrive largely based on strategy that they adopt. Management and organizational communication theorists point out that traditional and widely adopted understandings of strategy and being *strategic* are related to power and decision making (Mintzberg, 1979, 1988) focussed on organizational survival and efficiency (Perrow, 1992). Without broader thinking, this leads to an organization-centric focus and a 'command and control' approach in management, which is reflected in communication as well as other operations. As noted in Chapter 1, Kirk Hallahan et al. (2007) acknowledge that strategic communication by an organization is widely understood as "purposeful use of communication to fulfil its mission" (p. 3) and serve its interests, but go on to note that "alternative and more positive notions of strategy have … emerged since the 1950s" (p. 27) based on two-way symmetrical models of public relations (Dozier et al., 1995; Grunig et al., 2002). Similarly, in corporate communication literature Joep Cornelissen states that "strategy is about the organization and its environment" and that strategy involves "balancing the mission and vision of the organization … with what the environment will allow or encourage it to do. Strategy is therefore often adaptive" (2011, p. 83). However, there is considerable evidence, including the findings of research reported in this analysis, that organizations still have a way to go to realize Hallahan's and Cornelissen's rehabilitated notion of strategic communication.

A number of researchers have called for new approaches to strategy. At an International Communication Association seminar on strategic communication, Jesper Falkheimer and Mats Heide (2011) called on scholars and practitioners to "break the dominant approach to strategic communication" and adopt a participatory approach (p. 14) drawing on Stanley Deetz's (1992) identification of the twin purposes of communication as *participation* and *effectiveness*. In summary, Falkheimer and Heide propose that organizations rightly focus on organizational effectiveness, but this must be balanced with participation by key stakeholders and publics to gain their input and support. Priscilla Murphy (2011) similarly proposed that a "network view" of strategic communication provides a "holistic view of the opinion arena" and recognizes the interconnected, fluid, and participatory nature of this environment (p. 14). Perhaps the most significant argument for changing business approaches to strategy and communication is Cynthia King's (2010) call for "emergent communication strategies". While acknowledging that communication strategy is at least partly or even largely *planned* actions by organizations to achieve desired results, she notes that strategies also *emerge* regardless of an organization's intent. She defines emergent communication strategies as "a communicative construct derived from interaction between reader/hearer response, situated context, and discursive patterns" (p. 20). In short, organizations need to consider and adapt to their stakeholders and their environment. The concepts of *emergent strategy* and *emergent communication strategy* offer ways for businesses and other types of organizations to pursue their interests in a dynamic, interrelated way with their stakeholders and publics that overcomes the organization-centricity of traditional strategic communication and creates equitable, sustainable relationships. It is these interpretations and implementations of strategic communication that organizations need to adopt. And effective ethical organizational listening is a prerequisite for emergent strategy.

In a 2015 analysis of communication in public diplomacy and its broadening definition to include *corporate diplomacy*, Michael Schneider "stressed the importance of 'active listening' and sustained engagement with relevant stakeholders" (2015, pp. 18–19). Corporations as well as governments need to "listen first and talk second", according to Nancy Snow (2015, p. 87), arguing that this will improve relationships including international relations. As Bruce Dayton and Dennis Kinsey (2015) say in relation to public diplomacy and public relations: "If you aren't listening … your communication is fundamentally one-way". They add: "One-way communication is not generally effective for building positive relationships" (p. 267).

Listening to Create 'the Social Organization'

In 2011 the respected business consultancy firm Gartner Inc. published a book titled *The Social Organization: How to Use Social Media to Tap the Collective Genius of Your Customers and Employees* (Bradley & McDonald, 2011a). Shortly afterwards, IBM published a white paper titled 'The Social Business: Advent of a New Age' and the company formally committed itself to the mantra of being a "social business" (IBM Software Group, 2011). While being a commercial enterprise, IBM management statements and reports claim that the corporate giant's social business mantra is more than a glib slogan or market positioning statement. IBM's 'Social Business' Web site states:

> A social business isn't just a company that has a Facebook page and a Twitter account. A social business is one that embraces and cultivates a spirit of collaboration and community throughout its organization—both internally and externally. (IBM, 2013, para. 7)

Expanding this definition, IBM has identified three distinct characteristics of a social business, claiming (1) a social business is engaged, deeply connecting people, including customers, employees, and partners in productive, efficient ways; (2) a social business is transparent, removing boundaries to information, experts, and assets; and (3) a social business is nimble, which speeds up business with information and insights to anticipate and address evolving opportunities (IBM, 2013). Bradley and McDonald (2011a) on behalf of Gartner define a social organization as "one that strategically applies mass collaboration to address significant business challenges and opportunities". They add: "A social organization is able to be more agile, produce better outcomes, and even develop entirely new ways of operating that are only achievable through mobilizing the collective talent, energy, ideas, and efforts of communities" (p. 5). In a video available online, Mark McDonald further states: "A social organization is one that is able to bring together all the talents, interests, experience, insights [and] knowledge of their people in ways that are independent of the vertical top to bottom hierarchy or end to end process orientation to create sustained value" (McDonald, 2012).

From these definitions and descriptions, it can be seen that a social organization and a social business are not simply ones that use social media. Bradley and McDonald note this in a *Harvard Business Review* blog post, saying that "all organizations are social, but few are social organizations" (2011b, headline). The literature available suggests that the essence of a social organization—business or other—is the collaborative energy and resulting outputs that it is able to harness, drawing on its networks and stakeholders. Collaboration, networks and community are core elements of the social organization. In their book, the Gartner executives presented case studies showing that some companies are allegedly gaining significant benefits from collaboration enabled by social media and social networks.

A cynical view suggests that the concept of a social business is little more than another business buzzword describing a strategy to advance the commercial interests of a company, particularly when it refers to "productive", "efficient" ways, and addressing "opportunities". It begs the questions, whose productions, whose opportunities, and efficient for whom—citizens and society, or IBM? Nevertheless, what is relevant to this analysis is that, to be a social business, a company must listen to its stakeholders and publics and participate in two-way communication, dialogue, and engagement. Not listening is not social—in fact, it is anti-social in any context. Without listening, businesses will fail in any attempt to become a social business and miss out on benefits that Gartner and IBM claim to flow from that process.

Listening to Gain Trust and Maintain Relationships

As well as being important for government, trust is also a foundation stone of businesses. A substantial body of management research shows that trust is a key driver of relationships within and between organizations affecting employee loyalty, productivity and retention, and business partnerships (e.g., Tomlinson & Mayer, 2009). Marketing research also shows that trust is a significant, if not pivotal, aspect of customer relationships (Ganesan, 1994; Moorman, Deshpandé, & Zaltman, 1993). However, there is evidence that corporations and business generally are 'in the red' in terms of trust. In a post on the 2015 World Economic Forum blog titled 'Why Trust Matters in Business', the chairman of Baker & McKenzie USA, Eduardo Leite, wrote:

> Lack of public trust runs deep and it extends to both individual leaders and institutions. Perhaps more worrying, the trend looks set to continue, if the opinions of the next generation are anything to go by …. [L]ack of trust is something we should all be worried about, because trust matters. For many companies, particularly professional services firms like the one where I work, trust is at the centre of the business model. (Leite, 2015, paras 3, 5)

Leite went on to say that "in business, trust is the glue that binds employees to employers, customers to companies—and companies to their suppliers, regulators, government, and partners" (para. 6). He also said:

> Most companies appreciate that high trust levels lead to a stronger reputation, sustainable revenues, greater customer advocacy and increased employee retention. It is also likely that companies with higher levels of trust will bounce back from future crises far quicker than others. (para. 7)

However, Harvard University's 2015 annual study of trust reported continuing low levels of trust in business among young Americans, particularly in relation to the finance industry led by Wall Street, as well as in traditional media (see Table 5.1). The media industry could well look to such data to understand why many news consumers are abandoning press, radio, and TV. The Edelman Trust Barometer (2014, 2015a) confirms this trend across many countries including the UK, Australia, and many European nations.

Can listening contribute to and rebuild trust? There is substantial empirical evidence to show that it can. For example, a detailed study of 20 companies—10 selected from a *Fortune* list of 'most admired companies' and 10 from the list of 'most hated companies' in America—reported "a significant positive association existed between the perceived quality of dialogic communication and the level of trust" (Yang, Kang, & Cha, 2015, p. 187). The study further reported that openness to stakeholders and publics is "especially germane in engendering public trust" (p. 189).

Henry Jenkins writing with Sam Ford and Joshua Green (2013) says that companies that "listen to ... their audiences" will thrive (p. xii). However, recent research shows that senior management in business does not seem to have gotten the message and has a lot to learn and a lot to gain. In a paper presented to the annual International Public Relations Research Conference in Miami, Florida, in 2014, Ansgar Zerfass and Muschda Sherzada (2014) reported a survey of 602 CEOs and board members in Germany that found:

- 92.2 per cent of CEOs believe that mass media coverage influences corporate reputation, with comparatively few actively focussed on engagement and dialogue with stakeholders and publics;
- CEOs and board members focus on primary stakeholders, particularly customers and employees, and largely ignore other stakeholders including activists; and
- Top executives rate speaking as more important than listening in corporate communication.

The beat goes on! Speaking, talking, transmitting messages! There needs to be transformational change in business based on an understanding of communication. Subjects on communication should be included in all MBA programs and in all leadership and management courses. These currently exist to some extent, but are focussed mostly on interpersonal communication. Management education needs to be broadened to address the challenges of large-scale listening as part of two-way organization-public communication, dialogue, engagement, and building stakeholder relationships and public trust. It has to be acknowledged that there are some listening CEOs out there. But there are also many technocrat senior executives such as engineers, accountants, technologists, architects, and so on who are not trained in communication. They need to find themselves the right kind of communication professionals to work with them as advisers. But the fields of corporate and marketing communication and public relations are not well equipped to meet this need.

Professional public communication practices also need to undergo transformational change.

Listening to Transform Professional Communication Practice

We are already seeing the 'end of advertising' in terms of traditional advertising as we have known and endured it for many decades. While Roland Rust and Richard Oliver (1994) prematurely predicted the end of advertising some time ago, and John Seely Brown and Paul Duguid (2000) warn against the false prophets of *endism*, advertising is changing from a dominance of mass broadcast commercials and print advertisements to incorporate a wide range of interactive formats as well as embedded content that is integrated into programming. These new formats could hardly be said to involve listening as defined in this study. However, they are examples of a shift from one-way transmissional models to more interactive and user-orientated approaches.

The public relations industry explicitly claims to conduct two-way communication and dialogue, even to the point of symmetry, as outlined in Chapter 2. However, a number of critical scholars have exposed huge holes in these claims (e.g., Demetrious, 2013; Edwards & Hodges, 2011; Fawkes, 2015; L'Etang, 2008; L'Etang et al., 2015; Pieczka, 2006, 2011). Robert Brown (2006) argues that contemporary PR theory is ahistorical and proclaims "the myth of symmetry". This study indicates that the claims of PR theory for two-way communication, dialogue, and symmetry between organizations and their stakeholders and publics are farcical in many cases. Many of the same criticisms can be made of corporate communication and organizational communication.

Genuine commitment to, and resourcing of, listening would give meaning to the normative theories of public relations and provide a much more ethical form of practice. Recently, proponents of rhetorical theories of PR have argued for a synthesis of interests to "create and co-create the conditions that enact civil society" (Taylor, 2010, p. 7), and critical PR theorists have conceptualized a 'sociocultural turn' in public relations that seeks to reposition PR as societally orientated (Edwards & Hodges, 2011; Ihlen, van Ruler, & Fredriksson, 2009). Organizational listening is a fundamental element of two-way communication and dialogue—not to mention an essential component of corporate citizenship and corporate social responsibility. A 'social integration' model of PR incorporating the application of *standpoint theory*, principles of diplomacy, and listening is proposed in Macnamara (2016). Alternatively, theorists and practitioners of PR and corporate communication need to be honest and recognize that the locus of these practices is representing the voice of organizations. Another view is that corporate communication, by virtue of its name and focus, is the function of speaking for an organization, while public relations should focus on relationships and interaction. There is much for public relations, corporate communication, and organizational communication scholars and practitioners to think about based on the findings of this study.

There are also lessons for researchers in this analysis. Qualitative researchers in particular are required to be—and usually are—sensitive to human interpretation and subjectivities and implement a range of methods and analysis techniques designed to explore how people think and feel in an open-ended way, including paying attention to diversity and 'outliers'. Quantitative researchers need to ask whether the methods they employ and the statistical data they produce truly represent and reflect the diversity, depth, and nuance of the human conditions that they study. More use of mixed methods is one solution to combine the rigour of the scientific method with humanistic, social, and cultural perspectives. Many researchers now acknowledge that "the complexity of our research problems calls for answers beyond simple numbers ... a combination of both forms of data can provide the most complete analysis of problems" (Creswell & Plano Clark, 2007, p. 13). Researchers also need to question the common, almost default, use of surveys, interviews, and focus groups and consider other methods such as ethnography, participatory action research, in-depth case studies, conversation analysis, critical social inquiry, and grounded theory as ways of improving listening. Despite a heavy focus on quantitative research in late modernity (Giddens, 1991), numbers and proven hypotheses rarely if ever tell the full story about people and their concerns. As well, there is always more that all researchers can do to listen including being conscious of our own unavoidable subjectivity and applying reflexivity.

The 'Bottom Line' of Listening

A number of management studies and independent academic studies show that two-way communication including listening leading to dialogue and engagement provides a number of bottom line outcomes for organizations. National Business Hall of Fame member Peter Nulty (1994) says that "of all the skills of leadership, listening is one of the most valuable" and, in turn, he points to leadership as a vital element of business success. Sadly and instructively, he adds that listening is "one of the least understood" skills. Marvin

Bower, former McKinsey & Company senior executive and author of *The Will to Lead*, lends support to the findings of this research saying that, particularly in 'command and control' companies, "a high proportion of CEOs ... don't listen very well .... [I]n fact, chief executives of command companies are generally ... poor listeners" (Bower, 1997/2014, para. 22).

It is not possible in one short chapter to state and substantiate all the potential benefits of organizational listening and, as with government and political communication, it has to be recognized that business success and sustainability are determined by a range of factors. But there are well-supported arguments to show significant benefits, including tangible 'bottom line' benefits, from improved listening. The following are just some of the studies and reports that attest to the tangible and significant benefits of listening.

- Human resources management expert Avraham Kluger (2012) concludes from his research and experience that "truly listening to one's workers is good for business".
- Specifically, Michael Lowenstein (2006) says that internal communication by managers with employees motivates their subordinates to provide superior service to customers.
- A study by Sheila Bentley (2010) reported that improving listening in an organization can have positive outcomes for customer satisfaction and even profitability of a business.
- Research shows that productivity and profitability increase when employees are motivated and engaged (Benner & Tushman, 2003; Gallup, 2013). However, a 2013 Gallup 'State of the Global Workplace' study found that only 13 per cent of employees are engaged at work (Gallup, 2013) and concluded that "increasing workplace engagement is vital to achieving sustainable growth for companies, communities, and countries" (Crabtree, 2014, para. 9).
- It has been shown that employees' knowledge about their jobs and the organization (i.e., their level of engagement) contributes to the creation of organizational advocates, who can enhance the organization's reputation and increase sales (Gronstedt, 2000).
- The 2013 Edelman Trust Barometer survey reported that listening is the highest rated attribute for establishing trust in organizations (Edelman, 2013, p. 9). Successive annual Edelman Trust Barometer studies indicate that if there is one thing that increases satisfaction, trust, and reputation, listening is near the top of the list.

There is also a strong case that improved organizational listening can make a significant contribution to:

- Customer retention;
- Reduced staff turnover;
- Improved morale leading to increased productivity;
- Reduced industrial and workplace disputation; and
- Crisis avoidance through early detection of critical issues.

A number of studies have concluded that ineffective or lack of organizational listening can lead to financial costs and damage (such as dealing with problems and even crises), dysfunctional organizational communication (e.g., internal communication breakdowns), and organizations that clash with communities rather than work cooperatively with them, leading to resentment, loss of trust, reputational damage, and lost opportunities for collaboration (Brownell, 2003; Hunt & Cusella, 1983). In *Building a Magnetic Culture*, Kevin Sheridan (2012) says that, even in in the best companies to work for in the US, less than 40 per cent of employees are 'highly engaged'. In 'The 5 New Rules of Employee Engagement' Paul Keegan (2014) says that, overall, only 30 per cent of American employees are fully engaged at work and he estimates associated costs, such as those created by absenteeism and workplace accidents, at US\$450 billion to US\$550 billion a year. Chicago-based communication consultant David Grossman (2014) puts the costs higher, saying disengagement of employees is costing business between US\$450 million and \$1 billion a year. Conversely, a *Harvard Business Review* survey reported that 71 per cent of participants rated "high level of employee engagement" as a factor most likely to bring business success, exceeded only by high levels of customer service and effective communication (Harvard Business School, 2013, p. 4).

Governments also can gain 'bottom line' results from better listening. The UK Health and Social Care Bill fiasco cited in Chapter 3 illustrates clearly the cost of not listening. As a senior UK health communication executive summarized:

> What happened with the Health and Social Care Bill was a classic. We'll save time on engagement because we know what we want to do. That was the assumption. Of course, then having to do consultation and engagement with stakeholders retrospectively meant it took longer and if you look at the Bill itself, I think it has the world record for the most amount of amendments on a Bill ever. It's had something in the region of 1,800 to 2,000 amendments. That is a huge cost in time for government and stakeholders. (personal communication, February 2, 2015)

Such a process cost huge amounts of time and money—albeit not as much as the catastrophic failure to listen to UK hospital complaints that led to the death of an estimated 300 people, several major inquiries, and millions of pounds in legal costs (Stationery Office, 2013).

Listening for Social Equity

John Dewey warned of "the eclipse of the public" in 1927 in his important book *The Public and Its Problems*. In it, he pointed to a number of changes in society that are responsible for this eclipse, including the decline of leisure time, new forms of mass entertainment that distract people from politics and civic life and duty, institutionalization of politics, and the dynamic force of the economy and the growing power of big business that turns people into workers and consumers. Because of such forces and structural change, he argued that the important concept of the public has been lost. He observed that politics is mainly organized through political parties and campaign committees that operate as 'political machines' (1927, p. 137).

Dewey could not have foreseen the omniscient force of neoliberalism within government as well as capitalism, the massive expansion of 24/7 entertainment via the Internet and cable and satellite TV, the rise of celebrity politics, and the "permanent campaign" (Canel & Sanders, 2012, p. 87) focussed on winning and holding power rather serving the public interest. He wrote in 1927 that the public had become shadowy and formless. Given the escalation of the above forces and developments that have occurred since, it is reasonable to conclude that the gradual eclipse of the public viewed with concern by Dewey is in danger of becoming complete.

Concern about the role and influence of the growing professional public communication industry, such as advertising and PR, has been expressed for half a century or more since analyses such as Vance Packard's (1957) *The Hidden Persuaders*. However, Leon Mayhew (1997) was one of the first to critically examine contemporary public communication practices and show how, paradoxically, they have reduced rather than increased communication. Mayhew argued that professional specialists use market research and rhetorical techniques to dominate and control public communication. He pointed to "sound bite journalism, thirty second political advertising, one-way communication [i.e., information transmission], evasive spin control by public figures who refuse to answer questions, and the marketing of ideas and candidates by methods developed in commercial market research" (1997, p. 4). He said that in place of the modern public of the Enlightenment and the normative Habermasian notion entitled to free open discussion, communication professionals have created a "new public" that is subjected to mass persuasion and denied opportunities for two-way dialogue and debate. While Mayhew's analysis focussed on the public sphere and political communication, the findings of this study suggest that this malaise extends across all sectors—the public sphere, the marketplace, and civil society.

In many ways, Mayhew's *new public* is a return to an old public, a pre-Enlightenment, pre-modern public that is spoken to and spoken for by authorities such as public officials and church leaders, royalty, and their town criers, a public vanquished to the perimeters of power. There are nascent emancipatory movements such as the *prosumers* (Toffler, 1970, 1980) and *produsers* (Bruns, 2008) of social media; vocal activists who refuse to be silenced or ignored; and many well-meaning organizations committed to representing various constituencies. However, public communication involving dialogue and debate that contributes to citizen satisfaction and trust requires much greater commitment to listening by the organizations that dominate our industrialized, information age world. In addition to the practical and commercial arguments for organizational listening outlined in the previous sections, ultimately listening to stakeholders and publics is a matter of social equity and justice.

Listening to Marginalized Voices

In particular, organizational listening needs to recognize and focus more on marginalized voices through more open and simplified consultation procedures including outreach and other strategies recommended in this study. Marginalized voices vary from country to country and area to area, but typically include the poor; indigenous communities; gay communities in many societies; refugees; remote communities; as well as culturally and linguistically diverse (CALD) and Black, Asian, and Minority Ethnic (BAME) communities; and people from non-English-speaking backgrounds (NESB). But they can also include minorities of all shapes and forms whose voices are lost in the construction of consensus and majority rule.

Listening to the Silent Majority

Popular culture has long recognized the 'silent majority', but it seems that this group is growing and bifurcating. Democracy and social equity depend on having as many citizens participate in politics and civil society as possible. This ensures fair and equitable representation and creates a greater sense of community. But of even more concern than the silent majority of people who may choose to be silent are the *silenced majority*—those who are sidelined, ignored, and excluded from political and media representation.

Listening Across Cultures

Increasingly in multicultural societies—and that means most societies today— organizations need to listen across cultures. This is not discussed in detail here as there are many excellent texts and articles devoted to cross-cultural communication, or what some now prefer to call intercultural and multicultural communication (Beall, 2010; Crossman, Bordia, & Mills, 2011; Holliday, Hyde, & Kullman, 2010; Kim & Ebesu Hubbard, 2007). Listening across cultures involves listening across difference and also listening across borders, as discussed in the following concluding sections.

Dame Freya Stark, a widely respected travel writer who died at age 100 in 1993, said in her book *Journey's Echo* that the best advice when encountering new and different cultures is "hold your tongue and develop your listening skills" (as cited in Lee, n.d.). Noted authority on sustainable economic development, Ernesto Sirolli, is even blunter about how so-called experts and organizations should operate when working across cultures. In describing his experiences in aid work, he said well-intentioned aid workers often hear of a problem and go to work to prescribe solutions because they are the 'experts'. He says this is naïve and unproductive. He advises that the best way to help someone is to "shut up and listen" to tap into local knowledge and the ideas of those directly involved and affected (Sirolli, 2012).

Listening Across Difference

Tanja Dreher (2009) has championed the need for listening across difference and her work is cited and commended for that. The differences that can separate people and lead to the voices of some not being listened to include culture, as well as language skills, abilities, and religion, faith, or belief systems. An approach that is often advocated to restore social equity, fair representation, and justice is to give voice to marginalized groups. But, giving them voice is of little benefit if no one is listening. Giving people voice is not enough; it's listening to them that counts. Listening is what makes their voices effective and have value—or matter, as Nick Couldry (2010) says in his important book *Why Voice Matters*.

Dreher calls for a shift of "focus and responsibility from marginalized voices on to the conventions, institutions and privileges which shape who and what can be heard" (2009, p. 445). She focusses on media as important forums that should be receptive to difference, and indeed so-called mainstream media are collectively a site of limited representation and privileged voices. However, Dreher's call for a focus on "the institutions and conventions which enable and constrain receptivity and response" (p. 456) cited near the beginning of this book can and should be applied much more broadly. It applies to government departments and agencies, corporations, NGOs, and even non-profit organizations that, as this analysis shows, regularly fail to listen and, therefore, deny effective voice. In constructing an architecture of listening, organizations need to be mindful of the need to listen across difference.

Listening Across Borders

In today's globalized world, organizational listening by governments, corporations, and NGOs also needs to occur across borders. Not only are borders geographic, but they also exist as political and ideological borders. Communication is the primary mechanism for breaching borders without unwelcome incursion. But communication across borders must involve open, ethical listening, not simply intelligence gathering or selective listening to serve one's own interests. We hear often of 'communication breakdowns' and there is a tendency to believe that these are caused by not making a case well enough. But rarely are communication breakdowns caused by a lack of talking; they are usually the result of a lack of listening.

Conclusions

This analysis has presented extensive evidence that there is a marked and concerning lack of listening by organizations—government, corporate, and some NGOs and non-profits—in contemporary societies. It argues that the crisis of voice identified in developed democratic Western societies studied is, more specifically, a crisis of listening. Furthermore, while being conscious of the pitfalls of 'crying wolf' and moral panics, this analysis warns of an escalating crisis for democratic government, business, and civil society if present trends continue.

Importantly, this analysis has gone beyond critique to identify the key elements needed for effective ethical listening by organizations, which often requires large-scale listening. It has conceptualized these as an architecture of listening to emphasize the need for listening to be designed into organizations, rather than tacked on as an afterthought. It also has proposed that, with an architecture of listening in place, organizations need to undertake the work of listening, rather than being focussed on the work of speaking, which is the preoccupation of most fields of public communication practice and the predominant mode of public communication.

Third, it has outlined and overviewed some examples of innovation and best practice that can serve as exemplars and 'road maps' to effective ethical organizational listening and to a virtuous circle leading to transformation, rather than the vicious circle that begins with not listening to others, which devalues, demeans, and disenfranchises them. Fourth, it has indicated and given some evidence to show that there are significant benefits of organizational listening including tangible 'bottom line' returns.

The final part of this analysis presented in this last chapter has been relatively brief. Many will no doubt seek more details of how an architecture of listening can be implemented, how it might be scaled, what specific benefits it can bring, and how public communication disciplines should be transformed. But this study has done its work. This book reports two years of intense data collection and analysis, and space and time demand a pause for discussion, listening, and reflection before journeying on. Further research is necessary and proposed to build 'real life' models applying the architecture of listening outlined to test its efficacy and cost-effectiveness in various situations. No doubt there will be challenges and doubters. But the need is great and the quest worthy.

Today we have the skills and technologies to listen to the universe. But often we don't listen to people around us. While being respectful of the legacy given to us by Aristotle, it is useful and necessary to contrast his focus on the ability to speak as innately human, with Epictetus (circa 100/2007) who said: "Nature hath given men one tongue but two ears, that we may hear from others twice as much as we speak". Perhaps that is an unrealistic hope. However, the pioneering postmodernist Jean-Francois Lyotard well summed up the status quo and a more desirable future in *Au Juste: Conversations*, translated as *Just Gaming* in English, saying:

> For us, a language is first and foremost someone talking. But there are language games in which the important thing is to listen, in which the rule deals with audition. Such

a game is the game of the just. And in this game, one speaks only inasmuch as one listens. (Lyotard, 1979/1985, pp. 71–72)

Now is the time to stop, and listen.

Notes

1. The Localism Act 2011, which was passed in the UK Parliament and received Royal Assent in late 2011 and came into effect in early 2012, is designed to facilitate the devolution of decision making powers from central government to individuals, communities, and local government (Department of Communities and Local Government, 2011).
2. The phrase is derived from lines of Psalm 74:21 of the Bible and from 'The New Colossus', the sonnet by Emma Lazarus that is engraved on a bronze plaque inside the Statue of Liberty.

APPENDICES

Appendix 1: Interview Question Guide

The Organizational Listening Project

Introduction and Organization-Public Communication Overview:
1. **Name:** [to be de-identified post analysis]
2. **Title/role:**
3. **Organization:** [to be de-identified post analysis]
4. **Time in role:**
5. Do you have a **strategic communication plan** with clear objectives and targets?
6. What are the **main public communication activities** that your organization engages in as part of its public communication? (*List major communication activities in overview*)
7. Is your organization committed to **two-way communication**? (*Yes/no; if yes, where is this stated?*)
8. Do you attempt to or profess to achieve **engagement, dialogue, or conversation** with stakeholders and/or key publics in your public communication?

9. **How do you attempt two-way communication, engagement, dialogue, and/or conversation?** *(in overview, note details are sought in the next section)*

10. **Do you have a KPI** in your organization's strategic communication plan or other plans (e.g., stakeholder engagement, customer service) that relates to listening in the sense of seeking, receiving, considering, acknowledging, and responding to stakeholders or members of the public?

Methods of Organizational Listening:

Which of the following do you use?

1. **Formative research** such as market research, social research, reputation studies, or other types of research. If so, specify which:
   a. Surveys *(of whom, how often)*
   b. Focus groups *(of whom, how often)*
   c. Interviews *(of whom, how often)*
   d. Reputation tracking *(of whom, how often)*
   e. Other research *(please specify)*.
2. **Social media monitoring.** If so:
   a. How is this done (e.g., by monitoring service provider, free services such as Google Alerts, internally)?
   b. How extensively is this done *(monitor all mentions of key issues, some, or only monitoring of specific media on specific issues)*?
3. **Customer relations**—do you have a dedicated unit or department?
4. **Other client facing staff** who are charged with listening, not just distributing information or services or selling *(name department or unit such as Client Services Manager, Service Manager, field staff, Call Centres, etc.)*?
5. **Formal public consultations** *(if so, name examples and issues)*?
6. **Informal public consultation** *(such as public/'town hall' meetings, online forums or 'conversation' sites, 'listening posts', etc.)*?
7. **General Web site questions/comments sections** *(e.g., 'Contact us', 'Tell us your views')*? *(Who monitors, who responds?)*
8. **Feedback mechanisms** *(e.g., online forms, physical forums, suggestion boxes)*?
9. **Letters** *(are letters accepted; if so, who processes them, how many a year)*?
10. **Other** *(please specify)*?

Challenges, Obstacles, Requirements, and Benefits of Organizational Listening:

1. **Time**?
2. **Resources** (*i.e., staff*)?
3. **Systems/technology** (*such as social media monitoring services, text analysis software, sense making tools, specialist consultation or argumentation software*)?
4. **Culture** (*e.g., is there a culture of wanting to listen and respond to stakeholders and publics, or does management want communication to persuade stakeholders to the organization's point of view, nothing more*)?
5. **Politics** (*e.g., are you given policies and told to implement them regardless of public views; is it unpopular/career limiting to provide feedback to higher levels*)?
6. **Diversity** (*e.g., is there such a wide range of views/no consensus that responding to stakeholders and publics is seen as difficult or impossible*)?
7. **Articulation** (*i.e., does management want to hear and respond to what stakeholders and publics think and feel, or is management resistant or ignoring of public views*)?
8. Do you have any **examples of successful organizational listening**?
9. Being honest, what **proportion of your total public communication effort** (time, resources, technologies, etc.) is committed to producing and distributing information (i.e., *speaking* for the organization) and what proportion is committed to *listening* to stakeholders? (*e.g., 50/50, 60/40, 70/30, 80/20, 90/10, 100/0*)
10. Can you see **benefits in increased organizational listening**—if so, what are they?

Appendix 2: The 'Top 100' Terms Discussed by Participants in Interviews

(Nouns and verbs only, with the article, pronouns, and prepositions deleted as 'stop' words in NVivo)

No.	Word/term	Count	Similar words included
1	like	453	likes, liked, liking
2	social	434	socially
3	media	423	medium
4	communication	393	communications, comms, communicate, communicated, communicating, communicator, communicators
5	engagement	365	engage, engaged, engagements, engages, engaging
6	listening	312	listen, listens, listened
7	talk	291	talks, talked, talking
8	digital	233	digitally
9	call	232	call, called, calling, calls
10	consultation	230	consultations, consult, consultancy, consultant, consultancies, consultants, consulted, consulting
11	informed	199	inform, informs, information, informational, informing
12	response	184	responses, responsive
13	stakeholder	177	stakeholders
14	conversation	167	conversations, conversational, converse, conversing
15	campaign	160	campaigns, campaigning, campaigned
16	question	141	questions, questioning, questioned
17	data	135	big data
18	number	135	numbers, figures
19	saying	132	says, said
20	research	127	researched, researcher, researchers
21	story	125	stories
22	ask	120	asks, asked, asking
23	tell	115	tells, telling, told
24	survey	111	surveys, surveying, surveyed
25	online	102	
26	understand	101	understands, understanding, understood
27	comment	97	comments, commented, commenting
28	respond	97	responds, responded, respondents, responding
29	support	95	supports, supported, supporter, supporters, supporting

No.	Word/term	Count	Similar words included
30	insight	93	insights
31	monitoring	92	monitor, monitored, monitoring, monitors
32	community	91	communities
33	content	87	contents
34	view	87	views, viewed, viewing
35	open	82	opens, opened, openness
36	care	77	cares, cared, caring
37	message	73	messages, messaged, messaging
38	resource	69	resources, resourced, resourcing
39	meeting	68	meetings, meet, meets, met
40	answer	67	answers, answered, answering
41	post	65	posts, posted, posting, postings
42	audience	64	audiences
43	speak	64	speaks, speaking, spoke, spoken
44	evaluation	61	evaluate, evaluated, evaluating
45	feedback	61	response
46	consumer	59	consumers, consuming, consumption
47	analysis	57	analyses
48	forum	57	forums, fora
49	relations	57	relate, related, relates, relation
50	cost	55	costs, costing, costed
51	letter	55	letters
51	phone	55	phones, phoned, telephone, telephoning
53	relationship	54	relationships, relations
54	culture	53	cultures, cultural, culturally
55	measuring	52	measure, measures, measureable, measured, measurement, measurements
56	presentation	52	present, presents, presentations, presentational, presented, presenters, presenting
57	discussion	50	discuss, discussions, discussed, discussing
58	reach	50	reaches, reached, reaching
59	broadcast	47	broadcasts, broadcaster, broadcasting
60	fact	48	facts
61	share	47	shares, shared, sharing
62	write	48	writes, writing, wrote, written
63	news	46	
64	announcement	45	announce, announced, announcements, announcing
65	follow	45	follows, followed, followers, following

No.	Word/term	Count	Similar words included
66	impact	45	impacts, impacted, impacting
67	sense	45	senses
68	influence	44	influences, influenced, influencer, influencers, influencing
69	link	42	links, linked, linking
70	metrics	42	metrics
71	dashboard	40	dashboards
72	effect	40	effects, effective, effectively, effectiveness
73	interactive	40	interact, interaction, interactions, interactivity
74	positive	39	positives, positively
75	push	39	pushes, pushed, pushing
76	send	40	sent, sending
77	publish	38	published, publishes, publishing
78	read	38	reads, reading
79	behaviour	37	behaviours, behaviour, behavioural
80	produce	37	produces, produced, producer, producing
81	user	37	users
82	advertising	36	advertise, advertised, advertisers
83	power	36	powers, powered, powerful
84	test	36	tests, tested, testing
85	deliver	35	delivered, delivering
86	hear	35	hears, heard, hearing
87	perception	35	perceptions
88	structure	35	structures, structural, structurally, structured
89	civil	34	civic
90	trust	34	trusted, trusting
91	value	34	values, valued, valuable
92	access	33	accesses, accessed, accessible, accessing
93	citizen	33	citizens
94	explain	33	explains, explained, explaining
95	standard	33	standards
96	study	33	studies, studied, studying
97	human	32	humans, humanity, humanize
98	mention	32	mentions, mentioned, mentioning
99	volume	32	volumes
100	receive	31	receives, received, receiver, receiving

REFERENCES

Aarts, N. (2009). *Een gesprek zonder einde* [A never ending conversation]. Amsterdam, the Netherlands: Vosspuspers.

Aarts, N., & Van Woerkum, C. (2008). *Strategische communicatie* [Strategic communication]. Assen, the Netherlands: Van Gorcum.

Abelson, J., Forest, P., Eyles, J., Smith, P., Martin, E., & Gauvin, F. (2001, June). *Deliberations about deliberation: Issues in the design and evaluation of public consultation processes.* Research working paper 01–04. Ottawa, ON: McMaster University Centre for Health Economics and Policy Analysis.

Aberbach, J., & Rockman, B. (1994). Civil servants and policymakers: Neutral or responsive competence? *Governance, 7*(4), 461–469.

Abercrombie, N., & Longhurst, B. (1998). *Audiences: A sociological theory of performance and imagination.* London, UK: Sage.

Adams, A., & McCorkindale, T. (2013). Dialogue and transparency: A content analysis of how the 2012 presidential candidates used Twitter. *Public Relations Review, 39*(4), 357–359.

Adler, R., & Rodman, G. (2011). *Understanding communication* (11th ed.). New York, NY: Oxford University Press.

Adler, R., Rodman, G., & du Pré, A. (2013). *Understanding communication* (12th ed.). New York, NY: Oxford University Press.

AFSC (American Friends Service Committee) & Rustin, B. (1955). *Speak truth to power: A Quaker search for an alternative to violence.* Philadelphia, PA: Author. Retrieved from https://afsc.org/document/speak-truth-power

Akhtar, O. (2014, June 20). Social@Ogilvy partners with Sysomos to offer social media monitoring and analytics for campaigns. *The Hub*. Retrieved from http://www.thehubcomms.com/socialogilvy-partners-with-sysomos-to-offer-social-media-monitoring-and-analytics-for-campaigns/article/357012

Alberts, J., Nakayama, T., & Martin, J. (2007). *Human communication in society*. Upper Saddle River, NJ: Pearson-Prentice Hall.

AMEC [Association for Measurement and Evaluation]. (2015, March 24). *Cutting through the confusion! AMEC announce new industry metrics initiative*. London, UK: Author. Retrieved from http://amecorg.com/2015/03/cutting-through-the-confusion-amec-announce-new-industry-metrics-initiative

American University. (2015). What is public communication? Retrieved from http://www.american.edu/soc/communication/what-is-public-communication.cfm

Anderson, B. (1991). *Imagined communities: Reflections on the origin and spread of nationalism* (Rev. ed.). New York, NY: Verso. (Original work published 1983)

Anderson, B. (2015). What kind of thing is resilience? *Politics, 35*(1), 60–66.

Anderson, C. (2006). *The long tail*. New York, NY: Hyperion.

Argenti, P. (2003). *Corporate communication* (3rd ed.). Boston, MA: McGraw-Hill Irwin.

Argenti, P., & Forman, J. (2002). *The power of corporate communication: Crafting the voice and image of your business*. New York, NY: McGraw-Hill.

Argunet. (2015). Editor. Retrieved from http://www.argunet.org/editor

Argyle, M. (2009). *Social interaction* (2nd ed.). Piscataway, NJ: Transaction. (Original work published 1969)

Arnett, R. (2010). Defining philosophy of communication: Difference and identity. *Qualitative Research Reports in Communication, 11*(1), 57–62.

Arnstein, S. (1969). A ladder of citizen participation. *JAIP, 35*(4), 216–224.

Arthur Page Society. (2009). The dynamics of public trust in business: Emerging opportunities for leaders. Retrieved from http://www.awpagesociety.com/insights/trust-report

Atwill, J. (1998). *Rhetoric reclaimed: Aristotle and the liberal arts tradition*. Ithaca, NY: Cornell University Press.

Back, L. (2007). *The art of listening*. Oxford, UK: Berg.

Bakhtin, M. (1981). *The dialogic imagination: Four essays*. Austin: University of Texas Press.

Bakhtin, M. (1984). *Problems of Dostoevsky's poetics* (C. Emerson, Ed. & Trans.). Minneapolis: University of Minnesota Press. (Original work published 1963)

Bakhtin, M. (1986). *Speech genres and other late essays* (C. Emerson & M. Holquist, Eds., V. McGee, Trans.). Austin: University of Texas Press. (Original work published 1979)

Baloh, E. (1976). *A comparison of direct and indirect listening activities on the listening efficiency of fourth grade students*. Los Angeles: California State College.

Barthes, R. (1977). Death of the author: Structural analysis of narratives. In *Image, music, text* (pp. 142–148; S. Heath, Trans.). London, UK: Fontana. (Original work published 1968).

Bartholomew, D. (2012). Where is your organization on the social media listening maturity model. London, UK: Association for Measurement and Evaluation of Communication.

Retrieved from http://amecorg.com/2012/10/where-is-your-organization-on-the-social-media-listening-maturity-model

Bauman, Z. (1993). *Postmodern ethics*. Oxford, UK: Blackwell.

Baumgartner, F., & Jones, B. (2009). *Agendas and instability in American politics* (2nd ed.). Chicago, IL: University of Chicago Press. (Original work published 1993)

Baxter, L. (2011). *Voicing relationships: A dialogic perspective*. Thousand Oaks, CA: Sage.

Bazemore, G., & Schiff, M. (2001). *Restorative community justice: Repairing harm and transforming communities*. Cincinnati, OH: Anderson.

Beall, M. (2010). Perspectives on intercultural listening. In A. Wolvin (Ed.), *Listening and human communication in the 21st century* (pp. 225–238). Chichester, UK: Wiley-Blackwell.

Beard, D. (2009). A broader understanding of the ethics of listening: Philosophy, cultural studies, media studies, and the ethical listening subject. *International Journal of Listening, 23*(1), 7–20.

Beatty, J. (1999). Good listening. *Educational Theory, 49*(3), 281–298.

Bekkers, V. (2004). Virtual policy communities and responsive governance: Redesigning online debates. *Information Polity, 9*(3/4), 193–203.

Bellamy, R. (2010). Democracy without democracy: Can the EU's democratic 'outputs' be separated from the democratic 'inputs' provided by competitive parties and majority rule? *Journal of European Public Policy, 17*(1), 2–19.

Benner, M. J., & Tushman, M. L. (2003). Exploitation, exploration, and process management: The productivity dilemma revisited. *Academy of Management Review, 28*, 238–256.

Bennett, L., & Segerberg, A. (2012). The logic of connective action: Digital media and the personalization of contentious politics. *Information, Communication & Society, 15*(5), 739–768.

Bennett, W. (2008). Changing citizenship in the digital age. In W. Bennett (Ed.), *Civic life online: Learning how digital media can engage youth* (pp. 1–24). Cambridge, MA: MIT Press.

Bennett, W., Wells, C., & Freelon, D. (2011). Communicating civic engagement: Contrasting models of citizenship in the youth Web culture. *Journal of Communication, 61*(5), 835–856.

Bentley, S. (2010). Listening practices: Are we getting any better? In A. Wolvin (Ed.), *Listening and human communication in the 21st century* (pp. 181–192). Malden, MA: Wiley-Blackwell.

Berelson, B., & Steiner, G. (1964). *Human behaviour*. New York, NY: Harcourt, Brace & World.

Berger, A. (2000). *Media and communication research methods*. Thousand Oaks, CA: Sage.

Berger, B. (2005). Power over, power with, and power to relations: Critical reflections on public relations, the dominant coalition and activism. *Journal of Public Relations Research, 17*(1), 5–28.

Berger, B. (2007). Public relations and organizational power. In E. Toth (Ed.), *The future of excellence in public relations and communication management: Challenges for the next generation* (pp. 221–234). Mahwah, NJ: Lawrence Erlbaum.

Berger, B., & Reber, B. (2006). *Gaining influence in public relations: The role of resistance in practice*. Mahwah, NJ: Lawrence Erlbaum.

Berlo, D. (1960). *The process of communication: An introduction to theory and practice.* New York, NY: Harcourt/Holt, Rinehart & Winston.

Bernal, M. (1987). *Black Athena: The Afroasiatic roots of classical civilisation.* Piscataway, NJ: Rutgers University Press.

Berry, D. (2014). Study to test the content of the most effective SMS reminder message to reduce missed appointments in hospital outpatient clinics. *BioMed Central.* ISRCTN. Retrieved from http://www.isrctn.com/ISRCTN49432571

Berry, L. (1983). *Relationship marketing.* Chicago, IL: American Marketing Association.

Bickford, S. (1996). *The dissonance of democracy: Listening, conflict and citizenship.* Ithaca, NY: Cornell University Press.

Bimber, B., Flanagin, A., & Stohl, C. (2012). *Collective action in organizations: Interaction and engagement in an era of technological change.* New York, NY: Cambridge University Press.

BIS [Department for Business Innovation and Skills]. (2015). Using digital in open policy making. Microsite. Retrieved from http://discuss.bis.gov.uk/opm/2013/09/18/sources-of-help-and-advice

Blumler, J., & Coleman, S. (2010). Political communication in freefall: The British case—and others. *International Journal of Press/Politics, 15*(2), 139–154.

Blumler, J., & Gurevitch, M. (1995). *The crisis of public communication.* Abingdon, UK: Routledge.

Bobbitt, P. (2003). *The shield of Achilles.* Harmondsworth, UK: Penguin.

Bodie, G. (2010). Treating listening ethically. *International Journal of Listening, 24,* 185–188.

Bodie, G. (2011). The understudied nature of listening in interpersonal communication. *International Journal of Listening, 25*(1–2), 1–9.

Bodie, G., & Crick, N. (2014). Listening, hearing, sensing: Three modes of being and the phenomenology of Charles Sanders Peirce. *Communication Theory, 24*(2), 105–123.

Boggs, C. (2000). *The end of politics: Corporate power and the decline of the public sphere.* New York, NY: Guilford.

Boler, M. (Ed.). (2008). *Digital media and democracy: Tactics in hard times.* Cambridge, MA: MIT Press.

Booth, R. (2015, April 24). Apathy central: Where young see no point in casting a vote. *The Guardian Weekly,* p. 15.

Bormann, E. (1982). The symbolic convergence theory of communication: Applications and implications for teachers and consultants. *Communication and Mass Media, 10*(1), 1–2.

Botan, C., & Hazelton, V. (Eds.). (2006). *Public relations theory II.* Mahwah, NJ: Lawrence Erlbaum.

Bourdieu, P. (1990). *In other words: Essays towards a reflexive sociology.* Cambridge, UK: Polity.

Bowen, S. (2008). A state of neglect: Public relations as 'corporate conscience' or ethics counsel. *Journal of Public Relations Research, 20*(3), 271–296.

Bower, M. (2014). Developing leaders in a business. *McKinsey Quarterly.* Retrieved from http://www.mckinsey.com/insights/leading_in_the_21st_century/developing_leaders_in_a_business (Original work published 1997)

Bradley, A., & McDonald, M. (2011a). *The social organization: How to use social media to tap the collective genius of your customers and employees.* Boston, MA: Harvard Business Review Press.

Bradley, A., & McDonald, M. (2011b, October 3). All organizations are social, but few are social organizations [Web log post]. *Harvard Business Review*. Retrieved from http://blogs.hbr.org/cs/2011/10/all_organizations_are_social_b.html

Brainard, L. (2003). Citizen organizing in cyberspace: Illustrations from health care and implications for public administration. *American Review of Public Administration, 33*(4), 384–406.

Braithwaite, J. (2002). Setting standards for restorative justice. *British Journal of Criminology, 42*(3), 563–577.

Brand, R. (2013, November 6). Russell Brand: We deserve more from our democratic system. *The Guardian*. Opinion. Retrieved from http://www.theguardian.com/commentisfree/2013/nov/05/russell-brand-democratic-system-newsnight

Breakenridge, D. (2008). *PR 2.0: New media, new tools, new audiences*. Upper Saddle River, NJ: FT Press, Pearson Education.

Broom, G. (1977). Co-orientational measurement in public issues. *Public Relations Review, 3*, 110–119.

Broom, G. (2009). *Cutlip & Center's effective public relations* (10th ed.). Upper Saddle River, NJ: Pearson Education.

Broom G., & Dozier, D. (1990). *Using research in public relations: Applications to program management*. Englewood Cliffs, NJ: Prentice-Hall.

Brown, B., Sikes, J., & Wilmott, P. (2013, August 14). Bullish on digital: McKinsey global survey results. Retrieved from http://www.mckinsey.com/insights/business_technology/bullish_on_digital_mckinsey_global_survey_results

Brown, J., & Duguid, A. (2000). *The social life of information*. Boston, MA: Harvard Business School Press.

Brown, R. (2006). Myth of symmetry: Public relations as cultural styles. *Public Relations Review, 32*(3), 206–212.

Brownell, J. (2003). Applied research in managerial communication: The critical link between knowledge and practice. *Cornell Hotel and Restaurant Administration Quarterly, 44*(2), 39–49.

Bruns, A. (2008). *Blogs, Wikipedia, Second Life and beyond: From production to produsage*. New York, NY: Peter Lang.

Bryant, D. (1953). Rhetoric: Its functions and its scope. *Quarterly Journal of Speech, 39*, 123–140.

Bryman, A. (1988). *Quantity and quality in social research*. London, UK: Unwin Hyman.

Buber, M. (1958). *I and thou* (R. Smith, Trans.). New York, NY: Scribner. (Original work published 1923)

Buber, M. (2002). *Between man and man* (R. Smith, Trans.). London, UK: Kegan Paul. (Original work published 1947)

Buck, T. (2015, May 22). Women on the verge of Barcelona and Madrid electoral triumphs. *The Financial Times*. Retrieved from http://www.ft.com/cms/s/0/8548a50e-ffc0-11e4-bc30-00144feabdc0.html#axzz3b8cih8eO

Bucy, E. (2004). Interactivity in society: Locating an elusive concept. *Information Society, 20*(5), 373–383.

Bucy, E., & D'Angelo, P. (1999). The crisis of political communication: Normative critiques and democratic processes. *Communication Yearbook, 22*, 301–340.

Bulwer-Lytton, E. (1830). *Paul Clifford*. London, UK: Henry Colburn and Richard Bentley.

Burke, K. (1969). *A rhetoric of motives*. Berkeley, CA: University of California Press.

Burnside-Lawry, J. (2011). The dark side of stakeholder communication: Stakeholder perceptions of ineffective organisational listening. *Australian Journal of Communication, 38*(1), 147–173.

Burnside-Lawry, J. (2012). Listening and participatory communication: A model to assess organisation listening competency. *International Journal of Listening, 26*(2), 102–121.

Burrell, G., & Morgan, G. (1979). *Sociological paradigms and organizational analysis*. London, UK: Heinemann.

Bussie, J. (2011). Reconciled diversity: Reflections on our calling to embrace our religious neighbours. *Intersections, 33*, 30–35.

Butler, J. (1999). *Gender trouble: Feminism and the subversion of identity*. New York, NY: Routledge.

Cabinet Office. (2009). *Power of information task force review final report*. London, UK: Author. Retrieved from http://webarchive.nationalarchives.gov.uk/20100413152047/http://www.cabinetoffice.gov.uk/reports/power_of_information.aspx

Cabinet Office. (2013, December 10). Government digital strategy. London, UK: Author. Retrieved from https://www.gov.uk/government/publications/government-digital-strategy/government-digital-strategy

Cabinet Office. (2014, October 20). *Social media guidance for civil servants*. London, UK: Author. Retrieved from https://www.gov.uk/government/publications/social-media-guidance-for-civil-servants/social-media-guidance-for-civil-servants

Calder, G. (2011). Democracy and listening. In M. Crumplin (Ed.), *Problems of democracy: Language and speaking* (pp. 125–135). Oxford, UK: Inter-Disciplinary Press.

Cameron, G., Wilcox, D., Reber, B., & Shin, J. (2008). *Public relations today: Managing conflict and competition*. Boston, MA: Allyn & Bacon.

Campbell, A. (2013, June 27). Why the world of PR is changing. *Huffington Post*. Retrieved from http://www.huffingtonpost.co.uk/alastair-campbell/pr-world-is-changing_b_3511449.html

Campbell, D. (2009, September 26). Trust in politicians hits all time low. *The Observer*. Retrieved from http://www.theguardian.com/politics/2009/sep/27/trust-politicians-all-time-low

Campbell, W. (Joseph). (2004). 1897: American journalism's exceptional year. *Journalism History, 29*(4), 1–9. Retrieved from http://academic2.american.edu/~wjc/exceptyear1.htm

Canel, M., & Sanders, K. (2011). Government communication. In W. Donsbach (Ed.), *International encyclopedia of communication online* (n.p.). New York, NY: Wiley Blackwell. Retrieved from http://www.communicationencyclopedia.com/public

Canel, M., & Sanders, K. (2012). Government communication: An emerging field in political communication research. In H. Semetko & M. Scammell (Eds.), *The SAGE handbook of political communication* (pp. 85–96). London, UK: Sage.

Carey, J. (1989). *Communication as culture: Essays on media and culture*. New York, NY: Unwin Hyman.

Carey, J. (2009). *Communication as culture: Essays on media and culture*. New York, NY: Routledge. (Original work published 1989)

Carpentier, N. (2007). Participation, access and interaction: Changing perspectives. In V. Nightingale & T. Dwyer (Eds.), *New media worlds: Challenges for convergence* (pp. 214–230). South Melbourne, Vic: Oxford University Press.

Carpentier, N. (2011). *Media and participation: A site of ideological democratic struggle*. Chicago, IL: Intellect.

Carpentier, N., & De Cleen, B. (2008). *Participation and media production*. Cambridge, UK: Cambridge Scholars.

Carter, A. (2001). *The political theory of global citizenship*. London, UK: Routledge.

Castells, M. (2010). The new public sphere: Global civil society, communication networks, and global governance. In D. Thussu (Ed.), *International communication: A reader* (pp. 36–47). London, UK: Routledge.

Castro, F., & Murray, K. (2010). Cultural adaptation and resilience: Controversies, issues, and emerging models. In J. Reich, A. Zautra, & J. Hall (Eds.), *Handbook of adult resilience* (pp. 375–403). New York, NY: Guilford Press.

Chadwick, A. (2006). *Internet politics: States, citizens, and new communications technologies*. Oxford, UK: Oxford University Press.

Chadwick, A., & May, C. (2003). Interaction between states and citizens in the age of the Internet: 'E-government' in the United States, Britain, and the European Union. *Governance: An International Journal of Policy and Administration, 16*(2), 271–300.

Chafee, S., & Rogers, E. (Eds.). (1997). *The beginnings of communication study in America: A personal memoir*. Thousand Oaks, CA: Sage.

Chapman, A. (2013, May 28). The MasterCard Conversation Suite, with Andrew Bowins, Senior VP. *SocialMediaToday*. Retrieved from http://www.socialmediatoday.com/content/mastercard-conversation-suite-andrew-bowins-senior-vp

Charalabidis, Y., & Loukis, E. (2012). Participative public policy making through multiple social media platforms utilization. *International Journal of Electronic Government Research, 8*(3), 78–97.

Chartered Institute of Marketing. (2010). Cost of customer acquisition vs. customer retention. Fact file. Maidenhead, UK: Author. Retrieved from http://www.camfoundation.com/PDF/Cost-of-customer-acquisition-vs-customer-retention.pdf

Chartier, R. (Ed.). (1989). *A history of private life: Passions of the Renaissance* (A. Goldhammer, Trans.). Cambridge, MA: Harvard University Press.

Chen, I., & Popovich, K. (2003). Understanding customer relationship management (CRM): People, process, and technology. *Business Process Management, 9*(5), 672–688.

Chenoweth, L., Forbes, I., Fleming, R., King, M., Stein-Parbury, J., Luscombe, G., … Brodaty, H. (2014). PerCEN: A cluster randomised controlled trial of person-centred residential care and environment for people with dementia. *International Psychogeriatrics, 26*(7), 1147–1160. Retrieved from http://www.ncbi.nlm.nih.gov/pubmed/24666667

Chenoweth, L., King, M., Jeon, Y., Brodaty, H., Stein-Parbury, J., Norman, R., … Luscombe, G. (2009). Caring for aged dementia care resident study (CADRES) of person-centred care, dementia-care mapping and usual care. *Lancet Neural, 8*, 317–325. Retrieved from http://www.ncbi.nlm.nih.gov/pubmed/19282246

Churchman, C. (1967). Wicked problems. *Management Science, 14*(4), 141–142.

City of Portland. (2015). Gentrification and displacement study. Portland, OR: Author. Retrieved from http://www.portlandoregon.gov/bps/62635

Cognitive Edge. (2015). About SenseMaker. Retrieved from http://cognitive-edge.com/sensemaker

Cohen, H. (1994). *The history of speech communication*: The emergence of a discipline, 1914–1945. Annandale, VA: Speech Communication Association.

Cohen, J., & Arato, A. (1994). *Civil society and political theory*. Boston, MA: MIT Press.

Coldewey, D. (2013, April 21). The dawn of the digilante. *Techcrunch*. Retrieved from http://techcrunch.com/2013/04/21/dawn-of-the-digilante

Coleman, S. (2008). Doing IT for themselves: Management versus autonomy in youth e-citizenship. In W. Bennett (Ed.), *Civic life online: Learning how digital media can engage youth* (pp. 189–206). Cambridge, MA: MIT Press.

Coleman, S. (2013a). *How voters feel*. New York, NY: Cambridge University Press.

Coleman, S. (2013b, February 1). The challenge of digital hearing. *Journal of Digital and Media Literacy*. Retrieved from http://www.jodml.org/2013/02/01/challenge-of-digital-hearing

Coles, R. (2004). Moving democracy: Industrial areas foundation social movements and the political arts of listening, traveling, and tabling. *Political Theory, 32*(5), 678–705.

Collison, C., & Parcell, G. (2004). *Learning to fly: Practical knowledge management from leading and learning organizations*. Chichester, UK: Capstone. (Original work published 2001)

Commission for Healthcare Audit and Inspection. (2007, October). *Is anyone listening? A report on complaints handling by the NHS*. London, UK: Author. Retrieved from http://www.bipsolutions.com/docstore/pdf/18646.pdf

Commission for Healthcare Audit and Inspection. (2008, April). *Spotlight on complaints: Report on second-stage complaints about the NHS in England*. London, UK: Author. Retrieved from http://webarchive.nationalarchives.gov.uk/20090104012205/http:/healthcarecommission.org.uk/_db/_documents/5632_HC_V18a.pdf

Conklin, J. (2006). *Dialogue mapping: Building shared understanding of wicked problems*. Chichester, UK: Wiley & Sons.

Connor, S. (2000). *Dumbstruck: A cultural history of ventriloquism*. Oxford, UK: Oxford University Press.

Conquergood, D. (1985). Performing as a moral act: Ethical dimensions of the ethnography of performance. *Literature in Performance, 5*(2), 1–13.

Conrad, C., & Scott Poole, M. (2012). *Strategic organizational communication in a global economy* (7th ed.). Malden, MA: Wiley-Blackwell.

Conrad, J. (2008). *Under Western eyes*. Oxford, UK: Oxford University Press.

Constitutional Reform and Governance Act 2010. (2010). London, UK: The Stationary Office. Retrieved from http://www.legislation.gov.uk/ukpga/2010/25/contents

Content is king: Bill Gates, 1996. (2014). *Silkstream*, [Web log post]. Retrieved from http://www.silkstream.net/blog/2014/07/content-is-king-bill-gates-1996.html

Coombs, T., & Holladay, S. (2007). *It's not just PR: Public relations in society*. Malden, MA: Blackwell.

Cooper, L. (1997). Listening competency in the workplace: A model for training. *Business Communication Quarterly, 60*(4), 7–85.

Cooper, L., & Husband, C. (1993). Developing a model of organisational listening competency. *International Journal of Listening, 7*(1), 6–34.

Cooren, F., & Sandler, S. (2014). Polyphony, ventriloquism, and constitution: In dialogue with Bakhtin. *Communication Theory, 24*(3), 225–244.

Corcoran, S. (2011, June 2). Introducing 'social maturity': How social media transforms companies [Web log post]. *Sean Corcoran's blog*, Forrester. Retrieved from http://blogs.forrester.com/sean_corcoran/11-06-02-introducing_social_maturity_how_social_media_transforms_companies

Cornelissen, J. (2004). *Corporate communications: Theory and practice*. London, UK: Sage.

Cornelissen, J. (2008). *Corporate communication: A guide to theory and practice* (2nd ed.). London, UK: Sage.

Cornelissen, J. (2011). *Corporate communication: A guide to theory and practice* (3rd ed.). London, UK: Sage.

Corner, J. (2007). Media, power and political culture. In E. Devereux (Ed.), *Media studies: Key issues and debates* (pp. 211–230). London, UK: Sage.

Corollary. (2015). *Merriam-Webster*. Retrieved from http://www.merriam-webster.com/dictionary/corollary

Couldry, N. (2009). Commentary: Rethinking the politics of voice. *Continuum: Journal of Media & Cultural Studies, 23*(4), 579–582.

Couldry, N. (2010). *Why voice matters: Culture and politics after neoliberalism*. London, UK: Sage.

Couldry, N. (2012). *Media, society, world: Social theory and digital media practice*. Cambridge, UK: Polity.

Couldry, N., Livingstone, S., & Markham, T. (2007). *Media consumption and public engagement*. Basingstoke, UK: Palgrave Macmillan.

Covey, S. (1989). *The seven habits of highly effective people: Powerful lessons in person change*. New York, NY: Free Press.

Crabtree, S. (2014). Worldwide, 13% of employees are engaged at work. Gallup Web site. Retrieved from http://www.gallup.com/poll/165269/worldwide-employees-engaged-work.aspx

Craig, R. (1999). Communication theory as a field. *Communication Theory, 9*, 119–161.

Craig, R. (2006). Communication as a practice. In G. Shepherd, G. St John, & T. Striphas (Eds.), *Communication as … Perspectives on theory* (pp. 38–49). Thousand Oaks, CA: Sage.

Craig, R., & Muller, H. (Eds.). (2007). *Theorizing communication: Readings across traditions*. Thousand Oaks, CA: Sage.

Crawford, K. (2009). Following you: Disciplines of listening in social media. *Continuum: Journal of Media & Cultural Studies, 23*(4), 525–535.

Creswell, J., & Plano Clark, V. (2007). *Designing and conducting mixed methods research*. Thousand Oaks, CA: Sage.

Crompton, A. (2015). Runaway train: Public participation and the case of HS2. *Policy and Politics, 43*(1), 27–44.

Crossman, J., Bordia, S., & Mills, C. (2011). *Business communication for the global age*. North Ryde, NSW: McGraw-Hill.

Curran, J. (2002). *Media and power*. London, UK: Routledge.

Curran, J. (2011). *Media and democracy*. Abingdon, UK: Routledge.

Curran, J. (2012). Reinterpreting the Internet. In J. Curran, N. Fenton, & D. Freedman (Eds.), *Misunderstanding the Internet* (pp. 3–33). Abingdon, UK: Routledge.

Curtin, P., & Gaither, T. (2005). Privileging identity, difference and power: The circuit of culture as a basis for public relations theory. *Journal of Public Relations Research, 17*(2), 91–115.

Dahl, R. (1971). *Polyarchy: Participation and opposition*. New Haven, CT: Yale University Press.

Dahlberg, L. (2014). The Habermasian public sphere and exclusion: An engagement with post-structuralist-influenced critics. *Communication Theory, 24*(1), 21–41.

Dahlgren, P. (2001). The public sphere and the net: Structure, space and communication. In W. Bennett & R. Entman (Eds.), *Mediated politics: Communication in the future of democracy* (pp. 33–55). New York, NY: Cambridge University Press.

Dahlgren, P. (2009). *Media and political engagement: Citizens, communication and democracy*. Cambridge, UK: Cambridge University Press.

Dalton, R. (2011). *Engaging youth in politics: Debating democracy's future*. New York, NY: Idebate Press.

Daniels, T., & Spiker, B. (1994). *Perspectives on organizational communication* (3rd ed.). Dubuque, IA: Wm. C. Brown.

Dayton, B., & Kinsey, D. (2015). Contextual meaning. In G. Golan, S. Yang, & D. Kinsey (Eds.), *International public relations and public diplomacy: Communication and engagement* (pp. 267–278). New York, NY: Peter Lang.

de Moor, A., & Aakhus, M. (2006). Argumentation support: From technologies to tools. *Communications of the ACM, 49*(3), 93–98.

Deacon, D., & Golding, P. (1994). *Taxation and representation: The media, political communication and the poll tax*. London, UK: John Libbey.

Debreu, G. (1959). *Theory of value: An axiomatic analysis of economic equilibrium*. New Haven, CT: Yale University Press.

Deetz, S. (1982). Critical interpretative research in organizational communication. *The Western Journal of Speech Communication, 46*, 131–149.

Deetz, S. (1992). *Democracy in an age of corporate colonization: Developments in communication and the politics of everyday life*. Albany, NY: SUNY Press.

Deetz, S. (2001). Conceptual foundations. In F. Jablin & L. Putnam (Eds.), *New handbook of organizational communication: Advances in theory, research, and methods* (pp. 3–46). Thousand Oaks, CA: Sage.

DEFRA [Department of Environment, Food and Rural Affairs]. (2007). GM dialogue. London, UK: National Archives. Retrieved from http://webarchive.nationalarchives.gov.uk/20081023141438/http:/www.defra.gov.uk/environment/gm/crops/debate/index.htm

Deibert, R. (2000). International plug 'n play? Citizen activism, the Internet, and global public policy. *International Studies Perspectives, 1*(3), 255–272.

Deibert, R., & Rohozinski, R. (2010). Liberation vs. control: The future of cyberspace. *Journal of Democracy, 21*(4), 43–57.

Deliberatorium: Crowd-based innovation. (2015). Mark Klein's home page. Retrieved from http://cci.mit.edu/klein/deliberatorium.html

DelReal, J. (2014, November 10). Voter turnout in 2014 was the lowest since WWII [Web log post]. *The Washington Post. Post Politics*. Retrieved from http://www.washingtonpost.com/blogs/post-politics/wp/2014/11/10/voter-turnout-in-2014-was-the-lowest-since-wwii

DeLuca, K., Lawson, S., & Sun, Y. (2012). Occupy Wall Street on the public screens of social media: The many framings of the birth of a protest movement. *Communication, Culture & Critique, 5*(4), 483–509.

DeMers, J. (2014, June 30). How to maximize your marketing campaign through storytelling. *Forbes*. Retrieved from http://www.forbes.com/sites/jaysondemers/2014/06/30/how-to-maximize-your-marketing-campaign-through-storytelling

Demetrious, K. (2013). *Public relations, activism, and social change: Speaking up*. New York, NY: Routledge.

Department of Communities and Local Government. (2011, November). *A plain English guide to the Localism Act*. London, UK: Author. Retrieved from https://www.gov.uk/government/uploads/system/uploads/attachment_data/file/5959/1896534.pdf

Department of Health. (2014). Communications Strategy 2014/15. London: UK Government.

Department of State. (2015). Selected US government information Web sites. Retrieved from http://www.state.gov/misc/60289.htm

Dervin, B. (1983, May). *An overview of sense-making research: Concepts, methods, and results to date*. Paper presented to the International Communication Association annual meeting, Dallas, TX. Retrieved from http://faculty.washington.edu/wpratt/MEBI598/Methods/An%20Overview%20of%20Sense-Making%20Research%201983a.htm

Dervin, B. (1992). From the mind's eye of the user: The sense-making qualitative-quantitative methodology. In J. Glazier & R. Powell (Eds.), *Qualitative research in information management* (pp. 61–84). Englewood, CO: Libraries Unlimited.

Dervin, B., Foreman-Wernet, L., & Lauterbach, E. (2003). *Sense-making methodology reader: Selected writings of Brenda Dervin*. Cresskill, NJ: Hampton Press.

Devin, B., & Lane, A. (2014). Communicating engagement in corporate social responsibility: A meta-level construal of engagement. *Journal of Public Relations Research, 26*(5), 436–454.

Dewey, J. (1916). *Democracy and education*. New York, NY: Macmillan.

Dewey, J. (1927). *The public and its problems*. New York, NY: Henry Holt.

Dewey, J. (1939). *Intelligence in the modern world* (collected works). New York, NY: Modern Library.

Dewey, J. (1972). *The early works of John Dewey, 1882–1898* (J. Boydston, Ed.). Carbondale: Southern Illinois University Press.

Dhawan, N. (2012). Hegemonic listening and subversive silences: Ethical-political imperatives. *Critical Studies, 36*, 47–60.

Diamond, P. (2014). *Governing Britain: Power, power, politics and the prime minister*. London, UK: I. B. Taurus.

Digital government: Building a 21st century platform to better serve the American people. (n.d.). Washington, DC: Executive Office of the President of the United States. Retrieved from https://www.whitehouse.gov/sites/default/files/omb/egov/digital-government/digital-government.html

Dimitrov, R. (in print). Silence and invisibility in public relations. *Public Relations Review*. doi: 10.1016/j.pubrev.2014.02.019

Dobson, A. (2010). Democracy and nature: Speaking and listening. *Political Studies, 58*(4), 752–768.

Dobson, A. (2014). *Listening for democracy: Recognition, representation, reconciliation*. Oxford, UK: Oxford University Press.

Dominiczak, P. (2013, June 10). Mid Staffs: Police investigating up to 300 deaths. *The Telegraph*. Retrieved from http://www.telegraph.co.uk/news/health/10111192/Mid-Staffs-Police-investigating-up-to-300-deaths.html

Donath, J. (2002). A semantic approach to visualizing online conversations. *Communications of the ACM, 45*(4), 45–49.

Dorgelo, C., & Zarek, C. (2014, June 27). Using citizen engagement to solve national problems [Web log post]. *Open Government Initiative, the White House*. Retrieved from http://www.whitehouse.gov/blog/2014/06/27/using-citizen-engagement-solve-national-problems

Dourish, P. (2007). *Responsibilities and implications: Further thoughts on ethnography and design*. ACM Conference Designing for the User Experience DUX 2007, Chicago, IL. Retrieved from http://www.dourish.com/publications/2007/dux2007-ethnography.pdf

Downing, J. (2007). Grassroots media: Establishing priorities for the years ahead. *Global Media Journal* (Australia edition), *1*(1), 1–16.

Dozier, D., Grunig, L., & Grunig, J. (1995). *Manager's guide to excellence in public relations and communication management*. Mahwah, NJ: Lawrence Erlbaum.

Drake, K. (2014, June 30). *CrowdAround*. Presentation. Retrieved from https://prezi.com/qujtzn_zxqyj/crowdaround

Dreher, T. (2008). Media, multiculturalism and the politics of listening. In E. Tilley (Ed.), *Power and place: Refereed proceedings of the Australian and New Zealand Communication Association Conference 2008* (pp. 1–14). Palmerston, New Zealand: Massey University.

Dreher, T. (2009). Listening across difference: Media and multiculturalism beyond the politics of voice. *Continuum: Journal of Media & Cultural Studies, 23*(4), 445–458.

Dreher, T. (2010). Speaking up or being heard? Community media interventions and the politics of listening. *Media, Culture and Society, 32*(1), 85–103.

Dreher, T. (2012). A partial promise of voice: Digital storytelling and the limit of listening. *Media International Australia, 142*, 157–166.

Dryzek, J. (2000). *Deliberative democracy and beyond: Liberals, critics, and contestations*. Oxford, UK: Oxford University Press.

du Gay, P. (Ed.). (1997). *Production of culture/cultures of production*. London, UK: Sage.

du Gay, P., Hall, S., James, L., Mackay, H., & Negus, K. (1997). *Doing cultural studies: The story of the Sony Walkman*. Thousand Oaks, CA: Sage.

Dulek, R., & Campbell, K. (2015). On the dark side of strategic communication. *International Journal of Business Communication, 52*(1), 122–142.

Durkheim, E. (1984). *Division of labour in society*. New York, NY: The Free Press. (Original work published 1893)

Durose, C., Justice, J., & Skelcher, C. (2015). Governing at arm's length: Eroding or enhancing democracy? *Policy and Politics, 43*(1), 137–153.

DWP [Department of Work and Pensions]. (2014 April). DWP communication strategy 2014/15. London, UK: Author.

Edelman. (2009). *Public engagement in the conversation age* (Vol. 2). New York, NY: Author. Retrieved from http://www.slideshare.net/EdelmanDigital/public-engagement-in-the-conversation-age-vol-2-2009

Edelman. (2013). Edelman Trust Barometer. New York, NY: Author. Retrieved from http://www.edelman.com/insights/intellectual-property/trust-2013

Edelman. (2014). Edelman Trust Barometer. New York, NY: Author. Retrieved from http://www.edelman.com/insights/intellectual-property/2014-edelman-trust-barometer/trust-around-the-world

Edelman. (2015a). Edelman Trust Barometer. New York, NY: Author. Retrieved from http://www.edelman.com/insights/intellectual-property/2015-edelman-trust-barometer/trust-around-world

Edelman. (2015b). Who we are. New York, NY: Author. Retrieved from http://www.edelman.com/who-we-are/about-edelman/the-details

Editorial Board. (2014, November 7). To raise voter turnout, simplify the voting process. *The Washington Post. The Post's View*. Retrieved from http://www.washingtonpost.com/opinions/to-raise-voter-turnout-simplify-the-voting-process/2014/11/07/83577b66-6606-11e4-9fdc-d43b053ecb4d_story.html

Edwards, L. (2012). Defining the 'object' of public relations research: A new starting point. *Public Relations Inquiry, 1*, 7–30.

Edwards, L., & Hodges, C. (Eds.). (2011). *Public relations, society and culture: Theoretical and empirical explorations*. Abingdon, UK: Routledge.

Edwards, M. (2009). *Civil society* (2nd ed.). Cambridge, UK: Polity.

Edwards, M. (2014). *Civil society* (3rd ed.). Cambridge, UK: Polity.

Einwiller, S., & Steilen, S. (2015). Handling complaints on social network sites: An analysis of complaints and complaint responses on Facebook and Twitter pages of large US companies. *Public Relations Review, 41*(2), 195–204.

Elance-oDesk. (2015). The 2015 Millennial majority workforce. Research report. Mountain View, CA: Author. Retrieved from http://www.elance-odesk.com/millennial-majority-workforce

Election Watch Australia. (2013, September 19). Informal vote is on the rise. Retrieved from http://electionwatch.edu.au/australia-2013/analysis/informal-voting-rise

Eliasoph, N. (2004). Can we theorize the press without theorizing the public? *Political Communication, 21*(3), 297–303.

Eliot, S. (2011). Attentive vs. active listening [Web log post]. *The Listening Resource*. Retrieved from http://www.qualitative-researcher.com/blog/

Elstub, S. (2010). The third generation of deliberative democracy. *Political Studies Review, 8*(3), 291–307.

Epictetus. (2007). *The golden sayings of Epictetus*. Charleston, SC: BiblioLife. (Historical reproduction of original work published pre-1923)

Erickson, T. (2008). *Plugged in: The generation Y guide to thriving at work*. Boston, MA: Harvard Business School.

Escobar, O. (2014). Towards participatory democracy in Scotland. *Post*. Retrieved from http://postmag.org/towards-participatory-democracy-in-scotland

Escobar, O., Faulkner, W., & Rea, H. (2014). Building capacity for dialogue facilitation in public engagement around research. *Journal of Dialogue Studies, 2*(1), 87–111.

Evans-Cowley, J. (2010). Planning in the age of Facebook: The use of social networking in planning processes. *Geojournal, 75*(3), 407–420.

Ewen, S. (1996). *PR! A social history of spin*. New York, NY: Basic Books.

Fairbanks, J., Plowman, K., & Rawlins, B. (2007). Transparency in government communication. *Journal of Public Affairs, 7*(1), 23–37.

Falconi, T. (2014). In T. Falconi, J. Grunig, E. Zugaro, & J. Duarte, *Global stakeholder relationships governance: An infrastructure* (pp. 1–55). New York, NY: Palgrave.

Falconi, T., Grunig, J., Zugaro, E., & Duarte, J. (2014). *Global stakeholder relationships governance: An infrastructure*. New York, NY: Palgrave.

Falkheimer, J., & Heide, M. (2011, May). *Participatory strategic communication: From one- and two-way communication to participatory communication through social media*. Paper presented at the International Communication Association pre-conference, Strategic Communication—A Concept at the Center of Applied Communications, Boston, MA.

Farsetta, D. (2005, March 9). Desperately seeking disclosure: What happens when public funds go to private PR firms? *PR Watch*. Madison, WI: Center for Media and Democracy. Retrieved from http://www.prwatch.org/news/2005/03/3348/desperately-seeking-disclosure-what-happens-when-public-funds-go-private-pr-firms

Fawkes, J. (2010). The shadow of excellence: A Jungian approach to public relations ethics. *Review of Communication, 10*(3), 211–227.

Fawkes, J. (2015). *Public relations ethics and professionalism: The shadow of excellence*. Abingdon, UK: Routledge.

Ferguson, M. (1984, August). *Building theory in public relations: Inter-organizational relationships as public relations paradigm*. Paper presented at the conference of the Association for Education in Journalism and Mass Communication, Gainesville, FL.

Festinger, L. (1957). *A theory of cognitive dissonance*. Palo Alto, CA: Stanford University Press.

Fishkin, J. (1995). *The voice of the people: Public opinion and democracy*. New Haven, CT: Yale University Press.

Fiske, J. (1994). Audiencing: Cultural practice and cultural studies. In N. Denzin & Y. Lincoln (Eds.), *Handbook of qualitative research* (pp. 189–198). Thousand Oaks, CA: Sage.

Fiumara, G. (1990). *The other side of language: A philosophy of listening*. London, UK: Routledge.

Flew, T. (2008). *New media: An introduction* (3rd ed.). South Melbourne, Vic: Oxford University Press.

Flew T. (2014). *New media* (4th ed.). South Melbourne Vic: Oxford University Press.

Flynn, J., Valikoski, T., & Grau, J. (2008). Listening in the business context: Reviewing the state of research. *International Journal of Listening, 22*(2), 141–151.

Foreman-Wernet, L., & Dervin, B. (2006). Listening to learn: 'Inactive' publics of the arts as exemplar. *Public Relations Review, 32*, 287–294.

Foss, S., & Griffin, C. (1995). Beyond persuasion: A proposal for an invitational rhetoric. *Communication Monographs, 62*, 2–18.

Foucault, M. (1990). *The history of sexuality: An introduction by Michel Foucault* (Vol. 1). New York, NY: Random House.

Foulger, M. (2012, November 7). Social media's role in the 2012 US election: Obama breaks Twitter records [Web log post]. *Hootsuite.* Retrieved from http://blog.hootsuite.com/election-tracker-results

Fox, M. (2010). Directgov 2010 and beyond: Revolution not evolution. London: UK Government. Retrieved from https://www.gov.uk/government/publications/directgov-2010-and-beyond-revolution-not-evolution-a-report-by-martha-lane-fox

Fraser, N. (1990). Rethinking the public sphere. *Social Text, 25/26,* 56–80.

Fraser, N. (1992). Rethinking the public sphere: A contribution to the critique of actually existing democracy. In C. Calhoun (Ed.), *Habermas and the public sphere* (pp. 109–142). Cambridge, MA: MIT Press.

Fraser, N., & Honneth, A. (2003). *Redistribution or recognition: A political-philosophical exchange.* London, UK: Verso.

Fredriksson, L. (1999). Modes of relating in a caring conversation: A research synthesis on presence, touch and listening. *Journal of Advanced Nursing, 30*(5), 1167–1176.

Freeman, R. (1984). *Strategic management: A stakeholder approach.* London, UK: Pitman.

French, J., Blair-Stevens, C., McVey, D., & Merritt, R. (2010). *Social marketing and public health: Theory and practice.* New York, NY: Oxford University Press.

French, T., LaBerge, L., & Magill, P. (2012, July). Five 'no regrets' moves for superior customer engagement. *McKinsey Insights.* Retrieved from http://www.mckinsey.com/insights/marketing_sales/five_no_regrets_moves_for_superior_customer_engagement

Freundt, T., Hillenbrand, P., & Lehmann, S. (2013, October). How B2B companies talk past their customers. *McKinsey Quarterly.* Retrieved from http://www.mckinsey.com/insights/marketing_sales/how_b2b_companies_talk_past_their_customers

Frey, L., Botan, C., & Kreps, G. (2000). *Investigating communication: An introduction to research methods.* Needham Heights, MA: Allyn & Bacon.

Friestad, M., & Wright, P. (1994). The persuasion knowledge model: How people cope with persuasion attempts. *Journal of Consumer Research, 21*(1), 1–31.

FTC [Federal Trade Commission]. (2015, February 27). *Identity theft tops FTC's consumer complaint categories again in 2014* [Press release]. Retrieved from https://www.ftc.gov/news-events/press-releases/2015/02/identity-theft-tops-ftcs-consumer-complaint-categories-again-2014

Fuchs, C. (2014). *Social media: A critical introduction.* London, UK: Sage.

Fuller, G., McCrea, C., & Wilson, J. (2013). Troll theory? *The Fibreculture Journal, 21,* 1–14.

Gadamer, H. (1989). *Truth and method* (2nd ed., J. Weinsheimer & D. Marshall, Trans.). New York, NY: Crossroad. (Original work published 1960)

Gallup. (2013). State of the global workplace. Retrieved from http://www.gallup.com/services/178517/state-global-workplace.aspx

Gamson, W., & Schmeidler, E. (1984). Organising the poor: An argument with Francis Fox Piven and Richard A. Cloward's *Poor people's movements: Why they succeed how they fail. Theory and Society, 13*(4), 567–584.

Ganesan, S. (1994). Determinants of long term orientation in buyer–seller relationships. *Journal of Marketing*, 58(2), 1–19

Garrison, J. (2010). Compassionate, spiritual, and creative listening in teaching and learning. *Teachers College Record*, 112(11), 2763–2776.

Garson, G., & Khosrow-Pour, M. (Eds.). (2008). *Handbook of research on public information technology*. Hershey, PA: IGI Global.

Gates, B. (1996, January 3). Content is king. Microsoft Web site. Retrieved from http://web .archive.org/web/20010126005200/http://www.microsoft.com/billgates/columns/ 1996essay/essay960103.asp

Gehrke, P. (2009). Introduction to listening, ethics, and dialogue: Between the ear and eye: A synaesthetic introduction to listening ethics. *International Journal of Listening*, 23(1), 1–6.

Getuiza, C. (2014, January 29). Californians grade the state with new report card app. CA *FWD*. Retrieved from http://www.cafwd.org/reporting/entry/californias-citizens-grade-the-state-with-new-report-card-app

Gibson, J., & Hodgetts, R. (1991). *Organizational communication: A management perspective* (2nd ed.). New York, NY: HarperCollins.

Gibson, M. (2009). Noel Pearson and the 'Cultural Left': Between listening and deaf opposition. *Continuum: Journal of Media and Cultural Studies*, 23(4), 465–476.

Gibson, R., & Cantijoch, M. (2011). Comparing online elections in Australia and the UK: Did 2010 finally produce the Internet election? *Communication, Politics & Culture*, 44(2), 4–17.

Gibson, R., Cantijoch, M., & Ward, S. (2010). Citizen participation in the e-campaign. In R. Gibson, A. Williamson, & S. Ward (Eds.), *The Internet and the 2010 election: Putting the small 'p' back in politics* (pp. 5–16). London, UK: Hansard Society.

Gibson, R., Lusoli, W., & Ward, S. (2008). The Australian public and politics online: Reinforcing or reinventing representation. *Australian Journal of Political Science*, 43, 111–131.

Gibson, R., Williamson, A., & Ward, S. (2010). *The Internet and the 2010 election: Putting the small 'p' back in politics*. London, UK: Hansard Society.

Giddens, A. (1984). *The constitution of society: Outline of the theory of structuration*. Berkeley: University of California Press.

Giddens, A. (1991). *Modernity and self-identity: Self and society in the late modern age*. Cambridge, UK: Polity.

Giddens, A. (1994). *Beyond left and right: The future of radical politics*. Cambridge, UK: Polity.

Gilder, G. (1994). *Life after television*. New York, NY: Norton.

Gilens, M., & Page, B. (2014). Testing theories of American politics: Elites, interest groups, and average citizens. *Perspectives on Politics*, 12(3), 564–581.

Gillmor, D. (2004). *We the media: Grassroots journalism by the people, for the people*. North Sebastopol, CA: O'Reilly Media.

Gitlin, T. (1998). Public spheres or public sphericles? In T. Liebes & J. Curran (Eds.), *Media, ritual and identity* (pp. 170–173). New York, NY: Routledge.

Glaser, B. (1978). *Theoretical sensitivity*. Mill Valley, CA: Sociology Press.

Glaser, B., & Strauss, A. (1967). *The discovery of grounded theory: Strategies for qualitative research*. Chicago, IL: Aldine.

Glenn, E. (1989). A content analysis of fifty definitions of listening. *The International Journal of Listening, 3*(1), 21–31.

Global Alliance. (2014). The Melbourne Mandate. Retrieved from http://www.globalalliancepr .org/website/page/melbourne-mandate

GNM [Guardian New Media]. (2011, June 17). Guardian News & Media to be a digital-first organisation [Press release]. London, UK: Author. Retrieved from http://www .theguardian.com/gnm-press-office/guardian-news-media-digital-first-organisation

Goldman, E. (1948). *Two-way street: The emergence of the public relations counsel.* Boston, MA: Bellman.

Goodin, R. (2008). *Innovating democracy: Democratic theory and practice after the deliberative turn.* Oxford, UK: Oxford University Press.

Goodman, D. (1992). Public sphere and private life: Toward a synthesis of current historiographical approaches to the old regime. *History and Theory, 31*(1), 1–20.

Goodman, M. (1994). *Corporate communication.* Albany, NY: SUNY Press.

Gouldner, A. (1960). The norm of reciprocity: A preliminary statement. *American Sociological Review, 25*(2), 161–178.

Government Communication Service. (2014a, July). *Government Communication Service efficiency report.* London, UK: Author.

Government Communication Service. (2014b). *Government Communication Service (GCS) handbook.* London, UK: Author.

Government Digital Service. (n.d.). *Social media playbook.* Retrieved from https://gdssocialmedia.blog.gov.uk/playbook

Gov.UK. (2013). Consultation outcome: Equal marriage consultation. London, UK: Department of Culture, Media & Sport. Retrieved from https://www.gov.uk/government/ consultations/equal-marriage-consultation

Gov.UK. (2014). Consultation outcome: Northern futures. London, UK: Office of the Deputy Prime Minister. Retrieved from https://www.gov.uk/government/consultations/ northern-futures

Gov.UK. (2015). Mid Staffordshire NHS Foundation Trust. London, UK: HM Government. Retrieved from https://www.gov.uk/government/groups/mid-staffordshire-nhs-foundation-trust

Graber, D. (2003). *The power of communication: Managing information in public sector organizations.* Washington, DC: CQ Press.

Graybar, S., & Leonard, L. (2005). In defence of listening. *American Journal of Psychotherapy, 59*(1), 1–18.

Great unwashed. (2015). *Phrase Finder.* Retrieved from http://www.phrases.org.uk/meanings/ the-great-unwashed.html

Green, J. (2010). *The eyes of the people: Democracy in an age of spectatorship.* New York, NY: Oxford University Press.

Gregory, A. (2012). UK government communications: Full circle in the 21st century. *Public Relations Review, 38*(3), 367–375.

Gregory, A. (in print). Practitioner-leaders' representation of roles: The Melbourne Mandate. *Public Relations Review.* Retrieved from http://dx.doi.org/10.1016/j.pubrev.2014.02.030

Gregory, A., & Willis, P. (2013). *Strategic public relations leadership*. London, UK: Routledge.

Greenhouse, S. (2009). *The big squeeze* (2nd ed.). New York, NY: Anchor.

Greenwood, M. (2007). Stakeholder engagement: Beyond the myth of corporate responsibility. *Journal of Business Ethics, 74*(4), 315–327.

Griffin, E. (2009). *A first look at communication theory* (7th ed.). Boston, MA: McGraw-Hill.

Gronstedt, A. (2000). *The customer century: Lessons from world-class companies in integrated marketing communication*. New York, NY: Routledge.

Grossman, D. (2014, November–December). *Employee engagement*. International Association of Business Communicators (IABC) seminar series, Sydney, Australia.

Grunig, J. (1966). The role of information processing in economic decision making. *Journalism Monographs*, 3, 1–51.

Grunig, J. (Ed.). (1992). *Excellence in public relations and communication management*. Hillsdale, NJ: Lawrence Erlbaum.

Grunig, J. (1997). A situational theory of publics: Conceptual history, recent challenges and new research. In D. Moss, T. MacManus, & D. Verčič (Eds.), *Public relations research: An international perspective* (pp. 3–48). London, UK: International Thomson Business Press.

Grunig, J., Grunig, L., & Dozier, D. (2006). The excellence theory. In C. Botan & V. Hazelton (Eds.), *Public relations theory II* (pp. 21–62). Mahwah, NJ: Lawrence Erlbaum.

Grunig, J., & Hunt, T. (1984). *Managing public relations*. Orlando, FL: Holt, Rinehart & Winston.

Grunig, L., Grunig J., & Dozier, D. (2002). *Excellent organizations and effective organizations: A study of communication management in three countries*. Mahwah, NJ: Lawrence Erlbaum.

Guth, D., & Marsh, C. (2007). *Public relations: A values-driven approach* (3rd ed.). Boston, MA: Pearson Education.

Habermas, J. (1984). *Theory of communicative action: Vol. 1. Reason and the rationalization of society* (T. McCarthy, Trans.). Boston, MA: Beacon Press. (Original work published in German 1981)

Habermas, J. (1987). *The theory of communicative action: Vol. 2. Lifeworld and system: A critique of functionalist reason* (T. McCarthy, Trans.). Boston, MA: Beacon Press. (Original work published in German 1981)

Habermas, J. (1989). *The structural transformation of the public sphere*. Cambridge, UK: Polity. (Original work published 1962)

Habermas, J. (1990). *Moral consciousness and communicative action* (C. Lenhardt & S. Nicholsen, Eds. & Trans.). London, UK: Polity.

Habermas, J. (1991). *The structural transformation of the public* sphere (T. Burger, Trans.). Cambridge, MA: MIT Press. (Original work published 1962 in German).

Habermas, J. (1992). Concluding remarks. In C. Calhoun (Ed.), *Habermas and the public sphere* (pp. 462–479). Cambridge, MA: MIT Press.

Habermas, J. (1996). *Between facts and norms: Contributions to a discourse theory of law and democracy* (W. Regh, Trans.). Cambridge, MA: Polity.

Habermas, J. (2006). Political communication in media society: Does democracy still enjoy an epistemic dimension? The impact of normative theory on empirical research. *Communication Theory, 16*(4), 411–426.

Hallahan, K., Holtzhausen, D., van Ruler, B., Verčič, D., & Sriramesh, K. (2007). Defining strategic communication. *International Journal of Strategic Communication, 1*(1), 3–35.

Hallsworth, M., Berry, D., & Sallis, A. (2014, September). *Reducing missed hospital outpatient appointments through an SMS intervention: A randomised controlled trial in a London hospital.* Paper presented at the Division of Health Psychology annual conference, New York, NY. Retrieved from http://abstracts.bps.org.uk/index.Cfm?&Resultstype=abstracts&resultset_id=12039&formdisplaymode=view&frmshowselected=true&localaction=details

Hallsworth, M., Berry, D., Sanders, M., Sallis, A., King, D., Vlaev, I., & Darzi, A. (2015). Stating appointment costs in SMS reminders reduces missed hospital appointments: Findings of two randomized controlled trials. *PLoS ONE, 10*(10): e0141461.

Hansson, M. (2007). *The private sphere: An emotional territory and its agent.* New York, NY: Springer.

Hardy, T. (1874). *Far from the madding crowd.* London, UK: Cornhill Magazine.

Harker, M. (1999). Relationship marketing defined? An examination of current relationship marketing definitions. *Marketing Intelligence & Planning, 17*(1), 13–20.

Harlow, R. (1976). Building a public relations definition. *Public Relations Review, 2*(4), 34–42.

Harper, H. (2013). Applying behavioural insights to organ donation: Preliminary results from a randomized controlled trial. Retrieved from http://www.behaviouralinsights.co.uk/sites/default/files/Applying_Behavioural_Insights_to_Organ_Donation_report.pdf

Harris, J. (2015, June 26). A very English revolt. *The Guardian Weekly,* p. 30.

Hartley, R. (2010). Freedom not to listen: A constitutional analysis of compulsory indoctrination through workplace captive audience meetings. *Berkeley Journal of Employment & Labor Law, 31*(1), 65–125.

Harvard Business School. (2013). *The impact of employee engagement on performance.* Retrieved from https://hbr.org/resources/pdfs/comm/achievers/hbr_achievers_report_sep13.pdf

Harvard University. (2015). Trust in institutions and the political process. Boston, MA: Institute of Politics. Retrieved from http://www.iop.harvard.edu/trust-institutions-and-political-process

Haworth, A. (2004). *Understanding the political philosophers: From ancient to modern times.* London, UK: Routledge.

Hazelton, V., Harrison-Rexrode, J., & Keenan, W. (2008). New technologies in the formation of personal and public relations: Social capital and social media. In S. Duhé (Ed.), *New media and public relations* (pp. 91–105). New York, NY: Peter Lang.

Hazelwood Mine Fire Inquiry. (2014). *Hazelwood mine fire inquiry report.* Melbourne, Vic: Government of Victoria. Retrieved from http://report.hazelwoodinquiry.vic.gov.au/print-friendly-version-pdf

Hazelwood Mine Fire Inquiry. (2015). Hazelwood mine fire inquiry 2015–16. Retrieved from http://hazelwoodinquiry.vic.gov.au

Heath, R. (1992). The wrangle in the marketplace: A rhetorical perspective of public relations. In E. Toth & R. Heath (Eds.), *Rhetorical and critical approaches to public relations* (pp. 17–36). Mahwah, NJ: Lawrence Erlbaum.

Heath, R. (1997). *Strategic issues management.* Thousand Oaks, CA: Sage.

Heath, R. (2001). A rhetorical enactment rationale for public relations: The good organization communicating well. In R. Heath (Ed.), *Handbook of public relations* (pp. 31–50). Thousand Oaks, CA: Sage.

Heath, R. (2002). Issues management: Its past, present and future. *Journal of Public Affairs*, 2(2), 209–214.

Heath, R. (Ed.). (2005). *Encyclopaedia of public relations* (Vol. 1). London, UK: Sage.

Heath, R. (2006). A rhetorical theory approach to issues. In C. Botan & V. Hazelton (Eds.), *Public relations theory II* (pp. 63–99). Mahwah, NJ: Lawrence Erlbaum.

Heath, R. (2007). Management through advocacy: Reflection rather than domination. In E. Toth (Ed.), *The future of excellence in public relations and communication management* (pp. 41–65). Mahwah, NJ: Lawrence Erlbaum.

Heath, R. (2009). The rhetorical tradition: Wrangle in the marketplace. In R. Heath, E. Toth, & D. Waymer (Eds.), *Rhetorical and critical approaches to public relations II* (pp. 17–47). New York, NY: Routledge.

Heath R. (Ed.). (2010). *The SAGE handbook of public relations* (2nd ed.). Thousand Oaks, CA: Sage.

Heath, R. (2013). The journey to understand and champion OPR takes many roads, some not yet well travelled. *Public Relations Review*, 39(5), 426–431.

Heath, R., & Coombs, T. (2006). *Today's public relations: An introduction*. Thousand Oaks, CA: Sage.

Heath, R., & Ni, L. (2010). *Corporate social responsibility: Different fabrics*. Gainesville, FL: Institute for Public Relations. Retrieved from http://www.instituteforpr.org/essential_knowledge/detail/corporate_social_responsibility_different_fabrics

Heider, F. (1958). *The psychology of interpersonal relations*. New York, NY: Wiley.

Held, D. (1996). *Models of democracy*. Stanford, CA: Stanford University Press.

Held, D. (2006). *Models of democracy* (3rd ed.). Cambridge, UK: Polity Press.

Helmore, E. (2014, December 12). Anger grips America's streets. *The Guardian Weekly*, pp. 1, 4.

Hepburn, P. (2014). Local democracy in a digital age: Lessons for local government from the Manchester congestion charge referendum. *Local Government Studies*, 40(1), 82–101.

Hetherington, M. (2005). *Why trust matters*. Princeton, NJ: Princeton University Press.

Hiebert, R. (1966). *Courtier to the crowd: The story of Ivy Lee*. Ames: Iowa State University Press.

Himelboim, I. (2011). Civil society and online political discourse: The network structure of unrestricted discussions. *Communication Research*, 38(5), 634–659.

Hindess, B. (1993). Citizenship in the modern West. In B. Turner (Ed.), *Citizenship and social theory* (pp. 19–35). London, UK: Sage.

Hirst, M., & Harrison, J. (2007). *Communication and new media: From broadcast to narrowcast*. South Melbourne, Vic: Oxford University Press.

HM Government. (2014a). Government Communications Plan 2014/15. London, UK: Author. Retrieved from https://gcn.civilservice.gov.uk/wp-content/uploads/2014/05/Government-Communications-Plan_201415_webSmll.pdf

HM Government. (2014b). *The future of public service communications: Report and findings 1.0* (draft). London, UK: Government Communication Service.

Hobbes, T. (1946). *Leviathan*. Oxford, UK: Basil Blackwell. (Original work published 1651)

Hobolt, S., & Klemmensen, R. (2005). Responsive government? Public opinion and government policy preferences in Britain and Denmark. *Political Studies*, 53(2), 379–402.

Hoggart, R. (2004). *Mass media in a mass society: Myth and reality*. London, UK: Continuum.

Hoi polloi. (2015). *Oxford dictionaries*. Retrieved from http://www.oxforddictionaries.com/definition/english/hoi-polloi

Holliday, A., Hyde, M., & Kullman, J. (2010). *Intercultural communication: An advanced resource book for students* (2nd ed.). London, UK: Routledge.

Holquist, M. (Ed.). (1981). *The dialogic imagination: Four essays by M. M. Bakhtin* (C. Emerson & M. Holquist, Trans.). Austin: University of Texas Press. (Original work published 1975)

Holtzhausen, D. (2000). Postmodern values in PPR. *Journal of Public Relations Research, 12*(1), 93–114.

Holtzhausen, D. (2002). Towards a postmodern research agenda for PR. *Public Relations Review, 28*(3), 251–264.

Hon, L., & Grunig, J. (1999). Guidelines for measuring relationships in public relations. Gainesville, FL: Institute for Public Relations. Retrieved from http://www.instituteforpr.org/measuring-relationships

Honneth, A. (2007). *Disrespect*. Cambridge, UK: Polity Press.

Howard, C. (2010). *The organizational ombudsman: Origins, roles and operations, a legal guide*. Chicago, IL: American Bar Association.

Howell, A. (2015). Resilience as enhancement: Governmentality and political economy beyond responsibilization. *Politics, 35*(1), 67–71.

Howley, K. (2007). Community media and the public sphere. In E. Devereux (Ed.), *Media studies: Key issues and debates* (pp. 342–360). London, UK: Sage.

Hudson, W. (2000). Differential citizenship. In W. Hudson & J. Kane (Eds.), *Rethinking Australian citizenship* (pp. 15–25). Cambridge, UK: Cambridge University Press.

Hudson, W., & Kane, J. (2000). *Rethinking Australian citizenship*. Cambridge, UK: Cambridge University Press.

Huitt, W. (2009). Empathetic listening. *Educational Psychology Interactive*. Valdosta, GA: Valdosta State University. Retrieved from http://www.edpsycinteractive.org/topics/process/listen.html

Hunt, G., & Cusella, L. (1983). A field study of listening needs in organizations. *Communication Education, 32*(4), 393–401.

Husband, C. (1996). The right to be understood: Conceiving the multi-ethnic public sphere. *Innovation: The European Journal of Social Sciences, 9*(2), 205–215.

Husband, C. (2000). Media and the public sphere in multi-ethnic societies. In S. Cottle (Ed.), *Ethnic minorities and the media* (pp. 199–214). Buckingham, UK: Open University Press.

Husband, C. (2009). Commentary: Between listening and understanding. *Continuum: Journal of Media & Cultural Studies, 23*(4), 441–443.

Iandoli, L., Klein, M., & Zolla, G. (2009). Enabling online deliberation and collective decision making through large-scale argumentation: A new approach to the design of an Internet-based mass collaboration platform. *International Journal of Decision Support System Technology, 1*(1), 69–92. Hershey, PA: IGI Global.

IAP2 [International Association for Public Participation]. (2015). The IAP2 public participation spectrum. Retrieved from http://www.iap2.org.au/resources/iap2s-public-participation-spectrum

IBM. (2013). Social business. Retrieved from http://www.ibm.com/smarterplanet/au/en/social-business/overview/index.html

IBM Software Group. (2011). *The social business: Advent of a new age.* Retrieved from http://www.ibm.com/smarterplanet/global/files/us__en_us__socialbusiness__epw14008usen.pdf

ICCO [International Communications Consultancy Organization]. (2011). *ICCO world report: A return to growth.* Retrieved from http://www.iccopr.com/fckeditor/editor/filemanager/connectors/aspx/fckeditor/userfiles/file/ICCOWR2011_Return2Growth_final.pdf

Ihlen, Ø., van Ruler, B., & Fredriksson, M. (2009). *Public relations and social theory: Key figures and concepts.* New York, NY: Routledge.

Innovator 25: Andrew Bowins. (2014). *The Holmes Report.* Retrieved from http://www.holmesreport.com/ranking-and-data/innovator-25-2014/2014/the-innovator-25/andrew-bowins

Internet World Statistics. (2014). World Internet users and population statistics. Retrieved from http://www.internetworldstats.com/stats6.htm

IPR [Institute for Public Relations]. (2010). Barcelona declaration of measurement principles. Gainesville, FL: Author. Retrieved from http://www.instituteforpr.org/topics/barcelona-declaration-of-measurement-principles

Ipsos-MORI. (2015). Ipsos-MORI Veracity Index. London, UK: Author. Retrieved from https://www.ipsos-mori.com/researchpublications/researcharchive/3504/Politicians-trusted-less-than-estate-agents-bankers-and-journalists.aspx

James, R., & Gilliland, B. (2013). *Crisis intervention strategies* (7th ed.). Belmont, CA: Cengage.

James, W. (1952). *The principles of psychology.* Chicago, IL: William Benton.

Jenkins, H. (2006a). *Fans, bloggers, and gamers.* New York, NY: New York University Press.

Jenkins, H. (2006b). *Convergence culture: Where old and new media collide.* New York, NY: New York University Press.

Jenkins, H., Ford, S., & Green, J. (2013). *Spreadable media: Creating value and meaning in a networked culture.* New York, NY: New York University Press.

Jensen, R. (2015, March 24). *Media, crisis, and public communication from disasters and war to public outreach and engagement.* Public lecture at the University of Technology, Sydney, Australia.

Jiang, H. (2015). Ethics visions for public diplomacy as international public relations. In G. Golan, S. Yang, & D. Kinsey (Eds.), *International public relations and public diplomacy: Communication and engagement* (pp. 167–186). New York, NY: Peter Lang.

Johannesen, R. (2001). *Ethics in human communication* (5th ed.). Prospect Heights, IL: Waveland Press.

Johnston, J., Zawawi, C., & Brand, J. (2009). Public relations: An overview. In *Public relations: theory and practice* (3rd ed., pp. 3–25). Sydney, NSW: Allen & Unwin.

Johnston, K. (2014). Public relations and engagement: Theoretical imperatives of a multidimensional concept. *Journal of Public Relations Research, 26*(5), 381–383.

Kafka, F. (1917). A report for an academy (I. Johnston, Trans.). *The works of Franz Kafka.* Retrieved from http://www.kafka-online.info/a-report-for-an-academy.html

Kane, J. (2000). Communitarianism and citizenship. In W. Hudson & J. Kane (Eds.), *Rethinking Australian Citizenship* (pp. 215–230). Cambridge, UK: Cambridge University Press.

Kang, M. (2014). Understanding public engagement: Conceptualizing and measuring its influence on supportive behavioural intentions. *Journal of Public Relations Research, 26*(5), 390–416.

Kaplan, R., & Haenlein, M. (2010). Users of the world, unite! The challenges and opportunities of social media. *Business Horizons, 53*(1), 59–68.

Karim, F. (2014, September 26). Energy firms "awful" at customer service. *The Times,* p. 22.

Kaye, B. (2011). Between Barack and a net place: Motivations for using social network sites and blogs for political information. In Z. Papacharissi (Ed.), *A networked self: Identity, community, and culture on social network sites* (pp. 208–231). New York, NY: Routledge.

Keane, J. (2009a). *The life and death of democracy.* New York, NY: Norton.

Keane, J. (2009b). Monitory democracy and media-saturated societies. *Griffith Review, 24.* Retrieved from https://griffithreview.com/articles/monitory-democracy-and-media-saturated-societies

Keegan, P. (2014). The 5 new rules of employee engagement. *Inc.* Retrieved from http://www.inc.com/magazine/201412/paul-keegan/the-new-rules-of-engagement.html

Kellen, A., & Kellen, S. (2015, April). *What now? 2015: The politics of listening.* Presentation as part of the curatorial focus theme, Vera List Center for Art and Politics, New York, NY. Retrieved from http://events.newschool.edu/event/what_now_2015_the_politics_of_listening

Kennedy, G. (1994). *A new history of classical rhetoric.* Princeton, NJ: Princeton University Press.

Kenning, G. (2015a). Fiddling with threads: Craft-based textile activities and positive well-being. *Textiles: Journal of Cloth and Culture, 13*(1), 50–65.

Kenning, G. (2015b, August). *Art, affect and ageing: Creativity versus deficit.* Paper presented at the International Symposium of Electronic Arts (ISEA), Vancouver, BC, Canada.

Kent, M. (2013). Using social media dialogically: Public relations role in reviving democracy. *Public Relations Review, 39,* 337–345.

Kent, M., & Taylor, M. (2002). Toward a dialogic theory of public relations. *Public Relations Review, 28*(1), 21–37.

Khosrow-Pour, M. (Ed.). (2008). *Encyclopedia of information science and technology* (2nd ed.). Hershey, PA: IGI Global.

Kim, M., & Ebesu Hubbard, A. (2007). Intercultural communication in a global village: How to understand 'the other'. *Journal of Intercultural Communication Research, 36*(3), 223–235.

Kim, S., Choi, M., Reber, B., & Kim D. (2014). Tracking public relations scholarship trends: Using semantic network analysis on PR Journals from 1975 to 2011. *Public Relations Review, 40*(1), 116–118.

King, C. (2010). Emergent communication strategies. *International Journal of Strategic Communication, 4*(1), 19–38.

King, M. (2015). *Corporate blogging and microblogging: An analysis of dialogue, interactivity and engagement in organization-public communication through social media* (Unpublished doctoral dissertation). University of Technology, Sydney, Australia.

Kitchen, P. (1997). *Public relations: Principles and practice.* London, UK: International Thomson Business Press.

Klein, M. (2007, December 31). *The MIT Collaboratorium: Enabling effective large-scale deliberation for complex problems* (Working Paper 4679–08). Cambridge MA: MIT Sloan School of Management. Retrieved from http://ssrn.com/abstract=1085295

Klein, M. (2011). *How to harvest collective wisdom on complex problems: An introduction to the MIT Deliberatorium.* (CCI Working Paper). Boston, MA: Massachusetts Institute of Technology. Retrieved from http://cci.mit.edu/klein/deliberatorium.html

Klein, M., & Iandoli, L. (2008). Supporting collaborative deliberation using a large-scale argumentation system: The MIT Collaboratorium, MIT Sloan Research Paper No. 4691-08. Boston, MA: MIT Sloan School of Management. Retrieved from http://papers.ssrn.com/sol3/papers.cfm?abstract_id=1099082

Klein, M., Malone, T., Sterman, J., & Quadir, I. (2006, June 22). *The climate Collaboratorium: Harnessing collective intelligence to address climate change issues.* Cambridge MA: Massachusetts Institute of Technology. Retrieved from http://cci.mit.edu/klein/papers/collaboratorium.pdf

Kluger, A. (2012). I'm all ears: Improving your organization through active listening. Melbourne, Vic: University of Melbourne. Retrieved from http://upclose.unimelb.edu.au/episode/186-i-m-all-ears-improving-your-organization-through-active-listening#transcription

Kochhar, S., & Molleda, J. (2015). The evolving links between international public relations and corporate diplomacy. In G. Golan, S. Yang, & D. Kinsey (Eds.), *International public relations and public diplomacy: Communication and engagement* (pp. 51–71). New York, NY: Peter Lang.

Kompridis, N. (2011). Receptivity, possibility, and democratic politics. *Ethics and Global Politics, 4*(4), 255–272.

Kornhauser, W. (1959). *The politics of mass society.* Glencoe, IL: The Free Press.

Kosar, K. (2014, June 23). *Advertising by the federal government: An overview.* Washington, DC: Congressional Research Service. Retrieved from https://www.fas.org/sgp/crs/misc/R41681.pdf

Kreps, G. (1990). *Organizational communication* (2nd ed.). White Plains, NY: Longman.

Krippendorff, K. (2003). *Content analysis: An introduction to its methodology.* Thousand Oaks, CA: Sage.

Kundra, V. (2015, March 27). Panel presentation to the Digital Innovation Forum 2015, University of Technology, Sydney, Australia.

Lacey, K. (2013). *Listening publics: The politics and experience of listening in the media age.* Malden, MA: Wiley Blackwell/Polity.

Larsson, S., & Nordvall, H. (2010). *Study circles in Sweden: An overview with a bibliography of international literature.* Linköping, Sweden: Linköping University Electronic Press. Retrieved from http://liu.diva-portal.org/smash/get/diva2:328351/FULLTEXT01

Lazarus, E. (1883). The new colossus. Retrieved from http://www.libertystatepark.com/emma.htm

Leavis, F. (1930). *Mass civilization and minority culture.* Cambridge, MA: The Minority Press.

LeCompte, M., & Preissle, J. (1993). *Ethnography and qualitative design in educational research* (2nd ed.). New York, NY: Academic Press.

Ledingham, J. (2006). Relationship management: A general theory of public relations. In C. Botan & V. Hazelton (Eds.), *Public relations theory II* (pp. 465–483). Mahwah, NJ: Lawrence Erlbaum.

Ledingham, J., & Bruning, S. (1998). Relationship management and public relations: Dimensions of an organisation-public relationship. *Public Relations Review, 24*(1), 55–65.

Ledingham, J., & Bruning, S. (Eds.). (2000). *Public relations as relationship management: A relational approach to the study and practice of public relations.* Mahwah, NJ: Lawrence Erlbaum.

Lee, H. (n.d.). Communicating across culture. Extract from F. Stark (1988), *Journey's echoes: Selections from Freya Stark (Ecco Travels).* New York, NY: Ecco Press. Retrieved from http://www.hodu.com/across.shtml

Lee, M. (2012). The president's listening post: Nixon's failed experiment in government public relations. *Public Relations Review, 38*(1), 22–31.

Lee, S., & Desai, M. (2014). Dialogic communication and media relations in non-government organizations. *Journal of Communication Management, 18*(1), 80–100.

Leitch, S., & Walker G. (Eds.). (1997). Public relations on the edge. *Australian Journal of Communication, 24*(2), vii–ix.

Leite, E. (2015, January 19). *Why trust matters in business.* Address to the World Economic Forum, Davos-Klosters, Switzerland. Retrieved from https://agenda.weforum.org/2015/01/why-trust-matters-in-business

L'Etang, J. (2008). *Public relations: Concepts, practice and critique.* London, UK: Sage.

L'Etang, J. (2009). Radical PR: Catalyst for change or an aporia? *International Journal of Communication Ethics, 6*(2), 13–18.

L'Etang, J., McKie, D., Snow, N., & Xifra, J. (2015). *The Routledge handbook of critical public relations.* London, UK: Routledge.

L'Etang, J., & Pieczka, M. (1996). *Critical perspectives in public relations.* London, UK: International Thomson Business Press.

Levine, P. (2008). A public voice for youth: The audience problem in digital media and civic education. In W. Bennett (Ed.), *Civic life online: Learning how digital media can engage youth* (pp. 119–138). Cambridge, MA: MIT Press.

Lexer. (2015). (Web site). Retrieved from http://lexer.com.au

Leys, C. (2001). *Market-driven society.* London, UK: Verso.

Liang, H. (2014). The organizational principles of online political discussion: A relational event stream model for analysis of Web forum deliberation. *Human Communication Research, 40*(4), 483–507.

Lincoln, Y. (1997). Self, subject, audience, text: Living at the edge, writing in the margins. In W. Tierney & Y. Lincoln (Eds.), *Representation and the text: Reframing the narrative voice* (pp. 37–54). Albany, NY: SUNY Press.

Lincoln, Y. (2001, November). *Audiencing research: Textual experimentation and targeting for whose reality? Opinion Papers (120)—Speeches/Meeting Papers (150).* Paper presented to Association for the Study of Higher Education annual meeting, Richmond, VA.

Lincoln, Y., & Guba, E. (1985). *Naturalistic inquiry.* Beverly Hills, CA: Sage.

Lipari, L. (2009). Listening otherwise: The voice of ethics. *International Journal of Listening, 23*(1), 44–59.

Lipari, L. (2010). Listening, thinking, being. *Communication Theory, 20*(3), 348–362.

Lipari, L. (2012). Rhetoric's other: Levinas, listening, and the ethical response. *Philosophy & Rhetoric, 45*(3), 227–245.

Lipari, L. (2014). *Listening, thinking, being: Towards an ethics of attunement.* State College, PA: Penn State University Press.

Lippmann, W. (1922). *Public opinion.* New York, NY: Macmillan.

Littlejohn, S., & Foss, K. (2008). *Theories of human communication* (9th ed.). Belmont, CA: Thomson-Wadsworth.

Lloyd, J. (2012, March 21). The rich versus the seething masses [Web log post]. *Reuters. Analysis & Opinion.* Retrieved from http://blogs.reuters.com/john-lloyd/2012/03/21/the-rich-versus-the-seething-masses

Loader, B., Vromen, A., & Xenos, M. (2014). The networked young citizen: Social media, political participation and civic engagement. *Information, Communication & Society, 17*(2), 143–150.

Louw, E. (2010). *The media and political process* (2nd ed.). London, UK: Sage.

Lovari, A., & Parisi, L. (2015). Listening to digital publics: Investigating citizens' voices and engagement within Italian municipalities' Facebook pages. *Public Relations Review, 41*(2), 205–213.

Lowenstein, M. (2006, February 14). The trust equation: Build employee relationship credibility, rapport and integrity to leverage customer advocacy. *CRMGuru.* Retrieved from http://customerthink.com/201

Lu, X. (1998). *Rhetoric in ancient China fifth to third century BCE: A comparison with classical Greek rhetoric.* Columbia: University of South Carolina Press.

Lucas, C. (2013, August 7). You are not listening, say young voters. *The Sydney Morning Herald,* p. 14.

Lundsteen, S. (1979). *Listening: Its impact on language and the other language arts.* Urbana, IL: ERIC Clearing House on Reading and Communication Skills.

Lyons, M. (2001). *Third sector: The contribution of non-profit and cooperative enterprise in Australia.* Crows News, NSW: Allen & Unwin.

Lyotard, J. (1985). *Just gaming* (W. Godzich, Trans.). Manchester, UK: Manchester University Press. (Original work published 1979 in French as *Au juste*)

Macey, W., & Schneider, B. (2008). The meaning of employee engagement. *Industrial and Organizational Psychology, 1*(1), 3–30.

Macfadyen, P. (2014). *Flatpack democracy: A guide to creating independent politics.* Bath, UK: Eco-Logic Books.

Macnamara, J. (1992). Evaluation: The Achilles heel of the public relations profession. *International Public Relations Review, 15*(4), 17–31.

Macnamara, J. (1999). Research in public relations: A review of the use of evaluation and formative research. *Asia Pacific Public Relations Journal, 1*(2), 107–133.

Macnamara, J. (2005). *Jim Macnamara's public relations handbook* (5th ed.). Sydney, NSW: Archipelago Press.

Macnamara, J. (2010, June). The quadrivium of online public consultation: Policy, culture, resources, technology. *Australian Journal of Political Science, 45*(2), 227–244.

Macnamara, J. (2011). Pre- and post-election 2010 online: What happened to the conversation? *Communication, Politics, Culture, 44*(2), 18–36. Retrieved from http://search .informit.com.au/documentSummary;dn=627292905802447;res=IELHSS

Macnamara, J. (2012a). *Public relations theories, practices, critiques.* Sydney, NSW: Pearson.

Macnamara, J. (2012b). Corporate and organizational diplomacy: An alternative paradigm to PR. *Journal of Communication Management, 16*(3), 312–325.

Macnamara, J. (2013). Beyond voice: Audience-making and the work and architecture of listening. *Continuum: Journal of Media and Cultural Studies, 27*(1), 160–175.

Macnamara, J. (2014a). *The 21st century media (r)evolution: Emergent communication practices.* New York, NY: Peter Lang.

Macnamara, J. (2014b). *Journalism and PR: Unpacking 'spin', stereotypes, and media myths.* New York, NY: Peter Lang.

Macnamara, J. (2014c, June). *A review of public communication by the mine owner (GDF SUEZ Australian Energy) and government departments and agencies during the 2014 Hazelwood coal mine fire.* Report to the Hazelwood Coal Mine Fire Board of Inquiry, Morwell, Victoria. Retrieved from http://hazelwoodinquiry.vic.gov.au/wp-content/uploads/2014/08/Report-of-Prof-MacNamara.pdf

Macnamara, J. (2014d). Organizational listening: A vital missing element in public communication and the public sphere. *Asia Pacific Public Relations Journal, 5*(1), 90–108.

Macnamara, J. (2014e, July). Being social: Missing pre-requisites for online engagement, exchange and inclusion. In D. Bossio (Ed.), *Referred proceedings of the Australian and New Zealand Communication Association Conference 2014.* Symposium conducted at Swinburne University, Melbourne. Retrieved from http://www.anzca.net/conferences/past-conferences/2014-conf/p2.html

Macnamara, J. (2015a, June). *Creating an 'architecture of listening' in organizations: The basis of trust, engagement, healthy democracy, social equity, and business sustainability.* Sydney, NSW: University of Technology Sydney. Retrieved from http://www.uts.edu.au/sites/default/files/fass-organizational-listening-report.pdf

Macnamara, J. (2015b). The work and 'architecture of listening': Requisites for ethical organization-public communication. *Ethical Space, 12*(2). Retrieved from http://journals .communicationethics.net

Macnamara J. (2016). Socially integrating PR and operationalizing an alternative approach. In J. L'Etang, D. McKie, N. Snow, & J. Xifra (Eds.), *The Routledge handbook of critical public relations* (Chapter 26). London, UK: Routledge.

Macnamara, J., & Dessaix, A. (2014, July). The ethics of 'embedded' media content: Product placement and 'advertorial' on steroids. In D. Bossio (Ed.), *Refereed proceedings of the Australian and New Zealand Communication Association conference: The digital and the social: Communication for inclusion and exchange.* Symposium conducted at Swinburne University, Melbourne. Retrieved from http://www.anzca.net/conferences/past-conferences/2014-conf/p2.html

Macnamara, J., & Kenning, G. (2011). E-electioneering 2010: Trends in social media use in Australian political communication. *Media International Australia, 139*, 7–22.

Macnamara, J., & Kenning, G. (2014). E-electioneering 2007–2014: Trends in online political communication over three elections. *Media International Australia, 152,* 57–74.

Macnamara, J., & Zerfass, A. (2012). Social media communication in organisations: The challenges of balancing openness, strategy and management. *International Journal of Strategic Communication,* 6(4), 287–308.

Magna Global. (2014). *Magna Global advertising forecasts: 2014.* Retrieved from http://news.magnaglobal.com/ipgmediabrands/press-releases/magna-global-advertising-forecast-2014-ipg-mediabrands.print

Maier, C. (2015). Public relations as humane conversation: Richard Rorty, stakeholder theory, and public relations practice. *Public Relations Inquiry,* 4(1), 25–39.

Mancini, C., & Buckingham Shum, S. (2006). Modelling discourse in contested domains: A semiotic and cognitive framework. *International Journal of Human-Computer Studies,* 64(11), 1154–1171.

Mansell, R. (2012). *Imagining the Internet: Communication, innovation, and governance.* Oxford, UK: Oxford University Press.

Marshall, T. (1950). *Citizenship and social class.* London, UK: Cambridge University Press. Retrieved from http://www.jura.uni-bielefeld.de/lehrstuehle/davy/wustldata/1950_Marshall_Citizenship_and_Social_Class_OCR.pdf

Masten, A. (2001). Ordinary magic: Resilience processes in development. *American Psychologist,* 56(3), 227–238.

MasterCard. (2014). The Engagement Bureau, the MasterCard Conversation Suite. Retrieved from http://newsroom.mastercard.com/videos/mastercard-conversation-suite-video

Mattelart, A. (2007). The invention of communication. In R. Craig & H. Muller (Eds.), *Theorizing communication: Readings across traditions* (pp. 29–36). Thousand Oaks, CA: Sage.

Maude, F. (2014, October). *Foreword to social media guidance for civil servants: October 2014.* Retrieved from https://www.gov.uk/government/publications/social-media-guidance-for-civil-servants/social-media-guidance-for-civil-servants

Mayer, B. (2000). *The dynamics of conflict resolution: A practitioner's guide.* San Francisco, CA: Jossey-Bass.

Mayhew, L. (1997). *The new public: Professional communication and the means of social influence.* London, UK: Cambridge University Press.

Mayo, E., & Steinberg. T. (2007). *Power of information review.* Retrieved from http://webarchive.nationalarchives.gov.uk/20100413152047/http://www.cabinetoffice.gov.uk/reports/power_of_information.aspx

Mazur, M. (2013, March 1). The huge difference between communication and communications [Web log post]. *Communication Rebel.* Retrieved from http://www.drmichellemazur.com/2013/03/difference-between-communication-communications.html

McAllister-Spooner, S. (2009). Fulfilling the dialogic promise: A ten-year reflective survey on dialogic internet principles. *Public Relations Review,* 35(3), 320–322.

McChesney, R. (2008). *The political economy of media: Enduring issues, emerging dilemmas.* New York, NY: Monthly Review Press.

McChesney, R. (2013). *Digital disconnect: How capitalism is turning the internet against democracy.* New York, NY: The Free Press.

McCorkindale, T. (2010). Can you see the writing on my wall? A content analysis of the Fortune 50's Facebook social networking sites. *Public Relations Journal, 4*(3), 1–13.

McCrae, C. (2015). *Performative listening: Hearing others in qualitative research.* New York, NY: Peter Lang.

McDonald, M. (2012). Gartner's definition of the social organization [Video]. *Social Business News.* Retrieved from http://www.socialbusinessnews.com/gartners-definition-of-the-social-organization

McKinsey. (2015, February). How Google breaks through. *Insights.* Retrieved from http://www.mckinsey.com/insights/marketing_sales/how_google_breaks_through?cid=other-eml-nsl-mip-mck-oth-1503

McQuail, D. (2010). *McQuail's mass communication theory* (6th ed.). London, UK: Sage.

McWilliams, A., & Siegel, D. (2001). Corporate social responsibility: A theory of the firm perspective. *Academy of Management Review, 26*(1), 117–127.

Melissen, J. (2005). *The new public diplomacy: Soft power in international relations.* New York, NY: Palgrave Macmillan.

Meyer, J., & Smith, C. (2000). HRM practices and organisational commitment: A test of a mediation model. *Canadian Journal of Administrative Services, 17*, 319–331.

Miège, B. (2010). *L'espace public contemporain: Approche info-communicationnelle.* Grenoble, France: PUG.

Miles, M., & Huberman, M. (1994). *Qualitative data analysis.* Thousand Oaks, CA: Sage.

Miliband, E. (2009, July 27). *Ed Miliband muses on his experience as a 'keynote listener' at the Transition Network conference.* Address to Transition Network conference, London, UK. Retrieved from http://transitionculture.org/2009/07/27/ed-miliband-muses-on-his-experience-as-a-keynote-listener-at-the-transition-network-conference

Mill, J. (1859). *On liberty.* London, UK: John W. Parker & Sons.

Miller, K. (2009). *Organizational communication: Approaches and processes* (5th ed.). Boston, MA: Wadsworth.

Miller, L., & Williamson, A. (2008). *Digital dialogues: Third phase report August 2007–August 2008.* London, UK: Hansard Society.

Mintzberg, H. (1979). *The structure of organizations.* Englewood Cliffs, NJ: Prentice Hall.

Mintzberg, H. (1988). Five Ps for strategy. In J. Quinn, H. Mintzberg, & R. James (Eds.), *Readings in the strategy process* (pp. 10–18). Englewood Cliffs, NJ: Prentice Hall.

Mishra, K., Boynton, L., & Mishra, A. (2014). Driving employee engagement: The expanded role of internal communications. *International Journal of Business Communication, 51*(2), 183–202.

Mommsen, W. (1984). *Max Weber and German politics: 1890–1920.* Chicago, IL: University of Chicago Press. (Original work published in German 1959)

Monnoyer-Smith, L. (2007). Citizen's deliberation on the Internet: A French case. In D. Norris (Ed.), *E-government research: Policy and management* (pp. 230–253). New York, NY: IGI.

Monnoyer-Smith, L. (2015, January). *Institutionalizing public deliberation: Empowerment or appeasement?* Public lecture at London School of Economics and Political Science, London, UK.

Mooney, D. (2011, May 19). Derek Mooney: Queen is nice, but it's Obama we're really looking forward to. *The Evening Herald* [Dublin, Ireland]. Retrieved from http://www .herald.ie/incoming/derek-mooney-queen-is-nice-but-its-obama-were-really-looking-forward-to-27980302.html

Moorman, C., Deshpandé, R., & Zaltman, G. (1993). Factors affecting trust in market research relationships. *Journal of Marketing, 57*(1), 81–101.

Morozov, E. (2014, August 15). How big data will belittle democracy. *The Guardian Weekly*, pp. 27–29.

Morrison, M., Haley, E., Sheehan, K., & Taylor, R. (2002). *Using qualitative research in advertising.* Thousand Oaks, CA: Sage.

Mouffe, C. (1999). Deliberative democracy or agonistic pluralism. *Social Research, 66*(3), 745–758.

Mouffe, C. (2005). *On the political.* London, UK: Routledge.

Muldoon, J. (2004). *The architecture of global governance: An introduction to the study of international organizations.* Boulder, CO: Westview.

Murphy, P. (1991). Limits of symmetry. In J. Grunig & L. Grunig (Eds.), *Public relations research annual, 3* (pp. 115–131). Hillsdale, NJ: Lawrence Erlbaum.

Murphy, P. (2011, May). *Contextual distortion: Strategic communication vs. the networked nature of everything.* Paper presented at the International Communication Association 2011 pre-conference, Strategic Communication: A Concept at the Center of Applied Communications, Boston, MA.

Napoli, P. (2011). *Audience evolution: New technologies and the transformation of media audiences.* New York, NY: Columbia University Press.

Nasri, W. (2012). Conceptual model of strategic benefits of competitive intelligence process. *International Journal of Business and Commerce, 1*(6), 25–35.

Nathan, G. (2014, August 1). Garner died from chokehold while in police custody. *Time.* Retrieved from http://time.com/3071288/eric-garner-chokehold-death-nypd-medical-examiner/#3071288/eric-garner-chokehold-death-nypd-medical-examiner

National Audit Office. (2014). NHS waiting times for elective care in England. London, UK: Author. Retrieved from http://www.nao.org.uk/wp-content/uploads/2014/01/NHS-waiting-times-for-elective-care-in-England.pdf

NCCMT [National Collaborating Centre for Methods and Tools]. (2011). Engaging citizens for decision making. Hamilton, ON: McMaster University. Retrieved from http://www .nccmt.ca/registry/view/eng/86.html

NCDD. [National Coalition for Dialogue and Deliberation]. (2015a). What we're all about. Retrieved from http://ncdd.org/about

NCDD [National Coalition for Dialogue and Deliberation]. (2015b). City of Portland's Restorative Gentrification Listening Project. Retrieved from http://www.portlandoregon.gov/ bps/62635

NCPD [National Commission for Public Debate]. (2015). Giving you a voice and making it heard [Brochure]. Paris, France: Author.

Nesterak, E. (2014, July 13). Head of White House "Nudge Unit" Maya Shankar speaks about newly formed social and behavioral sciences team. *ThePsychReport.* Retrieved from http://

thepsychreport.com/current-events/head-of-white-house-nudge-unit-maya-shankar-speaks-about-newly-formed-us-social-and-behavioral-sciences-team

Net Promoter Community. (2015). The net promoter score and system. Retrieved from http://www.netpromoter.com/why-net-promoter/know

Neuendorf, K. (2002). *The content analysis handbook.* Thousand Oaks, CA: Sage.

Neuman, W. (2006). *Social research methods: Qualitative and quantitative approaches* (6th ed.). Boston, MA: Pearson Education.

Newsom, D., Turk, J., & Kruckeberg, D. (2007). *This is PR: The realities of public relations* (9th ed.). Belmont, CA: Wadsworth.

NGO. (2010). Web log. Retrieved from http://www.ngo.in

NHS England. (2014). Quarterly hospital activity data. Retrieved from http://www.england.nhs.uk/statistics/statistical-work-areas/hospital-activity/quarterly-hospital-activity/qar-data

Nielson, J. (2006, October 9). Participation inequality: Encouraging more users to contribute. *Jakob Nielsen' Alertbox.* Nielsen Norman Group. Retrieved from http://www.useit.com/alertbox/participation_inequality.html

Nietzsche, F. (2009). *Thus spake Zarathustra: A work for everyone and nobody.* Blacksburg, VA: Wilder. (Original work published 1883)

Nixon, S., & du Gay, P. (2002). Who needs cultural intermediaries. *Cultural Studies, 16*(4), 495–500.

Njoku, P. (2014). *GCS mandatory evaluation project (MEP), Phase 2. Presentation to GCS Evaluation Workshop.* London, UK: Government Communication Service.

Noelle-Neumann, E. (1974). The spiral of silence: A theory of public opinion. *Journal of Communication, 24*(2), 43–51.

Noelle-Neumann, E. (1993). *The spiral of silence: Public opinion—our social skin* (2nd ed.). Chicago, IL: University of Chicago Press. (Original work published 1984)

Norris, P. (2001). Political communication. In N. Smelser & P. Baltes (Eds.), *International encyclopaedia of the social and behavioural sciences* (pp. 11631–11640). Amsterdam, the Netherlands: Elsevier.

Norris, P. (2011). *Democratic deficit: Critical citizens revisited.* New York, NY: Cambridge University Press.

Northern Futures. (2014). Consultation. London, UK: UK Government. Retrieved from https://www.gov.uk/government/consultations/northern-futures

Nothhaft, H. (2010). Communication management as a second-order management function: Roles and functions of the communication executive—results from a shadowing study. *Journal of Communication Management, 14*(2), 127–140.

Noughayrède, N. (2014, December 19). The year the people stood up. *The Guardian Weekly,* pp. 1, 24–25.

Nulty, P. (1994, April 4). The National Business Hall of Fame. *Fortune,* p. 118.

Nye, J. (2004). *Soft power: The means to success in world politics.* New York, NY: Public Affairs.

Nye, J. (2010a), Public diplomacy and soft power. In D. Thussu (Ed.), *International communication: A reader* (pp. 333–344). London, UK: Routledge.

Nye, J. (2010b). The new public diplomacy. Project Syndicate. Retrieved from http://www
.project-syndicate.org/commentary/nye79/English

O'Carroll, E. (2010, February 5). Centralia, PA: How an underground coal fire erased
a town [Web log post]. The Christian Science Monitor. Bright Green. Retrieved from
http://www.csmonitor.com/Environment/Bright-Green/2010/0205/Centralia-Pa.-
How-an-underground-coal-fire-erased-a-town

OECD [Organisation for Economic Co-operation and Development]. (2003). Promise and
problems of e-democracy: Challenges of online citizen engagement. Paris, France: Author.
Retrieved from http://www.oecd.org/dataoecd/9/11/35176328.pdf

Ogilvy & Mather. (2015). Listening and analytics. Social@Ogilvy. Retrieved from https://
social.ogilvy.com/expertise/solutions/listening-post

OGP. (2015). Open government partnership. Retrieved from http://www.opengovpartnership
.org

Oliver, S. (1997). Corporate communication: Principles, techniques and strategies. London, UK:
Kogan Page.

OneWorld South Asia. (2010). India: More NGOs, than schools and health centres.
Retrieved from http://southasia.oneworld.net/news/india-more-ngos-than-schools-and-
health-centres

O'Neill, O. (2002). A question of trust. Reith Lectures 2002. Retrieved from http://www.bbc
.co.uk/radio4/reith2002/lecture4.shtml

O'Reilly, T. (2005, September 30). What is Web 2.0: Design patterns and business models for
the next generation of software [Web log post]. O'Reilly. Retrieved from http://oreilly.com/
pub/a/web2/archive/what-is-web-20.html?page=1

Ornatowski, C. (2003). Between efficiency and politics: Rhetoric and ethics in technical
writing. In T. Peeples (Ed.), Professional writing and rhetoric: Readings from the field
(pp. 172–182). New York, NY: Longman.

Oullier, O. (2014, June). The science of engagement. Paper presented to the International
Summit on Measurement, Association for Measurement and Evaluation, Amsterdam,
the Netherlands. Retrieved from http://amecorg.com/2014/09/amec-2014-summit-
presentations

Ovaitt, F. (2008, November 3). Is public engagement the future of public relations? [Web
log post]. Gainesville, FL: Institute for Public Relations. Retrieved from http://www
.instituteforpr.org/is-public-engagement-the-future-of-public-relations

Owyang, J. (2009, March 24). Social media marketing storyboard #1: Fish where the fish
are [Web log post]. Jeremiah Owyang. Retrieved from http://www.web-strategist.com/
blog/2009/03/24/social-media-marketing-storyboard-1-fish-where-the-fish-are

Owyang, J. (2010). The career path of the social media strategist (Research report). Retrieved from
http://www.slideshare.net/jeremiah_owyang/career-social-strategist

Pace, R., & Faules, D. (1994). Organizational communication (3rd ed.). Englewood Cliffs, NJ:
Prentice Hall.

Packard, V. (1957). The hidden persuaders. Harmondsworth, UK: Penguin.

Palmatier, R. (2008). Relationship marketing. Cambridge, MA: Marketing Science Institute.

Papacharissi, Z. (Ed.). (2011). *A networked self: Identity, community, and culture on social network sites.* New York, NY: Routledge.

Patton, M. (2002). *Qualitative research and evaluation methods* (3rd ed.). Thousand Oaks, CA: Sage.

Payne, J. (2009). Reflections on public diplomacy: People-to-people communication. *American Behavioural Scientist, 53*(4), 579–606.

Pearce, J. (2012). Power and the activist. *Development, 55*(2), 198–200.

Pelias, R., & VanOosting, J. (1987). A paradigm for performance studies. *Quarterly Journal of Speech, 73*(2), 219–231.

Penman, R., & Turnbull, S. (2012a). From listening … to the dialogic realities of participatory democracy. *Continuum: Journal of Media & Cultural Studies, 26*(1), 61–72.

Penman, R., & Turnbull, S. (2012b). Socially inclusive processes: New opportunities with new media? *Media International Australia, 142,* 74–86.

Pentagon spending billions on PR to sway world opinion. (2009, February 5). *Fox News.* Retrieved from http://www.foxnews.com/politics/2009/02/05/pentagon-spending-billions-pr-sway-world-opinion

Perelman, C., & Olbrechts-Tyteca, L. (1969). *The new rhetoric: A treatise on argumentation* (J. Wilkinson & P. Weaver, Trans.). Notre Dame, IN: University of Notre Dame Press.

Perrow, C. (1992). Organizational theorists in a society of organizations. *International Sociology, 7*(3), 371–379.

Peters, J. (1999). *Speaking into the air: A history of the idea of communication.* Chicago, IL: University of Chicago Press.

Peters, J. (2006). Media as conversation: Conversation as media. In J. Curran & D. Morley (Eds.), *Media and cultural theory* (pp. 115–126). Abingdon, UK: Routledge.

Peters, T., & Waterman, R. (1982). *In search of excellence.* New York, NY: Warner.

Petty, R., & Cacioppo, J. (1986). *Communication and persuasion: Central and peripheral routes to attitude change.* New York, NY: Springer-Verlag.

Phillips, S., & Orsini, M. (2002). *Mapping the links: Citizen involvement in policy processes* (Discussion Paper No. F21). Ottawa, ON: Canadian Policy Research Networks. Retrieved from http://rcrpp.org/documents/ACFRJK8po.PDF

Phillips, W. (2015). *This is why we can't have nice things: Mapping the relationship between online trolling and mainstream culture.* Cambridge, MA: MIT Press.

Phillips, W., & Milner, R. (forthcoming). *Between play and hate: Antagonism, mischief, and humor online.* Boston, MA: Polity.

Picone, I. (2007). Conceptualizing online news use. *Observatorio Journal, 3,* 93–114.

Pieczka, M. (1996). Paradigms, systems theory and public relations. In J. L'Etang & M. Pieczka (Eds.), *Critical perspectives in public relations* (pp. 124–156). London, UK: International Thomson Business Press.

Pieczka, M. (2006). Paradigms, systems theory and public relations. In J. L'Etang & M. Pieczka (Eds.), *Public relations: Critical debates and contemporary practice* (pp. 331–358). Mahwah, NJ: Lawrence Erlbaum.

Pieczka, M. (2011). Public relations as dialogic expertise? *Journal of Communication Management, 15*(2), 108–124.

Poole, M., Seibold, D., & McPhee, D. (1985). Group decision making as a structurational process. *Quarterly Journal of Speech, 71*, 74–102.

Porter, L. (2010). Communicating for the good of the state: A post-symmetrical polemic on persuasion in ethical public relations. *Public Relations Review, 36*(20), 127–133.

Pranis, K. (2001). Restorative justice, social justice, and the empowerment of marginalized populations. In G. Bazemore & M. Schiff (Eds.), *Restorative community justice* (pp. 287–306). Cincinnati, OH: Anderson.

Punch, K. (1998). *Introduction to social research: Quantitative and qualitative approaches*. London, UK: Sage.

Purdy, M. (2000). Listening, culture, and structures of consciousness: Ways of studying listening. *International Journal of Listening, 14*(1), 47–68.

Purdy, M. (2004, April). *Qualitative research: Critical for understanding listening*. Paper presented at the International Listening Association conference, Fort Meyers, FL.

Purdy, M., & Borisoff, D. (1997). *Listening in everyday life: A personal and professional approach* (2nd ed.). Lanham, MD: University of America Press.

Putnam, R. (1993). *Making democracy work*. Princeton, NJ: Princeton University Press.

Putnam, R. (1995). Bowling alone: America's declining social capital. *Journal of Democracy, 61*(1), 65–78.

Putnam, R. (2000). *Bowling alone: The collapse and revival of American community*. New York, NY: Simon & Schuster.

Putnam, R. (Ed.). (2004). *Democracies in flux: The evolution of social capital in contemporary societies*. Oxford, UK: Oxford University Press.

PWC [PriceWaterhouseCoopers]. (2014). *Global entertainment and media outlook 2014–2018: Internet advertising*. Retrieved from http://www.pwc.com/gx/en/global-entertainment-media-outlook/segment-insights/internet-advertising.jhtml

Qualman, E. (2009). *Socialnomics: How social media transforms the way we live and do business*. Hoboken, NJ: Wiley.

Quodling, A. (2015, April 22). Doxxing, swatting and the new trends in online harassment. Retrieved from http://theconversation.com/doxxing-swatting-and-the-new-trends-in-online-harassment-40234

Rainie, L., Smith, A., Schlozman, K., Brady, H., & Verba, S. (2012, October). *Social media and political engagement*. Washington, DC: The Internet & American Life Project. Retrieved from http://www.pewinternet.org/Reports/2012/Political-engagement.aspx

Rancière, J. (1998). *Disagreement: Politics and philosophy*. Minneapolis: University of Minnesota Press.

Reader, T., Gillespie, A., & Mannell, J. (2014). Patient neglect in 21st century health-care institutions: A community health psychology perspective. *Journal of Health Psychology, 19*(1), 137–148.

Reader, T., Gillespie, A., & Roberts, J. (2014). Patient complaints in healthcare systems: A systematic review and coding taxonomy. *BMJ Quality and Safety*, 1–12. doi: 10.1136/bmjqs-2013-002437

Redding, W., & Tompkins, P. (1988). Organizational communication: Past and present tenses. In G. Goldhaber & G. Barnett (Eds.), *Handbook of organizational communication* (pp. 5–33). Norwood, NJ: Ablex.

Regan, R. (1971). Effects of a favor and liking on compliance. *Journal of Experimental Social Psychology, 7*(6), 627–639.

Reichheld, F. (2003, December). One number you need to grow. *Harvard Business Review.* Retrieved from https://hbr.org/2003/12/the-one-number-you-need-to-grow/ar/1

Renton, A., & Macintosh, A. (2007). Computer-supported argument maps as a policy memory. *The Information Society, 23*(2), 125–133.

Rhoades. L., Eisenberger, R., & Armeli, S. (2001). Affective commitment to the organisation: The contribution of perceived organisational support. *Journal of Applied Psychology, 86,* 825–836.

Rice, S., & Burbules, N. (2010). Listening: A virtue account. *Teachers College Record, 112*(11), 2728–2742.

Rigg, J. (2015, March 27). Endless reform: Is it time to look beyond efficiencies on Whitehall? *This Week in Westminister.* London, UK: Keene Communications. Retrieved from http://www.publicaffairsnetworking.com/news/endless-reform-is-it-time-to-look-beyond-efficiencies-on-whitehall

Riordan, S. (2003). *The new diplomacy.* Cambridge, UK: Polity Blackwell.

Rittel, H., & Webber, M. (1973). Dilemmas in a general theory of planning. *Policy Sciences, 4,* 155–169.

Roberts, J., & Escobar, O. (2014, June). *Citizens' juries on wind farm development in Scotland: Interim report.* Retrieved from http://www.climatexchange.org.uk/reducing-emissions/citizens-juries-wind-farm-development-scotland-interim-report

Rodrigo, D., & Amo, P. (2006). *Background document on public consultation.* Paper prepared for the Regulatory Policy Division, Public Governance and Territorial Development Directorate, Organization for Economic Cooperation and Development, Paris, France.

Rogers, C., & Farson, R. (1987). Active listening. In R. Newman, M. Danzinger, and M. Cohen (Eds.), *Communicating in business today* (pp. 589–598). Lexington, MA: D. C. Heath.

Rogers, E. (1962). *Diffusion of innovations.* New York, NY: Free Press.

Rogers, E., & Chaffee, S. (2006). The past and the future of communication study: Convergence or divergence? *Journal of Communication,* (43)4, 125–131.

Rorty, R. (1979). *Philosophy and the mirror of nature.* Princeton, NJ: Princeton University Press.

Rosanvallon, P. (2008). *Counter-democracy.* Cambridge, UK: Cambridge University Press.

Rosen, J. (2006, June 27). The people formerly known as the audience [Web log post]. *Press-Think.* Retrieved from http://journalism.nyu.edu/pubzone/weblogs/pressthink/2006/06/27/ppl_frmr.html

Rosenstiel, T., & Mitchell, A. (2012, August). *How the presidential candidates use the web and social media.* Washington, DC: Pew Research Center Project for Excellence in Journalism. Retrieved from http://www.journalism.org/analysis_report/how_presidential_candidates_use_web_and_social_media

Rowe, G., Horlick-Jones, T., Walls, J., & Pidgeon, N. (2005). Difficulties in evaluating public engagement initiatives: Reflections on an evaluation of the UK GMNation? Public debate about transgenic crops. *Public Understanding of Science, 14,* 331–352.

Ruddock, A. (2007). *Investigating audiences.* London, UK: Sage.

Russell Brand: I've never voted, never will. (2013, October 23). BBC *Newsnight.* Retrieved from http://www.bbc.com/news/uk-24648651

Russell, D., Stefik, K., Pirolli, P., & Card, S. (1993). The cost of sense-making. In *Refereed proceedings of the INTERCHI'93 Conference on Human Factors in Computer Systems* (pp. 269–276). New York, NY: Association for Computing Machinery (ACM).

Rust, R., & Oliver, R. (1994). The death of advertising. *Journal of Advertising, 23*(4), 71–77.

Rutter, M. (1985). Resilience in the face of adversity. Protective factors and resistance to psychiatric disorder. *British Journal of Psychiatry, 147*, 598–611.

Sack, W. (2000). Conversation map: A content-based Usenet newsgroup browser. In *Proceedings of the 5th International Conference on Intelligent User Interfaces* (pp. 233–240). New York, NY: Association for Computing Machinery (ACM).

Saebo, O., & Nilsen, H. (2004). The support for different democracy models by the use of a Web-based discussion board. *Electronic Government, Proceedings, 3183*, 23–26.

Saha, L., Print, M., & Edwards, K. (Eds.). (2007). *Youth and political participation*. Rotterdam, the Netherlands: Sense.

Said, E. (1978). *Orientalism*. New York, NY: Penguin.

Sanders, K., & Canel, M. (Eds.). (2014). *Government communication: Cases and challenges*. New York, NY: Bloomsbury.

Satell, G. (2013, November 17). 4 failed marketing buzzwords that you really shouldn't use. *Forbes*. Retrieved from http://www.forbes.com/sites/gregsatell/2013/11/17/4-marketing-buzzwords-that-you-really-shouldnt-use

Schneider, M. (2015). US public diplomacy since 9–11: The challenges of integration. In G. Golan, S. Yang, & D. Kinsey (Eds.), *International public relations and public diplomacy: Communication and engagement* (pp. 15–36). New York, NY: Peter Lang.

Schudson, M. (1997). Why conversation is not the soul of democracy. *Critical Studies in Mass Communication, 14*(4), 320–329.

Schudson, M. (1998). *The good citizen: A history of American civic life*. New York, NY: Free Press.

Schudson, M. (2003). Click here for democracy: A history and critique of an information-based model of citizenship. In H. Jenkins & D. Thorburn (Eds.), *Democracy and new media* (pp. 49–60). Cambridge, MA: MIT Press.

Scott, L. (2014, July 8). Gavin Newsom and a Berkeley professor are trying to disrupt public opinion polls. *San Francisco Magazine*. Retrieved from http://www.modernluxury.com/san-francisco/story/gavin-newsom-and-berkeley-professor-are-trying-disrupt-public-opinion-polls

Searle, S., & Cormick, C. (2015, March 11). Engaging the disengaged with science. *The Conversation*. Retrieved from https://theconversation.com/engaging-the-disengaged-with-science-38435

Sendbuehler, F. (1994). *Silence as discourse in 'Paradise Lost'*. Paper presented at the GEMCS conference, Rochester, NY. Retrieved from https://facultystaff.richmond.edu/~creamer/silence.html

Sentiment. (2015). *Merriam-Webster*. Retrieved from http://www.merriam-webster.com/dictionary/sentiment

Severin, W., & Tankard, J. (2001). *Communication theories: Origins, methods, and uses in the mass media*. New York, NY: Addison Wesley Longman.

Shannon, C., & Weaver, W. (1949). *The mathematical theory of communication*. Urbana: University of Illinois Press.

Shapiro, I., Stokes, S., Wood, E., & Kirshner, A. (Eds.). (2009). *Political representation*. New York, NY: Cambridge University Press.

Shenton, A. (2004). Strategies for ensuring trustworthiness in qualitative research projects. *Education for Information, 22*(2), 63–75.

Sheridan, K. (2012). *Building a magnetic culture: How to attract and retain top talent to create an engaged, productive workforce*. New York, NY: McGraw-Hill.

Shields, B. (2015, January 5). Abbott government spends up big on media monitoring. *The Sydney Morning Herald*. Retrieved from http://www.smh.com.au/federal-politics/political-news/abbott-government-spends-up-big-on-media-monitoring-20150104-12hj88.html

Shockley-Zalabak, P. (1994). *Understanding organizational communication: Cases, commentaries, and conversations*. White Plains, NY: Longman.

Shoemaker, P., & Reese, S. (1996). *Mediating the message: Theories of influences on mass media content* (2nd ed.). White Plains, NY: Longman.

Siapera, E. (2012). *Understanding new media*. London, UK: Sage.

Silverman, D. (2000). *Doing qualitative research: A practical handbook*. London, UK: Sage.

Silverstone, R. (2007). *Media and morality: On the rise of the mediapolis*. Cambridge, UK: Polity.

Simon, G. (2009). Selective listening and attention: Hearing what you want to hear as a manipulation tactic. *Counselling resource* [Web site]. Retrieved from http://Counsellingresource.com/features/2009/03/30/selective-listening

Sirolli, E. (2012). Want to help someone out? Shut up and listen. *Ted Talk*. Retrieved from http://www.ted.com/talks/ernesto_sirolli_want_to_help_someone_shut_up_and_listen?language=en

Sissons, H. (2014). Whose news? Investigating public relations between journalists and public relations practitioners (Unpublished doctoral dissertation). School of Communication Studies, Auckland University of Technology, New Zealand.

Smith, A., & Rainie, L. (2008, June). *The Internet and the 2008 election* (Pew Internet & American Life Project Report). Washington, DC: Pew Research Center. Retrieved from http://www.pewinternet.org/files/old-media/Files/Reports/2008/PIP_2008_election.pdf.pdf

Smith, C. (2010). *Presidential campaign communication: The quest for the White House*. Cambridge, UK: Polity.

Smith, T. (2015, April 13). Employee communications: More than top down communications. Gainesville, FL: Institute for Public Relations, Organizational Communication Research Center. Retrieved from http://www.instituteforpr.org/employee-communications-top-communications

Smythe, D., & Van Dinh, T. (1983). On critical and administrative research: A new critical analysis. *Journal of Communication, 33*(3), 117–127.

Snow, N. (2009). Rethinking public diplomacy. In N. Snow & P. Taylor (Eds.), *Routledge handbook of public diplomacy* (pp. 3–11). London, UK: Routledge.

Snow, N. (2015). Public diplomacy and public relations: Will the twain ever meet? In G. Golan, S. Yang, & D. Kinsey (Eds.), *International public relations and public diplomacy: Communication and engagement* (pp. 73–90). New York, NY: Peter Lang.

Solis, B. (2008). Foreword. In D. Breakenridge, *PR 2.0: New media, new tools, new audiences* (pp. xvii–xx). Upper Saddle River, NJ: FT Press, Pearson Education.

Solis, B. (2011). *Engage: The complete guide for brands and businesses to build, cultivate, and measure success in the new web.* Hoboken, NJ: Wiley.

Solis, B., & Breakenridge, D. (2009). *Putting the public back in public relations: How social media is reinventing the aging business of PR.* Upper Saddle River, NJ: FT Press/Pearson Education.

Sommerfeldt, E., Kent, M., & Taylor, M. (2012). Activist practitioner perspectives of website public relations: Why aren't activist websites fulfilling the dialogic promise? *Public Relations Review, 38,* 303–312.

Sonnenfeld, J. (1982). Public affairs execs: Orators or communicators? *Public Relations Review,* 8(3), 3–16.

Sorrell, M. (2008, November 5). *Public relations: The story behind a remarkable renaissance.* Speech to the Yale Club, New York, NY. Retrieved from http://www.instituteforpr.org/edu_info/pr_the_story_behind_a_remarkable_renaissance1

Spicer, C. (2000). Public relations in democratic society: Value and values. *Journal of Public Relations Research, 12*(1), 115–130.

Spicer, C. (2007). Collaborative advocacy and the creation of trust: Toward an understanding of stakeholder claims and risks. In E. Toth (Ed.), *The future of excellence in public relations and communication management: Challenges for the next generation* (pp. 27–40). Mahwah, NJ: Lawrence Erlbaum.

Spivak, G. (1990). *The postcolonial critic.* London, UK: Routledge.

Sriramesh, K. (2004). *Public relations in Asia: An anthology.* Singapore: Thomson.

Sriramesh, K., Rivera-Sánchez, M., Soriano, C. (2011). Websites for stakeholder relations by corporations and non-profits. *Journal of Communication Management,* 17(2), 122–139.

Stake, R. (2008). Qualitative case studies. In N. Denzin & Y. Lincoln (Eds.), *The Sage handbook of qualitative research* (3rd ed., pp. 119–149). London, UK: Sage.

Stationery Office. (2013). *Report of the Mid Staffordshire NHS Foundation Trust Public Inquiry.* Retrieved from http://www.midstaffspublicinquiry.com/sites/default/files/report/Executive%20summary.pdf

Statista. (2014). Statistics and facts about the global advertising market. Retrieved from http://www.statista.com/topics/990/global-advertising-market

Stone, D., Patton, B., & Heen, S. (2000). *Difficult conversations: How to discuss what matters most.* New York, NY: Penguin.

Strauss, A., & Corbin, J. (1990). *Basics of qualitative research: Grounded theory procedures and techniques.* Newbury Park, CA: Sage.

Strauss, W., & Howe, N. (2000). *Millennials rising: The next great generation.* New York, NY: Vintage.

Street, J. (2004). Celebrity politicians: Popular culture and political representation. *The British Journal of Politics & International Relations,* 6(4), 435–452.

Strother, R. (2014, June 11). *How Lenovo set up a global analytics hub and social media listening command centers to get closer to the customer.* Presentation the International Summit on Measurement, Association for Measurement and Evaluation of Communication, Amsterdam, the Netherlands.

Surma, A. (2005). *Public and professional writing: Ethics, imagination and rhetoric.* Basingstoke, UK: Palgrave Macmillan.

Taachi, J. (2009). Finding a voice: Digital storytelling as participatory development in South-East Asia. In J. Hartley & K. McWilliam (Eds.), *Story circle: Digital storytelling around the world* (pp. 167–175). Oxford, UK: Wiley-Blackwell.

Tashakkori, A., & Teddlie, C. (2003). *Handbook of mixed methods in social and behavioural research*. Thousand Oaks, CA: Sage.

Taylor, C. (1992). *Multiculturalism and 'the politics of recognition'*. Princeton, NJ: Princeton University Press.

Taylor, M. (2010). Public relations in the enactment of civil society. In R. Heath (Ed.), *The Sage handbook of public relations* (pp. 5–15). Thousand Oaks, CA: Sage.

Taylor, M., & Kent, M. (2014). Dialogic engagement: Clarifying foundational concepts. *Journal of Public Relations Research, 26*(5), 384–398.

Teddlie, C., & Yu, F. (2007). Mixed method sampling: A typology with examples. *Journal of Mixed Methods Research, 1*(1), 77–100.

Tench, R., & Yeomans, L. (2009). *Exploring public relations* (2nd ed.). Harlow, UK: Prentice Hall-Pearson Education.

Tench, R., & Yeomans, L. (2013). *Exploring public relations* (3rd ed.). Harlow, UK: Pearson Education.

Thaler, R., & Sunstein, C. (2008). *Nudge: Improving decisions about health, wealth, and happiness*. New Haven, CT: Yale University Press.

Theunissen, P., & Noordin, W. (2012). Revisiting the concept of dialogue in public relations. *Public Relations Review, 38*, 5–13.

Thill, C. (2009). 'Courageous' listening, responsibility for the other and the Northern Territory intervention. *Continuum: Journal of Media and Cultural Studies, 23*(4), 537–548.

Thompson, A., Peteraf, M., Gamble, J., & Strickland, A. (2013). *Crafting and executing strategy: The quest for competitive advantage* (19th ed.). New York, NY: McGraw-Hill Irwin.

Tilley, C. (2005). *Trust and rule*. New York, NY: Cambridge University Press.

Tilley, C. (2007). *Democracy*. New York, NY: Cambridge University Press.

Tilley, E. (2015). The paradoxes of organizational power and public relations ethics: Insights from a feminist discourse analysis. *Public Relations Inquiry, 4*(1), 79–98.

Timmins, N. (2012). *Never again? The story of the Health and Social Care Act 2012: A study in coalition government and policy making*. London, UK: Institute for Government and the Kings Fund.

Toffler, A. (1970). *Future shock*. New York, NY: Random House.

Toffler, A. (1980). *The third wave*. New York, NY: William Morrow.

Tomlinson, E., & Mayer, R. (2009). The role of causal attribution dimensions in trust repair. *Academy of Management Review, 34*, 85–104.

Toulmin, S. (1959). *The uses of arguments*. Cambridge, UK: Cambridge University Press.

Tourish, D., & Hargie, O. (Eds.). (2004). The crisis of management. In *Key issues in organisational communication* (pp. 1–16). New York, NY: Routledge.

Transform. (2010, September 29). *Directgov strategic review: Executive summary*. London, UK: Author. Retrieved from https://www.gov.uk/government/uploads/system/uploads/attachment_data/file/60995/Directgov_20Executive_20Sum_20FINAL.pdf

Treadaway, C., Kenning, G., & Coleman, S. (2014, November). *Designing for positive emotion: Ludic artefacts to support wellbeing for people with dementia.* Paper presented at the 9th Design and Emotion conference: Colours of Care, Bogota, Colombia.

Trenholm, S. (2008). *Thinking through communication: An introduction to the study of human communication* (5th ed.). Upper Saddle River, NJ: Pearson Education.

Tuchman, G. (1978). The symbolic annihilation of women by the mass media. In G. Tuchman, A. Daniels, & J. Benet (Eds.), *Hearth and home: Images of women and the media* (pp. 3–17). New York, NY: Oxford University Press.

Turnbull, M. (2015, March 27). *Opening address.* Digital Innovation Forum 2015, University of Technology Sydney, Australia.

Turnbull, N. (2007). Perspectives on government PR. In S. Young (Ed.), *Government communication in Australia* (pp. 113–129). Port Melbourne, Vic: Cambridge University Press.

Turner, B. (Ed.). (1994). *Citizenship and social theory.* London, UK: Sage.

Turner, B. (2001). Outline of a general theory of cultural citizenship. In N. Stevenson (Ed.), *Culture and citizenship* (pp. 11–32). London, UK: Sage.

UC [University of California] Berkeley. (2013). Opinion space. Retrieved from http://opinion.berkeley.edu

UCL [University College London]. (2014). What is public engagement? [Web page]. Retrieved from http://www.ucl.ac.uk/public-engagement/whatispublicengagement

Ulbig, S. (2002, November 6). *Is having your say enough? The importance of voice and influence in political trust and policy assessments.* Paper presented to the North Eastern Political Science Association, Philadelphia, PA. Retrieved from http://citation.allacademic.com/meta/p_mla_apa_research_citation/0/8/9/6/0/p89600_index.html

United Nations. (2014). NGO database. Retrieved from http://csonet.org

United Nations Foundation. (2013, July 31). Social good summit 2013 announced new speakers, first group of 'keynote listeners' and massive open online course (MOOC). News and media. Retrieved from http://www.unfoundation.org/news-and-media/press-releases/2013/social-good-summit-2013.html

University of Melbourne. (2013, May 13). Australian voters are dissatisfied, distrustful and disengaged. Melbourne, Vic: Author. Retrieved from http://newsroom.melbourne.edu/votertrust

US Army. (2015). Army public affairs. Washington, DC: Author. Retrieved from http://www.army.mil/info/institution/publicaffairs

US Department of State. (2012). *Fact sheet: Non-governmental organizations (NGOs) in the United States.* Washington, DC: Author. Retrieved from http://www.humanrights.gov/fact-sheet-non-governmental-organizations-ngos-in-the-united-states.html

US Department of State. (2015). Selected US government information web sites. Washington, DC: Author. Retrieved from http://www.state.gov/misc/60289.htm

US spends millions on overseas propaganda, but no one is buying it. (2015, February 25). *RT* [Web site]. Retrieved from http://rt.com/op-edge/235719-us-kerry-rt-media-russia

Van Dijck, J. (2013). *The culture of connectivity: A critical history of social media.* Oxford, UK: Oxford University Press.

Van Riel, C. (1995). *Principles of corporate communication.* London, UK: Prentice Hall.

Van Riel, C., & Fombrun, C. (2007). *Essentials of corporate communications*. New York, NY: Routledge.

van Ruler, B., & Verčič, D. (2005). Reflective communication management, future ways for public relations research. In P. Kalbfleisch (Ed.), *Communication yearbook 29* (pp. 238–273). Mahwah, NJ: Lawrence Erlbaum.

van Ruler, B., Verčič, D., Bütschi, G., & Flodin, B. (2001). Public relations in Europe: A kaleidoscopic picture. *Journal of Communication Management, 6*(2), 166–175.

Vargas, J. (2008, November 20). Obama raised half a billion online. *The Washington Post*. Retrieved from http://voices.washingtonpost.com/44/2008/11/20/obama_raised_half_a_billion_on.html

Verba, S., Scholzman, K., & Brady, H. (1995). *Voice and equality: Civic voluntarism in American politics*. Cambridge, MA: Harvard University Press.

Vergeer, M. (2013). Politics, elections and online campaigning: Past, present … and a peek into the future. *New Media and Society, 15*(1), 9–17.

Viteritti, J. (1997). The environmental context of communication: Public sector organizations. In J. Garnett & A. Kouzmin (Eds.), *Handbook of administrative communication* (pp. 79–100). New York, NY: Marcel Dekker.

Waks, L. (2007). Listening and questioning: The apophatic/cataphatic distinction revisited. *Learning Inquiry, 1*(2), 153–161.

Waks, L. (2010). Two types of interpersonal listening. *Teachers College Record, 112*(11), 2743–2762.

Walton, D. (1989). *Informal logic: A handbook of critical argument*. New York, NY: Cambridge University Press.

Walton, D. (2006). *Fundamentals of critical argumentation: Critical reasoning and argumentation*. New York, NY: Cambridge University Press.

Walzer, M. (1992). The civil society argument. In C. Mouffe (Ed.), *Dimensions of radical democracy: Pluralism, citizenship, community* (pp. 89–107). London, UK: Verso.

Wanless review into UK child sex abuse claims finds no evidence of cover-up over missing dossier. (2014, November 12). *ABC News*. Retrieved from http://www.abc.net.au/news/2014-11-12/review-finds-no-evidence-of-cover-up-over-uk-sex-abuse-dossier/5884012

Ward, I. (2003). An Australian PR state? *Australian Journal of Communication, 30*(1), 25–42.

Watson, T. (2012). The evolution of public relations measurement and evaluation. *Public Relations Review, 38*(3), 390–398.

Watzlawick, P., Beavin, J., Jackson, D. (1967). Some tentative axioms of communication. In *Pragmatics of human communication: A study of interactional patterns, pathologies and paradoxes* (pp. 48–71). New York, NY: W. W. Norton.

Waymer, D. (2013). Democracy and government public relations: Expanding the scope of 'relationship' in public relations research. *Public Relations Review, 39*, 320–331.

Weatherall, A. (2002). *Gender, language and discourse*. Hove, UK: Routledge.

Weick, K. (1995). *Sensemaking in organizations*. London, UK: Sage.

Weiner, M. (2012, September). Showcase to the social media world. *Kommunikations Manager, 3*, 6–10.

Welch, D. (2013). *Propaganda: Power and persuasion*. London, UK: British Library.

Wiener, N. (1950). *The human use of human beings*. Cambridge, MA: Da Capo Press.

Wiener, N. (1954). *Cybernetics*. New York, NY: Wiley.

Wilcox, D., & Cameron, G. (2010). *Public relations: Strategies and tactics* (9th ed.). Boston, MA: Allyn & Bacon.

Wilde, O. (1888). The remarkable rocket. In *The happy prince and other tales*. Retrieved from http://www.eastoftheweb.com/short-stories/UBooks/RemRoc.shtml

Williams, R. (1976). *Communications*. Harmondsworth, UK: Penguin. (Original work published 1962)

Williams, R. (1980). Base and superstructure in Marxist cultural theory. In *Problems in materialism and culture: Selected essays* (pp. 3–49). London, UK: Verso.

Wintour, P. (2014, July 11). Home Secretary orders broad inquiry into handling of abuse. *The Guardian Weekly*, p. 15.

Wolvin, A. (Ed.). (2010). *Listening and human communication in the 21st century*. Chichester, UK: Wiley-Blackwell.

Wolvin, A., & Coakley, G. (1994). Listening competency. *Journal of International Listening Association*, 8(1), 148–160.

Wolvin, A., & Coakley, G. (1996). *Listening* (5th ed.). Madison, WI: Brown & Benchmark.

Woolgar, S. (2002). Five rules of virtuality. In *Virtual society? Technology, cyberbole, reality* (pp. 1–22). Oxford, UK: Oxford University Press.

World Bank. (2013). Citizen report card and community score card. Retrieved from http://web.worldbank.org/WBSITE/EXTERNAL/TOPICS/EXTSOCIALDEVELOPMENT/EXTPCENG/0,,contentMDK:20507680~pagePK:148956~piPK:216618~theSitePK:410306,00.html

World PR Report. (2014). Top 250. *The Holmes Report*. Retrieved from http://worldreport.holmesreport.com/top-250

Wright, D., Gaunt, R., Leggetter, B., Daniels, M., & Zerfass, A. (2009). *Global survey of communications measurement 2009: Final report*. London, UK: Association for Measurement and Evaluation of Communication. Retrieved from http://amecorg.com/wp-content/uploads/2011/08/Global-Survey-Communications_Measurement-20091.pdf

Wright, D., & Hinson, M. (2012). Examining how social and emerging media have been used in public relations between 2006 and 2012: A longitudinal analysis. *Public Relations Journal*, 6(4), 1–40.

Xenos, M., Vromen, A., & Loader, B. (2014). The great equalizer? Patterns of social media use and youth political engagement in three advanced democracies. *Information, Communication, Society*, 17(2), 151–167.

Yackee, W. (2006). Sweet-talking the fourth branch: The influence of interest group comments on federal agency rulemaking. *Journal of Public Administration Research and Theory*, 16(1), 103–124.

Yang, S., Kang, M., & Cha, H. (2015). A study on dialogic communication, trust, and distrust: Testing a scale for measuring organization-public dialogic communication (OPDC). *Journal of Public Relations Research*, 27(2), 175–192.

Yin, R. (2009). *Case study research: Design and methods* (4th ed.). Thousand Oaks, CA: Sage.

Young, I. (2000). *Inclusion and democracy.* Oxford, UK: Oxford University Press.

Young, S. (Ed.). (2007). *Government communications in Australia.* Melbourne, Vic: Cambridge University Press.

Zald, M., & McCarthy, D. (1987). *Social movements in an organizational society.* Fredericton, NB: Transaction Books.

Zerfass, A. (2008). Corporate communication revisited: Integrating business strategies and strategic communication. In A. Zerfass, B. van Ruler, & K. Sriramesh (Eds.), *Public relations research* (pp. 65–96). Wiesbaden, Germany: VS Verlag für Sozialwissenschaften.

Zerfass, A., & Sherzada, M. (2014, March). *Corporate communications from the CEO's perspective: How top executives conceptualize and value strategic communication.* Paper presented to the International Public Relations Research conference, Miami, Florida.

Zerfass, A., Verčič, D., Verhoeven, P., Moreno, A., & Tench, R. (2012). *European communication monitor 2012: Challenges and competencies for strategic communication.* Brussels, Belgium: Helios Media and EACD/EUPRERA.

Zerfass, A., Verčič, D., Verhoeven, P., Moreno, A., & Tench, R. (2015). *European communication monitor 2015: Creating communication value through listening, messaging and measurement: Results of a survey of 41 countries.* Brussels, Belgium: EACD/EUPRERA and Helios Media.

Zugaro, E. (2014). From the field: Six steps toward stakeholder relationships listening. In T. Falconi, J. Grunig, E. Zugaro, & J. Duarte, *Global stakeholder relationships governance: An infrastructure* (pp. 83–103). New York, NY: Palgrave.

INDEX